Women in American Religion

Women in Amer...

Edited by Janet Wilson James

NEW LON...

Copyright © 1976, 1978 by the Trustees of the University of Pennsylvania
Janet W. James, "Women in American Religious History: An
Overview," and Gerald F. Moran, " 'Sisters' in Christ: Women
and the Church in Seventeenth-Century New England,"
copyright © 1980 by the University of Pennsylvania Press, Inc.

Second printing 1982

Substantial portions of this book were originally published in the
American Quarterly under the editorship of Bruce Kuklick and are
reprinted here by exclusive arrangement.

Library of Congress Cataloging in Publication Data
Main entry under title:

Women in American religion.

1. Women in Christianity—United States—Addresses, essays,
lectures. 2. Women in Church Work—United States—Addresses,
essays, lectures. 3. Women in Judaism—United States—Addresses,
essays, lectures. 4. United States—Religion—Addresses, essays,
lectures. I. Boyer, Paul. II. James, Janet Wilson, 1918-
BR515.W65   1980   261.8'344   79-5261
ISBN 0-8122-7780-5 (cloth)
ISBN 0-8122-1104-9 (paper)

Contents

Janet Wilson James

Women in American Religious History
An Overview

An exploration of women's part in the history of religion soon encounters two constants: women usually outnumber men; men exercise the authority. For a long time historians have been preoccupied with the authority, particularly with clerical officialdom: the men who preached and administered the sacraments, expounded theology, and ran the affairs of the larger organized faiths. The preponderance of female communicants has been recognized but seldom discussed, and their subordination has been taken for granted.

Today the shock waves of the 1960s have weakened the familiar authority structure. Adherents of many systems of belief flock to pentecostal revivals, participate in liturgical experiments, and search out the liberating promises of scripture to revise theologies. Among them women are conspicuous. Convent doors have swung open for a mass exodus of women religious, some revoking their vows, others living them in smaller, more informal communities in the secular world. Within and outside the professional seminaries, some women contend for the right to be ordained and to exercise sacerdotal authority. Others have rejected the Judeo-Christian tradition altogether and are endeavoring to construct a new theology and a new ethics.

Even before they witnessed this upheaval, historians of religion had been extending their range. Protestants, letting the scales of denominationalism fall from their eyes, began to see the Protestant culture whole; Roman Catholic historians lowered their defenses; and each began to engage in dialogue with the other and with their Jewish counterparts. Now the more venturesome are extending their attention to disgruntled churchgoers of the past and to seekers of new Jerusalems, groups formerly dismissed as eccentric. Historians of religion have begun to shift their focus from the institutions and their pastors to the people: the laity, receiver of the word; the parishioner, supporter of its corporate form; and even the unchurched. How have religious experience and behavior in past times expressed their needs? What are the social implications of neglect of religious duties or rebellion against them?[1]

In another quarter of historical scholarship, social historians with an interest in women's history have been aware of religion as both a liberating and a repressive force in women's lives. Anne Scott follows the course of the Southern woman, from self-abnegation under the stern code of evangelical Protestantism in the antebellum period to liberation through service under religion's umbrella in the postwar world. Nancy Cott has shown how the Second Great Awakening enabled a generation of young New England women cast adrift from premodern society to find a new identity, and Donald Mathews has analyzed the effect of the Southern Awakening on the family and women's status. Barbara Welter and Ann Douglas have described the "feminization" of Protestantism that followed the nineteenth-century bifurcation of sex roles.[2]

Building on these insights, this collection of essays attempts to expand our understanding of the history of women and religion in America by considering not only Protestant women but Catholic and Jewish women as well, in

[1] Moshe Davis, review in *Union Seminary Quarterly Review*, 27 (Summer 1972); Sydney E. Ahlstrom, "The Problem of the History of Religion in America," *Church History*, 39 (June 1970); Moses Rischin, "The New American Catholic History," *Church History*, 41 (June 1972); Henry J. Browne, "American Catholic History," *Church History*, 26 (Dec. 1957); David J. O'Brien, "American Catholic Historiography: A Post-Conciliar Evaluation," *Church History*, 37 (Mar. 1968), and "American Catholicism and American Religion," *Journal of the American Academy of Religion*, 40 (1972); William A. Clebsch, "A New Historiography of American Religion," *Historical Magazine of the Protestant Episcopal Church*, 32 (1963), and "American Religious Studies: Towards a Morphology of American Religion," *Criterion*, 2, no. 3 (1972); William R. Hutchison, "Ol Ark's A-Creakin'," *Reviews in American History*, 2 (Sept. 1974), and reviews in *Journal of Interdisciplinary History*, 3 (Spring 1973), and 5 (Autumn 1974); Don Yoder, "Historiography of Religion in America," *American Quarterly*, 18 (Summer 1966); Martin E. Marty, "Religious Behavior: Its Social Dimension in American History," *Social Research*, 41 (Summer 1974); Edwin S. Gaustad, Darline Miller, and G. Allison Stokes, "Religion in America," *American Quarterly* 31 (bibliography 1979), 250-83.

[2] Anne Firor Scott, *The Southern Lady* (Chicago: Univ. of Chicago Press, 1970), and "Women, Religion, and Social Change in the South, 1830–1930," in Samuel S. Hill, Jr., et al., *Religion and the Solid South* (Nashville: Abingdon Press, 1972); Nancy F. Cott, "Young Women in the Second Great Awakening," *Feminist Studies*, 3 (Fall 1975), and *The Bonds of Womanhood: "Woman's Sphere" in New England, 1780–1835* (New Haven: Yale Univ. Press, 1977); Donald G. Mathews, *Religion in the Old South* (Chicago: Univ. of Chicago Press, 1977); Barbara Welter, "The Feminization of American Religion, 1800–1860," in her *Dimity Convictions* (Athens: Ohio Univ. Press, 1976); Ann Douglas, *The Feminization of American Culture* (New York: Knopf, 1977). See also Kathryn Kish Sklar, *Catharine Beecher* (New Haven: Yale Univ. Press, 1973).

the belief that their experiences in institutionalized religion had much in common. In this way we may be able to examine some elements of religious life that cross theological and institutional borders. The experience of women as individuals and as a distinct social group can illumine much of the scene outside the sanctuary in past time: the social status of the clergy, the dynamics of congregational life, the functions of lay leadership, the nature of the churches' social outreach and of the missionary impulse, even the tension between piety and knowledge. Our effort will be to indicate some avenues of research and interpretation.

*T*he Protestants who came to Boston in the 1630s found themselves living on a frontier in a fragment of their customary social structure, a congregation with the capstones of authority an ocean's distance away. This is the setting for the aborted mini-Reformation of the first generation of Puritan women, which Mary Maples Dunn describes in "Saints and Sisters," the first study in our collection. In this spontaneous movement we can identify features that recur in subsequent confrontations of American women with ecclesiastical power. Anne Hutchinson began her teaching in her home, to gatherings of women. These gatherings grew larger and soon attracted men. Her Antinomian doctrine would inevitably have increased the authority of laymen or laywomen at the ministers' expense, since only the Holy Spirit and the individual would be parties to God's gift of grace and the individual the only witness to the proceeding. Hutchinson also publicly defied the minister of the church in Boston by rising when he began to preach and leading her followers outside. The ministers, unable to best her on theological grounds, fell back on denigrating and discrediting her as a woman. She and her female followers were accused simultaneously of usurping their husbands' authority and using the wiles of Eve to convert them to Antinomianism. The ministers implied that their doctrine would lead to sexual promiscuity and seized upon the birth of "monsters" to Hutchinson and Mary Dyer as God's special punishment for women heretics.

What Anne Hutchinson had claimed both as theologian and as feminist, the Society of Friends realized to the fullest extent conceivable for Protestants of that day. By rejecting theological and social distinctions that Puritans considered essential to an orderly society, the Quakers were able partly to free themselves from the concept of women's subordination. Individuals could avail themselves of revelation and salvation; the priesthood was cast off with the sacraments and the remnants of ritual. A lay ministry to which women as well as men might be called undertook the missionary endeavor that made the Quakers world-famous. The separate women's meetings for discipline gave them their own area of church governance (though not financial independence). This interesting innovation, perhaps the first Protestant women's organization, was a mixture of old and new, traditional in its family-bounded view of women, modern in its assignment of important church business and its expectation of action. Meeting and ministry gave Quaker women a range of responsibilities. God's call might require the wife and mother to leave her family for an extended period.[3] He could send the single woman on mission as well.

Every aspect of Quakerism was abhorrent to the Puritan establishment in Massachusetts, which extinguished this threat as it had that of the women seekers of the pioneer generation. After 1675, a now safely rooted society generated no new threats. From studies of congregational records, both Dunn and Gerald F. Moran, in "'Sisters' in Christ," his chapter in this book, establish that women came increasingly to outnumber men in the churches. Moran further surmises that during this generation conversion was linked to the passage into adult life through marriage and parenthood, and suggests that submission of one's will to God was easier for women, who also reached for religious assurance in the face of the dangers of childbirth. With Laurel Thatcher Ulrich, who in her essay "Vertuous Women Found" surveys ministerial writings about women in the late seventeenth and early eighteenth centuries, Moran concludes that Puritans, unlike the later Victorians, did not discern sexual differences in psyche or soul.

Ulrich argues convincingly that the absence of sex-role typing in these clerical portraits of women indicates some measure of equality, at least in spiritual status. This was a natural emphasis for Cotton Mather and other sympathetic pastors of largely female congregations, who, appreciating women's resources of mind and spirit and mindful of their physical perils, were inclined to soften traditional indictments of Eve's daughters. Yet it implied no alteration in the standing order. As Dunn points out, the decline in male conversions likely indicates the increasing divergence of secular from spiritual affairs. But church and state were still united; traditional mechanisms of control would continue even if a majority of men failed to experience grace.

It was otherwise in times of revival. During the Great Awakening in New England, contemporaries reported, male converts rebalanced the sex ratio, especially in churches that returned to stern Calvinist doctrine. There is evidence that women's activity quickened, that they voted in some church business meetings and undertook exhortation or religious teaching in their own or others' homes, customs that subsequently fell again into disuse.[4]

The American Revolution set in motion waves of social change that were

---

[3] Janis Calvo, "Quaker Women Ministers in Nineteenth Century America," *Quaker History*, 63 (Autumn 1974), 78, 80–83.

[4] Ezra Stiles, *The Literary Diary of Ezra Stiles*, ed. Franklin B. Dexter (New York: Scribner's, 1901), I, 145–47; Charles Chauncy, *Enthusiasm Described and Cautioned Against*

profoundly to affect the nation's religious life. In her essay for this volume, "A Women's Awakening," Mary P. Ryan notes some of the changes that occurred in Utica, New York, during the Second Great Awakening. Utica never had a church establishment; the congregations Ryan reconstitutes are Presbyterian or Baptist. Their theologies were competitive: all offered the certainty of salvation once repentance was complete. During successive phases of the revival, the number of male church members predictably rose, but women now constituted the majority of both converts and members. While the pastors preached and prayed, the purposeful influence of Utica's wives and mothers within the family played a key role in the conversion of their flocks.

Redemption now imposed on lay people more obligations than godly behavior or indoctrination by learned ministers. An expanding faith imparted a sense of mission. As early as 1806 these same women formed a charitable society, awakened to a sense of their duty to aid and save local unfortunates by the revival and, doubtless, by the example of women in the English evangelical movement.[5] But the greater need was for spreading the word to unconverted westerly regions. By 1824 their organization was a regional body with seventy auxiliaries supporting eleven missionary evangelists, including the soon-to-be-famous Charles G. Finney.

After the revival, little was left unchanged. Although the doctrine of female subordination remained and the familiar religious and family values were reaffirmed, in the dynamics of the home a revolution was taking place. Women of this generation were seldom taxed with Eve's transgression. A society with new definitions of purity attempted to deny the existence of female sexuality, judging its manifestations pathological or lower class. Women's influence in the nineteenth century was to derive from spirituality, not sex appeal. The home became woman's special mission field; motherhood was sacralized. The minister and the father abdicated their responsibility for religious nurture. Thus the female majority was officially accepted and the secularization of the Protestant lay male recognized. Ryan's study helps us to see that this development was well under way before the Victorian era; what happened in the 1830s and after, as Ann Douglas's work relates, was its popularization by the agencies of mass culture.

Women in other areas were experiencing the same process of identity for-

---

[1742], in Alan Heimert and Perry Miller, eds., *The Great Awakening* (Indianapolis: Bobbs-Merrill, 1967), 239–41; Mary Beth Norton, "'My Resting Reaping Times': Sarah Osborn's Defense of Her 'Unfeminine' Activities, 1767," *Signs*, 2 (Winter 1976); Cedric B. Cowing, "Sex and Preaching in the Great Awakening," *American Quarterly*, 20 (Fall 1968).

[5] For the English evangelicals, and particularly the influence of Hannah More, see J. W. James, "Changing Ideas about Women in the United States, 1776–1825" (Diss. Radcliffe College, 1954), and Jill K. Conway, "Evangelical Protestantism and Its Influence on Women in North America, 1790–1860," paper delivered at the annual meeting of the American Historical Association, New Orleans, Dec. 30, 1972.

mation during the Second Great Awakening, as Nancy Cott has documented for New England and Donald Mathews for the evangelical communities of the Old South.[6] Organized groups were slower to form in the rural South, but the egalitarian spirit of the revival early raised women's consciousness. She who stood out from the revival crowd with the assurance of salvation had earned respect and acquired new obligations to herself, her family, and her community. As an individual, she fed, sheltered, and nursed the Methodist circuit riders, besides using her home and gathering neighbors for meetings. Women's religious societies provided peer companionship for self-measurement and protection in new endeavors. The seminary movement for women's education, both North and South, was one outgrowth of this women's Awakening.[7]

The missionary preachers in western New York had their zealous counterparts abroad, men confident that the gospel must prevail, not only within America's Christian borders, but among the heathen sitting in darkness in ancient lands. Barbara Welter's chapter in this collection, "She Hath Done What She Could," explores women's position in the Protestant foreign missionary movement.[8] For the educated woman convert with half-articulated yearnings for adventure and a wider field of action, or even for personal fame, the role of missionary wife seemed ideal. Few realized such an ambition, but the myth of the martyred missionary attests to the appeal of a role that combined sacrifice, submission, and self-assertion—at a safe distance. Dead at nineteen on an island in the Indian Ocean, Harriet Newell became a Protestant saint.[9]

The foreign missionary field had a compelling fascination for nineteenth-century Protestants, who found in those unprogressive lands the reverse image of themselves. Women in the Christian homes of the United States were moving to higher planes of influence, if not of power, while the Asian woman, hobbling on bound feet, immured in a seraglio, or prostrate on a husband's funeral pyre, was the helpless victim of man's oppression. At the same time she was credited, as a woman, with the power to influence. Her conversion therefore would be the key to the evangelization of the whole society. Male missionaries, however, like the male anthropologists of a later day, had no access to the domestic world. The only solution was to accept the single woman's call and admit her to paraclerical status. Eager to serve

[6] Cott, "Young Women in the Second Great Awakening" and *Bonds of Womanhood*, chap. 4; Mathews, *Religion in the Old South* and "The Second Great Awakening as an Organizing Process," *American Quarterly*, 21 (Spring 1969).

[7] Mathews, *Religion in the Old South*; Sidney Thomas Davis, "Woman's Work in the Methodist Church" (Diss. Univ. of Pittsburgh, 1963).

[8] See also Welter, "Feminization of American Religion," 91ff.

[9] Cott, *Bonds of Womanhood*, 140–41; Douglas, *Feminization of American Culture*, 106. See also Joan Jacobs Brumberg, *Mission for Life: The Judson Family and American Evangelical Culture, 1790–1900* (New York: Free Press, 1980).

in the field or to raise money for the cause, American ladies took up this limited mandate. As early as 1855, "female assistant missionaries" outnumbered the ordained males.[10]

The great revivalists seized upon other new ways to spread the word. Charles G. Finney encouraged women to speak in mixed prayer meetings and presided over the radical experiment in coeducation at Oberlin College that produced Antoinette Brown, the first woman to be ordained. In the 1840s, weekly parlor meetings for prayer in Phoebe Palmer's New York home became the core of a spreading holiness movement within the Methodist church. Influential laymen and ministers in the city listened to Mrs. Palmer call for sanctification through a second conversion; others read the message in her books and articles. By the 1850s, with the supportive presence of her husband as a second lay preacher, Phoebe Palmer was exhorting camp meeting crowds. Finney's conversion to holiness helped the Palmers carry the movement far beyond the bounds of Methodism.[11]

Women preachers might be an anomaly, but the female majority was becoming a steadily more active force in American Protestantism. Not surprisingly, the relationship between women and the clergy grew ambiguous. The minister retained his authority, solidly backed by the elders, deacons, or vestry, but found himself isolated in the increasingly female world of church and family. Inevitably, the women's predilections helped to alter the form and content of worship. Barbara Welter, in her article on "The Feminization of American Religion, 1800–1860," noted the softening of harsh dogma, the exaltation in sermons and hymns of meekness, humility, love, and forgiveness, and the reinterpretation of Christ as an embodiment of these sex-linked virtues. In a broader study of *The Feminization of American Culture*, Ann Douglas depicted the battleground created by the overlapping of female and clerical roles within the literary world of the Northeast between 1820 and 1875.[12] Douglas found a drastic decline in ministerial prestige with the fading of state support, habits of deference, and Calvinist theology on the one hand, and, on the other, the rise of aggressive female writers purveying a sentimen-

[10] See Robert Baird's figures for the American Board of Commissioners for Foreign Missions in his *Religion in America* (New York: Harper & Brothers, 1856), 610. Among recent works are Irwin T. Hyatt, *Our Ordered Lives Confess* (Cambridge: Harvard Univ. Press, 1976), and Helen Emery Falls, "Baptist Women in Missions Support in the Nineteenth Century," *Baptist History and Heritage*, 12 (Jan. 1977).

[11] Timothy L. Smith, *Revivalism and Social Reform* (1957; reprint ed., New York: Harper and Row, 1965) and *Called Unto Holiness* (Kansas City: Nazarene Publishing House, 1962); Anne C. Loveland, "Domesticity and Religion in the Antebellum Period: The Career of Phoebe Palmer," *The Historian*, 39 (May 1977); Conway, "Evangelical Protestantism"; Nancy Hardesty, Lucille Sider Dayton, and Donald W. Dayton, "Women in the Holiness Movement: Feminism in the Evangelical Tradition," in Rosemary Ruether and Eleanor McLaughlin, eds., *Women of Spirit: Female Leadership in the Jewish and Christian Traditions* (New York: Simon and Schuster, 1979).

[12] See also Barbara Welter, "Defenders of the Faith: Women Novelists of Religious Controversy in the Nineteenth Century," in her *Dimity Convictions*.

talized religion. A popular culture came into being as these intellectually deprived women and status-deprived clergy vied for the mass market for soft religion.

The ministers reserved their fire, however, for more direct threats. They could applaud Dorothea Dix, who observed the most self-effacing proprieties in her crusade for humane treatment of the insane, but in 1837 clerical wrath fell on the Grimké sisters for their advocacy of the antislavery cause through the radical means of speaking to mixed audiences in churches and public halls. When the pastoral letter of the Congregational ministers of Massachusetts forced the female abolitionists to a defense on feminist grounds, the battle was joined on the issue of women's independence.

The feminists thus took up a position not unlike that of the motley company of extremists who had abandoned the traditional churches in favor of experimental religious societies that promised to equalize relationships between the sexes. The new religions promised (as had Quakerism) direct inner spiritual experiences without the mediation of a clerical caste of educated males—indeed, they sometimes questioned whether God was masculine and made woman a priest or messiah. The individual was subordinated to the welfare of the community, thus discouraging male aggressiveness. Most important, celibacy among the Shakers, complex marriage and male continence in the Oneida Community, and even Mormon polygamy were approaches to fertility control.[13] Mother Ellen G. White of the Seventh-day Adventists, Mother Ann Lee, and Jemima Wilkinson, the Universal Friend, offered healing, comfort, and love, release from anxiety, guilt, and subservience, and a millennium close at hand. The cults were a refuge for the rootless, and for women without families and those trapped in intolerable marriages.

*P*rotestantism in all its variety had taken the continent for its own when masses of immigrants professing other faiths began to arrive. Their customs and beliefs would now face the exposure to the American environment that Protestantism had undergone through two hundred years. They would experience the temptations of economic opportunity, moral relativism, and evasion of authority. Their institutions, too, would have to adjust to the voluntary system. The Protestantism of Calvin had been much altered; it remained to be seen how the collective identity of Catholics, Jews, and the last large Protestant group, the Lutherans, would withstand the centrifugal force of American individualism.

The newcomers were numerous but poor, with little more than family

---

[13] Through celibacy, wrote Hannah Adams in her *A View of Religions*, 3d ed. (Boston: Manning and Loring, 1801), 256, "heaven begins upon earth," and the Shakers "thereby lose their earthly and sensual relation to Adam the first, and come to be transparent in their ideas, in the bright and heavenly visions of God."

and religion to keep body and spirit alive. The Catholic and Jewish faiths had not been born of a modern-age revolution and democratized by revivalism, and they carried the authority of ancient tradition. The Lutherans were the most conservative of the Protestant sects. Women in these groups were not preachers, and family relationships were slow to change.

The adjustments of religious groups and institutions, established and arriving, took place amid another revolution. In the crowded cities, where industrialization had been under way at least since the 1840s, casualties were already familiar: families broken by privation and unemployment, leaving orphaned children, rootless young people, the helpless, sick, and aged. Suffering became endemic when large-scale immigration resumed after the Civil War, and intensified with the onset in the mid-eighties of the great migration from Italy and eastern Europe. Each of the faiths made its own response to the crisis, but the size of the task and its social implications shaped their work along similar lines. The physical deprivation of the poor seemed inseparable from their spiritual needs; the relief effort took on the proportions of a religious crusade.

Looking at changes in Protestantism during the years after the Civil War, William McLoughlin identifies a third great American revival, running from about 1870 to 1915. Its landmarks included the Social Gospel and Progressive movements, but other features were debates over the higher criticism of the Bible, religious searches for health and healing, and the spread of adventist, holiness, and pentecostal sects. The Catholic church's responses to the times were in many ways similar. The growing middle class took up social reform under the aegis of the Church, while, as Jay P. Dolan has shown, working-class parishes found solace in revivalistic "missions" offering emotional release and faith healing.[14]

Among Protestants, the revival spirit continued to loosen institutional structures and thereby create opportunities for women. In the mainline churches they expanded their own missionary agencies and gained a new field for leadership in nondenominational enterprises like the Woman's Christian Temperance Union and the Young Women's Christian Association. Among the sects and schismatics, religious initiatives by women were encouraged. Men often shared the pulpit, and women preached freely. Some charismatics, like Alma White, Mary Baker Eddy, and Aimee Semple McPherson, became founders of new churches, and Mrs. Eddy's Church of Christ, Scientist, rising from a middle-class base, developed into a denomi-

---

[14] See McLoughlin, "Revivalism," in Edwin S. Gaustad, ed., *The Rise of Adventism: Religion and Society in Mid-Nineteenth-Century America* (New York: Harper and Row, 1974), 135. McLoughlin's larger study, *Revivals, Awakenings and Reform: An Essay on Religion and Social Change in America, 1607–1977* (Chicago: Univ. of Chicago Press, 1978), proposes a later date, 1890, for the beginning of this awakening. See also Jay P. Dolan, *Catholic Revivalism: The American Experience, 1830–1900* (Notre Dame, Ind.: Univ. of Notre Dame Press, 1978).

nation. Women in liberal religion, more sophisticated feminists, borrowed from the higher criticism under Elizabeth Cady Stanton's direction to prepare a *Woman's Bible*.[15]

Yet a counteracting tendency was unfavorable to female leadership: the bureaucratizing trend that in religion as well as in business and government accompanied the growth of ever-larger institutions. Within the older denominations this led to a tightening rather than a loosening of authority. After the turn of the century, church administrators, doubtless attracted by the cult of efficiency that Samuel Hays and others have identified as part of the Progressive movement, imposed financial controls on or absorbed many of the formerly independent women's mission boards and put up a stiff resistance to laity rights for women. Only in the sects or traditionally liberal churches like the Unitarian was ordination of women possible, and even the Methodists curtailed the licensing of women as lay preachers.[16] Nor did the Social Gospel's middle-class concern for the underprivileged extend to women. (As spokesman for the movement, Walter Rauschenbusch declared that Christianity had already achieved the ideal family.) And the last phase of what might be called the social action revival was the Men and Religion Forward Movement, which by preaching a muscular Christianity sought to bring men back into the mainline churches and restore the balance of the sexes.[17]

The bureaucratizing trend became manifest as religion gathered its resources for a crusade against poverty. Local undertakings moved toward cooperation, consolidation, and federation. The voluntary system ensured a variety of approaches: denomination-wide, interdenominational, or nondenominational; by lay people and religious; by men's groups, women's societies, or both together. Catholic sisterhoods had many obligations and were being increasingly diverted to parochial education; social action would require serious commitment by laywoman volunteers. As the Catholic and Jewish middle class grew, women of these faiths began joining together in local groups as Protestant women had in an earlier era, while Protestants moved

[15] Introduction by Barbara Welter, "Something Remains to Dare," in *The Original Feminist Attack on the Bible: The Woman's Bible* (New York: Arno Press, 1974); James H. Smylie, "The Woman's Bible and the Spiritual Crisis," *Soundings*, 59 (Fall 1976); and Lois W. Banner, "Elizabeth Cady Stanton, Religion, and the Woman's Bible," unpublished paper.

[16] Catherine F. Hitchings, *Universalist and Unitarian Women Ministers* (vol. 10 of the *Journal of the Universalist Historical Society*, 1975); Rosemary Skinner Keller, "Alternative Forms of Leadership by Women in the Protestant Tradition," paper delivered at the Berkshire Conference of Women Historians, Mount Holyoke College, Aug. 24, 1978.

[17] Robert T. Handy, ed., *The Social Gospel in America, 1870–1920: Gladden, Ely and Rauschenbusch* (New York: Oxford Univ. Press, 1966), 12; Dorothy Bass Fraser, "The Feminine Mystique, 1890–1910," *Union Seminary Quarterly Review*, 27 (Summer 1972); publicity booklet for Men and Religion Forward movement enclosed with Raymond Robins to Margaret Dreier Robins, Apr. 1, 1913, microfilm edition of Papers of the Women's Trade Union League and Its Principal Leaders, Margaret Dreier Robins Papers, Univ. of Florida Library, Reel 53, frames 583–85.

into the "connectional" stage of federation, creating large-scale enterprises requiring advanced management skills. A third phase would be the formal training and the professionalization of social workers—the majority of them women.

Two of the nineteenth-century immigrant groups brought with them distinctive institutions for women's work, particularly in charity and religious education. Catholics had long had an auxiliary force in the sisterhoods devoted to spiritual exercises and good works, including the schooling of children and young women. German Lutherans earlier in the century had revived the early Christian office of deaconess to create communities of single women dedicated to the relief of the sick and poor. This institution, transplanted with some difficulty to the United States, was also adopted by the Methodists. Celibacy was not a part of the Jewish tradition; for American needs the Jewish community adopted other models worked out by the Protestants.

Until the present generation, Catholic sisters were, to Protestants at least, the most visible presence of the Church, an exotic sight as they appeared in black-robed pairs on American streets. The Sisters of Charity, founded in 1808 by the convert Elizabeth Seton as the first order native to America, were in evidence in their hospitals, orphanages, foundling homes, and parish schools, as were the Sisters of the Good Shepherd, working with "magdalens," and the Little Sisters of the Poor. Yet less is known about their lives and work than about Catholic laywomen's activities. Sister Elizabeth Kolmer's bibliographical essay on "Catholic Women Religious and Women's History" points out the parlous state of the historical art for these communities and suggests sources for the study of the orders and their connection with the current feminist movement. Mary J. Oates's essay, "Organized Voluntarism," is a challenging example of research from a modern perspective. Socialized as women to unequal sacrifices, the sisters in effect subsidized the parish schools and ended by losing control of their work and institutions. This suggests parallels with industry and the exploitation of female labor in the same era.

Out of a grudging admiration for the work of the Catholic sisterhoods and an uneasy fear of their competition, an interest gradually arose in the formation of Protestant counterparts.[18] For this there was a famous model at Kaiserswerth in the German Rhineland, where the Lutheran pastor Theo-

[18] Charles Golder, *History of the Deaconess Movement in the Christian Church* (Cincinnati: Jennings and Pye, 1903), 305; Lucy Rider Meyer, *Deaconesses: Biblical, Early Church, European, American* (Cincinnati: Cranston and Stowe, 1892), 68–69; Jane M. Bancroft, *Deaconesses in Europe and Their Lessons for America* (New York: Hunt and Eaton, 1889), 230.

dor Fliedner and his wife, Friederike, in the 1830s had built a cluster of hospitals and asylums staffed by an order of deaconesses. Another pattern emerged in England, as the Anglo-Catholic revival prompted Anglicans to reinstitute religious orders of women. A sign of the times was an interest among English and American intellectuals in the life of St. Teresa of Avila.

The American movement had its early beginnings in the 1840s when the Reverend William A. Passavant secured Fliedner's help in planning a Lutheran hospital in Pittsburgh and imported Kaiserswerth deaconesses to staff it. Passavant's friend William A. Muhlenberg, a social-minded Episcopal priest in New York, at the same time founded the first American sisterhood in his denomination, consecrating his associate, the English-born Anne Ayres, as a Sister of the Holy Communion. Evidently the need for such communities was not sufficient to overcome Protestant prejudice, for they attracted little support.

A quarter of a century later, the Methodist laywoman Annie Wittenmyer attempted to introduce deaconesses into her denomination. A veteran of women's work with the United States Christian Commission, a Civil War relief agency, Wittenmyer had visited Kaiserswerth. Her Ladies and Pastors Christian Union (1868), which she hoped would lay the groundwork for deaconess communities, lapsed after the Methodist General Conference refused its backing.

The need for jobs for single women, fears aroused by industrial strife, and the rising new revivalism finally overcame prejudice and inertia in the 1880s. German-Americans of the Lutheran and Reformed churches, and German congregations of the mainline Protestant denominations, began to establish deaconess communities in the Middle West. A new Methodist advocate, Bishop James Thoburn, won the cooperation of successive General Conferences, and the recently founded denomination-wide Women's Home Missionary Society provided a network of support. At the grass roots, a Chicago group set up the first deaconess home and training school in 1885, under the direction of Lucy Rider Meyer, with Bishop Thoburn's sister Isabella, on leave from her missionary post in India, as superintendent; while from the top the society's Deaconess Bureau, guided by the scholarly Jane Bancroft, a student of Kaiserswerth and the Anglican sisterhoods, undertook a vigorous social program.

In the long run, as Virginia L. Brereton and Christa R. Klein indicate in "American Women in Ministry," their essay in this volume, deaconesses were at best a partial success, an innovation that for all its timeliness went against the grain of the Protestant community. The female majority turned naturally to religious work, but in the familiar and autonomous lay societies. The overseas missions held the spotlight and often the main attention of the elite of the mainline denominations, but their concern and their means extended also to work among the poor and the "pagan" within the borders of the United

States: blacks and highlanders in the South; Indians, Mexican-Americans, and Mormons in the West.

In the industrializing cities middle-class women found a variety of opportunities. Through the Young Women's Christian Association they offered a religious environment and education and employment services for female immigrants from rural America. The directors of the New York City Mission and Tract Society turned from distributing tracts to building foreign-language chapels in immigrant neighborhoods, while the society's Woman's Branch saw to it that the chapels provided missionary nurses in tenements (the earliest form of public health nursing), day nurseries, vacation homes for working girls, and dry saloons where workingmen could enjoy nontoxic sociability.[19]

A number of religious fraternal and sororal organizations were formed in response to a middle-class impulse to reach across class barriers while remaining safely sex-segregated. The Society of the King's Daughters, founded in 1886, grew to a membership of half a million ladies and white-collar workers, enabled to recognize each other by a small silver cross worn on a purple ribbon. The workers gained such advantages as home study courses and settlement house hospitality.[20]

In immigrant neighborhoods ladies of the mainline churches might encounter holiness missions where dedicated laymen and laywomen of the middle or working class preached sanctification through disciplined personal behavior. In the Salvation Army, an offshoot of the English holiness movement, the Booth family, inspired by Phoebe Palmer's ministry, preached and practiced equality of the sexes: women officers worked on an equal plane with men in the rescue of inhabitants of Skid Row, alcoholics, and fallen women, urban poverty's worst victims. And Frances Willard in her charismatic leadership of the WCTU owed much to Mrs. Palmer, whose preaching she had heard, as well as to the great revivalist Dwight L. Moody, a precursor of pentecostalism. On a program of "Do Everything" for the sake of "Home Protection," Willard's evangelism carried thousands of middle-class followers from temperance on to crusades for suffrage, health and hygiene, better treatment of female offenders, drug control, and social purity (opposition to prostitution and sex crimes against women). Strongly Methodist in ambience, the WCTU enjoyed the hearty approval of churchmen, presumably because as an independent organization it offered no in-house competition.

The advent of the settlement house at the end of the eighties shifted the balance in Protestant charity from a religious to a secular spirit. The spiritual force behind Jane Addams's Hull House was a kind of civil religion. This

[19] See Aaron I. Abell, *The Urban Impact on American Protestantism* (Cambridge: Harvard Univ. Press, 1943).
[20] Ibid., chap. 5, 194–202, 219–22.

faith, regardless of denominational ties or the lack of them, infused the middle-class Protestants who dominated the Progressive movement. Churches, especially in the South, sponsored settlement houses with a strong religious atmosphere. Secular leaders in the movement were evangelists, too, but with an environmental and humanitarian message. This faith was to be the new social cement; significantly, nowhere in Addams's account of her Italian and Jewish neighbors in Chicago does she mention churches or synagogues, priests or rabbis. For Protestant women good works and organized religion had begun to part company, at least in the white community.

Because black community life centered in the churches, pastor and congregation constituted an island of self-determination in a hostile world. Black ministers could be autocratic, because only they had access to power. Yet the large female majority held its own. Aware that the money they raised built and supported the church, conscious too that their loyalty fortified the ministers, the women were respectful but not submissive. "Take the women of the Church as a whole and they are the means by which the Church succeeds and the gospel is promulgated," declared Dr. Mattie Coleman in 1918 as she presided over the first meeting of the women's missionary council of the Colored Methodist Episcopal Church.

In the black church, religion and social services were of necessity intertwined. Anna Still recalled proudly in her old age that the women of "Mother Bethel," the Philadelphia congregation that became the nucleus of the African Methodist Episcopal Church, helped to "carry up" its first building in 1794, at the same time founding a mutual benefit society. In antebellum towns African Dorcas societies sewed clothing for destitute children; later, women's mission groups gathered and eventually, spreading with black migrations, came together in federations. The older denominations sent missionaries to Africa, but mission work most often began at home, with the relief of the aged, orphaned, or homeless; a legendary line of mother-teachers gathered in waifs, washed and fed them, and read them Bible stories. Accepting help from white women coreligionists, black churchwomen improvised auxiliary institutions: Sunday schools, summer institutes for church workers, vacation Bible schools, and, as blacks moved into the cities, settlement houses.[21]

[21] Theressa Hoover, "Black Women and the Churches: Triple Jeopardy," in Alice Hageman, ed., *Sexist Religion and Women in the Church: No More Silence* (New York: Association Press, 1974); W. E. B. DuBois, *Darkwater* (New York: Harcourt, Brace, and Howe, 1920), esp. 174–75, and *The Philadelphia Negro* (1899; reprint ed., New York: Schocken Books, 1967); Sara J. McAfee, *History of the Woman's Missionary Society in the Colored Methodist Episcopal Church*, rev. ed. (Phenix City, Ala.: Phenix City Herald, 1945); Hylan Lewis, *Blackways of Kent* (Chapel Hill: Univ. of North Carolina Press, 1955); Allen Hartvik, "Catherine Ferguson, Black Founder of a Sunday School," *Negro History Bulletin*, 35 (Dec. 1972); Letitia W. Brown, "Battles Won and Evil Overcome," in Doris J. Mitchell and Jewel H. Bell, eds., *The Black Woman: Myths and Realities* (Cambridge: Radcliffe College, 1978).

In Catholic America, as a middle class rose from the immigrant ranks, a body of prescriptive literature came into being, stressing women's place at home and condemning their individuation through suffrage, education, and labor organization. James J. Kenneally's chapter in this volume, "Eve, Mary, and the Historians," is a counterpart to Barbara Welter's well-known essay, "The Cult of True Womanhood," which reviewed the standards held up to the women of the Protestant culture of the antebellum era. Despite official warnings, some Catholic women did undertake nondomestic activities.

In the eighties and nineties a variety of initiatives for social action came from upper-class Catholic women in touch with the white Protestant world. Mary Theresa Elder, scion of an old Maryland family and an archbishop's niece, became widely known for her articles in Catholic journals demanding that the Church act on social problems. The convert Mary Hoxsey and other St. Louis laywomen founded the Society of Queen's Daughters on the Protestant model; the organization spread and won papal approval in 1908. In the 1890s "Catholic women of refinement and leisure" were joining the Protestant philanthropist Grace Dodge in promoting her working girls' clubs. And in the ecumenical atmosphere of the Chicago World's Fair of 1893, Alice T. Toomy of California led the Woman's Catholic Congress in founding a National League of Catholic Women, modeled upon the WCTU. Eliza Allen Starr, a convert and noted Chicago art teacher and lecturer, who was made secretary, declared that women who declined to contribute to the social good "in the cloister or under the protection of the religious habit" had a duty to move out into the world.

An adaptation of the settlement house proved to be the laywomen's bridge into a new era of more clearly defined Catholic social policy. Marion F. Gurney, another convert, working with the pastor of the Dominican Church of St. Catherine of Siena in a crowded Italian district on New York's West Side, organized the first Catholic settlement, St. Rose's, in 1898. Catholics were slow to see settlement work as a religious vocation. Immigrants from southern Italy, however, largely hostile to their clergy, were immune to priestly approaches, and the success of St. Rose's, with its classes in English and Church doctrine comfortably coexisting with clubs and other recreational activities, prompted imitation. In 1908 Gurney founded a religious order, the Sisters of Our Lady of Christian Doctrine, and as Mother Marianne of Jesus continued settlement work on the Lower East Side.

As clerical advocates built upon the encyclical *Rerum novarum* to strengthen the Church's commitment to social justice, laywomen's groups moved into the mainstream of the movement. In keeping with precedent set by the Society of St. Vincent de Paul, they could reach out to work with secular-Protestant groups against child labor and oppressive working conditions for women, in common recognition of the fact that under the present economic system "women's work in the domain of industry and general business cannot be done away with." Oregon's legislature passed the first minimum wage law for women because of the research of Caroline Gleason, field secretary of the League of Catholic Women, founded in Portland by Father Edwin V. O'Hara. Gleason had attended the pioneer Chicago School of Civics and Philanthropy under the Reverend Graham Taylor and worked at Taylor's settlement house, the Chicago Commons.

Father John A. Ryan, his fellow reformer-priests, and their women co-workers steered a Catholic course through the Progressive era. Though a popular feeling persisted that to do charitable work for pay was mercenary, they recognized the limitations of volunteerism and the necessity of more elaborate organization and professionalism in social service, as well as the fact that the majority of social workers were women. Several Catholic colleges opened professional schools in the 1910s, but additional effort went into separate training programs, beginning with the American Academy of Christian Democracy for Women, founded in 1915 by Father Peter E. Dietz of the German-American Catholic community and located in Cincinnati. The World War I emergency brought into being the National Catholic Social Service School for women, in Washington, D.C., supported by the National Council of Catholic Women until its merger in 1947 with the school of social work at Catholic University. Women professionals like Rose McHugh, a leading expert on case work in the Social Action Department of the National Catholic Welfare Conference, and Agnes Regan, executive secretary of the National Council of Catholic Women, were essential in the functioning of the new bureaucratic structure.[22]

The adjustment of women's role in the Jewish community under the pressures of American life is particularly illuminating. Religion and the family defined the Jews as a people, and ancient tradition supported an extreme differentiation of male and female roles. This the Jews brought with them. In the United States, men continued to participate in religious affairs, but as they were drawn into secular pursuits they ceased to monopolize religion. Like their Christian counterparts, they turned to women for aid in providing charity and religious education, and then adjusted to a shift in family equilibrium as this work led women into the public domain.

To be sure, the Jewish family clung to the comforts of tradition. Women continued the supportive domestic role of ministering to basic physical and emotional needs, a role that their responsibility for observance of the dietary and hygienic laws had long acknowledged. In this way they had helped to hold family and community together through many traumas before the last

---

[22] Aaron I. Abell, *American Catholicism and Social Action: A Search for Social Justice, 1865–1950* (Garden City, N.Y.: Doubleday, 1960); J. G. Shaw, *Edwin Vincent O'Hara* (New York: Farrar, Straus and Cudahy, 1957).

migration. The pattern endured until by the mid-twentieth century the Jewish mother had become the symbol for a national malady.

But Jews also responded to the openness of America. The managerial skills developed in fending for their families stood Jewish women in good stead. In the past this consciousness of competence had done something to ease the psychological burdens imposed by the theology of inferiority and subordination; now it enabled them to function confidently through a process of modernization that produced a partial role reversal and even in some cases a female majority. Accustomed to the congregational form of religious government, Jews easily split into sociologically differentiated denominations, each with its variant role for women. And it was easy to adopt the organizational forms the Protestants had worked out, as Rebecca Gratz had done as early as 1818 by starting a Jewish Sunday school movement in Philadelphia.

Norma Fain Pratt's chapter, "Transitions in Judaism," gives us an overview of this process. Modernization and Americanization once again came through organization, under the initial leadership of well-to-do German-Jewish women of the second generation. Biographies and studies of Jewish communities indicate that the process of federation began early.[23] Bostonians organized a citywide group, the Hebrew Ladies' Sewing Circle, in 1869, in order to support a work-relief project for poor women; Kansas City's Hebrew Ladies' Relief Society got its start in 1871.

In the 1880s and 1890s, under pressure from the mass immigration of Eastern European Jews, the women's program expanded to include religious education: Lina Hecht in 1889 started a Sunday school for girls at the new synagogue in Boston's North End; by 1897 the Boston Council of Jewish Women was coordinating efforts for Jewish education. The temple sisterhoods followed, establishing a function for women within these once masculine precincts.

Compared with women of other faiths, Jewish women appear to have worked more closely with men in charitable undertakings, and to have held memberships earlier on boards representing the religious community as a whole. When Boston's Federated Jewish Charities organized in 1895, the old sewing society was one of its components and three women were appointed to the board. Impelled by the same combination of concern for the preservation of the faith and Progressive reform, the Jewish community likewise adopted the settlement house and then encouraged the training of social workers. Though Judaism was a nonproselytizing faith, its women found their own missionary outlet in organizing medical aid for Jewish Palestine. Their society, Hadassah, under the charismatic leadership of Henrietta Szold, became an independent force in Zionism.

[23] See Barbara Miller Solomon, *Pioneers in Service* (Boston: Associated Jewish Philanthropies, 1956); Howard F. Sachs, "Development of the Jewish Community of Kansas City, 1864–1908," *Missouri Historical Review*, 60 (Apr. 1966).

When we turn from the churches' social outreach to their interior life, we enter largely uncharted territory. Only for Protestants do we have even a modicum of historical information about the interplay between women's concerns and masculine authority. It would be a mistake to think of the churches as a battleground between the sexes, but undertones of conflict run through the denominational history of this era, long anticipating today's controversies.

One identifiable area of tension has been the issue of family limitation, an issue still very much alive in the contemporary debates over birth control and the even more explosive question of abortion. To churches and clergy this has always been a moral question, to which their opposition was only partly articulated. Much was said about the breakdown of the family: separating sex from procreation raised the specter of female promiscuity and desertion of the home. Less was heard about birth control's separating sex from subordination, thereby threatening masculine, and ultimately clerical, authority. Alan Graebner's essay, "Birth Control and the Lutherans," follows the retreat of Missouri Synod clergy from outright opposition in the early 1900s to silence in the 1930s, and then to outright advocacy by the 1960s. As Graebner indicates, the experience of the Missouri Synod Lutherans, the most conservative of the Protestant denominations, has parallels within the Roman Catholic church: traditional outlooks preserved in immigrant enclaves gradually modernize under pressure from an upwardly mobile laity in a secular environment. The wife and mother's part—and indeed the collusion of husbands—in this evasion of clerical authority is hidden in the statistics of shrinking family size after 1885.

Another historical tension was created by women's aspirations for leadership. As local church programs came under the supervision of the growing denominational bureaucracies, women too were attracted by the advantages of centralization, particularly by the prospect of increasing power to do good through their beloved missions. Such prospects raised questions of status and authority, and these questions grew weightier through association with other issues involving women that occasionally made their way up to the church boards and then to the general assembly or conference platform. If the ladies administered their own denomination-wide missionary empire, should they be given laity rights of representation and suffrage in church conferences? To the male establishment, such prospects seemed pregnant with the ultimate challenge to power: female ordination. In "American Women in Ministry," Virginia Brereton and Christa Klein survey a century of muted conflict in the mainline denominations.

Much of the hostility engendered was suppressed, particularly by the women, who came onto the stage of power politics in a state of political innocence. Their deep commitment to the church bespoke the conservative social outlook they shared with their husbands. Whatever latent feminism they harbored had ample outlet in their work for sisters "cowering in the gloom of paganism."[24] This involvement, however, made them possessive. Where religion and the home were concerned, the authority, they felt, was theirs; and in the local or regional female mission groups of earlier generations they had enjoyed considerable autonomy, raising and disbursing their own funds, appointing and supporting their own missionaries.

Investigation of denominational records in the 1860s and 1870s, the years when church centralization began, might suggest how the issues of authority and collegiality emerged and were discussed behind the scenes. Perhaps it was the women's wartime service that led Congregationalists to approve an autonomous women's board of foreign missions in 1868, and the Northern Methodists and Northern Baptists to follow suit in 1869 and 1871. At the same time, strong opposition appeared to this or any further degree of independence.

In Northern Methodism, even the Women's Foreign Missionary Society, headed by the wives, daughters, and other female relatives of bishops and other church leaders, had difficulty in getting a spot on a conference schedule. "Let us only think our evening secure," wrote one lady in 1881, "when suddenly a telegram for Dr. Rust, Dr. Fowler, Chaplain McCabe, or some of the other comets or meteors of the great connectional work of Methodism moves us out of our inheritance, and puts us in a less desirable corner. But we are *only women*, you know," she concluded, "and have been used to it for ages and ages."[25]

The Methodist General Conference in 1880 confirmed women's entitlement to positions as Sunday school superintendents and class leaders, but discontinued licensing women as local preachers and turned down Anna Howard Shaw's appeal for ordination. The General Conference of 1888 approved deaconesses, but refused to seat Frances Willard and three other locally accredited female delegates. It was 1904 before Northern Methodist women gained laity rights.[26]

At the Southern Methodist General Conference of 1898, women were authorized to be Sunday school superintendents, and the Woman's Parsonage and Home Mission Society was reorganized into the Woman's Board of Home Missions with virtual autonomy. Its independence was short-lived,

[24] Keller, "Alternative Forms of Leadership."
[25] Theodore Lee Agnew, "Reflections on the Woman's Foreign Missionary Movement in Late Nineteenth-Century American Methodism," *Methodist History*, 6 (Jan. 1968), 15.
[26] Keller, "Alternative Forms of Leadership."

however. In 1910 the Conference placed the women's groups under control of the church's mission board and defeated a movement to give women laity rights, declaring that such a step ran counter to "the view our people hold in regard to woman's place in the church and in society. . . ."[27]

At the Southern Baptist Convention in 1885, two of seven Arkansas "messengers" (delegates) turned out to be women. Amid expressions of fear that women would "take possession of the Convention and occupy the president's chair," the delegates changed the constitution to make it clear that only "brethren" could be messengers. Not until 1888 were women able to centralize in a Woman's Missionary Union. And when the union's president at last gained the privilege of reporting directly to the Convention in 1929, a number of male delegates walked out, necessitating a compromise whereby that session was held in the Sunday school rooms of the host church rather than violate the dictum of St. Paul.[28]

Black Baptists furnish an interesting variation on the pattern. Their National Baptist Convention was formed in 1895 by uniting older foreign missionary, home missionary, and religious education organizations. Black women had been pressing the foreign missionary group to authorize an organization of their own, but though allowed to present their case at the meetings, they were voted down. By 1900, filled with "a righteous discontent," they launched a campaign for independence with an address by Nannie H. Burroughs on "How the Sisters are Hindered from Helping." Refusing to accept an auxiliary under the control of the church board, they won their own Woman's Convention and launched a social program similar to that of the WCTU. They established a vocational training school for girls in conjunction with a settlement house in Washington, D.C., discussed the mixed evils of racism and sexism, and by 1915 had issued a report grading the denomination's clergy. Those ministers in the lowest of three categories they condemned as "intellectually inept" or as having "exploited the membership for self-gratification." Since, as they pointed out, "women provided the greatest financial as well as numerical support to the churches," they had the right "to endorse only well-trained clergymen."[29]

---

[27] Howard Grimes, "The United States, 1800–1962," in Stephen C. Neill and Hans-Ruedi Weber, eds., *The Layman in Christian History* (Philadelphia: Westminster Press, 1963), 248–49; Douglas R. Chandler, "Belle Harris Bennett," in Edward T. James, Janet Wilson James, and Paul Boyer, eds., *Notable American Women* (Cambridge: Harvard Univ. Press, 1971); Norma Taylor Mitchell, "From Social to Radical Feminism: A Survey of Emerging Diversity in Methodist Women's Organizations, 1869–1974," *Methodist History*, 13 (Apr. 1975), 30.

[28] Harry L. McBeth, "The Role of Women in Southern Baptist History," *Baptist History and Heritage*, 12 (Jan. 1977), 5, 7–8, 6, 15–16.

[29] Evelyn Brooks Barnett, "The Feminization of the Black Baptist Church, 1890–1920," paper delivered at the Berkshire Conference of Women Historians, Mount Holyoke College, Aug. 24, 1978.

It is perhaps more than coincidental that at a time when women of the mainstream denominations were finding male clerical leadership increasingly frustrating a female-oriented church should arise. Like Ann Lee before her, Mary Baker Eddy spoke of a God who was both father and mother. For a time she and other women served as ministers of the Church of Christ, Scientist, but she soon did away with clergy altogether. Twin lecterns replaced the pulpit, and local officials holding office in rotation, a man and a woman, read prescribed selections from the Bible and Mrs. Eddy's *Science and Health*. In Christian Science the authority was a woman's. The male-dominated churches had given Mrs. Eddy no help in her time of physical and spiritual travail. In her theology woman could heal herself through affirming the feminine element—spirituality—over materialism.

On another level of society, the loosely structured Protestant sects picked up the mantle of the early Quakers and Methodists, who, when called to carry a new message, had welcomed women's evangelizing gifts. Preaching the second blessing and the baptism of Pentecost in the Wesleyan or the Reformed tradition, women appeared, like the men, as God's instruments.

She whom the spirit visited would have wrestled with her earthly affections, even her love for husband and children, until she could accept God's overriding claims. Phoebe Palmer, Catherine Booth, Alma White, Mary Cole of the Church of God, the black itinerant Amanda Smith, may have been traditionalists in their concept of woman's place, but they vigorously defended their right to preach and were defended by their male associates. Married couples worked in the gospel together: William and Mary Boardman with Robert Pearsall Smith and Hannah Whitall Smith in the English Higher Life movement, Seth and Hulda Rees of the Pilgrim Holiness church, the Booths and their married children.[30]

In the faith healing movement of the post–Civil War generation, women were prominent as cult leaders, practitioners, and presiding geniuses of faith cure homes and hospitals. Mrs. Eddy's Christian Science and the related New Thought movement, some of whose leaders were her former lieutenants, offered a mind cure attractive to the middle class. Mrs. Eddy's theology and the healing center founded by Dorothea Trudel in Switzerland influenced several prominent Reformed clergymen in eastern cities who in the 1880s sponsored faith cure homes under female direction.[31]

[30] Loveland, "Domesticity and Religion"; Smith, *Called Unto Holiness*; Hardesty, Dayton, and Dayton, "Women in the Holiness Movement"; Edith L. Waldvogel, "The 'Overcoming Life': A Study in the Reformed Evangelical Origins of Pentecostalism" (Diss. Harvard Univ., 1977).

[31] Donald Meyer, *The Positive Thinkers* (Garden City, N.Y.: Doubleday, 1965); Gail T. Parker, *Mind Cure in New England* (Hanover, N.H.: Univ. Press of New England, 1973); Ernest R. Sandeen, *The Roots of Fundamentalism* (Chicago: Univ. of Chicago Press, 1970); Raymond J. Cunningham, "From Holiness to Healing: The Faith Cure in America,

In the same decade followers of Mary Woodworth-Etter in central Indiana experienced remarkable healings and began speaking in tongues; her ministry may have been the origin of the worldwide pentecostal movement. Florence Crawford, breaking with her teacher, the black holiness preacher William Seymour, left Los Angeles for Portland about 1908 and launched pentecostalism in the Pacific Northwest. She later established her new sect, the Apostolic Faith, in the northern Midwest, although this group rejected her principle of celibacy and split away, calling itself the Open Bible Standard. In the 1920s Aimee Semple McPherson built a religious superworld called the Church of the Foursquare Gospel for the rootless of Los Angeles. Her gifts reappeared in Kathryn Kuhlman, a wandering evangelist from the age of sixteen. In 1955, in middle life, Kuhlman began a ministry of healing in Pittsburgh, and through the use of radio and television she attracted a nationwide following.[32]

Where the sects coalesced into organized churches, women's leadership and influence dwindled. In denominational structures, church life was routinized; charisma randomly distributed no longer provided sufficient authority. The holiness Church of the Nazarene and the pentecostal Assemblies of God ruled that female evangelists could no longer administer the sacrament, and many lapsed into the secondary role of teachers and missionaries.

Today we find ourselves in the third decade of another great revival. Like those of the past, it both renews and reforms, strengthening elements of the old order as lifelines to the past and carrying society in new directions toward the future.

A neo-Victorian idealization of domesticity asserted itself in the 1950s with the middle-class flight to suburbia, the rise in the birth rate, and the commercialized cult of togetherness. This was the audience for the inspirational writings that Paul Boyer describes in his essay in this volume, "Minister's Wife, Widow, Reluctant Feminist: Catherine Marshall in the 1950s." Marshall typified the mainline Protestant woman's most sex-

---

1872–1892," *Church History*, 43 (Dec. 1974); Waldvogel, "The 'Overcoming Life.'" The health reformism of Seventh-day Adventist leader Ellen G. White, elaborated in the 1860s and 1870s, was a different phenomenon. See Ronald L. Numbers, *Prophetess of Health* (New York: Harper and Row, 1976).

[32] I am indebted to Grant Wacker for information about pentecostalism and its preachers. See also Robert M. Anderson, *Vision of the Disinherited* (New York: Oxford Univ. Press, 1979). Other sources are William G. McLoughlin, "Aimee Semple McPherson," in *Notable American Women*, and "Aimee Semple McPherson: 'Your Sister in the King's Glad Service,'" *Journal of Popular Culture*, 1 (Winter 1967); and David Edward Harrell, Jr., *All Things Are Possible: The Healing and Charismatic Revivals in Modern America* (Bloomington: Indiana Univ. Press, 1975), 190–91.

linked role: the pastor's tireless, self-denying, and unremunerated better half. At the same time, she belonged to the group of energetic and am- bitious writers who have made money by preaching conservative ideals of womanhood.

All revivals, as we have seen, have simultaneously reflected and cre- ated change in women's lives and in their self-consciousness. The current revival differs from its predecessors in the close identification of many churchwomen, lay and religious, with a feminist movement that goes beyond demands for equality to express a search for new values. Unlike the anticlericalism of such freethinking outsiders as Frances Wright and Elizabeth Cady Stanton, feminist criticism is now a conscious and delib- erate force within the churches. The ordination of women is the symbolic issue, challenging oppressive, male-oriented authority patterns linked to narrow concepts of the family and sex roles. The churches have fought a long battle to preserve the old forms and sanctions, but traditional family relationships are poorly adapted to life in modern societies. Caught be- tween the denigration of authority and the celebration of sexuality, the ranks of the celibate priesthood are thinning; religious and lay women, along with laymen, are moving to meet ecclesiastical needs. Feminist scholars, now trained in seminaries, offer a new theology and a new understanding of God based on changing sex roles, reminding us of the culture's habit of shaping God in its own image.

In the historical record, we can find the forerunners of today's femi- nists. Presbyterian history records a striking example of the birth of fem- inist consciousness among churchwomen. The Presbyterians long refused to countenance a woman's missionary board. "Some of the most thought- ful minds are beginning to ask what is to become of this Woman's Move- ment in the church," one Presbyterian churchman commented in 1870, but his advice was: "Let it alone—all through her history like movements have started. Do not oppose these women and it will die out." Women's organizations nevertheless came into being, and under the energetic lead- ership of Katharine Bennett, an auxiliary called the Woman's Board of Home Missions won legal independence through incorporation in 1915. The event occasioned much uneasiness in the church, and in the early 1920s the all-male General Assembly combined the women's boards and integrated them with the Presbyterian Board of National Missions. The female majority (60 percent) watched the absorption of their mission so- cieties without an outcry, but within two years morale and revenues plum- meted. Alarmed, the General Council commissioned a report on "Causes of Unrest among Women of the Church." The authors, Katharine Bennett and Margaret Hodge, the former heads of the women's home and foreign mission boards respectively, deplored the constant male reminders that women were not "intellectually or spiritually equal to responsibilities in the church" and asked for opportunities to serve according to ability. Perhaps as a result, the church in 1930 permitted women to be ordained as elders, thus opening its legislative councils to them; for ordination as ministers they waited until 1956. The Bennett-Hodge report was rediscovered in the 1970s when Presbyterian churchwomen turned to history for help in their campaign against tokenism.[33]

The feminist tide has run strong in Protestantism and also in contemporary Judaism. In recent years a significant body of recruits has come from the Catholic church. Dawning consciousness of the disparity between the lives of sisters and those of churchmen came about through the Sister Formation movement of the 1950s, which strove to improve professional training and thereby both encouraged personal growth and attracted the disapproving attention of conservative prelates. The Second Vatican Council opened other windows on the world and the work to be done in it. Among Catholic feminists, Sidney Callahan led the way. Her mild reasonableness in *The Illusion of Eve* (1965) attracted little attention, but the publication of Mary Daly's *The Church and the Second Sex* (1968) was an event of the first magnitude, attesting to the accumulated anger of women both within and outside institutional religion. Sister Marie Augusta Neal, as a sociologist, documents the new reformation "calling the sister out of the cloister and the wife out of the nuclear family." Rosemary Ruether, as a writer and seminary teacher, searches out neglected religious traditions that are more positive for women and applies feminist insights to the human condition.[34]

Today women of all faiths are practicing ecumenicity in feminism. Theirs is the mission of resolving the central paradox of women's religious history. Both for religion and for women, America has been a new theater. Religious revivals have strengthened female identity, called forth female charisma, and encouraged social reforms through which women found places in modern society. The Judeo-Christian heritage, however, while imparting common

[33] Elizabeth Howell Gripe, "Women, Restructuring and Unrest in the 1920s," *Journal of Presbyterian History*, 52 (Summer 1974); and, on Presbyterianism, Elizabeth Howell Verdesi, *In But Still Out: Women in the Church* (Philadelphia: Westminster Press, 1976), 85–90, 101–8, 133–37.

[34] Sidney Cornelia Callahan, *The Illusion of Eve* (New York: Sheed and Ward, 1965); Mary Daly, *The Church and the Second Sex* (1968), and reprint ed., *With a New Feminist Postchristian Introduction by the Author* (New York: Harper and Row, 1975). See also Daly, *Beyond God the Father: Toward a Philosophy of Women's Liberation* (Boston: Beacon Press, 1973) and *Gyn/Ecology: The Metaethics of Radical Feminism* (Boston: Beacon Press, 1978); Sister Marie Augusta Neal, "Women in Religion: A Sociological Perspective," *Sociological Inquiry*, 45 (Dec. 1975), 33. Among Rosemary Ruether's writings see *Liberation Theology: Human Hope Confronts Christian History and American Power* (New York: Paulist Press, 1972); *New Woman New Earth: Sexist Ideologies and Human Liberation* (New York: Seabury Press, 1975); Ruether, ed., *Religion and Sexism: Images of Woman in the Jewish and Christian Traditions* (New York: Simon and Schuster, 1974); and Ruether and McLaughlin, eds., *Women of Spirit*.

hopes for freedom, has blocked women's way through ancient teachings about women's place and male-female relationships. Ever millennialists, we seem to see the day approaching when femaleness will be no more than a biological distinction, when the people of the churches, men and women, will have forged new concepts of religious authority and the majority will be silent no longer.*

* For help in the preparation of this introduction, I would like to thank Clarissa Atkinson, Sandra Boyd, William R. Hutchison, Edward T. James, Sydney V. James, and Leila Zenderland.

Mary Maples Dunn

Saints and Sisters
Congregational and Quaker Women in the Early Colonial Period

*I*t is frequently observed in Christian societies that the women go to church. The implication is that the church, or even religion, is in some way more necessary to women than to men, although women are submissive to the men who dominate the priesthoods. But how and why this gender differentiation develops in respect to religion is imperfectly understood; we are not certain that it is inherent in Christianity itself; we do not know why it becomes part of a social-religious order, what functions it might have in that society, nor what conditions produce the dichotomy. American experience in the seventeenth and early eighteenth centuries offers the historian two Protestant cases to investigate and contrast, the Puritan Congregationalists and the Quakers. Puritans and Quakers pursued different routes to settlement in America, with different results for women.[1]

The religious intensity and excitement in England prior to and during the Civil War gave rise to both Puritanism and Quakerism, and provided a

[1] There is now a considerable literature on what Patricia Martin Doyle calls "the role of religion . . . in shaping the traditional cultural images that have degraded and suppressed women" in Rosemary Radford Ruether, ed., *Religion and Sexism: Images of Woman in the Jewish and Christian Tradition* (New York: Simon and Schuster, 1974), 9. Interest in the "feminization" of religion has been created by Barbara Welter, "The Feminization of American Religion: 1800–1860," in Mary S. Hartman and Lois Banner, eds., *Clio's Consciousness Raised: New Perspectives on the History of Women* (New York: Harper and Row, 1974), 137–57. See also Nancy F. Cott, *The Bonds of Womanhood: Woman's Sphere in New England, 1780–1835* (New Haven: Yale Univ. Press. 1977), 126–59.

background in which a rethinking of Christian doctrine was taking place and church governance and church-state relationships were being questioned. This fluid situation was particularly important to women. The Protestant dismissal of the cult of Mary and of the nunneries opened up questions about the position of women, both in society and in the structure of the church, and destroyed the most powerful female religious symbol and role model. The result was a period of intense religious activity in which Puritan and Quaker women in America took part. Indeed, removal to America may have been particularly invigorating to the Protestant women who took part in these religious migrations, because of the sense shared by both men and women that they were free from traditional restraints. But in Puritan Congregationalism, despite the vigor and enthusiasm of the first-generation women, women were disciplined to accept male authority, socialized to submission, and accustomed to filling the churches. Amongst Quakers we discover religious experience and church governance more equally shared by women and men.[2]

There were at least three factors that determined these different outcomes for women in the "City on a Hill" and the "Holy Experiment." First, it was necessary to the development of a predominantly female piety that there be some objectives of the society that required female piety, and at least to some extent excused it in men. Second, scripture had to be interpreted in a way that asserted female inferiority. Therefore, the interests of those who had the power to formulate doctrine and interpret the word of God were determinants of the female role. The third factor is related to the second. Those who had the power to exert discipline over women had power to socialize them in the church.

*T*he Puritan development precedes the Quaker one. The first generation of Puritan immigrants to America were not yet sectarians; they were groping their way toward a form of church governance which would be free from the evils of episcopacy. The godly, both inside and outside the ministry, were making their way toward a doctrinal position that would explain their sense of communion with God. The lines between lay and clerical authority were blurred. Puritans certainly

---

[2] For the effects of the Reformation, see Jane Dempsey Douglass, "Women and the Continental Reformation," in Ruether, *Religion and Sexism*, 292–318, and for early Calvinism. Nancy L. Roelker, "The Appeal of Calvinism to French Noblewomen in the Sixteenth Century," *The Journal of Interdisciplinary History*, 2 (Spring 1972), 391–418. England is discussed in Christopher Hill, *The World Turned Upside Down* (New York: Viking, 1972), 247–60, and Keith Thomas, "Women and the Civil War Sects," *Past and Present*, 13 (1958), 42–62.

brought in their baggage a sense of the inferiority of women; but belief in female equality before the Lord also made it uncertain what role women would play in a new religious order.

The fundamental statement of female inferiority was, of course, found in Genesis. Eve, the first to listen to Satan and the seducer of Adam, brought to women a heavy share of original sin; and to Adam, to man, the message that he should have known better than to listen to woman. Woman in this case was also a vehicle for Satan, not able to see through his wiles, wanting in intellect, needing protection. Genesis 3:16 imposed the correction and punishment: "Unto the woman he said, I will greatly increase thy sorrows, & thy conceptions. In sorrow shalt thou bring forth children, and thy desire shall be subject to thine husband, and he shall rule over thee."[3] The Calvinist sense of original sin was powerful, and it was unlikely that Puritans could ever reject the notion that God required submission of women.

The traditional Christian rules which might govern the place and conduct of a woman in the church, and the authorities she should seek in matters of doctrine, were asserted for Puritans by St. Paul. Paul was widely accepted as authority by those who wished to recapitulate in their own time the primitive Christian church, and he was therefore important to New World Puritans. Paul seemed to make his position clear in his letters to the Corinthians and, later, to Timothy and Titus. In I Cor. 14:34–35 he said, "Let your women keep silence in the Churches: for it is not permitted unto them to speak: but they ought to be subject, as also the Law saith. And if they will learn any thing, let them ask their husbands at home: for it is a shame for a woman to speak in the Church."[4] It was not possible to construe this injunction narrowly as to time and place, that is, only to Corinth, since the Apostle was equally specific in the later letter to Timothy (1 Tim. 2:11–12), "Let the women learn in silence with all subjection. I permit not a woman to teach, neither to usurp authority over the man, but to be in silence."

Paul apparently derived these rules from the customs with which he was familiar; he may have asserted them at first only for Corinth, and later reaffirmed them in the realization that the end of human time was not, after all, at hand. This could account for the fact that in other ways Paul had a more liberating message for women. In Titus 2:3–4, older women were given a teaching function: "teachers of honest things, they may

---

[3] Lloyd E. Berry, ed., *The Geneva Bible: A Facsimile of the 1560 Edition* (Madison: Univ. of Wisconsin Press, 1969), the Bible used in New England, is used here for all Biblical quotations. I have modernized spelling.

[4] Compare the English text of I Cor. 14:34 in the King James version: "Let your women keep silence in the churches: for it is not permitted unto them to speak; but *they are commanded* to be under obedience, as also saith the law." Italics added.

instruct the young women to be sober minded, that they love their husbands, that they love their children." Paul also insisted that women were to share equally in the benefits of the new order. He wrote to the Galatians (3:28), "There is neither Jew nor Grecian: there is neither bond nor free: there is neither male nor female: for you are all one in Christ Jesus." Furthermore, even in the first letter to the Corinthians there is some confusion, since he said in 1 Cor. 11:3–5, "But I will that you know, that Christ is the head of every man: & the man is the woman's head: and God is Christ's head. Every man praying or prophecying having any thing on his head, dishonoreth his head. But every woman that prayeth or prophecieth bareheaded, dishonoreth her head: for it is even one very thing, as though she were shaven." The implication of inferiority is clear; but so is the possibility of speaking in the church, and the ancient Biblical tradition of women prophets receives recognition.

The people of New England could, if they wanted, find in Paul a situation parallel to their own: a radical spiritual message of equality in tension with social custom. It was not certain how the tension between these two views of women would be resolved in New England, and in this situation (which may have obtained at all times and on all frontiers in the Christian religion) many women engaged themselves in both experiments in church governance and in the discussion of doctrine. A few of them made their marks.[5]

Women shared fully in the excitement that creation of a new religious settlement produced, and they responded to the challenge with intelligence, vigor, and enthusiasm. The covenanted or gathered church was a source of a feeling of equality. Women also tried to control doctrines in many areas, including those relating specifically to women. Unfortunately, heresy trials constitute much of the evidence that women tried to assert themselves. This is unfortunate because those charged with heresy were considered extremists whom the Puritans rejected and because these women were more apt to perish than to publish. Their trial records are our only evidence of their doctrinal positions, and those records were written by male opponents. Nevertheless, they are ample testimony that women were neither silent nor submissive.

Anne Hutchinson is the most famous of these women, because the doctrine that she, John Cotton, and their followers tried to bring to general acceptance in Boston would have changed profoundly the thrust of the Massachusetts experiment. Hutchinson and the Antinomians rejected the doctrine of sanctification or the "Covenant of Works" (the idea that

---

[5] Paul's ambivalence and change through time are presented in Constance F. Parvey, "The Theology and Leadership of Women in the New Testament," in Ruether, *Religion and Sexism*, 123–37.

outward behavior or a righteous life was a sign of justification or redemption of one's soul by Christ). Their own doctrine, or "Covenant of Grace," insisted that redemption came only through the gift of grace. Hutchinson's own knowledge of this was her sense of direct communion with the Holy Spirit. In the Antinomian view, the Covenant of Works had a deadening effect on the spiritual life of the community because it encouraged too much scrutiny of behavior and led to formalism or legalism in establishing rules of behavior which, consistently observed, would prepare for or offer evidence of election by God to sainthood. The Antinomians acquired a following that threatened a breakdown in Massachusetts' ideological unity, an overturning of the authority of law and therefore of social discipline, and a real revolution in the norms for Christian (Puritan) behavior. It was possible for a woman to share in the leadership of such a movement because the Covenant of Grace could free her from restraints emanating from a rigid application of the rules of a Covenant of Works.

The story of Hutchinson's trial and defeat is too well known to need retelling here. However, it is worth pointing out again that she was a tough woman, intelligent and learned, determined to remake the church. She had remarkable vigor and a charisma that might have changed the course of Massachusetts history had she been a man. It was clear that her judges, particularly John Winthrop, thought she headed a "potent party" and was a formidable enemy. They were determined to get rid of her. She was a good match for them in all theological discussions, and over and over again in the trial they were forced to revert to the issue of women speaking and teaching. Hutchinson insisted that she worked within the Pauline rules; her judges were sure she did not.

At the heart of their disagreement was the fact that Hutchinson applied Paul in a positive way to her situation, while her judges were determined to stick to the reading most restricting for women. For example, she maintained that in the large meetings held in her house to discuss sermons, she could speak because this was private, that is, not in the church; that she could, as an older woman, teach younger women; that she could, when asked, teach and counsel men in private. But she also declared a right to public utterance in exercising a gift of prophesy, for which she found Biblical precedent. Her judges decided that the age of prophesy was over. Finally, ". . . to justify this her disordered course, she said she walked by the rule of the Apostle, Gal. which she called *the rule of the new creature*. . . ." [italics added], that is, Gal. 3:28 "there is neither male nor female: for you are all one in Christ Jesus." Hutchinson insisted, then, in applying the broadest possible definition of Christian responsibility to women's roles in religion. Because she argued in the context of a situation which seemed to her judges to be threatening to the Puritan establishment, they were not able to consider the problem dispassionately, and the judgment against her was the most important decision Puritans made about women's place in the formulation of doctrine.[6]

Aggressive women were also evident in conservative New Haven seven years after Hutchinson's defeat, which had influenced attitudes toward women everywhere in the Puritan settlements. In 1644 a heretic woman of high status disturbed the peace of New Haven. Anne Eaton, daughter of an English bishop and the unhappy wife of Theophilus Eaton, the governor, was tried and excommunicated. Her fall from grace first arose from her disavowal of infant baptism; she had been led to error by reading and failure to seek guidance from her husband. Because she was the wife of the governor, her example was considered important to the development of the community. When the governor's wife walked out of church, there was hell to pay. Minister, elders, and husband were quick to go to work to convince her of the error of her ways. She was steadily hounded, particularly by the minister, John Davenport, who had played a small role in the trial of Anne Hutchinson.

Anne Eaton either could not or would not argue her own case, and while she refused to accept the authority of her male opponents in a matter of doctrine, the trial record does not give any evidence that she argued for her own ability to make decisions. But heresy on the question of infant baptism was not the only ground on which the church moved against her. In the end, Eaton was excommunicated for lying and stubbornness (that is, for refusal to discuss the matter) and censured on additional charges which sprang from bad relations with other members of her household: her mother-in-law, her grown stepdaughter, and several servants. It would appear that by 1644 intellectual error alone would not serve as grounds to proceed against a woman because, strictly speaking, heresy was beyond her capacity. Women had lost the battle for control over doctrine, which now belonged to men.[7]

[6] The documents have been collected by David D. Hall, *The Antinomian Controversy, 1636–1638: A Documentary History* (Middletown: Wesleyan Univ. Press, 1968). The introduction is an excellent brief summary of the doctrinal issues involved, 5–20. For Anne Hutchinson's defense of herself from Galatians see pp. 268–69. The most recent study is Lyle Koehler, "The Case of the American Jezebels: Anne Hutchinson and Female Agitation during the Years of Antinomian Turmoil, 1636–1640," *William and Mary Quarterly*, 3d Series, 31 (Jan. 1974), 55–78, which discusses Antinomianism in feminist terms. See also Ben Barker-Benfield, "Anne Hutchinson and the Puritan Attitude Toward Women," *Feminist Studies*, 1: no. 2 (1973).

[7] Anne Lloyd Yale Eaton had been married previously to David Yale; her children by Yale came to America with her, and her grandson Elihu, founder of Yale, was born in Boston. Her daughter Anne Yale Hopkins was the woman of whom Winthrop made the famous remark, "If she had attended her household affairs, and such things as belong to women, and not gone out of her way and calling to meddle in such things as are proper for men,

Both Hutchinson and Eaton found supporters among women, a fact that argues convincingly that the Puritan experience in America was a liberating one for women. However, these supporters were also silenced by prosecution and punishment. The most notable case was that of Mary Dyer, who became a Quaker and was hanged. If these examples were not enough to still female dissent, a startling and damaging condemnation of Hutchinson and Dyer, the one to which was attached the highest symbolic power, was the birth of monsters. Few people in Puritan New England could believe that accident caused their two most vigorous female dissenters to give birth to "monsters." John Cotton had advised keeping Mary Dyer's unnatural birth a secret, believing that God intended such things only as warnings to parents. John Winthrop, however, had no doubt that public judgment was involved, and ordered exhumation and examination. He also sent for details of the banished Anne Hutchinson's childbirth, and believed it to be the final evidence against her.[8]

The cases of Eaton and Hutchinson are both tied into social and political factors that overwhelmed the women, increased the bias of their judges, and prejudiced their communities. The question whether women may have played a more active "mainstream" role in religion and church governance is difficult to answer; women who achieved small-scale successes didn't so readily break into the records.

However, some evidence of aggressive females and a church seemingly more open to the formulation of less limiting policies for women is found in the notebook or diary of John Fiske (1637–1675), a clergyman of Wenham. In this church, in which the pastor always referred to his congregation as "the brethren and sisters," and usually fully identified women (that is, he used both the father's and husband's names and the woman's Christian name), there was brisk debate in the 1640s over female membership. It was argued first that women themselves had publicly to

---

whose minds are stronger, etc., she had kept her wits. . . ." James Kendall Hosmer, ed., *Winthrop's Journal* (New York: Barnes and Noble, 1953), 2:225. For Anne Eaton's trial, see Newman Smyth, ed., "Mrs. Eaton's Trial (in 1644); As It Appears Upon the Records of the First Church of New Haven," *Papers of the New Haven Historical Society*, 5 (1905), 133–48. It was suggested at the time that Eaton was influenced by Lady Deborah Moody, who was excommunicated in Salem for the same heresy and moved to Long Island.

[8] Koehler, "The Case of the American Jezebels," 69–72, identifies Hutchinson's supporters and their treatment. In 1646 a Mrs. Brewster was accused of sympathizing with Eaton and of saying that Davenport made her "sermon sick"; Mrs. Moore, another Eaton sympathizer, was accused of denying the minister's authority. See Charles J. Hoadly, ed., *Records of the Colony and Plantation of New Haven, from 1638 to 1649* (Hartford, 1857), 1:243–59. In the case of Mary Dyer, modern analysis is difficult. See Hall, *The Antinomian Controversy*, 280–82, and for Winthrop's opinion, 214. See Emery Battis, *Saints and Sectaries: Anne Hutchinson and the Antinomian Crisis in the Massachusetts Bay Colony* (Chapel Hill: Univ. of North Carolina Press, 1963), 346–48, for modern medical opinion of Hutchinson's misfortune.

relate their religious experiences and their sense of election, if the church were to judge their fitness for membership. Therefore the act of qualification seemed to require women to speak in church. The diary noted that in some churches men, elders or ministers, were reading the women's statements, on the grounds that women should keep silent; and Wenham produced scriptural examples of female prophets to justify female public speaking of this kind. The case was similar to the one made by Anne Hutchinson.

Secondly, Wenham church decided that women were not automatically transferred from one church to another when their husbands moved, and it badgered the Salem church to get individual dismissions for women. The issue appears to have been pushed by one Joan White, who also took an active role in church governance; she spoke in church meetings and made motions which the congregation acted upon. In her relation, she said that she "was brought up in a poore Ignorant place," and although she came to New England because she believed good people came there, she was "for a long space of time living far in ye woods, from the means; and reading on Rom. 10, Faith commeth by hearing; put her affections onward ye desire of ye means." In short, she wanted to get out of the woods and into a church, and was enjoying every minute of it. Wenham, too, had to face the difficulty of an "unnatural birth." In 1646 John Fiske examined a stillborn child who might have been judged a monster, but Fiske proved a careful observer. In the presence of female witnesses, he performed a partial autopsy, decided that the child was basically normal, and cleared the mother.[9]

Wenham church gives us a number of aggressive women, behaving independently, taking an active role in church governance, and being taken seriously. Then in late 1655, Fiske and a number of his followers moved from Wenham to Chelmsford, where they started a new church. In establishing local practices, they concluded in early 1656, "this day agrrd [sic] by ye church yt ye officer should repeate & declare ye Relation of ye wo: to ye church." In the following decade fewer and fewer women appear in Fiske's pages, and in Chelmsford as in almost all churches, women were referred to as "wife of"; first names generally went unrecorded. Women lost not only voice, but also identity. Furthermore, the experience in Chelmsford was not unique. By 1660, in all of the church records examined for this study, silence had been enjoined on women in the matter of the relation. Silence also prevented them from having a voice in cases of discipline. Judgment was in the hands of men, and more

---

[9] John Fiske, "Notebook (Diary) of Church Matters, 1637–1675," Fam MSS, Essex Institute, on prophesy, f. 28 (25.8.1644) and on Joan White's membership, f. 66–68 (10.2.1645), and on the autopsy, f. 94.

and more the minister instructed the brethren in their voting. Women seem to have been disciplined in numbers out of proportion to their share of congregational populations, and their offenses were increasingly connected with social behavior, not with heresy. What had happened?[10]

Certainly women continued to respond positively to the church, far more so than the men. Scattered admissions data for 28 Congregational churches (18 from Massachusetts and 10 from Connecticut) show a steady growth in the proportion of female admissions. In the 1630s and 1640s male and female admissions were fairly equal, but a shift began in the 1650s, and after 1660 female admissions exceed male. This numerical superiority holds both in rural and urban areas and throughout the period investigated, as Tables 1 and 2 show.[11]

Before 1660 women probably joined the church in numbers somewhat out of proportion to their part of the total population. However, by 1640 women may have accounted for as much as 40 percent of the population,[12] and by 1660, at least in Massachusetts, the sex ratio would have narrowed still further. In any case, the more important point to be developed is women's preponderance in the church population, even after their attempts to share in governance were defeated and male membership shrank.

The best explanation for this phenomenon may come from the anthropologists, who have suggested that all societies tend to esteem male roles more than female ones; and that there is a universal tendency to make what the man does a matter of public importance, what the woman does a domestic matter, carrying less status.[13] New England allows us to add another dimension to these statements: when a society as a whole suffers from a serious conflict in its goals, it can *use* gender role differences to resolve that conflict. It can do this by assigning one set of goals to men, and another to women. This guarantees that those goals which are

[10] For Chelmsford, see Fiske, "Notebook," f. 181 (29.4.1656). My conclusions about discipline are still impressionistic, but I hope to verify them in a future study. They are partially confirmed by Emil Oberholzer, *Delinquent Saints* (New York: Columbia Univ. Press, 1956), who reports more heresies pre-1660 and during the Great Awakening, 78–110. For church records that lead to this conclusion, see Table 1.

[11] I am not the first to check the records for female membership. See Edmund S. Morgan, "New England Puritanism: Another Approach," *William and Mary Quarterly*, 3d Series, 18 (Apr. 1961), 238–39. Robert G. Pope, *The Half-Way Covenant: Church Membership in Puritan New England* (Princeton: Princeton Univ. Press, 1969) has also observed this imbalance from 1660–1690, but he does not interpret it beyond remarking that religion continued to be important in women's lives (p. 218) and that "The tendency to leave religion to women is normal in a relatively stable society" (p. 213).

[12] Koehler, "The Case of the American Jezebels," 71.

[13] Michelle Zimbalist Rosaldo, "Woman, Culture, and Society: A Theoretical Overview," in Michelle Zimbalist Rosaldo and Louise Lamphere, eds., *Woman, Culture and Society* (Stanford: Stanford Univ. Press, 1974), 17–42.

Table 1. PERCENTAGE OF FEMALE CHURCH ADMISSIONS*

	1632–1639	1640–1649	1650–1659	1660c–1669	1670–1679	1680–1689	1690–1699	1700–1709	1710–1719	1720–1729	1730–1739	1740–1749	1750–1759
Mass.a	50	55	61	64	71	66	68	65	63	67	62	66	71
Mass. and Conn.b	46	51	60	65	67	60	65	63	64	66	63	65	70

a 18 congregations

b 28 congregations

c Figures after 1660 generally include those members who came in under the Half-Way Covenant; many records do not distinguish classes of admissions.

* *Sources for Massachusetts:* Beverly, First Church, MSS Records, and Beverly, Second Church, MSS Records, Essex Institute (Essex, hereafter); Boston, Second Church, Records, Vols. I, 8, Massachusetts Historical Society (MHS); Boston, Fourth Church, Brattle Street, John Homans, 2d, et al., eds., *Records of the Church in Brattle Square Boston* (Boston: The Benevolent Fraternity of Churches, 1902); Boston, Eighth Church, Hollis Street, Records 1732–1788, Edes Papers, MHS; Brockton, First Parish, Records 1740–1805, Congregational Library, Boston; Charlestown, James Frothingham Hunnewell, ed., *Records of the First Church in Charlestown, Massachusetts, 1632–1789* (Boston: David Clapp, 1891); Dorchester, Charles H. Pope, ed., *Records of the First Church at Dorchester in New England 1636–1734* (Boston: George H. Ellis, 1891); Essex, First Church, # 10, Records 1725–1869; and Essex First Church Separates, # 10, Records 1745–1810, Essex; Hanover, Vernon L. Briggs, *History and Records of the First Congregational Church, Hanover, Mass., 1727–1865* (Boston: Wallace Spooner, 1895); Hingham, First Church, Box # 8, Vital Records 1717–1865, MHS; Hingham, Second Church, in Hingham First Church, Box # 10, Records 1635–1897, MHS; Ipswich, First Church, Records, Ipswich Historical Society; Plymouth, *Plymouth Church Records, 1620–1859* (New York: New England Society, 1920, 1923), 2 vols.; Topsfield, First Church, Records 1729–1759, Essex; Salem, First Church, and Salem, Separates, Records, 1629–1772, Barnard Copy, Essex. *For Connecticut:* Branford, First Church, Records, 1687–1889, I, Connecticut State Library (CSL); Farmington, First Church, Records 1652–1938, II, CSL; Greenfield, First Church, Records 1741–1763, I, CSL; Guilford, First Church, Records 1717–1921, I(A), CSL; New Haven, Franklin B. Dexter, *Historical Catalogue of the Members of the First Church of Christ in New Haven, Connecticut, 1639–1914* (New Haven, 1914); New London, First Church, Records 1698–1917, I, CSL; Preston, Separate, Ruby Parke Anderson, ed., *The Parke Scrapbook* (Baltimore: Portlitz, 1965), I; Stonington, First Church, Records 1674–1925, CSL; Windsor, First Church, Records 1636–1932, I, CSL. Obviously, only a few records span the whole period.

Table 2. PERCENTAGE OF FEMALE CHURCH ADMISSIONS
IN THREE MASSACHUSETTS CONGREGATIONS*

	1660–1669	1670–1679	1680–1689	1690–1699
Salem	62	63	70	73
Charlestown	65	69	64	71
Boston Second Church	72	77	63	68

* Salem was chosen because of interest in the response amongst women and men to the end-of-century crisis; Charlestown, as a stable but old church; and Boston Second to represent the urban churches because of Cotton Mather's frequently quoted observation that his congregation was largely female, in *Ornaments for the Daughters of Zion* (London: Tho. Parkhurst, 1694), 54–56.

feminine will become domestic issues and command less social importance. The men can ignore them and apply themselves to male goals.

The Puritans had not been long in New England before the ministry began to murmur about some decline in piety. When it became clear that they would not be called home to England in triumph, men turned to building a permanent civil society. Historians have long tried both to explain the Puritans' loss of a sense of mission and to discover how they handled their guilt. But it is possible that what was seen as a "declension" was only a loss of *male* piety, that Puritans adopted more stringent gender role differences, and turned their church into a feminine institution. In this church, passive females, ruled over by ministers, would personify Christian virtue. One stage in defusing goal conflict, then, was female dominance in number in the church; it is well known that such organizations lose value when they lose male members.[14]

A number of issues are important in understanding the religious terms of the decline in male admissions. Some ministers understood (where historians have failed) that there were still many *people* joining the church; the problem was that there were fewer men. But they did not seem to comprehend that policies which they and the elders espoused would have the effect of discouraging male admissions. This was because their thrust in church governance was to reduce the role played by lay men, just as the role of women had been reduced.

Ministers had responded to the Antinomian crisis by resisting *all* claims to lay prophetic power, since it had produced extreme criticism of minis-

[14] There is a considerable literature and disagreement on this declension. The issues can be uncovered in Perry Miller, *The New England Mind: From Colony to Province* (Cambridge: Harvard Univ. Press, 1953), Book I, "Declension," 19–130; and Robert G. Pope, "New England Versus the New England Mind: The Myth of Declension," *Journal of Social History*, 3 (Winter 1969), 95–108.

ters during the crisis, and in general threatened the ministers' status in the church. This was much contested in the 1630s and '40s, but accepted by the 1660s, with the inevitable result that the lay contribution to the making of the church in New England was reduced. The issues of tests for membership and authority of the ministers over the congregations were also resolved in ways that led to expectations of male passivity.

Ministers wanted control over the vote and voice of the congregations. The Synod of 1637 opposed the practice of asking questions after sermons and lectures, an opposition certainly created by the Antinomians. The Cambridge Platform further decreased the laymen's right to speak (it required permission from the elders) or to participate in discipline cases; and in the 1640s the ministers took on a kind of veto power in church deliberations. Many ministers also wanted to relax the requirement, adopted in the 1630s, that full membership depend in part on a satisfactory account of conversion. They believed that an increase in membership would follow such relaxation, and the Half-Way Covenant of 1660 was a step in that direction. Later we find the suggestion that men who wanted full membership be allowed the women's "privilege"; that is, that they be excused from speaking, and allow the ministers to report their relations for them. The causes and means by which such positions were reached were complex, but the effect was to enjoin silence on the men, to lose the egalitarianism inherent in a company of saints, and to create a ministerial elite. No doubt this was easier to achieve when the majority of the devout were women.[15]

By the turn of the century ministerial rhetoric had validated this symbolic reduction of a Christian congregation to a company of women. Membership was increasingly referred to in terms of the old metaphor of a mystical marriage with Christ. Two funeral sermons illustrate the new emphasis. James Fitch, enumerating the virtues of Anne Mason in 1672, first described her constant attempts to improve her communion with God, in which both "Public Ordinances" and secret prayer and religious conversation played a part. The Lord "gifted her with a measure of Knowledge above what is usual in that Sex" and enabled her to help the afflicted in spirit. She was noted for her works of mercy and made a good death. Thus in 1672 a woman could still be commended for an intellectual

---

[15] This discussion of ministerial policy is based on David D. Hall, *The Faithful Shepherd: A History of the New England Ministry in the Seventeenth Century* (Chapel Hill: Univ. of North Carolina Press, 1972). See especially chapters 4 and 5. For churches that gave the women's "privilege" to men, see Hunnewell, *Records of the First Church in Charlestown*, ix (1684/85); Pope, *Records of the First Church at Dorchester*, 45–46 (1664); First Church at Danvers (Salem Village) Records, 1689–1845, f. 3, Essex (1689); Plymouth Church Records, I, 163 (1688) and 201 (1705); and Stonington, Conn., First Congregational Church, Records, I, 21, Connecticut State Library (1705).

and personal approach to religion and salvation, in which introspection and privacy were as important as public acts of faith. There is little to distinguish this from the virtues ascribed to men.

Fifty years later, Thomas Foxcroft drew up a list of female virtues. The virtuous woman should be a thorough Christian (not clearly defined); she should be a loving and obsequious wife; a careful, wise, tender mother; an affectionate and respectful sister; a discreet and condescending mistress; a true and constant friend; a courteous, benevolent, and obliging neighbor. The virtuous woman, therefore, has become the sum of these virtuous relationships. Feminine virtue has become a family affair. Indeed it is in these relationships, and through the family, that the Christian community would be preserved. We begin to find admonitions to mothers to teach sons civic duty (and it is clear that the mother's reward would be the virtue of her children). In regard to her no-longer-so-religious husband, she is to take on a private ministry. One minister suggests that, although a woman cannot speak in the church, "yet she may humbly repeat unto her husband at home what the minister spoke in the Church, that may be pertinent to his condition."[16]

Women after 1660 could find great reinforcement in religion for the female image most of them had always accepted, and which coincided with their traditional place in the family. To be a good woman was to be a good Christian. But to be a good man was to be a good citizen, active, competitive, self-confident. The women were given, and accepted, the task of preservation of as many values of the Christian community as could be discovered in the family. Only for women did religion and social goals maintain a close correlation. Puritan women, then, subscribed to a Christian role developed out of male needs to pursue social goals no longer validated by religion, out of ministerial determination to control doctrine and governance. They accepted it because of the defeat and discipline of female dissenters, because of the correlation between female socialization into family roles and their place in the church. Perhaps a new role was created, too: as members of the church, women became the keepers of the covenant and protectors of the idea of mission. Put histori-

---

[16] Margaret W. Masson, "The Typology of the Female as a Model for the Regenerate: Puritan Preaching, 1690–1730," *Signs*, 2 (Winter 1976), 304–15, and Laurel Thatcher Ulrich, "Vertuous Women Found: New England Ministerial Literature, 1668–1735," in this volume, both study the ministerial literature that defines female virtue. The two sermons are James Fitch, *Peace The End of the Perfect and Upright* (Cambridge, 1672) and Thomas Foxcroft, *The Character of Anna the Prophetess, Consider'd and Apply'd* (Boston: S. Kneeland, 1723). Cotton Mather made frequent use of the marriage metaphor; see *Ornaments for the Daughters of Zion*, 85, 88, and for women instructing husbands, 113.

cally, women accepted the burdens of the past, and men the burdens of the future. Put politically, gender differentiation could in this way be seen as a stage in the separation of church and state.[17]

Quaker women were not so bound by either scripture or society as Puritan women. When Pennsylvania was founded in 1682, and Quakers found themselves in control of an important settlement, the sect had already come through its experimental stage and had resolved most major questions of doctrine and of church governance as they applied to women. Quakers were persecuted before 1682, but not directly because of the role women played in the group. Policies in respect to women never threatened the society as a whole, and women had the support of the leaders of the Quaker movement. Both George Fox and Margaret Fell championed female equality and ministries and the inclusion of women in the governance of the Society. William Penn was committed to a policy of religious toleration, and religious unity was never a goal, even in Pennsylvania, as it had been in Massachusetts at the time of the Antinomian crisis. Moreover, Quakers early began to accept their identity as a "peculiar" people who marked themselves as social deviants by such characteristics as their speech, "hat honor" principle, and refusal to take oaths.[18]

Quakers, in common with other radical sects of seventeenth-century England, but unlike New England Puritans after the Antinomian crisis, believed in spiritual rebirth, direct inspiration by the Divine Light, and lay ministries. All three of these doctrinal positions were important to women. Friends insisted on the possibility of being reborn in the spirit, and on an informing, indwelling Divine Light. Sex bias had no place in this conversion experience; there was nothing inherent in the female to prevent her spiritual rebirth, to hinder the work of the Divine Light. As Fox

[17] If this analysis is correct, the situation was difficult for men until their civic concerns acquired a new ideological content. Robert N. Bellah, "Civil Religion in America," *Daedalus*, 96 (Winter 1967), 1–21, suggests the sort of development which later may have taken place among men, although he does not discuss the question in terms of gender.

[18] William C. Braithwaite, *The Beginnings of Quakerism* (London: Macmillan, 1912), still reliable and informative, includes some discussion of the role of women. For women in England see Richard T. Vann, *The Social Development of English Quakerism, 1655–1755* (Cambridge: Harvard Univ. Press, 1969), especially chap. 3, "Persecution and Organization," 88–121. Henry J. Cadbury, "George Fox and Women's Liberation," *The Friends Quarterly*, 18 (Oct. 1974), 370–76, considers Fox "sensitive and sympathetic" to women. For formation of English women's meetings, see Arnold Lloyd, *Quaker Social History, 1669–1738* (London: Longmans, Green, 1950), chap. 8, and Isabel Ross, *Margaret Fell: Mother of Quakerism* (London: Longmans, Green, 1949), chap. 19.

put it, in an interesting variation of Paul's message to the Galatians, "Ye are all one *man* in Christ Jesus [italics added]." [19]

Puritans, more ambivalent, believed in spiritual equality, too, but they did not make room for women in the ministry or church governance and did not allow revision of scriptural prescriptions for female behavior. But through emphasis on the Divine Light, viewed as a continuing revelation, Friends could ignore ancient limitations on women by claiming that the new Light could, at a minimum, serve as a guide to understanding earlier revelations. This was crucial to defining the female role. For example, the curse laid on women in Genesis, which was seen by Puritans as the fundament of inferiority and submission, was reinterpreted by Fox, who considered the spiritual regeneration of the converted as a triumph over this curse. His opinion was that, before the Fall, men and women were equal; after their rebirth, this equality returns: "For man and woman were helpsmeet, in the image of God and in Righteousness and holiness, in the dominion before they fell; but, after the Fall, in the transgression, the man was to rule over his wife. But in the restoration by Christ into the image of God and His righteousness and holiness again, in that they are helpsmeet, man and woman, as they were before the Fall." We have statements by women, too, emphasizing the curse and woman's role in redemption. Women could address each other as "you that are of the true Seed of the promise of God in the beginning, that was to bruise the Serpent's head." The emphasis here is not on guilt or original sin but on regeneration and triumph. [20]

Nor did Fox or the female Friends of the formative generation accept the restrictions that St. Paul laid on the women of Corinth and Puritans laid on the women of New England. The Quakers dismissed these rules as not pertaining to the regenerate, or to those in whom Christ dwells. As Fox put it, "and may not the spirit of Christ speak in the Female as well as in the Male? is he then to be limited?" Fell was certain that Paul spoke to Corinth alone, or to certain women only. On the issue of learning from their husbands, she pointed out that not all women marry; and in fact it was acceptable to Quakers that some women stay single. George Keith used as a text the woman from Samaria (John 4:28–30) who proclaimed

---

[19] Melvin B. Endy, Jr., *William Penn and Early Quakerism* (Princeton: Princeton Univ. Press, 1973) discusses early Quaker belief, particularly pp. 63–92. For Fox on Galatians see George Fox, *A Collection of Many Select and Christian Epistles, Letters and Testimonies* (London: T. Sowle, 1698), #291, II, 323–24.

[20] Ibid., Milton D. Speizman and Jane C. Kronick, eds., "A Seventeenth-Century Quaker Women's Declaration," *Signs*, 1 (Autumn 1975), 235. Quaker women were also released from the idea that childbirth was a curse; see J. William Frost, *The Quaker Family in Colonial America* (New York: St. Martin's, 1973), chap. 4.

Christ without a university education. Quakers produced other Biblical evidence, too, to prove that women often played active and prophetic roles: Miriam, Hannah, Mary Magdalen, Susannah, Mary, and Martha were only a few of their cloud of witnesses. This was an important doctrinal position for women, but also for all Quakers, who simply took their protest against an ordained ministry as authorities on revelation to its logical conclusion. In fact, having exposed and solved for themselves contradictions in Christian messages to women, Friends proceeded to go their own way. Fox's first disciple was probably a woman, and if Fox was the father of Quakerism, Fell was its mother.[21]

The first and most notable way in which Quaker women acted upon. their dispensation and through the spirit within was to engage in the lay ministry; through this ministry, they could influence doctrine. A woman first pursued an internal commitment to a public ministry. She had to be convinced of the presence of Christ within and that He spoke through her. She might be uncertain and need support and encouragement from other Friends. When her work as a public exponent of the truth was established she might then believe herself called to carry that truth abroad. In the early years of the Society, these missions were designed to proselytize; later, as the Friends became more withdrawn, they were intended to help keep strong the faith. Of the first 59 publishers of the truth who came to America from 1656 to 1663, nearly half (26) were women; of these, only four were travelling in ministry with their husbands. Many of these women exhibited enormous courage and bravery in the face of the frequently hostile environment and establishments. Mary Dyer may have been unusual in courting death in Massachusetts, but she was not unusual in her determination to spread the Quakers' message. The later ministry, in which women were equally active, could also take them far afield, although they travelled to established meetings to main-

---

[21] [George Fox], *Concerning Sons and Daughters, and Prophetesses Speaking and Prophecying, in the Law and in the Gospel* (London: MW, n.d.), 9; Margaret Fell, *A Brief Collection of Remarkable Passages and Occurrences Relating to the Birth, Education, Life, Conversion, Travels, Services, and the Deep Sufferings of that Ancient, Eminent, and Faithful Servant of the Lord, Margaret Fell* (London: J. Sowle, 1710), 339–40, 344. For single Quakers, see Robert V. Wells, "Quaker Marriage Patterns in a Colonial Prespective," *William and Mary Quarterly*, 3d Series, 29 (July 1972), 426–27. George Keith's opinion is in *Woman-Preacher of Samaria; A Better Preacher, and More Sufficiently Qualified to Preach than any of the Men Preachers of the Man-Made-Ministry of These Three Nations* (1674), 2. The cloud of witnesses is cited in Speizman and Kronick, "A Seventeenth-Century Declaration," 237–40. It was characteristic of Quakers to use these names for their daughters; they did not name them for the passive qualities (e.g., patience, content, submit) which are regularly found in Congregational baptismal registers.

tain a high level of religious experience. All of these women had the support of their own meetings and were heard with respect at others.[22]

The other area in which Quaker women engaged most actively was the women's meetings, and here we find them playing a part in church governance, the discipline of women, and the control of membership. Some historians have assumed that women's meetings were established to give women enough authority to keep them happy but not enough to make them powerful. The records of women's meetings do convey a sense of lesser bodies, with relatively little money, not given the quasi-judicial function which men's meetings had in dealing with controversy. However, Fox was concerned about the role of women, and his message to them was unconventional; and the Fell women, Margaret and her daughter Sarah, had a great deal to do with the formation of early women's meetings and saw them as an instrument for the expansion of woman's role.

This is not to say that all Friends agreed; a minority of males attacked the establishment of women's meetings, and believed in male superiority. The Wilkinson-Story schism was in part the result of some men's objections to the founding of women's meetings, and there was opposition to the principle of equality throughout the colonial period. However, men's meetings sometimes helped to assert the authority of the women's meetings. The Narragansett, Rhode Island, Men's Meeting was once asked to sign certificates of dismissal for women who were moving from one meeting to another, dismissals which had already been signed by the women's meeting. They replied that this would "degrade" the women's meeting, and stated their belief that "both male & female are all one in Christ Jesus."[23]

The Quaker meeting structure was complicated. As it developed in Pennsylvania, there was a local weekly meeting for worship and local preparative meetings, or business meetings which got ready for the monthly meeting. The monthly meetings were also business meetings, made up of representatives (sometimes called overseers) from several weekly meetings which formed a small geographic cluster within a county. Quarterly meetings were county based; and the Philadelphia yearly meeting was colony-wide, although it met in Burlington in alternate

---

[22] The early female ministers who came to America are calculated from the list in Frederick B. Tolles, "The Atlantic Community of the Early Friends," Supplement 24, *Journal of the Friends' Historical Society* (London, 1952), 35–38.

[23] For founding of women's meetings, see Mabel Richmond Brailsford, *Quaker Women, 1650–1690* (London: Duckworth, 1915), chap. 13, and Lloyd, *Quaker Social History*, chap. 8. Speizman and Kronick, "A Seventeenth-Century Declaration," a letter giving guidelines for forming a women's meeting, was probably written by Sarah Fell between 1675 and 1680, pp. 241–45, 233–34.

years until 1760. All of the meetings for business had separate meetings for men and women, except the Select Meeting (or meeting for ministers and elders) which also had yearly, quarterly, and monthly components. This was set up by the yearly meeting in 1714, but not until 1740 was there a requirement that women be included as elders as well as ministers. Thus women were included in every part of the Friends' meeting structure and hierarchy.[24]

The first women's monthly meetings were formed in 1681, on the advice of a yearly meeting held in Burlington, which decided that, as Friends were becoming more numerous, it was necessary to establish a woman's monthly meeting "for the better management of the discipline and other affairs of the church more proper to be inspected by their sex."[25] It is possible to watch through the records of monthly meetings the slow growth of organization and organizational skills at these "grass roots" levels. At first the women simply recorded the fact that they met, but soon they began to see what business they should undertake. They disciplined women who behaved questionably, or who were not attending meeting, and began to collect money to distribute to the poor. They appointed representatives to the quarterly and yearly meetings and decided who might go out on public ministries. Not all of these women's meetings were assertive; some seemed to defer to the men. The Bucks Quarterly Women's Meeting, for example, was uneasy about contributing to the yearly meeting without seeking consent from the men. Other meetings took pleasure in vigorous decision making, and in meetings with stable memberships, such as Chester, one finds older women, like Grace Lloyd, year after year accepting responsibility for female behavior and participation in quarterly and yearly meetings. They must have been influential in socializing young women to an active role.[26]

---

[24] Fox had made it clear that women should serve as elders; Fox, *Epistles*, #291, II, 324. The question whether women should be elders was debated in the Philadelphia Yearly Meeting in the 1730s. Bucks Quarterly from the beginning sent women as ministers to the Select Meeting; see records of the Quarterly Meeting of Ministers and Elders for the County of Bucks, 24, 3d month, 1710, Swarthmore MSS, Swarthmore College Library.

[25] Preface, Burlington Monthly Meeting, Women's Minutes, 1681–1747, Swarthmore MSS.

[26] Many Women's Minutes survive for the eighteenth century. Those on which this brief analysis is based were primarily part of the Philadelphia Yearly Meeting, and are housed at Swarthmore College. However, I have also used Minutes from Meetings in Maryland, New Jersey, New York, Virginia, and North Carolina. The Bucks Quarterly Meeting of Women Friends, Swarthmore MSS, expressed its concern on 26. 3 mo. 1709; 24. 9 mo. 1709; and 25. 3 mo. 1710. The Chester Monthly Meeting of Women Friends, 1695–1733, Swarthmore MSS, shows Grace Lloyd's activities; so does "A Short Narrative of the Life of Jane Hoskins," Haverford MSS. Hoskins was a servant in the Lloyd household, and records their concern for her and encouragement of her as a minister, f. 33–35; she remained close to Grace Lloyd until the latter died in 1760.

A notable symbolic act occurred in each meeting as women became accustomed to manage their affairs. They invariably decided to buy a record book (an important investment) and to appoint a clerk. Thereafter, the book was tangible evidence of their activity. Equally important, as Friends began to build permanent meeting houses, women acquired their own space. Typically, meeting houses were built with sliding partitions which could divide them down the center. Women sat on one side, men on the other. During meetings for worship, the partitions were open and all worshiped together, but during meetings for business the partitions would come down, thus providing women and men with separate spaces for the conduct of their separate business.[27]

But the most important function in American meetings, ultimately, was the female share in protection of the institution of marriage, and the maintenance of the unity of membership. Concern that partners be free to marry was important in a mobile group, and particularly in America, an immigrant society. Hence, people who wanted to marry, if they were not native to the meeting in which they expected to wed, had to produce certificates from their prior meetings showing them to be free. It was equally important to know that they were Friends to guarantee the marriage would be "in unity." That is, Friends had to marry Friends, both parties had to demonstrate membership in good standing, and they had to marry in meeting. Marriage out of the meeting, if not repented, led to exclusion from membership for the couple, and perhaps their parents, if they could be shown to have been negligent. This exclusiveness parallels the Puritans' attempt to maintain unity on a larger social scale by keeping dissenters out of the colony; but it prevented domination by either sex in membership in the Friends' meetings.

Women's meetings appointed several members to oversee a marriage. This involved interviews with the couple, not only to examine their intentions, but also to make certain both were convinced Quakers who would keep their family in the Society. Women looked into reputation and even into material considerations. The men's meeting cooperated in this, and the marriage could not take place until the meetings agreed. The women sent representatives to the wedding, to make sure all was done with dignity and decency, according to the Friends' mode. This rigorous protection of marriage in unity was combined with disciplining of men and

---

[27] I have not as yet precisely dated the sliding partitions, but I believe they originated in the early eighteenth century. In England, apparently, a separate room or loft for women's meetings was more common. See Hubert Lidbetter, *The Friends Meeting House* (York: Ebor, 1961), 15. The Meeting in Tuckerton, N.J., built in 1709, had a little wing for women's meetings. See T. Chalkley Matlack, "Brief Historical Sketches Concerning Friends Meetings" (1938), 1:158, Haverford MSS.

women who were not regular in meeting attendance. Through these disciplines women's meetings played a role in maintaining a family-based membership in the Society of Friends, one in which neither sex dominated in number, and women retained a share of power.[28]

We can conclude that Quaker women played a more forceful role in the Society of Friends than Puritan women did in the Congregational church. Quaker doctrine provided for a reinterpretation of scriptural prescriptions of female inferiority and submission; Puritans reaffirmed both Genesis and St. Paul. Quaker women, through the Divine Light and their lay ministry, maintained an important position for themselves in the formulation of doctrine; Puritan women were defeated in their attempts to influence doctrine. Quaker women had their own place in church governance, disciplined themselves, and shared control of membership; Puritan women were disciplined to silence, and socialized to accept moral responsibility for the continuation of a Christian community.

The Quakers may have developed an active and workable role for women, but they did not have a major influence on the American Protestant view of women. Never in the mainstream of American religious life, Friends did not retain their dominance in politics or culture even in Pennsylvania, and in the course of the eighteenth century they became more and more introspective, exclusive, and "peculiar." In the face of rigorous discipline numbers decreased, but the religious commitment of those who remained was enhanced. Quaker women, pious and active, may eventually have had some influence on American women as moral custodians; but women of other sects did not learn from the Friends what they needed to know to change their position in the church.[29]

The Puritans, on the other hand, *were* the mainstream of American religious life, and the congregational way, which marked the politics and culture of New England in such distinctive ways, had a far-reaching influence. Friends may have demonstrated the best that the religious revolution of the seventeenth century could do for women; but it was the Puritan mode of female piety and submission to ministerial authority that was to dominate both pew and pulpit in America.

---

[28] Fox, *Epistles*, #264, 282, said that marriages should be proposed *first* to the women's meeting, and by the women proposed to the men. Sarah Fell, in Speizman and Kronick, "A Seventeenth-Century Declaration," 242, also advises that proposals for marriages go first to the women, and this seems to have been the practice in American meetings.

[29] Sydney V. James, *A People Among Peoples* (Cambridge: Harvard Univ. Press, 1963), studies the Quaker turn to reforming humanitarian causes in the late eighteenth century. Quaker women were actively and publicly involved, had the organizational skills other women lacked, and could usefully serve as models to reformers in the early nineteenth century.

Gerald F. Moran

"Sisters" in Christ
Women and the Church
in Seventeenth-Century New England

*H*istorians often adopt the view that the Protestant church in nineteenth-century America became feminized as its membership shifted from male to female domination and congregations became densely populated with women, even though a historical background to feminization has not been supplied. No comprehensive statistical statements on earlier periods, including the colonial era, have been attempted.[1] What were the antecedents of this female predominance? Did it follow upon a history of male domination in religion, or did it merely sustain previous patterns? These questions could be approached effectively in the light of Puritan experience, but even seventeenth-century New England—that most thoroughly explored of colonial societies—has failed to inspire a demography of gender and church membership. Only studies restricted to a narrow time frame or sample cases have been undertaken, with the unfortunate consequence of a confusing literature on women and the New England church. Either women predominated as members from time to time or place to place in colonial New England, as some studies suggest,[2] or they emerged preponderant during a particular period, the late seventeenth century.[3] Or, conversely, they became less, not more, visible in membership after 1675, a theme echoed by several

---

[1] See Barbara Welter, "The Feminization of American Religion, 1800–1860," in her *Dimity Convictions* (Athens: Ohio Univ. Press, 1976); and Ann Douglas, *The Feminization of American Culture* (New York: Knopf, 1977), 98–99.

[2] See, for example, Edmund S. Morgan, "New England Puritanism: Another Approach," *William and Mary Quarterly*, 3d ser., 18 (Apr. 1961), 238–39.

[3] William Andrews, "The Printed Funeral Sermons of Cotton Mather," *Early American Literature*, 5 (Fall 1970), 32; and Mary Maples Dunn, "Saints and Sisters: Congregational and Quaker Women in the Early Colonial Period," in this volume.

recent articles on New England Puritanism.[4] Only the extant church records for the entire seventeenth century can disclose an accurate history, and they indicate that New England church membership became increasingly female. How and why this happened are the questions this essay explores.

*E*vidence obtained from the records of eighteen New England churches reveals that for the seventeenth century, Massachusetts and Connecticut churches admitted substantial proportions of women. As the last column of Table 1 shows, women made up roughly two-thirds of members added by the churches of Beverly, Boston Third, Rowley, and Salem, Massachusetts; and Hartford Second, New London, and Middletown, Connecticut. They made up about three-fifths of admissions in Boston First and Charlestown, Massachusetts; and Milford, Windsor, and Woodbury, Connecticut. Lower percentages prevailed elsewhere, but no lower than the 54 percent recorded by Farmington, Connecticut. Five other churches ranged between 55 and 57 percent: Dedham, Dorchester, and Roxbury, Massachusetts; and New Haven and Stonington, Connecticut.[5]

---

[4] Robert G. Pope, *The Half-Way Covenant: Church Membership in Puritan New England* (Princeton: Princeton Univ. Press, 1969), chap. 8; Margaret Masson, "The Typology of the Female as a Model for the Regenerate: Puritan Preaching, 1690–1730," *Signs: Journal of Women in Culture and Society*, 2 (1976), 315; Laurel Thatcher Ulrich, "Vertuous Women Found: New England Ministerial Literature, 1668–1735," in this volume, n. 65.

[5] All data on church membership come from the following records: Milford, Connecticut, First Congregational Church Records, Connecticut State Library (CSL), Hartford, I, 1–3, 7–10, 19–22; Henry Stiles, *The History and Genealogies of Ancient Windsor, Connecticut . . .* , 2 vols. (New York: Charles B. Norton, 1859), II, 873–74, 886–88; Franklin Bowditch Dexter, comp., *Historical Catalogue of the Members of the First Church of Christ in New Haven, Connecticut . . .* (New Haven: published by the author, 1914), 1–39; "Records of Farmington in Connecticut," *New England Historical and Genealogical Register*, 11 (Oct. 1857), 323–26, and 12 (Jan. 1858), 34–37; Stonington, Connecticut, First Congregational Church and Ecclesiastical Society Records, CSL, III, 1–8; Woodbury, Connecticut, First Congregational Church Records, CSL, 1, 3–22; Edwin P. Parker, *History of the Second Church of Christ in Hartford* (Hartford: Belknap & Warfield, 1892), 291–94; New London, Connecticut, First Congregational Church Records, CSL, I, 5–10; Middletown, Connecticut, First Congregational Church Records, CSL, I, 1–22; Don Gleason Hill, ed., *The Record of Baptisms, Marriages and Deaths, and Admissions to the Church . . . in the Town of Dedham, Massachusetts: 1638–1845* (Dedham: printed at the office of the Dedham Transcript, 1888), 21–39; Charles Pope, ed., *Records of the First Church at Dorchester in New England, 1636–1734* (Boston: George H. Ellis, 1891), 2–29; Richard D. Pierce, ed., *Records of the First Church in Boston 1630–1868*, the Colonial Society of Massachusetts Publications, 39 (Boston: Colonial Society, 1961), 13–98; "Early Records of Rowley, Mass.," Essex Institute Historical *Collections*, 34 (1898), 77–86; "Beverly First Church Records," Essex Institute Historical *Collections*, 35 (1899), 185–211; "Record Book of the First Church in Charlestown," *New England Historical and Genealogical Register*, 23 (April 1869), 190–91, (July 1869), 279–84, and (Oct. 1869), 435–42; *Roxbury Land and Church Records, Reports* of the Record Commissioners, 6 (Boston: Rockwell and Churchill, City Printers, 1881), 73–102; *An Historical Catalogue of the Old South Church* (Boston: David Clapp & Son, 1883); Richard D. Pierce, ed., *The Records of the First Church in Salem, Massachusetts, 1629–1736* (Salem: Essex Institute, 1974), 5–183.

Table 1. WOMEN ENTERING NEW ENGLAND CHURCHES: PERCENTAGE OF ALL ENTRANTS, WITH AVERAGE ANNUAL INCREMENTS OF NEW MEMBERS PER DECADE, 1630–99

Church	Date Organized	Percentages (with increments in parentheses)							
		1630–39	1640–49	1650–59	1660–69	1670–79	1680–89	1690–99	Total
Salem	1629	52 (40)	54 (17)	74 (5)	65 (8)	67 (6)	70 (15)	76 (11)	64 (12)
Boston First	1630	47 (45)	59 (30)	62 (8)	66 (15)	65 (18)	68 (13)	75 (22)	60 (21)
Dorchester	1630	58 (40)	49 (7)	43 (4)	64 (4)	57 (7)	54 (5)	63 (6)	56 (8)
Roxbury	1631	50 (20)	59 (8)	50 (4)	65 (4)	67 (5)	54 (9)	66 (8)	57 (8)
Charlestown	1632	56 (20)	57 (11)	67 (7)	68 (7)	71 (9)	65 (8)	70 (7)	63 (10)
Windsor	1636		53 (2)	64 (1)	56 (3)	53 (2)	63 (7)	57 (4)	59 (3)
Dedham	1638		54 (12)	64 (3)	58 (3)				56 (6)
Milford	1639		51 (8)	56 (2)	57 (7)	66 (7)	56 (4)	67 (9)	59 (6)
New Haven	1639		37 (17)	46 (3)	84 (4)		65 (14)	61 (15)	55 (11)
Rowley	1639				71 (4)	64 (3)	57 (5)	69 (9)	65 (5)
New London	1646					72 (3)	50 (1)	66 (8)	66 (4)
Farmington	1652			50 (4)			59 (4)	55 (6)	54 (5)
Beverly	1667				54 (8)	58 (2)	73 (6)	67 (12)	67 (7)
Middletown	1668					63 (4)	50 (1)	68 (8)	64 (5)
Boston Third	1669					79 (19)	63 (12)	64 (17)	70 (16)
Hartford Second	1669					68 (4)	75 (2)	59 (5)	65 (3)
Woodbury	1669					55 (1)	58 (2)	59 (3)	58 (2)
Stonington	1674					58 (4)	65 (2)	50 (5)	56 (4)

Table 2. DISTRIBUTION OF PERCENTAGES OF WOMEN ENTERING NEW ENGLAND CHURCHES, 1630–99

Female Entrants (Percent)	First-Generation Churches				Second-Generation Churches	
	1630–59		1660–99		1660–99	
	Number	Percent	Number	Percent	Number	Percent
35–39	1	4	0	0	0	0
40–44	1	4	0	0	0	0
45–49	3	13	0	0	0	0
50–54	8	33	4	10	3	16
55–59	6	25	9	22	6	32
60–64	3	13	5	12	3	16
65–69	1	4	15	37	4	21
70–74	1	4	5	12	1	5
75–79	0	0	2	5	2	11
80–84	0	0	1	2	0	0
Total	24	100	41	100	19	101

The sex ratio of admissions changed considerably over time. Before 1660, membership in some churches was less skewed along sexual lines or was even tipped in favor of men. Thus, fewer than one-half of the people entering Dorchester and New Haven in 1640–59 were women, as were fewer than one-half in Boston in 1630–1639. A rough sexual balance existed at Roxbury during the 1630s, Milford and Windsor during the 1640s, and Farmington during the 1650s. Only Charlestown started admitting a higher percentage of women than men at the beginning of settlement, and continued to add to the proportion subsequently.

From the 1660s to the end of the century, no first-generation church, including Farmington and New London, admitted more men than women in any one decade. In Boston First, Charleston, and Salem, a nearly step-by-step increase in female communicants took place from the 1630s through the 1690s, so much so that by the latter decade each church had about seven women joining for every three men. Sex ratios changed more erratically in other churches, but larger proportions of women were admitted per decade in 1660–99 than in 1630–59, as Table 2 reveals. For over half of the decades before 1660, less than 55 percent of those entering the church were women; while in well over half of the decades after 1660, more than 64 percent of new communicants were women. In 90 percent of the post-1660 decades, more than 54 percent were women.

This history can be clarified by combining data, as in Figure 1. The preponderance of women at admission increased substantially from 1640 to 1670, then leveled off and even dipped slightly during the 1670s and 1680s,

Figure 1. PERCENTAGE OF WOMEN ENTERING NEW ENGLAND CHURCHES, 1630–99

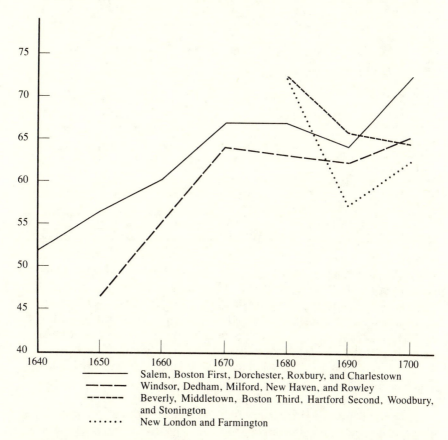

— Salem, Boston First, Dorchester, Roxbury, and Charlestown
– – – Windsor, Dedham, Milford, New Haven, and Rowley
– – – – Beverly, Middletown, Boston Third, Hartford Second, Woodbury, and Stonington
· · · · · · · New London and Farmington

although no fewer than three out of every five people becoming members were women. Farmington and New London together saw the sex ratio plummet during the 1680s, but they, along with other first-generation churches, underwent increases in the admission of women in the last decade of the century. These changes in the sexual composition of membership, with women acquiring more and more visibility at admission after mid-century, have escaped historians who have failed to consider long-range trends or the evidence open to statistical analysis.

Second-generation churches established after 1660 accepted more women than men from the very start, while several were even founded upon a surplus of them, contrary to the traditional practice of gathering a church around male "pillars." The Beverly church embraced 27 women and 24 men at its founding in 1667, and Hartford Second had 18 "sisters in full communion"

Table 3.   SURPLUSES OF WOMEN ADMITTED BY NEW ENGLAND CHURCHES, 1630–99

Churches	1630s	1640s	1650s	1660s	1670s	1680s	1690s	Total
Salem, Boston First, Dorchester, Roxbury, Charlestown	35	94	57	120	137	139	264	846
Windsor, Milford, New Haven		−43	2	42	22	66	68	157
Beverly, Middletown, Boston Third, Hartford Second, Woodbury, Stonington					134	80	133	347
Rowley, New London					20	6	60	86

consent to the new covenant along with 15 male "brethren" shortly after its separation from Hartford First in 1669.[6] Each continued to bring in high percentages of women during the last three decades of the century, as did other second-generation churches. Only two churches, each in a different decade, added an equal number of men and women. Nearly two-fifths of all decades in 1660–99 saw over 64 percent women admitted, and more than four-fifths over 54 percent. Moreover, as Figure 1 shows, these churches together maintained a very high, though slightly dwindling, proportion of women among new members during the 1680s and 1690s.

The combination of late-century increases in members and female preponderance at admission led to larger and larger surpluses of women with access to the Lord's Supper. Eleven of seventeen churches for which data exist averaged more annual admissions in the 1690s than in any other decade from 1650. Of these, the admissions for six were over 65 percent female, and for ten they were over 58 percent female. Table 3 shows that more churches added more women than men during this same decade than at any other time during the century, while they often added to their surplus of female communicants with each succeeding decade from 1630.

Female-dominated admissions meant female-dominated churches, even if women were more likely than men to disappear from membership because of death or emigration. Women predominated in those churches that recorded

---

[6] "Beverly First Church Records," 177; Parker, *History of Second Church in Hartford*, 290–91.

from time to time their existing membership. Farmington had 91 communicants in 1680, 53 percent of whom were women. In New London 54 percent of 24 members in 1670, and 65 percent of 31 members in 1691, were women; in Middletown 58 percent of 121 communicants in 1676; and in Boston First 63 percent of 302 full members in 1688.[7] By this time in Boston, nearly sixty years and two generations removed from its founding, none of the men who had joined First Church during the 1630s, and only ten of those who had entered in the 1640s, remained. As in other churches, the death or migration of first-generation males, together with the increasing visibility of women at admission, had created a church top-heavy with second- and third-generation females. By 1688, 42 percent of the membership consisted of women added in 1670–88 and 56 percent of women admitted in 1660–88, a period when their influx into communion rose.

The late-century upsurge in admissions thus enhanced the presence of women among new and existing members alike. Some fifty years before this time, during the 1630s and early 1640s, similar increases in membership had made for more sexually balanced churches. What happened between the "Great Migration" to New England and the turn of the seventeenth century to alter the sexual profile of membership is a question that requires some discussion of religious experience, attitudes, and institutions. Though this history is a circuitous one, it will nevertheless prove profitable for an understanding of how changes witnessed by successive generations of New Englanders produced a preponderance of women in the church.

*T*he English experience set precedents for widespread and sexually balanced religious participation in early New England. Drawing upon such sources of popular piety as Lollardy, English Puritanism was a movement largely of active lay men and women who sought to abolish religious ritual and undermine the power of the Anglican hierarchy.[8] In Puritan theory and practice, the laity as well as the family gained at the expense of the hierarchy. The household became the setting for bringing sinners around to Christ through family prayer and homily, while the father assumed the role of preacher to family members whose salvation now depended upon an effective presentation of the Word. Although this "spiritualization of the household" increased the power of the patriarch, it also improved the spiritual status of the woman. A woman became attractive for her piety rather than her property. After marriage she became an important religious companion to

[7] "Records of Farmington," 12:, 35–36; New London Congregational Church Records, I, 5, 7; Middletown Congregational Church Records, I, D; Pierce, *Records of First Church Boston*, 84–90.
[8] Patrick Collinson stresses the importance of the laity to English Puritanism in *The Elizabethan Puritan Movement* (Berkeley and Los Angeles: Univ. of California Press, 1967).

her husband, a source of spiritual support and comfort, as he was to her. At the same time, she became the special guardian of grace in children. The spiritualized household provided the energy for an aggressive English lay piety.[9]

This active English laity reasserted itself in the New World. In the course of establishing communities in Massachusetts Bay and Connecticut, lay men worked with preachers in creating covenants, organizing churches, selecting ministers, deacons, and elders, devising polity, and admitting new members. Some witnesses record the presence of an intense and extensive popular piety, a popular piety expressed in outbursts of spiritual enthusiasm, lay prophesying, and voluntary testimonies of conversion before congregations. Lay piety became channeled through legally established churches, and membership increased rapidly through the 1630s and into the early 1640s. Many husbands and wives joined the church together as the family continued to serve as an instrument of spiritual companionship and reinforcement. Ultimately the established church penetrated deeply within the community.[10]

With time, admissions began to decline, partly because few unchurched inhabitants remained. By the 1660s, however, many newcomers, along with second-generation sons and daughters who were reaching maturity, were failing to join the church. In many communities the ratio of communicants to inhabitants was slipping noticeably.[11]

Apparently the sons and daughters were having difficulty duplicating the experiences of their parents, and with reason. Most churches demanded that they testify to an experience of regeneration before gaining access to the Lord's Supper and baptism for their children; even after the introduction of the Half-Way Covenant in the 1660s, full membership was not easily attained. Many first-generation patriarchs survived through the 1660s to uphold strict admission standards and preside over the ceremony of admission, and thus the second generation had to face the scrutiny of its elders, rarely its

---

[9] Christopher Hill, *Society and Puritanism in Pre-Revolutionary England* (New York: Schocken Books, 1964), chap. 13; Charles H. George and Katherine George, *The Protestant Mind of the English Reformation 1570–1640* (Princeton: Princeton Univ. Press, 1961), 269–70; Lawrence Stone, *The Crisis of the Aristocracy 1558–1641*, abr. ed. (New York: Oxford Univ. Press, 1967), 281.

[10] In Dedham, for example, 70 percent of the town's taxpayers were church members by 1648. Kenneth Lockridge, "The History of a Puritan Church 1637–1736," *New England Quarterly*, 40 (Sept. 1967), 409. Also, in Milford, 82 percent of the male inhabitants in 1644, and 77 percent of their wives had joined the church by the end of 1644, and during the 1640s 66 percent of the married men and women who became communicants did so on the same day or within a year of their spouses. Gerald F. Moran, "Religious Renewal, Puritan Tribalism, and the Family in Seventeenth-Century Milford, Connecticut," *William and Mary Quarterly*, 3d ser., 36 (April 1979), 56–57.

[11] Slightly over 50 percent of Dedham's taxpayers were communicants in 1670, for example, and only 36 percent of Milford's male inhabitants in 1669. Lockridge, "History of a Puritan Church," 411; Moran, "Religious Renewal, Puritan Tribalism, and the Family."

peers. While preparing for this encounter, the sons and daughters could not anticipate receiving the kind of lay and communal support present during the 1630s, although the family and minister could, and often did, offer encouragement. They were also expected to duplicate the religious experiences of their forebears in a new set of social and cultural circumstances. Fathers and mothers might recall how their conversions had been framed by disorientation in pre–Civil War England and by the disruption accompanying resettlement in New England. In comparison to England, where Puritanism had evolved amid extreme social and religious tensions, mid-seventeenth-century New England was remarkable for its stability and social cohesion.

Eventually, as Table 1 shows, admissions turned upward; the second generation, often the children of communicants, became members with increasing frequency during the late 1660s, the 1670s, and beyond, and some participated in the formation of new churches.[12] The sons and especially the daughters decided to cross the barriers to admission once they entered a new stage of life. Where previously conversion had often accompanied social disorientation, now, in late seventeenth-century New England, it became geared to crucial developmental changes in the life of the individual and the family: in particular, betrothal, marriage, and then parenthood. These changes, taken together, betokened adulthood and guided church members who sought to admit mature and responsible individuals. As expectations concerning church candidates meshed with some of the more apparent transitions of life to relate admission to adulthood, the experiences peculiar to marriage and parenthood, among other things, led to the increasing visibility of women in church membership.

Puritan divines considered "middle age" to be the proper setting for regeneration and church candidacy. They felt that new members ought to be mature and of "years of discretion." "Children not being usually able to examine themselves, nor discern the Lord's body," Thomas Shepard observed, "hence they are not to be admitted to the use of this privilege." Although God's mercy was free and he extended his gracious hand to all age groups, "those whom God doth call it is most commonly in their middle age," Thomas Hooker believed, "before they come to their old age." Assurance must come through reason. "Though knowledg may be without grace," John Norton explained, "yet there can be no grace without knowledg." According to Thomas Hooker, when someone reached "the ripenesse of his yeares, from 20. years untill he come to be 40. or thereabouts, then the workes of reason put forth themselves, then his apprehension is quick to conceive a thing, and his

---

[12] Of the churches experiencing increases in admissions during the 1660s, Boston First added more than the average number of new members in 1661 and 1664–67; Salem did so in 1662–63 and 1666–67; and Milford did so in 1669, when 46 people became communicants. Boston First, Dorchester, Roxbury, and Charlestown saw membership increase during the 1670s, as Table 1 indicates.

Table 4.   AGE AT ADMISSION IN CONNECTICUT, 1660-99*

Age	Male		Female	
	Number	Percent	Number	Percent
Under 20	9	4	34	15
20-24	30	15	69	29
25-29	52	25	58	25
30-34	57	28	30	13
35-39	24	12	18	8
40-44	15	7	8	3
45-49	7	3	13	6
50 and above	11	5	5	2
Total				
	205	99	235	101

*This table is based upon the church records of Milford, Windsor, Woodbury, Stonington, and New London, and the vital statistics of the towns as contained in the Barbour Collection of births, marriages, and deaths in the Connecticut State Library, Hartford.

memory is strong and pregnant to retaine a thing apprehended. . . ." At middle age "a man is able to conceive and partake of the things of grace, and fadom them, and the power of his understanding comes on whereby he is able to embrace them." It was "the fittest time that God should bestow his graces upon man."[13]

Thus ministers and lay members alike were apt to depreciate youthful outbursts of piety; nor, as guardians of the keys to the church, were they willing to extend such privileges as voting at church meetings to wayward and irresponsible youths. In practice, individuals tended to become members at relatively late ages (see Table 4). Rarely in Connecticut churches during the 1660s and beyond were new members below the age of twenty; in many instances they were in their late twenties and early thirties. Although women were very often some years younger than men when admitted (as they were at marriage), most church candidates shared the common status of matrimony.[14] In Milford, 78 percent of the women and 77 percent of the men added by the church in 1660-99 were married; in Windsor, 83 and 81 percent respectively. Eighty-three percent of the women admitted to the Stonington church were married and 86 percent of the men; for the New London church the figures were 89 percent and 93 percent respectively, and for the Woodbury church, 79 percent and 83 percent. Many individuals had also become parents before admission; 49 percent of the married women and 52 percent

[13] The Church Membership of Children, The Works of Thomas Shepard, ed. John A. Albro, 3 vols. (New York: AMS Press, 1967), 3, 531; Thomas Hooker, The Unbelievers Preparing for Christ (London: T. Cotes for A. Crooke, 1638), 199-200. John Norton is quoted in Ross W. Beales, Jr., "In Search of the Historical Child: Miniature Adulthood and Youth in Colonial New England," American Quarterly, 27 (Oct. 1975), 386-87.

[14] In the four Massachusetts churches studied by Pope, for example, women nearly always became communicants at earlier ages than men. See Half-Way Covenant, Appendix.

of the married men had one to three children, while the mode for both groups was one child.[15]

In the absence of age-specific categories of life stages, marriage and parenthood marked an individual's passage from youth to adulthood, and from immaturity into the "years of discretion" expected of candidates for church membership. Through marriage and parenthood a person also became more and more exposed to life crises—the birth of a son or daughter, or the death of a child, spouse, or parent—events that either demanded a religious interpretation or raised interest in the church and salvation to a new level of intensity. Attitude and experience interacted at the moments of conversion and admission and were partly responsible for the timing of these important events.

Marriage and its aftermath altered the lives of women. Males were not untouched by the transition, for, among other things, they had to discard the role of obedient son for that of dominant husband and father. But women had a wider divide to cross between old and new familial arrangements, experiences, and demands as they relinquished the position of daughter for that of wife and mother. Even while courting, women perhaps faced new paternal pressures to close with the church and its discipline and to submit to the brethren in preparation for submission to their husbands. Once married, they were caught up in an inexorable biological and demographic cycle. Every two years or so between marriage and menopause they became pregnant, and thus often encountered the possibility of dying in childbirth. If they survived the ordeal, they faced another possibility, the loss of an infant or child. Anxieties about death, the afterlife of the soul, and the spiritual welfare of the child were the constant companions of women in marriage.

To say this might be to reject demographic evidence on the remarkable healthiness of early New England when weighed against contemporary England and Europe, especially if the benign disease environment of New England also made death appear less awesome. But recent studies show that Puritans were extremely fearful of death, and were tormented by thoughts of

---

[15] The numbers of children belonging to new members in Connecticut were distributed thus:

				Males				
Children	0	1	2	3	4	5	6	over 6
New Members	28	33	26	28	16	11	11	14

				Females				
Children	0	1	2	3	4	5	6	over 6
New Members	46	50	46	30	28	20	16	23

hell and the prospect of eternal damnation.[16] Besides, women often did die in childbirth—they had a shorter life span than men because of its rigors—and also chanced losing on the average several children through death in infancy or youth.[17] Moreover, because they were more mobile than men (for example, they often moved to another town on marriage), they had to cope with familial and religious crises in greater isolation from parents, siblings, and other kin.[18]

Thus, for women in particular, passage through betrothal, marriage, and parenthood resonated beyond the secular into the religious life. An example of this, though in some ways an atypical one, is provided by the autobiography of Elizabeth White, a woman who underwent conversion in mid-seventeenth-century New England. "From my Childhood," she begins her spiritual narrative, "the Lord hath inclined my Heart to seek after the best Things, and my Father's chiefest Care was to bring me up in the Nuture [sic] and Admonition of the Lord. My Nature being some-what more Mild than the rest of my Sisters, I was ready to think my self some Body."[19]

Like many other second-generation sons and daughters, White had parents who had joined the church and wished their children to do so. Her father felt that a daughter, upon considering marriage, should also consider committing herself to the church: "I remember about a Month before I was married, my Father would have me receive the Sacrament of the LORD's Supper." But when she began contemplating "what was requisite to be in those which did partake thereof," she hesitated, fearing "that I had not those Things which

[16] David E. Stannard, *The Puritan Way of Death: A Study in Religion, Culture, and Social Change* (New York: Oxford Univ. Press, 1977), esp. chap. 4. Because of their sensitivity to death, Puritans overestimated the rate of mortality in New England, as indicated by Maris A. Vinovskis, "Angels' Heads and Weeping Willows: Death in Early America," paper read at the meeting of the American Antiquarian Society, April 1974, esp. pp. 14–21.

[17] The recent literature on childhood mortality rates in early New England is surveyed in Stannard, *Puritan Way of Death*, 54–56. In Andover, Massachusetts, one of the healthier communities of New England, some three of nine children born to the average family during the seventeenth century died before attaining their twenty-first birthday. Mortality rates were considerably higher in port areas like Boston and Salem.

For mortality rates among women, see John Demos, *A Little Commonwealth: Family Life in Plymouth Colony* (New York: Oxford Univ. Press, 1970), 66; Philip J. Greven, Jr., *Four Generations: Population, Land, and Family in Colonial Andover, Massachusetts* (Ithaca: Cornell Univ. Press, 1970), 27–28, 109; Vinovskis, "Angels' Heads and Weeping Willows," 7, and "Mortality Rates and Trends in Massachusetts Before 1869," *Journal of Economic History*, 32 (1972), 201.

[18] Linda Auwers Bissell examines the mobility rates of women in "From One Generation to Another: Mobility in Seventeenth-Century Windsor, Connecticut," *William and Mary Quarterly*, 3d ser., 31 (Jan. 1974), 87–88. In Milford, 17 and 9 percent of the new members added by the church in 1660–84 and 1685–99 respectively were female newcomers, most of whom had entered town to marry. Moran, "Religious Renewal, Puritan Tribalism, and the Family."

[19] *The Experiences of God's Gracious Dealings with Mrs. Elizabeth White. As they were written under her own Hand, and found in her Closet after her Decease, December 5, 1669* (Boston: Kneeland and [Gleason], 1741), 3.

were requisite wrought in me, as Knowledge, Faith, Love, Repentance, etc." What to do? "I was loath," she says, "to disobey my Father, and more loath to eat and drink my own Damnation."

But in the end White was unable to disappoint her father. In "this Perplexity," she wrote, "I set my Self to seek the Lord for his Grace," working through the standard preparatory stages of conversion. In time, she continued, "I began to be comforted, verily thinking, now I had repented, and could believe in Christ Jesus," and had "some notional Knowledge of Things," and some hope that "when I was married, I should have more leisure to serve God." Such proved sufficient to carry her to the minister for examination, and then to the Lord's Table. After all, she believed, "I was in as good a Condition as any of the rest which did receive." This happened around the time of her marriage, in 1657.

Soon, though, White began to suffer spiritual anxiety and despair. She started imagining she "had a Heart worse than the Devil," and upon seeing a spider, a creature "most loathsome" to her, she desired to be "such a one, esteeming of it to be in a far happier Condition than I was." Fearing "to be in the Dark, lest I should meet the Devil," she doubted whether she was "Elected" and "thought if I were not Elected, is [*sic*] was to no Purpose to strive, for what God hath decreed must be." At one point she "began to see mine own Vileness more than ever, and found mine Heart ran out to the Lord Jesus in Love, but doubted very much of his Love to me." For over a year, she wrote, "I had scarcely any settled Peace, now and then a good Word thrown in which would revive me for the present, but the Comfort would be soon gone."

When she became pregnant, perhaps for the first time, she started to fear that she might die in childbirth before gaining true repentance, and the prospect of suffering everlasting damnation overwhelmed her: "once when I was in great Fear least [*sic*] my Heart should grow dead, and when I was with Child, I was much dejected, having a Sense of my approaching Danger, and wanting an Assurance of my everlasting Happiness." But even after having "speedy Deliverance" of her child "beyond my Expectation," she still was unable to cast aside her apprehensions. One evening, while recovering from the birth, and after suckling her child, she envisioned "Satan laughing at me, because I had no Sleep," and continued through the night "weak in Body, and comfortless in Mind, so that in the Morning I expected nothing but Death." But these impressions suddenly became fused with other, more reassuring ones: "I have cast my self wholly upon the Lord Christ, and in him only is my Hope, and here will I Rest, and if I perish, I perish, but sure I am such shall not perish, for Christ hath promised them eternal lief [*sic*]." Now aware of Christ's power and mercy, and "thus being assisted by the Lord, I vanquished Satan for that Time," she wrote, and being thus at peace, "quickly fell asleep," and dreamt "that I should die in Child-bed" (as she did twelve years later), and "that the Night before I died, I should have full Assurance." She then awoke, feeling an "inexpressible Joy," a sense of Christ's saving presence, "earnestly longing to be Dissolved, and to be with Christ . . . and yet willing, if the Lord pleased to suffer any Thing which might be inflicted on me."[20]

The latter phases of this spiritual journey embody a theme found time and again in sermons delivered by New England ministers: the will must submit to Christ in regeneration if true assurance is to be gained. White had gradually sensed this need as she sought spiritual comfort from the Word, her minister, and published sermons like Shepard's *The Sincere Convert*. Humiliation formed the central passageway through conversion: only after the self had been humbled, the sinful past of youth purged, could an individual feel the joy of assurance. The unregenerate were often exhorted by such as Thomas Shepard to "lie down under" the Lord, that "he may tread upon thee, and thereby exalt himself, as well as lift thee up and exalt thee." Because the natural soul was an unclean vessel, it had to be emptied of its impurities before it could begin to receive the benefits of God's grace. Thus for Thomas Hooker, the self, "now being full of abominations, full of covetousnesse, full of malice, full of pride, full of love of our selves, full of hypocrisie, full of carelessenesse, loosenesse, and prophaneness, full of all manner of lusts, and corruptions, and concupuscence of the flesh," is unable to receive God's saving faith. Only through humiliation—"the utter nothingness of the soul"—could the reprobate cut himself off from "all high conceits and self confidence of that good which is in him."[21]

The regenerate was to God what the woman was to man after marriage. "It is a marriage-covenant that we make with God," Peter Bulkeley said, "therefore we must doe as the Spouse doth, resigne up our selves to be ruled and governed according to his will."[22] Although Puritan wives and mothers perhaps enjoyed a higher status than English and European women,[23] New Englanders upheld the tradition of the natural subordination of the wife to the husband. "The proper conduct of a wife was submission to her husband's instructions and commands. He was her superior, the head of the family, and she owed him an obedience founded on reverence."[24] All other responsibilities in marriage were mutual: husbands and wives were to cohabit, to love,

---

[20] *Experiences*, 4, 6, 9–13.

[21] Shepard, *The Sound Believer, Works of Shepard*, I, 179, 186; Hooker, *The Unbelievers*, 94.

[22] *The Gospel-Covenant: or the Covenant of Grace Opened*, 2d ed. (London, 1651), 50, quoted in Edmund S. Morgan, *The Puritan Family: Religion and Domestic Relations in Seventeenth-Century New England*, rev. ed. (New York: Harper and Row, 1966), 161.

[23] See, especially, Demos, *A Little Commonwealth*, chap. 5, and Roger Thompson, *Women in Stuart England and America: A Comparative Study* (Boston: Routledge and Kegan Paul, 1974).

[24] Morgan, *Puritan Family*, 44–45.

honor, and respect one another, to demonstrate patience and devotion toward one another.[25] But mutual caring in marriage could only be ensured by the wife's submitting willingly to the gentle yet firm rule of the husband, a belief verified by the Puritan's reading of the Pauline epistles. Thus Cotton Mather preached that:

> The *Principal Direction* for a Good Carriage in the *Married State* is that: Eph.
> V. 24, 25. *As the Church is subject unto* CHRIST, *so let Wives be unto their own Husbands, in everything. Husbands, Love your Wives even as* CHRIST *also has loved the Church.* I do not stay upon the Observation, That the Duty of the *Wife* is here, as elsewhere prescribed before that of the *Husband*; Because there may be more of *Difficulty* in *Her* Duty than in *His*; And, Because His cheerful doing of *His* Duty, will very much depend upon Her doing of *Hers*.[26]

Partly because of striking analogies between the position of the woman in marriage and the proper role of the regenerate Christian, New England ministers often employed the metaphor of marriage to elucidate Puritan doctrine on conversion. No other image conveyed so intimately the nature of true piety. "In sermon after sermon," Edmund S. Morgan shows, "the ministers of New England explained to their congregations that the true believer was wedded to his God in a holy marriage." Redemption could be understood as marriage to Christ; imperfect holiness in contrast to sanctification, as betrothal versus marriage; the trinity, as the family under God paralleling the secular family under the father.[27] By resorting to such imagery from the pulpit, however, ministers only reinforced the existing social and cultural harmony between the religious life, the transitional episodes of adulthood, and the experiences of married women. Properly submissive wives could easily identify with marriage and humiliation to Christ in regeneration, while, for dominant husbands and fathers, the achievement of true piety demanded an abrupt reversal in roles.

New England ministers also used other types of images that at certain times seemed more applicable. In the 1650s, 1660s, and 1670s, when first-generation patriarchs controlled New England, the image of the angry and wrathful God the Father demanding obedience and submission from his children predominated as people sought to understand the apparent impiety and waywardness of the rising generation. Many divines turned to the Old Testament

---

[25] So said Benjamin Wadsworth in *The Well-Ordered Family* (Boston, 1712), 28, as noted by Ulrich, "Vertuous Women Found," 76.

[26] *A Glorious Espousal: A Brief Essay to Illustrate and Prosecute the Marriage, Wherein Our Great Saviour Offers to Espouse unto Himself the Children of Men . . .* (Boston: Kneeland, 1719), 42, quoted in Masson, "Typology of the Female as a Model for the Regenerate," 308.

[27] *The Puritan Family*, 161–65.

to decry the present backsliding, and found in another kind of familial arrangement—the required subordination of son to father—an image to aid in bringing about regeneration and the submission of people to the Lord.[28] Thomas Hooker had used the metaphor with special force:

> Thus the Lord deales with us as a wise father doth with his child, he seeth if he had his portion in his hands he would be riotous and carelesse, and therefore it is wisedome not to trust him with his estate, but to keep him low, and to keep him upon dependance, that he may have better subjection from his hands. So it is with the Lord, he seeth that we have unruly hearts, and that if we had that evidence of Gods mercy made knowne to us that we would have, we would be so proud, and so haughty, and so full of contempt, and so censorious, that there were no living with us; therefore the Lord keepes us only in some hope, to hold up our soules: and the more dependance the soule hath, the more observance hath the Lord from us.[29]

But to exhort this way meant to risk losing completely the religious support of second-generation sons, who were struggling to come to terms with a patriarchal God in regeneration and to live up to their fathers before admission.[30]

With the 1680s and 1690s, and the passing of the fathers, the Old Testament figure of a vengeful God became less pervasive than the New Testament one of a loving, gentle, and protective Christ—the brother, bridegroom, or husband to the saved.[31] Second-generation ministers sought to cure their parishioners of their spiritual inhibitions, comfort them in a time of social and political transition, but emerging confidence, and excite them into religious action. Ministers employed the metaphor of regeneration as marriage to Christ to inspire conversions and adopted new methods to encourage church membership. Some supported the Half-Way Covenant, believing that it might stir interest in full membership; others, a sacramental piety in the hope of

---

[28] Emory Elliott, *Power and the Pulpit in Puritan New England* (Princeton: Princeton Univ. Press, 1975), 13–15 and passim. Elliott notes (p. 14) that in the sermons "before 1650 passages from the New Testament concerning mercy and grace predominate; between 1650 and 1680 there were fifty-seven published sermons based on Old Testament texts and only fifteen on texts from the New Testament; from 1681 to 1695 verses from the Gospel served as the texts for eighty-nine sermons while there were fifty-six texts from the Old Testament."

[29] *The Soules Implantation* (London: R. Young, 1637), 133.

[30] John Murrin, in a "Review Essay," *History and Theory*, 11 (1972), 236, suggests that "most second-generation men (women had less difficulty) could not experience a psychologically convincing conversion so long as their fathers were still alive to provide thunderous comparisons from the 1630s. Viewed from this perspective, scrupulosity blends indistinguishably into awe of the patriarch."

[31] Elliott, *Power and the Pulpit*, 14, 129, 176–77.

assuaging scruples about partaking of the Lord's Supper.[32] During the 1690s
Cotton Mather began promoting a "New Piety" centered upon the experience
of the new birth, a piety that retained humiliation as a key spiritual event
but discarded the notion of preparation.[33] Moreover, Solomon Stoddard of
Northampton, Massachusetts, started using the Lord's Supper as a "converting ordinance" and as a means through which the people of the town could
grow in grace.[34]

Such efforts to bring about conversions and broaden church membership
perhaps touched off the predominantly female revivals in admission that occurred especially during the 1690s. Congregations were becoming top-heavy
with women, and some ministers, including Cotton Mather, attempted to
explain why they were so visible in membership. Maybe, he noted, there
was simply a greater abundance of women than men in the population. But
a deeper appreciation of their religious fervor demanded an inquiry into their
experiences apart from men. He observed that "the *Curse* in the *Difficulties*
both of *Subjection* and of *Child bearing* which the *Female Sex* is doom'd
unto, has been turn'd into a *Blessing*, by the *Free Grace* of our Most Gracious God. God Sanctifies the *Chains*, the *Pains*, the *Deaths* which they meet
withal; and furthermore, makes the *Tenderness* of their Disposition, a further
Occasion of Serious Devotion in them." In addition, most women "have more
Time to Employ in the more Immediate Service of [their] Souls, than the
Other Sex is owner of." They "are Ordinarily more within the *House*, and so
may more mind the Work within the *Heart*, then *We*."[35]

Benjamin Colman of Boston's Brattle Street Church made similar observations. Women were less a part of the world than men and hence more
religious (Puritan divines were always decrying the secular distractions created by man's involvement in the profane), but their zeal was particularly due
to their "MULTIPLIED SORROWS." The *"Curse pronounc'd upon our first
Mother* EVE," Colman explained to an assembly of women, has been *"turn'd
into the greatest Blessing to Your Souls."* He continued that *"Your frequent
Returns in Your own Apprehension towards the Gates of Death, by which We
all receive our* LIFE, *suitably leads you to a returning serious Tho'tfulness
for your Souls and of Your Spiritual State."* The fears of the mother awaiting
childbirth were more apt to *"terrify"* than the anxieties arising out of illness,

---

[32] E. Brooks Holifield, *The Covenant Sealed: The Development of Puritan Sacramental
Theology in Old and New England 1570–1720* (New Haven and London: Yale Univ. Press,
1974), chap. 7.

[33] Robert Middlekauff, *The Mathers: Three Generations of Puritan Intellectuals,
1596–1728* (New York: Oxford Univ. Press, 1971), chaps. 13, 17.

[34] Paul R. Lucas, *Valley of Discord: Church and Society in the Connecticut Valley,
1636–1720* (Hanover, N.H.: University Press of New England, 1976), chaps. 7–9.

[35] *Ornaments for the Daughters of Zion, or the Character and Happiness of a Vertuous
Woman* . . . (Cambridge, Mass.: Green, 1692), 44–45.

for the *"Impressions"* of *"Fits of Sickness"* soon disappear, while the experiences of pregnancy are of greater duration and tend not to vanish, but linger in the mind.[36]

At the close of the seventeenth century and beyond, ministers who faced congregations filled with regenerate women not only tried to understand the source of their piety, but also were increasingly willing to extol their sanctity and virtue. A "typology of the female as a model for the regenerate" emerged in the literature alongside an idealized picture of the virtuous woman. As portrayed especially by the funeral sermons of the period from 1690 to 1730, the ideal woman sought God early, prayed and fasted, attended church frequently, and submitted to the will of God. This does not mean that Puritan piety became "feminized" or that the woman's virtues began to be praised at the expense of the man's. Puritan divines stressed the need for a virtuous mankind and a common Christianity in working for the conversion of all New Englanders, and were quick to point out that experience, not nature, accounted for her more fervent piety.[37] At the same time, they were attempting to come to terms with the more noticeable, and perhaps unsettling, preponderance of women at admission.

Feminine piety had become a powerful source of religious renewal and the object of some scrutiny after the mid-seventeenth century, when conversion and admission into the Church became keyed to the transitional experiences of adulthood and attuned particularly to the situation of married women. Possibly the public recognition pious women received from the pulpit strengthened the trend toward female domination, and helped to perpetuate it into the eighteenth century, although how far into the century is unknown.[38] This one issue, then, needs to be explored, along with others also raised by our discussion of women and the early New England Church. What of the experiences of males apart from females? What explains the local variations in sex ratios, which were considerable at certain times and places?[39] By shift-

---

[36] *The Duty and Honour of Aged Women, Deliver'd . . . after the Funeral of the Excellent Mrs. Abigail Foster . . .* (Boston: Green, 1711), ii–iii.

[37] Masson, "Typology of the Female as a Model for the Regenerate," 304–15; Ulrich, "Vertuous Women Found," 67–87.

[38] Some evidence for Connecticut Colony suggests that the percentages of women at admission declined significantly during the 1720s and 1740s, and increased from then until the 1770s. See Gerald F. Moran, "The Puritan Saint: Church Membership, Religious Experience, and Piety in Connecticut, 1636–1776" (Diss. Rutgers Univ., 1974), chaps. 8 and 10.

[39] Such variations or sexual imbalances in church membership, however, were not the result of skewed sex ratios within the population. The Connecticut census of 1774 allows an examination of sex ratios by town and over time, and it reveals that women made up only 49.4 percent of the Colony's population. More than two-thirds of the towns listed on the census contained more men than women, while the percentages of women per town ranged from 46.2 to 55.7. Older communities tended to contain higher percentages of women than more recently settled towns, although the association proved insignificant $(r = +.26)$. The mean percentages of women residing in towns settled at 25 year intervals

ing focus from broad patterns over time to the parish, and by using techniques of comparative history, future studies might produce answers to these and other questions concerned with the possible connections between changes in communities and admission patterns. Additional demographies of gender and church membership can only deepen our understanding of the important historical background to feminine experience and behavior in antebellum America.*

---

from 1635 to 1774 were as follows: 49.7, 49.6, 49.9, 49.7, 48.5, and 48.3. Even if seventeenth-century communities differed from their eighteenth-century counterparts and often contained more women than men, we would be forced to look elsewhere to explain sex ratios in membership that frequently exceeded 65 percent women, and at times 70 percent. The 1774 census can be found in *The Public Records of the Colony of Connecticut*, vols. 1–3, ed. J. H. Trumbull; vols. 4–15, ed. C. J. Hoadly (15 vols.; Hartford: Case, Lockwood, and Brainard, 1850–90), 14, 485–91.

*An earlier version of this chapter was presented to the Comparative Studies Colloquium, Department of History, University of Michigan, Ann Arbor. I wish to thank John King and John Shy for their helpful suggestions at that session, and also Peter Amann, Leslie Tentler, Tom Tentler, and Maris Vinovskis for their useful comments in the course of revision.

Laurel Thatcher Ulrich

Vertuous Women Found
New England Ministerial Literature, 1668–1735

Cotton Mather called them "The Hidden Ones." They never preached or sat in a deacon's bench. Nor did they vote or attend Harvard. Neither, because they were virtuous women, did they question God or the magistrates. They prayed secretly, read the Bible through at least once a year, and went to hear the minister preach even when it snowed. Hoping for an eternal crown, they never asked to be remembered on earth. And they haven't been. Well-behaved women seldom make history; against Antinomians and witches, these pious matrons have had little chance at all. Most historians, considering the domestic by definition irrelevant, have simply assumed the pervasiveness of similar attitudes in the seventeenth century. Others, noting the apologetic tone of Anne Bradstreet and the banishment of Anne Hutchinson, have been satisfied that New England society, while it valued marriage and allowed women limited participation in economic affairs, discouraged their interest in either poetry or theology. For thirty years no one has bothered to question Edmund Morgan's assumption that a Puritan wife was considered "the weaker vessel in both body and mind" and that "her husband ought not to expect too much from her."[1] John Winthrop's famous letter on the insanity of bookish

---

[1] Edmund S. Morgan, *The Puritan Family: Religion and Domestic Relations in Seventeenth-Century New England* (New York: Harper and Row, 1966), 44. Recent works continue to rely on Morgan's study, which was first published in 1944. See, for example, John Demos, *A Little Commonwealth: Family Life in Plymouth* (New York: Oxford Univ. Press, 1970), 98. Morgan's description of male dominance within a loving marriage is consistent with descriptions taken from English prescriptive literature in Louis B. Wright, *Middle-Class Culture in Elizabethan England* (Chapel Hill, N.C.: Univ. of North Carolina Press, 1935), chap. 7, and in Charles H. and Katherine George, *The Protestant Mind of the English Reformation, 1570–1640* (Princeton, N.J.: Princeton Univ. Press, 1961), chap. 7.

Mistress Hopkins has been the quintessential source: ". . . if she had attended her household affairs, and such things as belong to women, and not gone out of her way and calling to meddle in such things as are proper for men, whose minds are stronger, etc., she had kept her wits."[2]

Yet there is ample evidence in traditional documents to undermine these conclusions, at least for the late seventeenth and early eighteenth centuries. For the years between 1668 and 1735, Evans' *American Bibliography* lists 55 elegies, memorials, and funeral sermons for females plus 15 other works of practical piety addressed wholly or in part to women.[3] Although historians have looked at such popular works as Cotton Mather's *Ornaments for the Daughters of Zion*, they have ignored the rest.[4] Thus, New England's daughters remain hidden despite the efforts of her publishing ministry. True, a collection of ministerial literature cannot tell us what New England women, even of the more pious variety, were really like. Nor can it describe what "most Puritans" thought of women. It can tell us only what qualities were publicly praised in a specific time by a specific group of men. Yet, in a field which suffers from so little data, there is value in that. A handful of quotations has for too long defined the status of New England's virtuous women. This interesting collection deserves a closer look.

Although 27 of the 70 titles are by Cotton Mather (who wrote more of everything in the period), the remaining 43 are the work of 21 authors. They range from a single sermon by Leonard Hoar, his only published work, to the six poems for women written over a 25-year period by ubiquitous elegist John Danforth. They include four English works republished in America. Only 12 of the titles were printed before 1700, but two others, Samuel Willard's short discourse on marriage from his *Complete Body of Divinity*, posthumously published in 1726, and Hugh Peter's *A Dying Father's Last*

---

[2] The Winthrop quote appears in Morgan (p. 44) as in many lesser summaries of Puritan attitudes toward women from Thomas Woody, *A History of Women's Education in the United States*, Vol. I (New York: Science Press, 1929), 106–7, to Lyle Koehler, "The Case of the American Jezebels: Anne Hutchinson and Female Agitation During the Years of Antinomian Turmoil, 1636–1640," *William and Mary Quarterly*, 3d ser., 31 (Jan. 1974), 58. Koehler's article exemplifies the common imbalance in favor of deviant women.

[3] Charles Evans, *American Bibliography: A Chronological Dictionary of all Books, Pamphlets and Periodical Publications Printed in the USA, 1639–1820* (New York: P. Smith, 1941); Roger Bristol, *Supplement to Charles Evans' American Bibliography* (Charlottesville, Va.: Univ. Press of Virginia, 1970).

[4] Mary Sumner Benson, in *Women in Eighteenth-Century America* (New York: Columbia Univ. Press, 1935), quotes extensively from Mather's *Ornaments*, using it as evidence that he believed in the "proper submission of women." Page Smith draws the opposite conclusion from the same document in *Daughters of the Promised Land* (Boston: Little, Brown, 1970), 47ff. Two of the three main sources for Edmund Morgan's description of marital ethics belong to this group of materials: Willard's *Complete Body of Divinity* and Wadsworth's *The Well-Ordered Family*, although he quotes rather selectively from them. William Andrews, "The Printed Funeral Sermons of Cotton Mather," *Early American Literature*, 5 (Fall 1970), 24–44, notes the high percentage of sermons on females and attempts some analysis of the materials but without relating it to the wider corpus of ministerial literature.

Legacy, first reprinted in Boston in 1717, originated earlier. Peter's treatise, written just before his execution, is especially interesting as a link to the first generation of New Englanders.

In spite of personal idiosyncracies and the acknowledged predominance of Mather, this literature is remarkably consistent. Thus, a crude woodcut decorating a broadside published for Madam Susanna Thacher in 1724 is identical to that ornamenting an elegy for Lydia Minot published in 1668. Nor are doctrinal distinctions of any consequence. Benjamin Colman could differ with his brethren over the precise meaning of New England, for example, yet share with them a common attitude toward women.[5] Because these works are so much a piece, however, subtle shifts in emphasis between authors and across time become significant. A patient examination of this seemingly static and formulaic material reveals nuances in ministerial thought of considerable interest, demonstrating that for women's history, as for so many aspects of social history, the real drama is often in the humdrum.

*I*n ministerial literature, as in public records, women became legitimately visible in only three ways: they married, they gave birth, they died. In the written materials, dying is by far the best-documented activity. Although a minister might have had a specific woman in mind as he prepared an idealized portrait of the good wife for a wedding or espousal sermon or as he composed a comforting tract for parishioners approaching childbed, it is only in the funeral literature that he is free to name names and praise individual accomplishments. Not that a funeral sermon is ever very specific. Circumlocution, even a certain coyness in referring to "that excellent person now departed from us," is the rule. Still, it is a rare sermon that does not contain a eulogy, however brief. Some append fuller biographical sketches often containing selections from the writings of the deceased.[6] From these materials a composite portrait emerges.

A virtuous woman sought God early. Hannah Meigs, who died in New London at the age of 22, was typical. She began while still a child to pay attention in church, acquiring the habit of reading and praying at night when the rest of her family was asleep. Becoming preoccupied with her own salvation, she bewailed her sinfulness, at last receiving an assurance of God's mercy. In the sickness which eventually claimed her, she submitted her will

---

[5] In his study of prescriptive literature in late seventeenth-century England, Levin L. Schucking noted a similar phenomenon. See *The Puritan Family: A Social Study from the Literary Sources* (London: Routledge and Kegan Paul, 1969), xiii. I have made no attempt to define the "Puritanism" of the authors. Although most of them belonged to the congregational majority, Samuel Myles was an Anglican. His eulogy for Elizabeth Riscarrick, though less detailed than many, follows the typical pattern.

[6] The funeral sermon with its accompanying biographical "lean-to" was a venerable form by this time. See William Haller, *The Rise of Puritanism* (New York: Harper, 1938), 101.

to God, from her death bed meekly teaching her brothers and sisters and other "Relatives, Acquaintances, & Companions."[7] Praise of early piety was not confined to sermons for young women. In his eulogy for Mary Rock, who died at the age of 80, Cotton Mather devoted considerable space to her early religiosity and the wise education of her parents.[8] The women eulogized typically found God before marriage, having been, in Danforth's phrase, first "Polish'd and Prepar'd" by pious parents.[9]

A virtuous woman prayed and fasted. Jane Colman was said to have lain awake whole nights mourning for sin, calling on God, praying.[10] Mrs. Increase Mather regularly prayed six times a day. After her death her husband wrote a tribute to her from his study, a spot which had become endeared to him when he discovered in some of her private papers that during his four years' absence in England she had "spent many whole Days (some Scores of them) alone with God there" in prayer and fasting for his welfare and that of her children.[11] Thomas Foxcroft characterized a praying mother as "One that *stood in the Breach* to turn away wrath" and concluded that the death of such women was a bad omen for the community.[12] Cotton Mather was fond of saying that good mothers travailed twice for their children, once for their physical birth, again for the spiritual.[13]

A virtuous woman loved to go to church. On the day of her death ailing Sarah Leveret went to hear the sermon even though the weather was bitter. When her friends tried to dissuade her, she answered: "If the Ministers can go abroad to Preach, certainly, it becomes the People to go abroad; and hear them."[14] Sarah was not alone among New England's pious matrons. The ministers who preached the funeral sermons for Anne Mason and Jane Steel both commented on the fact that they came to church even when they were ill.[15] Jabez Fitch said of Mrs. Mary Martin: "The feet of those that brought

---

[7] John Hart, *The Nature and Blessedness of Trusting in God* (New London, 1728), 45.

[8] Cotton Mather, *Nepenthes Evangelicum . . . A Sermon Occasion'd by the Death of a Religious Matron, Mrs. Mary Rock* (Boston, 1713), 41.

[9] John Danforth, "An Elegy upon the much Lamented Decease of Mrs. Elizabeth Foxcroft," appended to Thomas Foxcroft's *Sermon Preach'd at Cambridge after the Funeral of Mrs. Elizabeth Foxcroft* (Boston, 1721), 53.

[10] Benjamin Colman, *Reliquiae Turellae, et Lachrymae Paternae. Father's Tears over his Daughter's Remains . . . to which are added, some Large Memoirs of her Life and Death by her Consort, the Reverend Mr. Ebenezer Turell* (Boston, 1735), 116.

[11] Increase Mather, *A Sermon Concerning Obedience & Resignation To The Will of God in Everything* (Boston, 1714), ii, 39.

[12] Foxcroft, *Sermon Preach'd*, 14–15.

[13] This is a common theme throughout Mather's funeral sermons. A typical example is in *Virtue in its Verdure. A Christian Exhibited as a Green Olive Tree . . . with a character of the Virtuous Mrs. Abigail Brown* (Boston, 1725), 23.

[14] Cotton Mather, *Monica Americana, A Funeral-Sermon Occasioned by Death of Mrs. Sarah Leveret* (Boston, 1705), 27.

[15] James Fitch, *Peace the End of the Perfect and Upright* (Cambridge, 1672), 12; Benjamin Colman, *The Death of God's Saints Precious in His Sight* (Boston, 1723), 23.

the glad Tidings of the Gospel, were always beautiful in her Eyes, and it was her great Delight to attend on the Ministry of the Word."[16]

A virtuous woman read. Throughout the eulogies reading is mentioned as often as prayer, and the two activities are occasionally linked, as in John Danforth's praise of Hannah Sewall:

> *Observing Ladys* must keep down their Vail,
> 'Till They're as *Full* of Grace, *& Free* from Gall,
> As *Void* of Pride, as *High* in Vertue Rare
> As *much* in Reading, and as *much* in Prayer.[17]

After her children were grown, Maria Mather took renewed interest in reading the scriptures, more than doubling the prescribed pace by reading the Bible through twice in less than a year.[18] Her daughter Jerusha was a great reader of history and theology as well as scripture, having been given eyesight so excellent she could read in dim light.[19] Katharin Mather, Cotton's daughter, went beyond her grandmother and her aunt. She mastered music, penmanship, needlework, the usual accomplishments of a gentlewoman, "To which she added this, that she became in her childhood a Mistress of the Hebrew Tongue."[20]

A virtuous woman conversed. Mourning for Elizabeth Hatch, Joseph Metcalf lamented nothing so much as the loss of her pious discourse.[21] For John Danforth, Elizabeth Hutchinson's conversation was "sweeter than Hybla's Drops," while for Cotton Mather, the "fruitfulness" of Mary Rock's "Religious Conferences" made her sick room "A little *Anti-Chamber* of Heaven."[22] James Hillhouse said his mother could converse "on many subjects with the Grandees of the World, and the Masters of Eloquence" yet she was not haughty. "Her incessant and constant Reading, with her good Memory, and clear Judgment, made her expert (even to a degree) in the Bible. Insomuch, that she was capable on many occasions, very seasonably and suitably to apply it, and that with great facility and aptness, to the various Subjects of

[16] Jabez Fitch, *Discourse on Serious Piety. A Funeral Sermon . . . upon the Death of Mrs. Mary Martyn* (Boston, 1725), 18.

[17] John Danforth, "Greatness & Goodness Elegized, In a Poem upon the Much Lamented Decease of the Honourable & Vertuous Madam Hannah Sewall" (Boston, 1717), Broadside, 1.33ff.

[18] Increase Mather, *A Sermon Concerning Obedience*, ii.

[19] Cotton Mather, *Memorials of Early Piety* (Boston, 1711), 3–4, 13.

[20] "An Account of Mrs. Katharin Mather by Another Hand," in Cotton Mather, *Victorina: A Sermon Preach'd on the Decease and at the Desire of Mrs. Katharin Mather* (Boston, 1717), 50.

[21] [Joseph Metcalf,] "Tears Dropt at the Funeral of . . . Mrs. Elizabeth Hatch" (Boston, 1710), Broadside.

[22] John Danforth, "Honour and Vertue Elegized in a Poem Upon an Honourable, Aged, and Gracious Mother in Israel" (Boston, 1713), Broadside; Cotton Mather, *Nepenthes*, 45–46.

Discourse, that offered themselves."[23] James Fitch said that if he were to "rehearse the many Spiritual, Weighty, and Narrow Questions & Discourses" he had heard from Anne Mason, "it would fill up a large book."[24] Benjamin Wadsworth praised Bridget Usher for promoting "pious and savoury Discourse."[25] Godly matrons were meant to be heard.

A virtuous woman wrote. A quill as well as a distaff was proper to a lady's hand. Despite eight pregnancies in ten years, Katharin Willard was such a good manager and so industrious that she was "hindred not from the Use of her Pen, as well as of her Needle."[26] One form of writing was simply taking notes in church. Mary Terry wrote down the main points of the preacher's sermon, recalling the whole thing later from her notes, a habit which had apparently become less common by Foxcroft's time, for he commented that aged Bridget Usher and her associates had "practiced (even to the last) the good old way of *writing* after the Minister. They were *swift to hear*; and by this laudable (but not too unfashionable) Method, took care to hear *for the time to come*, as the Prophet Speaks."[27]

In preaching a funeral sermon Cotton Mather often included excerpts from the woman's writings. In Elizabeth Cotton's, for example, he drew from writings at several stages of her life, telling his audience that one of these selections was "so expressive and so Instructive, that it may well pass for the Best part of my Sermon, if I now give to you all, and particularly the Daughters of our *Zion*, the Benefit of hearing it Read unto you."[28] In 1711 he edited a selection of the writings of his sister Jerusha and published them with an introduction as *Memorials of Early Piety*. Such a practice was not uncommon. In 1681, Sarah Goodhue's husband published *The Copy of A Valedictory and Monitory Writing*, a letter of "sage counsel" and "pious instructions" which she had written for her family and hidden, having had a premonition of her death in childbirth.[29] Grace Smith's legacy to her children was supposedly "taken from her lips by the Minister of that Town where she died," a

---

[23] James Hillhouse, *A Sermon Concerning the Life, Death, and Future State of Saints* (Boston, 1721), 112, 117. Although Hillhouse's sermon was published in Boston after he had settled there, it was originally preached in Ireland.

[24] James Fitch, *Peace*, 11.

[25] Thomas Foxcroft, *The Character of Anna, The Prophetess Consider'd and Apply'd* (Boston, 1723), from the Preface by Benjamin Wadsworth, ii.

[26] Cotton Mather, *El-Shaddai . . . A brief Essay . . . Produced by the Death of That Virtuous Gentlewoman, Mrs. Katharin Willard* (Boston, 1725), 22.

[27] Thomas Reynolds, *Practical Religion Exemplify'd In the Lives of Mrs. Mary Terry . . . and Mrs. Clissould* (Boston, 1713), 4; and Foxcroft, *Anna*, 14.

[28] Cotton Mather, *Ecclesiae Monilia. The Peculiar Treasure of the Almighty King Opened . . . Whereof one is more particularly Exhibited in the Character of Mrs. Elizabeth Cotton* (Boston, 1726), 25.

[29] Sarah Goodhue, *The Copy of a Valedictory and Monitory Writing . . . Directed to her Husband and Children, with other Near Relations and Friends*, reprinted in Thomas Franklin Water, *Ipswich in the Massachusetts Bay Colony* (Ipswich, Mass.: Ipswich Historical Society, 1905), 519–24.

strange statement since it included in addition to predictable paragraphs of advice and motherly proverbs, two long passages in verse written in iambic tetrameter with a rather complex internal rhyme scheme.[30] Like the others, she had obviously been sharpening her pen after the spinning was done.

A virtuous woman managed well. Increase Mather said his father's greatest affliction was the death of his wife, "Which Afflication was the more grievous, in that she being a Woman of singular Prudence for the Management of Affairs, had taken off from her Husband all Secular Cares, so that he wholly devoted himself to his Study, and to Sacred Imployments."[31] Women were praised in the funeral sermons not only for being godly but for being practical. Even the saintly Jerusha Oliver was not above dabbling in investments. "When she sent (as now and then she did) her Little *Ventures to Sea*, at the return she would be sure to lay aside the *Tenth* of her gain, for Pious Uses."[32]

Anne Eliot's talents, which included nursing, were so valued that Danforth almost credited her with holding up the world:

Haile! Thou *Sagacious & Advant'rous* Soul!
Haile, Amazon Created to Controll
Weak Nature's Foes, & T'take her part,
The King of Terrours, Thou, (till the command
Irrevocable came to Stay thy Hand,)
Didst oft Repel, by thy Choice Art:
   By High Decree
   Long didst thou stand
An Atlas, in Heav'n's Hand
To th' World to be.[33]

Mrs. Eliot, like many of her sisters, was no less pious as an "Atlas."

A virtuous woman submitted to the will of God. Increase Mather told the story of a "Person of Quality" whose only son contracted smallpox. She called in the ministers to pray for him. When they prayed that if by God's will the child should die the mother would have the strength to submit, she interrupted, crying: "If He will Take him away; Nay, He shall then *Tear* him away." The child died. Some time later the mother became pregnant, but when the time for delivery arrived the child would not come and was consequently "Violently *Torn* from her; so she Died."[34] For the godly woman rebellion was not worth the risks. She learned to submit to God,

[30] Grace Smith, *The Dying Mother's Legacy, or the Good and Heavenly Counsel of that Eminent and Pious Matron* (Boston, 1712).
[31] Increase Mather, *The Life and Death of Richard Mather* (Cambridge, 1670), 25.
[32] Cotton Mather, *Memorials of Early Piety*, 45.
[33] John Danforth, "A Poem Upon the Triumphant Translation of a Mother in Our Israel," appended to *Kneeling to God* (Boston, 1697), 64.
[34] Increase Mather, *Sermon Concerning Obedience*, 34.

meekly acquiescing to the deaths of husband and children and ultimately to her own as well. Only one minister suggested that a departed sister was less than patient in her final sickness and Samuel Myles cautioned his reader lest he "Uncharitably, and Unchristianly impute that to the *Person*, which was justly chargeable on the *Disease*."[35] Cotton Mather's women were typically terrified of death until it approached; then they triumphed over the "King of Terrours." Jerusha Oliver sang for joy and sent a message to her sister in Roxbury telling her not to be afraid to die.[36] Rebeckah Burnet, age 17, expired crying, "Holy, Holy, Holy—Lord Jesus, Come unto Me!"[37] In her illness, Abiel Goodwin heard voices and music and was transported by the tolling of funeral bells. In her quieter moments she exhibited a wry sense of humor, agreeing with a visitor that, given her hydropical condition, she was "A going to Heaven by Water" and might soon sing that song with Jesus.[38]

Read directly, the qualities attributed to these women have little meaning. It is easy to conclude from the lavish praise bestowed upon them that they enjoyed an exalted position in the Puritan ethos. It is even more tempting to conclude the opposite, that the limited nature of their intellectual achievement and their continually lauded meekness and submission document a secondary role. It is helpful, then, to compare this portrait of a virtuous woman with a contemporary portrait of a godly man. Richard Mather, according to the eulogy written by his son Increase, found God early, prayed often, read the scriptures, and though he was learned "was exceeding low and little in his own eyes." Though well-educated, he was careful not to display his learning, and he always preached plainly. He loved to listen to sermons and in his last months continued to attend lectures in neighboring congregations until he was too sick to ride. "Yea and usually even to his old Age (as did Mr. Hildersham) he took notes from those whom he heard, professing that he found profit in it." He was patient in affliction, submitting to the will of God in death.[39] The inference is clear. While a godly woman was expected to act appropriately in all the relations in which she found herself, to be a dutiful daughter, an obedient and faithful wife, a wise parent and mistress, a kind friend, and a charitable neighbor, in her relationship with God she was autonomous. The portrait of Richard Mather, the first spiritual autobiography published in America, is duplicated in miniature in dozens of funeral sermons printed in Boston. But it did not originate there. It is a pattern of godliness

---

[35] Samuel Myles, *Sermon Preach't At the Funeral of Mrs. Elizabeth Riscarrick* (Boston, 1698).

[36] Cotton Mather, *Memorials of Early Piety*, 49.

[37] Cotton Mather, *Light in Darkness, An Essay on the Piety Which by Rememb'ring the Many Days of Darkness, Will Change Them Into a Marvelous Light* (Boston, 1724), 20.

[38] Cotton Mather, *Juga Jucunda* (Boston, 1728), 31–32.

[39] Increase Mather, *Richard Mather*, 33, 34.

basic to the English reformed tradition.[40] This much should be obvious to anyone familiar with Puritan literature, yet it bears repeating in a time when qualities such as "meekness" and "submissiveness" are presumed to have a sexual reference. In a very real sense there is no such thing as *female* piety in early New England: in preaching sermons for women, the ministers universally used the generic male pronouns in enlarging their themes, even when the text had reference to a scriptural Bathsheba or Mary; the same Christ-like bearing was required of both male and female.

Because dying is an individual rather than a social act, it is in the funeral literature that we see most clearly the equality of men and women before God. It is important, then, to try to determine whether this acknowledged spiritual equality impinged on the prescribed social roles described in the general works of practical piety.

*I*n 1709 there appeared in Boston a reprint of a wedding sermon preached at Sherbourn in Dorsetshire by a nonconformist minister named John Sprint. Called *The Bride-Woman's Counsellor*, it virtually ignored the groom. Marital troubles, the author concluded, were mainly the fault of women anyway. "You women will acknowledge that Men can learn to command, and rule fast enough, which as Husbands they ought to do, but tis very rare to find that Women learn so fast to Submit and obey, which as Wives they ought to do."[41] Like Sarah, women should call their husbands "Lord," never presuming to the familiarity of a Christian name lest they in time usurp his authority and place him under the discipline of an Apron-String. Although women might make light of this instruction to obey, he continued, "I know not of any duty belonging to any Men or Women, in the Whole Book of God, that is urged with more vehemency." Authority had been given to the husband as "absolutely and as peremptorily as unto Christ himself."[42]

This is a remarkable document, all the more remarkable because in the whole corpus of materials printed in Boston there is nothing remotely like it

[40] See, for example, Cotton Mather, *A Good Man Making A Good End* (Boston, 1698), on the death of a minister; and Thomas Foxcroft, *A Brief Display of Mordecai's Excellent Character* (Boston, 1727), on the death of a public official. For the English tradition (which placed less emphasis on early piety), see Haller, *Rise of Puritanism*, 93ff. Robert Middlekauff and David Hall both stress the prototypal quality of Richard Mather's biography. See *The Mathers: Three Generations of Puritan Intellectuals, 1596–1728* (New York: Oxford Univ. Press, 1971), 101–2, and *The Faithful Shepherd: A History of the New England Ministry in the Seventeenth Century* (Chapel Hill, N.C.: Univ. of North Carolina Press, 1972), 179.

[41] John Sprint, *The Bride-Woman's Counsellor, Being A Sermon Preached at a Wedding at Sherbourn, in Dorsetshire* (Boston, 1709), 2.

[42] Ibid., 16, 11.

in content or in tone. It makes a useful reference point for looking at three other works printed about the same time: Benjamin Wadsworth's *The Well-Ordered Family*, 1712; William Secker's *A Wedding Ring*, an English pamphlet reprinted in Boston in 1690, 1705, 1750, and 1773; and Samuel Willard's exposition of the fifth commandment in *A Complete Body of Divinity*, 1726.

Wadsworth's treatise must be looked at structurally. Like Sprint he reminded wives to "love, honour and obey," but his entire essay was organized around the notion of mutual responsibility, mutual caring. He listed seven duties of husbands and wives. The first six are reciprocal: to cohabit, to love one another, to be faithful to one another, to help one another, to be patient with one another, to honor one another. It is only with the seventh duty that there is any differentiation at all: the husband is to govern gently, the wife to obey cheerfully. It was thus within an ethic of mutual concern and sharing that Wadsworth developed the obedience theme, and he maintained the parallel structure of the essay even in these paragraphs. Both mates were scolded if they should lift up their hands against the other. A woman who struck her husband usurped not just his authority but that of God. A man who twitted his wife affronted not just a Woman but God.[43] Wadsworth thus undercut the subjection of women to their husbands even as he upheld it.

The same tendency is apparent in Secker. *A Wedding Ring* is a frothy bit of writing, a tiny little book which would have fitted a pocket or pouch. Its intention was not so much instruction as celebration, and it appropriated attractive quotations and metaphors at random, regardless of inconsistency. Although there are traditional proverbs enjoining submission, the great weight of the imagery falls on the side of equality. Eve is a "parallel line drawn equal" with Adam. A husband and wife are like two instruments making music, like two streams in one current, like a pair of oars rowing a boat to heaven (with children and servants as passengers), like two milch kine coupled to carry the Ark of God, two cherubims, two tables of stone on which the law is written.[44]

Willard accepted this two-sided view of the marriage relation and in his short disquisition on the family attempted to harmonize it. "Of all the Orders which are unequals," he wrote, "these do come nearest to an Equality, and in several respects they stand upon even ground. These do make a Pair, which infers so far a Parity. They are in the Word of God called *Yoke-Fellows*, and so are to draw together in the Yoke. Nevertheless, God hath also made an imparity between them, in the Order prescribed in His Word, and for that reason there is a Subordination, and they are ranked among unequals." Yet,

---

[43] Benjamin Wadsworth, *The Well-Ordered Family: or, Relative Duties, Being The Substance of Several Sermons About Family Prayer, Duties of Husband & Wives, Duties of Parents & Children, Duties of Masters & Servants* (Boston, 1712), 28.

[44] William Secker, *A Wedding Ring* (Boston, 1690), unpaged.

referring to the duties of the wife "as inferiour," he cautioned that "the word used there is a general word, and signified to be ordered under another, or to keep Order, being a Metaphor from a Band of Souldiers, or an Army." Further he explained that "the Submission here required, is not to be measured by the Notation or import of the Word itself, but by the Quality of the Relation to which it is applied." The husband-wife relation must never be confused with the master-servant or child-parent relation. A husband ought to be able to back his counsels with the word of God "and lay before her a sufficient Conviction of her Duty, to comply with him therein; for he hath no Authority or Compulsion." While in any relation it is the duty of inferiors to obey superiors unless a command is contrary to God, "a wife certainly hath greater liberty of debating the Prudence of the thing." Thus, the emphasis throughout is on discussion, on reasoning, on mediation. Wives as well as husbands have the responsibility to counsel and direct. Each should "chuse the fittest Seasons to Reprove each other, for things which their Love and Duty calls for."[45] The command to obedience, for Willard, was primarily a principle of order.

Sprint's sermon, bristling with assertive females and outraged husbands, is an oddity among the ministerial literature. Harmony, not authority, was the common theme. Thus, the marriage discourses support the implication of the funeral literature that women were expected to be rational as well as righteous, capable of independent judgment as well as deference, and as responsible as their spouses for knowing the word of God and for promoting the salvation of the family. A virtuous woman was espoused to Christ before she was espoused to any man.

*T*hat few tracts and sermons on childbirth survive is probably evidence in itself of the reluctance of the ministers to stress "feminine" or "masculine" themes over a common Christianity. The limited writing on parturition is worth examining, however, for here if anywhere authors had an opportunity to expound upon the peculiar failings or virtues of the weaker sex.

A pregnant woman in New England's godly community had two preparations to make for the day of her delivery. On the one hand she had to arrange for a midwife, ready a warm and convenient chamber, prepare childbed linen for herself and clothing for her infant, and plan refreshment for the friends invited to attend her. But she knew, even without a ministerial reminder, that these things could prove "miserable comforters." She might "perchance need no other linen shortly but a winding

---

[45] Samuel Willard, *A Complete Body of Divinity in Two Hundred and Fifty Expository Lectures* (Boston, 1726), 609–12.

sheet, and have no other chamber but a grave, no neighbors but worms."[46] Her primary duty, then, was preparing to die. Female mortality is the most pervasive theme of the childbirth literature. The elegists loved to exploit the pathos of death in birth—the ship and cargo sunk together, the fruit and tree both felled, the womb become a grave. In his poem for Mary Brown, for example, Nicholas Noyes dwelt at length on the fruitless pangs of her labor: "A BIRTH of *One*, to Both a Death becomes;/ A Breathless Mother the *Dead Child* Entombs."[47] Thus, it was often in a very particular sense that the ministers spoke of the "fearful sex." In stressing the need for a husband's tenderness, for example, Willard had singled out those bodily infirmities associated with the "breeding, bearing, and nursing" of children.[48]

Yet these grim realities had their joyous side. Cotton Mather was fond of saying that though an equal number of both sexes were born, a larger proportion of females were reborn.[49] He wondered why. Perhaps they had more time to spend in godly activities, "although I must confess, tis often otherwise." No, he concluded, it was probably because in childbirth the curse of Eve had turned into a blessing.[50] Given the spiritual equality of men and women, the only possible explanation for a disparity in religious performance had to be physical. Benjamin Colman resolved the same problem in a similar way in a preface to one of his sermons. Writing later in the period than Mather, he could toy with the idea of a "natural Tenderness of Spirit" given to women through the election of God, yet he too focused upon their bodily experience. Pregnancy and childbirth, by turning female thoughts frequently "towards the Gates of Death, by which We all receive our Life," increased women's susceptibility to the comforts of Christ. Pregnancy was superior to regular human ills in this regard, thought Colman, because it continued for months rather than surprising the victim with an acute attack forgotten as soon as it was over.[51]

Even here the ministers were ready to stress similarities between men and women. Though John Oliver urged husbands to be kind to their pregnant wives because of their increased vulnerability to "Hysterical vapours," his argument really rested on an analogy, not a contrast, between the sexes. Husbands should be tolerant of their wives, he insisted, because they "desire

---

[46] John Oliver, *A Present for Teeming American Women* (Boston, 1694), 3. This was an American edition of a pamphlet first printed in London in 1663.

[47] Nicholas Noyes, poem for Mrs. Mary Brown in Cotton Mather, *Eureka the Vertuous Woman Found*, 1. 15; See also "Upon the Death of the Virtuous and Religious Mrs. Lydia Minot" (Cambridge, 1668), an anonymous broadside.

[48] Willard, *Complete Body of Divinity*, 611.

[49] See, for example, *Tabitha Rediviva, An Essay to Describe and Commend The Good Works of a Virtuous Woman* (Boston, 1713), 21.

[50] Cotton Mather, *Ornaments for the Daughters of Zion* (Cambridge, 1692), 45.

[51] Benjamin Colman, *The Duty and Honour of Aged Women* (Boston, 1711), ii–iii.

or expect the like favour to themselves in their own sickness, wherein all men are lyable to many absurdities, and troublesome humours."[52] Eve in her troubles was no more unstable than Adam.

Thus, the ministers were able to acknowledge the reproductive role of women without giving a sexual content to the psyche and soul. They stressed the *experience* of childbirth, rather than the *nature* of the childbearer. It is significant that the one place where they openly referred to the "curse of Eve" (rather than the more generalized "sin of Adam") was in dealing with the issue of birth. In such a context, Eve's curse had a particular and finite meaning, and it could be overcome. Stressing the redemptive power of childbirth, they transformed a traditional badge of weakness into a symbol of strength. Locating the religious responsiveness of women in their bodily experience rather than in their eternal nature, they upheld the spiritual oneness of the sexes. The childbirth literature, though fragmentary, is consistent with the marriage and funeral sermons.

When New England's ministers sat down to write about women, they were all interested in promoting the same asexual qualities: prayerfulness, industry, charity, modesty, serious reading, and godly writing. From 1660 to 1730 the portrait of the virtuous woman did not change. Her piety was the standard Protestant piety; her virtues were those of her brothers. Although childbearing gave her an added incentive to godliness, she possessed no inherently female spiritual qualities, and her deepest reality was unrelated to her sex. Yet an examination of the ministerial literature is not complete without consideration of an important but subtle shift, not in content but in attitude. This begins around the turn of the century in the work of Cotton Mather and continues, though less strikingly, in the sermons of Foxcroft and Colman. Mather's elegy for Mary Brown of Salem, "Eureka the Vertuous Woman Found," marks the tone:

> Monpolizing HEE's, pretend no more
> Of wit and worth, to hoard up all the store
> The Females too grow wise & Good & Great.[53]

Everything Mather said about Mary Brown had been said before by other ministers about other women. But his open championship of her sex was new. All of the ministers believed in the inherent equality of men and

---

[52] John Oliver, *Teeming Women*, 4.
[53] Cotton Mather, *Eureka*, 1.

women, but for some reason first Mather, then others, seemed *compelled* to say so.

If we turn to the earliest of the advice literature, Hugh Peter's *A Dying Father's Last Legacy*, written for his daughter in 1660, this subtle shift becomes immediately apparent. The researcher who combs its tightly packed pages looking for specific comments on women will come away disappointed. Yet the entire work is a profound comment on his attitude toward the subject. That he would write a long and detailed treatise to Elizabeth without reference to her sex is evidence in itself that he considered her basic responsibilities the same as his. Know Christ, he told her. Read the best books. Study the scriptures, using the annotations of divines. Pray constantly. Keep a journal; write of God's dealings with you and of yours with him. Discuss the workings of salvation with able friends. Seek wisdom. Speak truth. Avoid frothy words. Do your own business; work with your own hands. The one explicit reference to feminine meekness is inextricable from the general Christian context: "Oh that you might be God-like, Christ-like, *Moses*-like. *Michael* contesting with the Dragon, maintained his Meekness; and Paul says, it is the Woman's Ornament." For Peter, virtue had no gender. In putting on the woman's ornament, Elizabeth was clothed in the armor of a dragon-fighter as well. In a short paragraph on marriage, he reminded his daughter that while it was the husband's duty to lead, hers to submit, these duties "need mutual supports." Husbands and wives "need to observe each others Spirits; they need to Pray out, not Quarrel out their first Grablings; They need at first to dwell much in their own duties, before they step into each others." When he told her to stay much at home, he was applying a judgment to his own stormy career and troubled marriage. "For my Spirit it wanted weight, through many tossings, my head that composure others have, credulous, and too careless, but never mischievous nor malicious: I thought my work was to serve others, and so mine own Garden not so well cultivated."[54] Thus, Peter's treatise epitomized the central sermon tradition.

Thirty years later Cotton Mather was promoting the same qualities—but with a difference. Clearly, a contrast between inherent worth and public position was at the heart of his attitude toward women. "There are People, who make no Noise at all in the World, People hardly known to be in the World; Persons of the *Female Sex*, and under all the Covers imaginable. But the world has not many People in it, that are fuller of the Truest Glory."[55] That

[54] Hugh Peter, *A Dying Father's Last Legacy* (Boston, 1717), 22, 34, 83. Lyle Koehler quotes merely the phrase "Woman's Ornament" in attempting to show that Hugh Peter shared a general Puritan belief in the subjection of women. See "The Case of the American Jezebels," 59.

[55] Cotton Mather, *Bethiah. The Glory Which Adorns the Daughters of God and the Piety, Wherewith Zion Wishes to see her Daughters Glorious* (Boston, 1722), 34.

women made no noise bothered Mather, and he was continually devising metaphorical detours around the Pauline proscriptions. "Yes, those who may not *Speak in the Church*, does our Glorious Lord Employ to *Speak*: to *Speak* to us, and *Speak* by what we *see* in them, such Things as we ought certainly to take much Notice of."[56] He made much of the fact that Abiel Goodwin, a little damsel half his age, had taught him much of salvation, and in her funeral sermon he expressed pleasure that she could finally "without any Disorder" speak in the Church.[57]

But there was a route to worldly honor open to women, one which no epistle denied. "They that might not without *Sin*, lead the Life which old stories ascribe to *Amazons*, have with much Praise done the part of *Scholars* in the World."[58] A long section in *Ornaments for the Daughters of Zion* was devoted to the promotion of female writing. Mather combed the scriptures and the classics for precedents and applauded the efforts of near contemporaries such as Anna Maria Schurman, a Dutch feminist whose tract *The Learned Maid* probably influenced his decision to teach Katharin Hebrew. Schurman's argument, deeply imbedded in traditional piety, would have been congenial to Mather. She excluded from discussion "*Scriptural Theology*, properly so named, as that which without Controversie belongs to all Christians," directing her attention to that wider scholarship commonly denied women. If you say we are weak witted, she wrote, studies will help us. If you say we are not inclined to studies, let us taste their sweetness and you will see. If you say we have no colleges, we can use private teachers. If you say our vocations are narrow, we answer they are merely private; we are not exempt from the universal sentence of Plutarch: "It becomes a perfect Man, to know what is to be Known, and to do what is to be done."[59] She concluded by suggesting that young women be exposed from their infancy to the "encouragement of wise men" and the "examples of illustrious women." In his tracts and in her sermons, Mather enthusiastically provided both.

It is important to understand that we are not dealing with a new concept of women in Mather's work, but a new visibility. Though in 1660, under sentence of death, Peter could hardly have recommended a public role for Elizabeth, there is evidence that he was as ready as Mather to value female scholarship and writing. In 1651 he had contributed a Prefatory letter to a revolutionary tract by Mary Cary, applauding her clear opening of the scriptures and her rejection of "naked Brests, black Patches" and "long Trains" in favor of a pen. He referred to "Two of this Sexe I have met with, very famous for more than their mother-tongue, and for what we call Learning, yet liv-

---

[56] Cotton Mather, *Undoubted Certainties, or, Piety Enlivened* (Boston, 1720), 26.
[57] Cotton Mather, *Juga*, 24.
[58] Cotton Mather, *Ornaments*, 5–6.
[59] Anna Maria Schurman, *The Learned Maid: or, Whether a Maid may be a Scholar? A Logick Exercise* (London, 1659), 1, 37.

ing." One of these women, "the glory of her sexe in Holland," was apparently Anna Maria Schurman, whom Peter may have met in Utrecht.[60]

As important as Mather's promotion of increased intellectual activity for women was the luster he gave to their more traditional roles. In beginning his funeral sermon for his own mother, he exclaimed: "Oh! The Endearments of our God! Beyond all the Endearments of the Tenderest Mother in the World!" Taking for his text Isaiah 49:15, "Can a Woman forget her Sucking Child, that she should not have Compassion on the Son of her Bowels? Yea, They may forget: yet will not I forget thee," he drew out the parallels between the love of God and the love of a mother. "The Disposition which the Glorious God has to provide for the *Comfort* of His People, has Two Resemblances, in *His Two Testaments*; And in both of them, 'tis Resembled unto the Provision which *Female-Parents* make for their Young-ones." Mothers comfort their children through their good instructions, through their good examples, and through their pious prayers. These, however, are temporary comforts. Mothers feed us, but God does more. Mothers clothe us, but God does more. Mothers guide us, but God does more. Mothers keep us out of harm's way, but God does more. Mothers confer ornaments upon us, but God confers upon us the lasting ornament. Thus God is a better mother than our earthly mothers. At this point, Mather drew back somewhat from his metaphor, assuring his audience that God was also our father. "What is the best of Mothers weigh'd in the Ballance with Such a *Father*? Our *Father* is now the Infinite God." But he went on:

> It has been a little Surprising unto me to find That in some of the Primitive Writers, the *Holy Spirit* is called, *The Mother*. Tertullian uses this Denomination for the *Holy Spirit; the Mother*, who is Invoked with the *Father* and the *Son*.[61]

Instead of recoiling from the heresy, Mather explained the reasonableness of the metaphor. It is through the Holy Ghost that we are born again. The Holy Ghost is spoken of in the scriptures as a comforter. Surely nothing is of greater comfort than a good mother.

Mather did not mean to deify women. In finding female as well as male virtues in the Godhead, he was simply reasserting the spiritual equality of men and women and the essentially asexual nature of godliness. But he was doing something else as well. He was openly and generously bolstering the public image of Boston's women.

If a person believes in the inherent equality of the sexes yet notes an inequity in the way they are regarded in society, he can resolve the discrepancy in three ways. He can try to change women, encouraging them

---

[60] The entire letter is quoted in Doris Mary Stenton, *The English Woman in History* (London: G. Allen and Unwin, 1957), 136–37.

[61] Cotton Mather, *Maternal Consolations of God* (Boston, 1714), 5, 8, 24, 25.

to enlarge those activities which might bring them honor and recognition. He can try to change society, urging recognition and praise for the unsung activities women already excel in. Or he can dismiss the whole problem, deny the importance of status altogether, and turn his attention to the spiritual realm. Mather tried all three. In praising the works of Anna Maria Schurman and in teaching his daughter Hebrew, he put himself on the side of enlarged opportunity. In eulogizing his mother, he gave public recognition to a specifically feminine role. But as a good minister he could not commit himself completely to any worldly activity. His real commitment had to be to the glory of God. Paradoxically, then, one of the attractions of women for Mather seems to have been their very lack of status. In praising them, he was not only encouraging their good works; he was demonstrating his own superiority to earthly standards. Thus he withdrew with one hand what he had given with the other.

Mather's work points to a difficulty in reconciling inherent worth and earthly position. For most of the ministers through most of the period this had been no problem. Either they had seen no discrepancy or they were unconcerned with questions of status. The reasons for Mather's position are not entirely clear, although several explanations suggest themselves. On the one hand, he may have been influenced by European feminist thought; in a letter to his sister-in-law, who was living in England, he mentioned not only Anna Maria Schurman but Marie de Gournay.[62] Yet even with an allowance for the Atlantic, the writings of neither were new. Gournay's essays were published in the 1620s, Schurman's in the 1650s. Nor was Schurman unknown to earlier ministers, as the Hugh Peter friendship shows. More probably, Mather was dealing with changes in his own provincial society. It is a commonplace that by the end of the seventeenth century, New England was becoming more secular as well as more prosperous. The presumed threat of leisure hangs over much of Mather's writing. In his first booklet, he noted that while women often had a great deal to do, "it is as *often* so, that you have little more Worldly Business, than to Spend (I should rather say, to Save) what others *Get*, and to *Dress* and *Feed* (should I not also say, to *Teach*) the Little Birds, which you are *Dams* unto. And those of you, that are *Women of Quality* are Excused from very much of *this* Trouble too."[63] He picked up the same theme in his tract for midwives, urging mothers to suckle their own infants. "Be not such an Ostrich as to Decline it, merely because you would be One of the Careless Women Living at Ease."[64]

[62] *Diary of Cotton Mather, 1709–1724*, Mass. Hist. Soc. Collections, 7th Series, VIII (Boston, 1911), 325.

[63] Cotton Mather, *Ornaments*, 45.

[64] Cotton Mather, *Elizabeth*, 35. James Axtel, *The School Upon a Hill: Education and Society in Colonial New England* (New Haven and London: Yale Univ. Press, 1974), 75–83, surveys English attitudes toward wet-nurses and speculates on colonial practice.

Clothing and jewels are pervasive metaphors not only in *Ornaments for the Daughters of Zion* but in *Bethiah*, a similar pamphlet written thirty years later. In both, women are told that if they will resist the temptation to worldly adornment they will be "clothed with the sun."[65] Perhaps changes in the provincial lifestyle gave new impetus to the traditional Puritan distrust of leisure. Such an explanation accounts for Mather's injunctions to piety and his warnings against worldliness, but it does not totally explain his preoccupation with status.

Cotton Mather's writings on women point to a much more fundamental problem, a paradox inherent in the ministerial position from the first. This paper began by noting the obvious—that New England's women could not preach, attend Harvard, or participate in the government of the congregation or commonwealth. It went on to argue that this circumscribed social position was not reflected in the spiritual sphere, that New England's ministers continued to uphold the oneness of men and women before God, that in their understanding of the marriage relationship they moved far toward equality, that in all their writings they stressed the dignity, intelligence, strength, and rationality of women even as they acknowledged the physical limitations imposed by their reproductive role. Cotton Mather may not have been fully conscious of this double view, yet all his writings on women are in one way or another a response to it. Such a position requires a balance (if not an otherworldliness) that is very difficult to maintain. In the work of his younger contemporaries, Benjamin Colman and Thomas Foxcroft, this is even more clearly seen.

Colman's daughter Jane was apparently fond of the sermons of Cotton Mather for she composed a tribute to him on his death. Certainly in her own life she exemplified his teaching, spurning balls, black patches, and vain romances for godly scholarship. She had the run of her father's library, which included, in addition to edifying tomes, the poetry of Sir Richard Blackmore and of Waller. At eleven she began composing rhymes of her own and as a young bride she wrote letters to her father in verse which he sometimes answered in kind. Although intensely religious, she began to measure her own writing against a worldly as well as a heavenly scale, a tendency that must have contributed to her own self-doubts and frequent headaches. In a letter to her father, she expressed the hope that she had inherited his gifts. His answer epitomized the possibilities and the limitations of the ministerial position:

[65] Cotton Mather, *Bethiah*, 37. Declension is of course a familiar theme. The sex ratio of church membership is worth further study in this regard. Robert Pope, "New England Versus the New England Mind: The Myth of Declension," *Journal of Social History*, 3 (1969–70), 102, argues that women were becoming less rather than more dominant after 1675. This would undercut the easy assumption made by Andrews, "Funeral Sermons of Cotton Mather," 32, that women were getting more attention from ministers because men had abandoned the churches.

My poor Gift is in thinking and writing with a little Eloquence, and a Poetical turn of Thought. This, in proportion to the Advantages you have had, under the necessary and useful Restraints of your Sex, you enjoy to the full of what I have done before you. With the Advantages of my liberal Education at School & College, I have no reason to think but that your Genious in Writing would have excell'd mine. But there is no great Progress or Improvement ever made in any thing but by Use and Industry and Time. If you diligently improve your stated and some vacant hours every Day or Week to read your Bible and other useful Books, you will insensibly grow in knowledge & Wisdom, fine tho'ts and good Judgment.[66]

Both the "useful Restraints" and the encouragement of study are familiar themes. If Colman saw no possibility for a university education, neither did he deny her ability to profit by it. Like the other ministers, he made no attempt to extrapolate a different spiritual nature from a contrasting social role. But he fully accepted that role and expected Jane to fulfill it.

In 1735, Jane Colman Turrel died in childbirth. In her father's sermons and in the biography written by her husband, there is little to distinguish her from Katharin Mather or even Jerusha Oliver. But in a poem appended to the sermons, there is a fascinating crack in the portrait. The Reverend John Adams wrote:

> Fair was her Face, but fairer was her Mind,
> Where all the Muses, all the Graces join'd.
> For tender Passions turn'd, and soft to please,
> With all the graceful Negligence of Ease.
> Her Soul was form'd for nicer Arts of Life,
> To show the Friend, but most to grace the Wife.[67]

Negligence, softness, ease! These are concepts alien to the virtuous woman. Jane Colman had been invited into her father's library as an intellectual equal, but to at least one of her male friends she had become only that much more attractive as a drawing-room ornament. It is tempting to conclude that by 1735, even ministers were seducing the Virtuous Woman with worldly standards. But the new prosperity was not entirely to blame. As an instrument of piety, scholarship had its limits. With no other earthly outlet available, dinner party conversation had to do.

Thomas Foxcroft was either less comfortable with the intellectual role than Mather or Colman or more concerned about its limits. In *Anna the Prophetess* he went to great lengths to deny the implications of his own text, arguing on the one hand that women were worthy of the title of prophet and on the

---

[66] Colman, *Reliquiae Turellae*, 69.
[67] Ibid., v.

other that they certainly should not be allowed to speak in church. His choice of a text and title were very much in the tradition of Mather, but his handling of it betrayed a discomfort his mentor never acknowledged. When he came to write of motherhood, however, his defense of women blossomed. In his sermon for his own mother, preached in 1721, he described women as the bastions of religion in the home and the community. "At the Gap, which the Death of a wise and good Mother makes, does many times enter a Torrent of Impieties and Vices." Some mothers were simply too good for this world: God might gather them home to prevent them seeing the "Penal Evils" about to befall their children. Foxcroft's praise overlay a more conservative base. He cautioned that the death of a mother might be a punishment for loving her too much as well as for loving her too little. But his own sermon is evidence of where he felt the greater danger lay. "Indeed Children's Love and Regard to their Parents living or dead, commonly needs a Spur, Tho' the Parents too often need a Curb."[68] As a good Puritan, he could not embrace mother love or any other form of human love as an unqualified good, but like Mather he was concerned that Boston's mothers receive the proper respect.

This is a crucial point. In the funeral literature there had been little mention of "motherhood" as opposed to the more generalized concept of "parenthood." Even Colman, who published a baptismal sermon entitled *"Some of the Honours that Religion Does Unto the Fruitful Mothers in Israel,"* was unable to maintain the sex differentiation much beyond the title. If a distinction between mothers and fathers is ever made in the literature, however, it is over the issue of respect. Wadsworth felt that "persons are often more apt to *despise a Mother*, (the weaker vessel, and frequently most indulgent) than a Father."[69] Despite its text, John Flavell's *A Discourse: Shewing that Christ's Tender Care of His Mother is an Excellent Pattern for all Gracious Children* is about parents rather than about mothers specifically. But the one direct comment on women echoes Wadsworth: "[S]he by reason of her blandishments, and fond indulgence is most subject to the irreverence and contempt of children."[70] Thus Boston's ministers showed a concern for neglect of women well before they identified or elaborated any sex-related virtues. Foxcroft built upon this concern, but with a subtle difference. Although his mother's piety was the traditional piety, it was as a *mother* rather than as a Christian that she was singled out. With a new set of values, a focus upon tenderness and love rather than on godliness and strength, Foxcroft's effusiveness would be indistinguishable from nineteenth-century sentimentality.

Thus, in New England sermons firmly rooted in the reformed tradition of the seventeenth century, we can see developing, as if in embryo, both the

---

[68] Foxcroft, *Sermon*, 14, 20.
[69] Wadsworth, *Well-Ordered Family*, 92.
[70] John Flavell, *A Discourse* (Boston, 1728), 5.

"genteel lady" of the eighteenth century and the "tender mother" of the nine-teenth. Adams' poem for Jane Turrel shows the short step from Puritan intel-lectuality to feminine sensibility. Foxcroft's eulogy for his mother demon-strates how praise for a single virtue might obliterate all others. If Puritan piety upheld the oneness of men and women, Puritan polity in large part did not. Nor, we assume, did the increasingly mercantile world of early eighteenth-century Boston. Unwilling or unable to transfer spiritual equality to the earthly sphere, ministers might understandably begin to shift earthly differences to the spiritual sphere, gradually developing sexual definitions of the psyche and soul.

It is important to remember here that the sermon literature deals with a relatively small group of people, that it reveals attitudes, not practices. Pre-sumably, few women experienced the conflicts of Jane Turrel. Most house-wives in provincial Boston were probably too occupied with the daily round to consider the nature of their position in society. Yet when a minister of the stature of Cotton Mather assumes a defensive tone, telling us that "those *Handmaids of the Lord*, who tho' they ly very much Conceal'd from the World, and may be called *The Hidden Ones*, yet have no little share in the *Beauty* and the *Defence* of the Land," as historians we ought to listen to him.[71] Attitudes are important. Subtle shifts in perception both reflect and affect social practice. Mather's advocacy of women suggests a real tension in early eighteenth-century New England between presumed private worth and public position. It demonstrates the need for closer study of the actual functioning of women within congregation and community. But it has rami-fications beyond its own time and place. Mather's work shows how discrete and ultimately confining notions of "femininity" might grow out of genuine concern with equality. Finally, the ministerial literature to which it belongs illustrates the importance of the narrow study, the need to move from static concepts like "patriarchal New England society" to more intricate questions about the interplay of values and practice over time. Zion's daughters have for too long been hidden.

[71] Cotton Mather, *El-Shaddai*, 31.

Mary P. Ryan

A Women's Awakening
Evangelical Religion and the Families of Utica, New York, 1800–1840

Writing more than a quarter century ago, Whitney Cross observed that women "should dominate a history of enthusiastic movements, for their influence was paramount."[1] Although Cross retreated from the question of the relationship between sex and revivalism, his history of religion and reform in western New York State was riddled with evocative references to women. The women of the "Burned-Over District" still stand in the sidelines of antebellum history ready to play a variety of roles. First of all, there is woman as convert, piously, at times hysterically, approaching the anxious seat. Then there is her more audacious sister, perhaps her alter ego, who grasped for social power under cover of religious enthusiasm as she led men in private prayer or even preached. Finally, hidden in the history of American revivalism, is woman the power behind the pulpit, the minister's financial and moral support, the convert's evangelizing wife or mother.

A trail of anecdotes leads out of this literature into the eastern section of the Burned-Over District, to the county of Oneida and its bustling regional

---

[1] Whitney R. Cross, *The Burned-Over District: The Social and Intellectual History of Enthusiastic Religion in Western New York, 1800 to 1850* (Ithaca: Cornell Univ. Press, 1950), 84.

marketplace, the town of Utica. The grand master of antebellum revivalism, Charles Finney, experienced childhood, courtship, and conversion in Oneida County. More to the point, Finney's career as an evangelist began with a tour of Oneida funded by the Female Missionary Society of the Western District. The direct antecedent of this organization had been established in 1806 at a tiny trading post in the frontier township of Whitestown, the village of Utica. For nearly 20 years the women of Utica carefully prepared the soil, planted and nourished the seeds for Finney's renowned evangelical harvest of 1825 and 1826. Utica, then, is an appropriate place to begin writing the women's history of the Burned-Over District.[2]

Utica and its environs, like other bounded localities, also provides the specific population and a concrete and manageable body of records through which to identify the precise roles women played in the Second Great Awakening. The names of converts were inscribed in the registries of four local churches: the First Presbyterian Church of Utica; its parent church, the First Presbyterian Society of Whitestown, located in the adjacent town of Whitesboro; its offshoot, the Second Presbyterian Church; and one of its denominational rivals, the Whitesboro Baptist Church. Each of these lists of church members was arranged according to the date when a parishioner formally professed his or her faith. Admissions to all churches clustered in a similar chronological pattern with each peak of new entries matching the dates of revivals designated by contemporary observers. Altogether, these lists yield a revival population consisting of over 1,400 men and women who proclaimed their salvation during the years 1814, 1819, 1826, 1830 to 1832, and 1838. The distribution of Christian names within this population indicates that women were in the majority during each revival and at every church. The proportion of female converts ranged from a low of approximately 52 percent in the Whitesboro Baptist Church in 1814 to a high of around 72 percent during the revival that occurred in the same church in 1838. All these proportions were above the sex ratio of the population at large: women constituted slightly less than 50 percent of the combined population of Utica and Whitestown at the beginning of the revival cycle and accounted for only 51.3 percent by 1838. Within the membership of each church, however, women outnumbered men by a larger margin, accounting for 62 to 65 percent of the total admissions. The ratio of females to males occasionally fell below this percentage during seasons of revival. In other words, most revivals, and particularly those of the 1820s and 1830s, saw a relative

[2] Charles Finney, *Memoirs of Reverend Charles G. Finney* (New York, 1876), chaps. 1 and 2; "Records of the Female Charitable Society of Whitestown," MS, The Whitestown Collection, Oneida Historical Society, Utica, N. Y. (hereafter OHS).

increase in the proportion of male church members and hence, an actual diminution of the female majority (see Tables 1 and 4).[3]

In addition to sex ratios, these simple church lists contain other demographic evidence: kin relationships as signaled by common surnames. The church records of Utica and Whitesboro are meshed with these suggestions of kin ties (see Tables 1 and 2).[4] Depending on which church or revival year is considered, from 17 to 54 percent of the converts professed their faith in the company of relatives. The same records suggest significant differences between men and women: on the one hand the majority of men, as opposed to only one third of the women, assumed full church membership during the same revival period as did persons of the opposite sex and same surname; on the other hand, approximately half the female converts, compared to 41 percent of the males, made their appearance in the church lists unaccompanied by relatives of either sex.

These data evoke at least two hypotheses about the position of women in Utica's evangelical history. First of all, the proportion of solitary female converts suggests that by joining a church independently of relatives many women exercised a degree of religious autonomy during seasons of revival. A second hypothesis can be shakily constructed around the propensity of men to profess their faith in the company of female kin. This statistic could be read as an indication that the male converts were led into the churches by pious wives, mothers, and sisters. This intriguing hypothetical relationship is given further credence by the analysis of the larger kin networks that laced the church membership. Approximately 30 percent of the revival converts were preceded into full church membership by persons who shared their surname. The first family member to enter the church was twice as likely to be female as male. It would follow that women, in addition to constituting the majority of revival converts, were also instrumental in a host of other conversions among their kin of both sexes.

---

[3] The records of the First Presbyterian, Utica, and the First Presbyterian, Whitesboro were transcribed from the original by the New York Genealogical and Biographical Society in 1920, edited by Royden Woodward Vosburgh; these typescripts along with the original records from the Second Presbyterian Church and the Whitesboro Baptist Church are found at the Oneida Historical Society and the Utica Public Library. Church records are unavailable for the local Methodist Congregation, which reportedly played a small role in Utica's revivals. The records of Trinity Episcopal Church revealed no significant increase in membership during revival years. Sex ratios were calculated from published summaries of the Federal Census, 1800–1840.

[4] Of the total number of converts 49.9 percent of the females entered the church alone, 17.6 percent in the company of relatives of the same sex, and 32.5 percent with relatives of the opposite sex; the comparable figures for males are 41.2 percent, 5.5 percent, and 53.3 percent.

Table 1. PERCENTAGE OF CONVERTS BY SEX AND BY SURNAME

Year of Revival	Utica First Presbyterian			Whitesboro Presbyterian			Utica Second Presbyterian			Whitesboro Baptist		
	N*	% Female	% with same surname	N	% Female	% with same surname	N	% Female	% with same surname	N	% Female	% with same surname
1814	65	69.2	41.5	45	69.6	36.9	—	—	—	44	52.3	52.2
1819	90	67.9	27.7	65	56.9	54.5	—	—	—	70	70.0	44.2
1826	123	59.3	35.1	134	67.1	26.9	53	71.6	30.0	87	63.2	40.2
1830	121	58.6	29.7	110	55.4	44.8	236	59.3	31.0	—	—	—
1838	57	56.1	42.1	—	—	—	76	69.7	17.0	82	71.9	46.0

* Total Number of Converts

Table 2. FAMILY PRECEDENTS OF CONVERSION 1800 TO 1838

	Utica First Presbyterian N = 456 %	Whitesboro Presbyterian N = 354 %	Whitesboro Baptist N = 201 %
Converts related to church members	29.7	29.3	30.0
Cases in which males are the first professors	20.7	15.3	29.5
Cases in which females are the first professors	48.3	61.2	43.1
Cases in which couples are the first professors	37.0	23.5	36.2

To test these hypotheses requires reference to the records that specify the kin relations that may underlie common surnames. Unfortunately, the volatile communities of antebellum New York are unlikely places in which to find reliable sets of vital statistics. The First Presbyterian Church of Utica compiled the only extensive series of marriage and baptismal records for the revival period. These parish records provide information about the 476 men and women who flocked into the church during the revival seasons. Upon initial examination, these records seem unpromising; more than 60 percent of the men and women admitted to the First Presbyterian church during the revivals left no trace in the birth and marriage records. There is no indication that they underwent baptism, married, or had their children christened in the same church in which they first professed their faith. Thus their age, marital status, and kin associations remain unknown. This poorly documented majority can be described only through a series of negative inferences.

In most cases these elusive church members left the First Presbyterian Church shortly after their revival experiences: fully 30 percent of the converts requested official letters of dismissal within five years of their conversions. Countless others must have left the church more hastily and without this formality. Although women registered their intention of leaving the church less frequently than men, more than a quarter of them had also removed from the place of their conversion within five years (see

Table 3. INDICES OF MOBILITY, AGE AND STATUS FOR
UTICA FIRST PRESBYTERIAN CONVERTS

Year of Revival	N	% in Church Records	% Dismissed within 5 Years	% in Directory	% (of Males) Boarders
1814	65	48	8	14 (1817)	—
1819	90	38	31	9 (1817)	—
1826	123	34	35	17 (1828)	—
1830	121	25	38	22 (1832)	28
1838	57	44	25	24 (1838)	44

Table 3).[5] Thus it is safe to draw one conclusion about this historically silent majority: they were, at least in the short run, a peripatetic lot with shallow roots in church and community.

There is reason to suppose that the bulk of revival converts was not only mobile but also young and of relatively low social status. Evidence of youth is convincing in the case of male converts. The low enumeration of converts in city directories compiled soon after the revivals cannot be attributed entirely to mobility. It is also plausible that large numbers of converts failed to meet the qualification for inclusion in the directory, namely, being a head of household. Conversely, when the compilers of the directories changed their policy and began to include young men 17 years of age and over regardless of family status, the number of identifiable converts tended to increase. For example, 44 percent of the male converts of 1838 appeared in that year's directory and were identified as boarders. Almost 65 percent of the male converts whose names appeared in the directory at all exhibited the status of boarder, one which often connoted not only youth but also deracination from the conjugal family.[6] There is little reason to believe that female converts differed markedly from males in age or family status. The absence of almost 60 percent of the female converts from the records either of marriage or of the parents of newly baptized infants suggests that few of them were adult married women.[7]

The inference that large numbers of Utica's converts were young and single was repeatedly affirmed by contemporary observers. Ministers

[5] The church records list formal professions of faith made several months after the peak of the revival and exclude professions made in a second church. As such they may underestimate the mobility of converts.

[6] Of the 13 known boarders who converted in 1830, 7 resided with persons of a different surname whereas 8 of the 11 boarders were in this position in 1838.

[7] See Tables 3 and 5.

Table 4. INDICES OF HOUSEHOLD AND FAMILY CHANGE

Year of Census	Mean Household Size	Sex Ratio*	Child/ Woman Ratio**	% Boarders (in Directory Listings)
1800 (Whitestown Township)	6.19	108.2	2,091	—
1810 (Whitestown Township)	6.22	107.8	2,018	—
1820 (Utica)	6.24	105.6	1,387	—
1830 (Utica)	6.48	103.1	1,008	28 (1835)
1840 (Utica)	6.82	96.9	885	30 (1845)

* Men per 100 women.
** Children aged 0–9 per 1,000 women aged 15–49.

sympathetic to the revivals admitted that only a choice minority of their converts ranked among the community's respectable heads of households. The opponents of revivalism unleashed apocalyptic rhetoric as they described the age and social status of Finney's recruits. The conservative ministers of Oneida County penned a pastoral letter in 1827 which indicted the leaders of the recent revival for "disregard of the distinctions of age and station," and charged the converts with acts of rebellion against patriarchal authority. A typical crime, the ministers alleged, was to address a church elder as follows: "You old, grey headed sinner, you deserved to have been in hell long ago."[8]

The religious history of Oneida county contains hints of evangelical disregard for the distinctions of sex as well as age. From the town of Paris, located a few miles south of Utica, came a defense of female preaching in the incendiary tones of Deborah Peirce. The author demanded that sinful males "remove the yoke from my sisters' necks," and challenged timid women to "rise up ye careless daughters," and give public testimony for Christ.[9] Another inspired and daring woman toured the environs of Utica

[8] "Pastoral Letter of the Ministers of the Oneida Association to the Churches under their Care on the Subject of Revivals of Religion" (Utica, 1827), 13–14.
[9] Deborah Peirce, "A Scriptural Vindication of Female Preaching, Prophesying, or Exhortation" (n.d., n.p.), OHS.

preaching against the practice of infant baptism. Martha Howell's evangelism elicited a jeremiad and the accolade Jezebel from James Carnahan, Utica's first Presbyterian minister. Yet a Baptist defender of Martha Howell pointed out that on at least one occasion a woman had spoken before a promiscuous audience in the Reverend Carnahan's own meetinghouse.[10]

These examples of bold female piety were concentrated in rural areas during the first decade of the nineteenth century and were typical of the relatively youthful Baptist and Methodist sects. As such they may be more a symptom of frontier leniency than an example of beneficent evangelical policy toward women. The revivals themselves occasioned only a minor expansion of woman's public role, her right to pray aloud and speak out during religious services. There is evidence that women exercised even this limited new freedom with constraint. In a report favorable to revivals, a committee of the Oneida Presbytery observed; "We have also had various small circles for prayer, as well as stated and public prayer-meetings, and in the former females, in some cases, though more seldom than we could wish, have taken part."[11] In short there is little direct evidence that the young women who swelled Utica's church rolls during the Second Great Awakening were in open and militant defiance of male authority.

These young women, and men, who passed so quickly and quietly through the evangelical history of Utica left little direct evidence of the motivations surrounding conversion. The personal meaning of conversion can only be illuminated by speculative references to the social world encountered during a sojourn in Utica between 1814 and 1838. The strongest reaction inspired by this time and place was probably a heady sense of change, bustle, and impermanence. The military post known as Fort Schuyler during the Revolution had become a village of some 3,000 inhabitants by 1817. Stimulated by the completion of the Erie Canal in 1825, the town of Utica had grown to a city of four times that population before 1840. Stores, workshops, banks, insurance companies, shipping offices, and law firms proliferated as quickly as the population and apace with the evangelical harvest. In sum, Utica was the archetypal commercial town, the bustling marketplace for a maturing agricultural economy.

---

[10] James Carnahan, "Christianity Defended Against the Cavils of Infidels and the Weakness of Enthusiasts" (Utica, 1808), 29; Elias Lee, "A Letter to the Rev. James Carnahan, Pastor of the Presbyterian Churches in Utica and Whitesborough, Being a Defense of Martha Howell and the Baptists Against the Misrepresentations and Aspersions of that Gentleman" (Utica, 1808), 22.

[11] "A Narrative of the Revival of Religion in the County of Oneida, Particularly in the Bounds of the Presbytery of Oneida" (Utica, 1826), 26.

The sheer volatility and newness of this way of life and making a living might well have augured uncertain futures for Utica's young of either sex.

Young Uticans, however, were spared the direct experience of industrialization and the accompanying challenge to traditional sex roles that beset their neighbors in Whitestown. The influx of young women into the cotton mills of this nearby village had made the men of Whitestown a minority group by the 1820s. Utica's men, by contrast, were nearly equal to women numerically until the advent of the city's first textile factories in 1845. Their preindustrial city offered young Uticans an expanding range of occupations and opportunities, which male converts seemed to have exploited to the fullest. Men entered the revival rolls from the ranks of merchants, shopkeepers, artisans, professionals, white collar workers, and clerks. The lowly class of common laborers, however, contributed only two converts to the entire revival roster. The city directory also recorded a twofold increase in female occupations during the revival era. Yet females still accounted for a mere 3.3 percent of the directory's entries in 1835. The limited ranks of female occupations, chiefly milliners, dressmakers, washerwomen, and teachers, sent only two women, both seamstresses, into the revivals of the First Presbyterian Church. Thus, whatever economic uncertainty might have propelled women to the anxious seat remained hidden in the homes and home economics of the busy city.[12]

Although the majority of the women of Utica remained in the households of shopkeepers and artisans, the advances of a market economy encroached upon their roles. First, the domestic manufactures that once occupied so much of woman's time were almost nonexistent in Utica. The entire town produced only 2,500 yards of homespun in 1835, or slightly more than a yard per household. The products of home gardens and dairies were also minuscule within the city limits, at a time when newspapers advertised everything from flour to candles to crockery, all for sale in cash. Utica's market economy was also absorbing the female roles of shopkeeper's assistant and artisan's helper. The cash revenues that accrued to the petty bourgeoisie could pay the wages of a growing number of clerks and hired laborers, all of whom were male. Finally, an increasing number of the town's women were removed from the source of their families' livelihood. As early as 1817 approximately 14 percent of the entries in the village directory listed separate addresses for home and

[12] Calculations based on: *Census for 1820* (Washington, 1821); *Census of the State of New York for 1835* (Albany, 1836); Manuscript Schedules of the Federal Census for 1840; *Utica City Directory*, 1817, 1837–38. Too few of Utica's converts were traceable in the city directories to provide a precise description of their class backgrounds. For an excellent portrait of male converts, see Paul Johnson, "A Shop Keepers' Millennium: Society and Revivals in Rochester, N.Y., 1815–1837" (Diss. UCLA, 1975).

workplace. Twenty years later this measure of the disintegration of the home economy combined with an extraordinarily high rate of boarding. According to the city directory of 1837–38 a full 28 percent of the entries identified boarders, men and women who resided apart from their kin and remote from their place of work.[13]

The structure of the family as well as the work force changed during the revival era. Although mean household size remained at the same high level (more than six resident members), household composition was changing in important ways. The practice of boarding brought the brittle monetary relations of commercial capitalism into the household itself. Moreover, the proliferation of boarders and boarding houses coincided with a decline in Utica's birth rate. Extrapolating from the federal census of 1820, there were 1,390 children between the ages of zero and ten for every thousand women of childbearing age. This crude measure of fertility had declined to 885, or by 36 percent, at the time of the 1840 census (see Table 4). This drop in the child-woman ratio is due in part to an increase in the proportion of young adult women in the city's population. These unmarried females, rather than shunning motherhood, had simply not yet begun the reproductive period of their life cycles. Nonetheless, the overall role of Utica's women in reproduction, as well as production, declined during the revival period.

Referring to a similar social setting, Nancy Cott has demonstrated how such changes in the history of the family and the economy worked a particular hardship on America's daughters.[14] Cott has argued that the young women who experienced or anticipated changes in their social and economic roles early in the nineteenth century might assuage their anxieties and affirm a modern identity in the act of religious conversion. This interpretation may constitute the best possible explanation for the behavior of the youthful and anonymous majority of Utica's converts. Such inferences do not, however, fully differentiate women's experience from that of the many men who converted at the same time and place. Nor do they account for the dense network of kin ties that riddled church membership lists, often linking male to female in one evangelical process. The kinship of conversion is particularly significant because it invites a revision of the frequent understanding of antebellum revivalism as exemplary of youthful, independent, and individualistic Jacksonian America.

Only an examination of the select minority of converts who left evidence of kin ties in Utica can yield a more satisfying description of the

[13] Calculations based on *Census of the State of New York for 1835; Utica City Directory*, 1817, 1837–38.
[14] Nancy F. Cott, "Young Women in the Second Great Awakening in New England," *Feminist Studies*, 3 (Fall 1975), 14–29.

relation between women and revivalism. Thus the remainder of this analysis is based on the experience of the 160 men and women who left more substantial testimony in the records of Utica's First Presbyterian Church. They may or may not be representative of the bulk of converts who made a minor appearance in the annals of local churches. Nonetheless, the minority commands attention both in its own right and because its more durable church ties insured a greater capacity to affect the course of evangelism itself. Many even of these converts, however, made but a single appearance in the vital records—at the time of their marriage, their baptism, or their children's christening. Thus any conclusions based solely on these fragmentary records are heuristic—rare and suggestive tracks through an uncharted historical landscape.

In the case of Utica's first revival, that of 1814, these tracks lead in a specific direction: toward a religious awakening among Utica's parents. Although less than half of those men and women who professed their faith in the 1814 revival left any trace in the vital records, 65 percent of these (or almost a third of all converts) left evidence of being married and 23 percent of them baptized an infant child within a year of their conversion. In addition more than a dozen older children were promptly brought forward to be christened by their newly converted parents. All these relationships reappeared with the second revival in 1819. The subsequent revivals seem to follow naturally upon these first two, as progeny came to supplant parentage as the predominant family status of converts. Despite an increase in the proportion of mobile and independent converts during and after the revival of 1826, approximately 20 percent of the new communicants can be identified as the children of church members. Many of the parents in question had presented these very children for baptism in the full flush of their own conversion in 1814 or 1819. By 1838 more than 40 percent of the converts could be identified as the offspring of this firmly entrenched first generation. In some cases the lineage of conversion had passed unbroken through each stage of the revival cycle. Seventy converts, 15 percent of the total, had a relative who joined the church during a previous or subsequent revival (see Table 5).

Thus beneath the febrile evangelism of Utica's First Presbyterian Church there lay a solid infrastructure, the family cycle of the church's first generation. During the revivals of the 1810s Utica's first settlers took the opportunity to plant religious roots in the frontier soil. These revivals of 1814 and 1819 also coincided with the highest marriage and birth rates in the church's history. The revivals of the 1820s and 1830s can then be attributed to the echo effect of this high birth rate, as the children of the prolific first generation came of age, grew in grace, and professed their faith in the church of their parents. In short, the family pattern of the

Table 5. PARENT/CHILD CONVERSIONS, UTICA
FIRST PRESBYTERIAN CHURCH

Year of Revival	N	Number of Converts in Vital Records	Infants baptized within year	Children of Church members
1814	65	31	15	0
1819	90	33	7	0
1826	123	41	1	25
1830	121	30	1	22
1838	57	25	0	24
Total	456	160	24	71

revivals is in part a reflection of the peculiar demographic history of the First Presbyterian Church.

The family cycle is a partial but hardly sufficient explanation of either revivalism or the conversion of Utica's second generation. Certainly the Presbyterian ministry did not rely on demography as a means of salvation. In fact, they were preoccupied with admonishing Oneida's parents of their obligation to guide their offspring into the church. The theologians of Oneida County steered a treacherous path through Calvinist dogma and simultaneously conducted pamphlet and sermon warfare against the local Baptists—all in defense of infant baptism and the Abrahamic covenant interpreted as a kind of birthright of salvation for their progeny. Every human agency, both pastoral and parental, was mobilized to bring the children of the frontier into full church membership. The Synod of Utica instructed pastors to preach every November on "the privileges and obligations of the Abrahamic covenant, presenting distinctly the duty of pious parents to dedicate their infant children to God in baptism." The annual sermon should also remind parents of their "responsibilities in connection with their [children's] religious training and the precious grounds of expectation and confidence that, if found faithful, saving blessings would follow." This rather Antinomian interpretation of the lineage of salvation was reinforced by the revival of 1826, which brought so many of the children of the first generation to the ranks of the elect. The report of the clergymen of Oneida on the Finney revival closed with this lesson: "One great end of the baptism of households is that parents and ministers and church may be impressed with the obligation of bringing [their children] up in the nurture and admonition of the Lord." Oneida County was littered with pamphlets, sermons, and ecclesiastical resolutions testifying to this same religious imperative, devising practical ways to guide a second generation toward salvation and full allegiance to the church of their parents.[15]

This same literature, addressed to "heads of households" or "parents," did not acknowledge the conscientious guardians of this religious inheritance, the mothers. A review of the records of Utica's First Presbyterian Church exposes the female agency of the Second Great Awakening with striking clarity. At the time of the first revival women constituted 70 percent of the church population. The mothers, in other words, first planted the families' religious roots on the frontier. Women certainly claimed a maternal role in the first revival, for 12 percent of all the converts of 1814 appear to have been pregnant when they professed their faith. Mothers, unaccompanied by their mates, also accounted for approximately 70 percent of the baptisms that followed in the wake of revivals in 1814 and 1819.[16] Nancy Lynde exemplified this maternal fervor. Within two years of her conversion in 1814, she had given six children to the Lord in baptism. The church records referred to the children's father, who was not a member of the congregation, by the perfunctory title of Mr. Lynde. This family failed to appear in the village's first directory, compiled in 1817.

Yet in some later revival, perhaps somewhere to the west, the children of Nancy Lynde may have swelled the membership of another evangelical church. At any rate many of Nancy Lynde's peers who remained in Utica enrolled their children in the church during the sequence of revivals that began in 1826. Of those children of church members who dominated the revival of 1838, for example, more than 60 percent professed the faith of their mothers, but not their fathers.[17] These later revivals brought some of Utica's mothers a pious sense of achievement, when after years of prayer and instruction their children pledged their souls to Christ. Harriet Dana must have felt this satisfaction when her son John joined the ranks of the saved in 1826, and again with the belated conversion in 1838 of her son James Dwight Dana, who would soon acquire a national reputation as a Yale professor of natural science. Mrs. Dana's own conversion had occurred in July of 1814, at the zenith of Utica's first revival. She was most likely pregnant at the time; her son James was baptized the following September, his brother John two years thereafter. The religious biog-

---

[15] P. H. Fowler, *Historical Sketch of Presbyterianism Within the Bounds of the Synod of Central New York* (Utica, 1844), 110; "Narrative of the Revival," 54.

[16] The Baptismal Records of the First Presbyterian Church reveal that 8 converts of 1814 baptized infant children within nine months of their profession of faith. Of the 28 children of recent converts baptized in 1814 and 1819, 15 had mothers among converts, 11 had 2 parents converting, and only 2 children had merely a father in full church membership.

[17] During this revival 24 children of church members converted; 16 of them were preceded into the church by a mother alone, 5 by two parents, and 3 by a father alone.

raphies of an additional eight children are outside the purview of Utica's church records and beyond the time span of the revival cycle.

Another episode in the private revival of Harriet Dana is worthy of note, however. In 1826 James Dana, Senior, joined the church in which his wife had been ensconced for a dozen years. This conjugal dimension of the kinship of conversion was not unusual. In the revival occasioned by Finney's appearance in Utica, for example, seven husbands followed their wives into full church membership after many years of recalcitrance. This trend continued in the revivals that followed, much to the delight of the local ministry, ever eager to snare a head of household. One church history written 40 years after the event recalled with special pride the conversion in 1838 of Mr. John H. Ostrom, lawyer, bank officer, and prominent Utica politician. The author failed to mention that Ostrom's wife, then the young Mary Walker (notable church member and community leader in her own right) had converted in a revival that occurred almost a quarter-century earlier.[18]

Another example illustrates the matrilineage that runs through the history of revivalism in the Utica Presbyterian Church. This story of domestic evangelism began with the conversion of Sophia Bagg, who professed her faith on July 7, 1814, in the company of seven women and two men. Her daughter Emma was baptized the following September; the baptismal covenant was recited for her son Michael 14 months later; and two more sons were christened before 1820. When Finney arrived in Utica, Emma Bagg was at least 11 years old and promptly entered the church. A Mary Ann Bagg who was examined for admission to the church at about the same time may have been another of Sophia's daughters whose baptism was not recorded in the church records. At any rate the family of Sophia Bagg figured prominently in the revival of 1826, for in that year Moses Bagg, the wealthy and respected son of one of Utica's very first entrepreneurs, joined his wife and children in church membership. Moses Bagg was one of those "gentlemen of property and standing" who helped to organize Utica's anti-abolitionist riot in 1835.[19] Amid the uproar of the 1830s the Bagg family continued quietly to play out the family cycle of revivals. Moses Junior ranked among the converts of 1831, and his brother Egbert enrolled in the church in 1838. The Bagg family may be atypical only in social stability, public prominence, and the consequent wealth of historical documentation. Perhaps countless anonymous women left a similar legacy of conversions across the frontier or in poorly documented evangelical denominations, the Baptist and the Methodist.

[18] Fowler, *Historical Sketch*, 222.
[19] See Leonard L. Richards, *Gentlemen of Property and Standing: Anti-Abolitionist Mobs in Jacksonian America* (New York: Oxford Univ. Press, 1970).

Nor do the church records reveal the more extended kinship ties that underpinned the revival. Utica supplies one anecdote illustrating this wider network of revivalism and at the same time suggests the modes of evangelism peculiar to women. The central female character in this religious homily generally appears in the church's history under the name of Mrs. C or Aunt Clark. During the revival of 1825 and 1826 Mrs. C was visited by a nephew, a student at nearby Hamilton College. The nephew in question came from conservative Calvinist stock and looked with disdain upon the vulgar evangelist Charles Finney, a friend and temporary neighbor of his aunt. Thus Aunt Clark resorted to a pious deception to entice her young kinsman to a revival meeting at the Utica Presbyterian Church. She persuaded him to attend a morning service on the pretense that Finney would not be preaching until later in the day. Once in the church and in the presence of the despised preacher, the young man realized that he was caught in a trap of woman's making. He recalled it this way: "When we came to the pew door [Aunt Clark] motioned me to go in and followed with several ladies and shut me in." When he attempted a second escape his pious and wily aunt whispered in his ear, "You'll break my heart if you go!" Woman's role in the conversion that ensued would have remained forever unrecorded were it not that the convert in question was none other than Theodore Dwight Weld.[20] The famed abolitionist's aunt was Sophia Clark, whose many accomplishments included the enrollment of at least three children among the revival converts.

Such anecdotes would have to be compounded hundreds of times in order to demonstrate a causal rather than a coincidental relationship between women's revival fervor and the subsequent conversion of their kin. Obtaining such proof would entail an exhaustive and probably futile search through women's diaries and letters for confessions of bringing extreme evangelical pressure to bear upon members of their families. This exercise is not entirely necessary in Utica, where woman's role in the revival was not confined to her private efforts. Rather, it was conducted publicly and collectively within two women's organizations, the Female Missionary Society and the Maternal Association. Both these organizations left membership lists, the first for the year 1814, the second dating from 1840 but including the names of deceased members. Despite the sporadic and incomplete nature of these records almost one third of the revival converts can be traced to one of these documents, either directly or through their mothers (see Table 6). For example, Harriet Dana, Mary

---

[20] Charles Beecher, ed., *Autobiography, Correspondence, Etc., of Lyman Beecher, D.D.* (New York, 1865), 2: 310–12.

Table 6. LINKS BETWEEN REVIVALS AND
WOMEN'S ORGANIZATIONS

Year of Revival	N*	Number of Female Converts	Converts in Female Missionary Society	Converts in Maternal Association	Mothers of Converts in Female Missionary Society	Mothers of Converts in Maternal Association
1814	65	45	23	3	0	0
1819	90	57	13	4	0	0
1826	123	73	1	4	18	16
1830	121	71	4	3	7	21
1838	57	32	0	1	6	18
Total	456	278	41	15	31	55

* Utica First Presbyterian Church only.

Walker Ostrom, Sophia Bagg, and Sophia Clark all subscribed to one or both of these organizations.

During the earliest revivals the strongest connection was between female converts and the Missionary Society. More than one third of the women who professed their faith in the revival of 1814 can be found among the members of the Female Missionary Society. In the 1820s and 1830s the links between women and revivalism were more often forged by mothers of converts enrolled in the Maternal Association. By 1838 over 30 percent of the converts had mothers in the Maternal Association alone. Neither missionary societies nor maternal associations were unique to Utica or to the Presbyterian Church. The city's Baptists, for example, established analogues to both these women's groups. Within these associations—the female contribution to the "new measures" of the Second Great Awakening—the historian can see women weaving the social and familial ties that ran through the revival.

Female missionary activity actually predated the formal organization of both the church and the village of Utica. In 1806 women associated with the First Religious Society of Whitestown met at the nucleus of stores and houses that would become the city of Utica and formed themselves into the Female Charitable Society. These women, who had assembled at the home of Sophia Clark, pledged a small annual contribution toward the support of missionary tours of the New York frontier. By 1824 this women's organization had evolved into the Female Missionary Society of the Western District, which spawned over 70 auxiliaries and contributed more than $1,200 annually for the support of eleven missionaries. The

Table 7. SOCIAL CHARACTERISTICS OF
MEMBERS OF WOMEN'S ORGANIZATIONS

Class Composition	Female Missionary Society (N = 55) %	Maternal Association (N = 65) %	Total Directory Listings 1817 %	1828 %
Merchants and Merchant Manufacturers	31	25	19	10
Professionals and White Collar	33	18	14	12
Artisans	16	35	40	42
Shopkeepers and Farmers	11	14	8	13
Laborers	—	—	15	14
Widows	7	5	4	6
Female Occupations	2	3	2	3

treasurer's report for 1824 revealed that $192 from the Society's coffers had gone to an untried young preacher named Charles Finney.[21]

The organizational and financial sophistication of this woman's organization invites comparison with the trading network built up by Utica's merchant capitalists. In fact the missionary society's officers almost mimic these entrepreneurs. The Female Charitable Society appeared under the heading of "Corporations" in the *Utica Almanack* for 1810,[22] in the company of a glass factory, a cotton factory, and a bank, as well as the village corporation. Throughout their history and in the style of businessmen the Female Missionary Society elected presidents, vice presidents, and trustees; met in formal meetings; and kept accounts.

The ties between female missionaries and male merchants were more substantial than such analogies. In fact 31 percent of the members of the missionary society were married to "merchants." The men who went by this title in the city directory were rarely shopkeepers but rather substantial retail and wholesale dealers involved in the regional market, men like James and Jerimiah Van Rensselaer, import merchants and scions of the

---

[21] "Minutes of the Whitestown Female Charitable Society," Oct. 21, 1806, MS, OHS; "Constitution of the Female Missionary Society of Oneida" (Utica, 1814); "First Annual Report of the Trustees of the Female Missionary Society of the Western District" (Utica, 1817); "Eighth Annual Report of the Trustees of the Female Missionary Society of the Western District" (Utica, 1824), 19, 20, 24.

[22] *Utica Almanack* (Utica, 1810), n.p.

New York aristocracy, or Samuel Stocking, shoe merchant and manufacturer who would amass one of Utica's largest fortunes. The wives of professional men had almost equal representation in the Missionary Society, and the wives of attorneys contributed almost one third of the membership (see Table 7).[23] Notable among these women were Ann Breese and Sophia Clark, who along with Susan and Adaline Van Rensselaer and Phoebe Stocking served as officers of the Society. By contrast, few wives of artisans, the largest occupational group in Utica, found berths among the officers or membership of the Female Missionary Society. Involvement in the missionary society seems characteristic of the sexual division of labor within Utica's more prominent merchant and professional families. By joining the Female Missionary Society women of the upper class publicly assumed the moral and religious responsibilities of their mercantile households. By efficiently and visibly fulfilling such social obligations these women enhanced the status of their busy mates.

At the same time these groups expanded woman's social role, and in a sphere that was organizationally independent of the male head of the household. Accordingly, another related social characteristic of the members of the Female Missionary Society is as significant as their husbands' class standing. Analysis of the city directories indicates that 66 percent of these women were married to men who maintained a business address detached from their place of residence. This percentage, which is too large to be attributed to a single class within the society's membership, compares with a figure of only 14 percent for the total population listed in the city directory (see Table 7). In other words, the members of the Female Missionary Society differed from the other women of Utica in that they had experienced the removal of basic economic activities from the household to the shops and offices of Genesee Street, hub of Utica's commercial life. It might follow that involvement in religious benevolence filled the consequent vacuum in woman's everyday life. To put it another way, participation in the Female Missionary Society might be one way of exercising the first breath of freedom from the duties and restrictions of a patriarchal home economy.

The alternative roles and activities that these women devised for themselves within the missionary society were more social than domestic. That is not to say that the society's officers eschewed heartrending appeals to women's domestic sensibilities. Their circular for 1819 begged the women of western New York to "imagine a pious mother, surrounded with a numerous family—none of them give evidence of possessing an interest in

[23] The term "shopkeepers" refers to such business designations as "grocery," "drug store," or "hardware store," and conveys fewer pretensions of economic stature than the self-proclaimed title of "merchant."

Christ.''[24] Yet, although this image may have reflected the personal sentiments of many of the society's members, it led rhetorically to some remote frontier town where a paid agent might save unknown children from damnation. The Female Missionary Society presented itself primarily as the financial support of male missionaries who wrought the conversion of other women's children. This approach typified the early female benevolence that subordinated personal domestic relations to a wider ranging, more highly rationalized, more hierarchical, and more characteristically masculine mode of organization. In 1827 the Female Missionary society was absorbed into a masculine organization. In that year the society voted to accept an invitation to consolidate with their recently founded male counterpart, the Western Domestic Missionary Society. In the process many of these enterprising women forfeited evangelical leadership to their own husbands. Before this abdication, however, the members of the female missionary society saw their homes, their churches, and the surrounding countryside set ablaze with the evangelical fervor of 1825 and 1826.

The demise of the Female Missionary Society did not mark the retirement of Utica women from the battle for souls. Three years earlier eight members of the First Presbyterian Church, including the ubiquitous Sophia Clark, had formed one of the first Maternal Associations outside New England. Utica's Maternal Association shared the evangelical purpose of its sister organization and contributed financially to the education of missionaries. Yet most of the association's energy focussed in a novel direction. The constitution pledged each member to perform religious and parental duties—praying for each of her children daily, attending meetings every other Wednesday, renewing her child's baptismal covenant regularly, reading systematically through the literature of Christian childrearing, setting a pious example to her offspring at all times, and, finally, spending the anniversary of each child's birth in prayer and fasting. With the formation of the Maternal Association, the evangelical energies of Utica's women seemed to change course. The current that once gushed forth from Utica to inundate countless villages of the Western District was now diverted toward the homes of individual women, where it nurtured grace in the souls of their own children and kindled private family revivals.[25]

This transition from the Female Missionary Society to the Maternal Association hardly occurred in a single movement. Only six of the women

---

[24] "The Third Annual Report of the Trustees of the Female Missionary Society of the Western District" (Utica, 1819), 26.
[25] "Constitution of the 'Maternal Association of Utica' Adopted June 30, 1824," printed copy, New York State Library, Albany.

associated with the revivals held membership in both organizations. These women represented the pioneer generation; all were converted before 1820 and half of them came from lawyer families. Yet the professional classes were poorly represented in the membership of the Maternal Association. In fact they were outnumbered by the wives of common mechanics. Women of the artisan class accounted for 35 percent of the association's identifiable members and assumed the dominant position granted to merchants' wives within the Missionary Society (see Table 7). The class composition of the Maternal Association reflected the social structure of Utica in the canal era, when the city's economy was geared to small-scale artisan production for the local farm market.

The presence of these representatives of Utica's middling sort introduced some distinctive domestic concerns and relations into the Maternal Association. Consider, for example, the case of the Merrill family, four of whose members (Harriet, Lucina, Maria, and Julia) enrolled in the Maternal Association of the First Presbyterian Church. All these women were linked by marriage to a family of artisan printers and bookbinders. The clan's partriarch, Bildad Merrill, Sr., constructed an extended family economy out of such materials as a series of business partnerships among his sons, brothers, and nephews, and two strategic marital alliances with the family of his first business partner, Talcott Camp. The women who married into this family network inhabited an intricate and difficult domestic environment. In 1834, for example, Julia Merrill appeared before the session meeting of the First Presbyterian Church to charge her mother-in-law, Nancy Camp Merrill, with acts of personal abuse. The trial that ensued brought several of Julia's in-laws to her defense and exposed a frenetic and embittered household to historical scrutiny.

Julia Merrill's home, inhabited by four small children and replete with visiting neighbors, relatives, and customers, was further cluttered by two boarders, her father-in-law and his cranky wife. Nancy Merrill's animosity toward her daughter-in-law became unbearable when the elder Mrs. Merrill, to use Julia's phrase, "Took hold of me with violence." Such domestic contention could not but interfere with the pious mother's fulfillment of her maternal responsibilities. Julia Merrill herself testified that "My little children have often asked why Gramma talked so to me and why mama cried so."[26] The turmoil in this household may have been rare among Utica's families. Yet there is reason to believe that many members of the Maternal Association inhabited equally complex if more harmoni-

---

[26] "Records of the Session Meetings of the First Presbyterian Church," MS, The First Presbyterian Church, Utica, Vol. II, Nov. 10–Nov. 28, 1834. The Merrill family history was reconstructed from church records, the city directories, and Moses Bagg, Jr., *Pioneers of Utica* (Utica, 1877).

ous households. Only 45 percent of the members of the Maternal Association, as opposed to 66 percent of the Missionary Society's members, resided in homes that were separated from the husband's place of work (see Table 7). These women, like Julia Merrill, were likely to reside and work in households that retained many of the economic functions of the "little commonwealth." For many women of the Maternal Association, then, the demands of what they called "Christian Motherhood" came as an addition to the "arduous duties" that continued to characterize the households of Utica's middling sort.

A busy mistress of one of these households, recently awakened to her responsibility for her child's salvation, would seek out a special kind of organization. Accordingly, the founders of the Maternal Association eschewed the elaborate system of officers, trustees, and corporate charters that typified the Female Missionary Society. They resorted instead to the cooperative style exemplified by Article Six of the Association's charter. It stipulated that each mother should "suggest to her sister members such hints as her own experience may furnish, or circumstances seem to render necessary."[27] The Maternal Association may have formalized a longstanding network of neighborly advice and consultation, yet the articulation of common maternal responsibilities and the intention of fulfilling them in such a systematic fashion marked a crucial historical twist both in woman's roles and the methods of evangelism.

The casual organizational structure of the Maternal Association resembles the female prayer groups that Charles Finney discovered in Utica in 1825. The First Presbyterian Church had employed this "new measure" as early as 1822, and there were rumors of a quickening of grace within the woman's prayer group during the same year.[28] The idea for a maternal association probably emerged in one of these religious circles as women shared their anxiety about their children's souls.

It is easy to discern the material conditions that might breed this anxiety. The first decade in the Maternal Association's history coincided with the opening of the Erie Canal, the doubling of the city's population, and the accompanying proliferation of grog shops, boarding houses, and brothels. Neither the social elite represented by the Female Missionary Society nor relics of the New England social order such as the Presbyterian church trials could successfully oversee public morality. By turning their religious fervor as well as methods of childhood education on their own offspring, the women of the Maternal Association hoped to reinforce the Abrahamic Covenant against the assaults of a secular and individualistic culture. The revivals of 1826, 1831, and 1838 seemed to proclaim their enterprise a success. Known members of the Maternal Association saw at least 55 of their children enter the church during these years.

---

[27] "Constitution of the Maternal Association."
[28] Session Records, I, Apr. 1822; II, July 10, 1822.

Toward the end of the revival cycle, Maternal Associations evangelized as much in behalf of their own institutions as for the church itself. In 1833 the Presbyterian Maternal Association voted to establish a magazine that would circulate advice to mothers throughout central New York. The early issues of *The Mother's Magazine* depicted women guiding children and husbands toward salvation. Yet ministers and revival churches that once mediated the kin relations of conversion rarely appeared in these accounts. In fact, the typical reference to clergymen was a polite rebuke for their failure to foster Maternal Associations within their congregations. The Maternal Association seemed to be outgrowing the need for ministers and revivals. In 1835 the female editor of *The Mother's Magazine* put it this way: "The Church has had her seasons of refreshing and her returns of decay; but here in the circle of mothers, it is felt that the Holy Spirit condescends to *dwell*. It seems his blessed 'rest.'"[29] In other words mothers may have ultimately supplanted ministers as the agents of religious conversion and of its functional equivalent, the Christian socialization of children.

More to the point, the experience of a small group of mothers in upstate New York suggests an alternative interpretation of antebellum revivalism. Propelled by the fervor of their own conversions and strengthened by the female institutions that grew up around revivals, Utica women conducted a systematic evangelical campaign. As wives and mothers, and earlier as the trustees of an extensive missionary organization, women's contribution to revivalism did not stop with their own conversions. It exceeded their numbers in the revival population as it expanded to gather in converts of both sexes and spread throughout the revival cycle. The success of this woman's evangelism contradicts the interpretation of the Second Great Awakening as a rite of youthful independence. Quite the contrary, maternal evangelism in particular led scores of young men and women to an active, intensive, and deeply personal affirmation of the faith of their parents. The proliferation of such conversions among the sons and daughters of the middling sort moderated nineteenth-century individualism as it demonstrated the internalization of parental values. Simultaneously, the women who orchestrated the domestic revivals played a central part in creating a narrowly maternal role and image for their sex, with all its attendant contradictions. Thus, if the case of Utica, New York, at all represents the hundreds of communities embroiled in antebellum revivalism, then women were more than the majority of the converts, more even than the private guardians of America's souls. The combination and consequence of all these roles left the imprint of a women's awakening on American society as well as on American religion.*

---

[29] *The Mother's Magazine*, Jan. 1833, 4–5; June 1833, 93–95.

* I would like to thank Paul Johnson, Louise Knauer, and Kathryn Kish Sklar for their helpful criticism of an earlier draft of this paper.

Barbara Welter

She Hath Done What She Could

Protestant Women's Missionary Careers in Nineteenth-Century America

Woman's entry into a field or occupation formerly closed to her was a prized goal of nineteenth-century feminists, who assumed that each new opportunity was a victory for their cause. It is possible, however, that woman's entry into certain fields represented less a victory than a strategic retreat by the opposition. Certain areas of societal concern were given over to woman not because of her efforts but because either society or the occupation had changed. As Olive Schreiner, the South African feminist, remarked with some irony, "Whenever there is a general attempt on the part of the women of any society to readjust their position in it, a close analysis will always show that the changed or changing conditions of that society have made women's acquiescence no longer necessary or desirable."[1] Through this "readjustment" of roles, certain occupations in nineteenth-century America were maintained by female succession. Three social phenomena played a part in this process: first, a need to place people in some area from which men were physically or socially barred but where women could be admitted; second, men's diminishing interest in certain work when other alternatives offered greater rewards of money or status; and third, a desire to maintain the rhetoric of certain institutions without any concomitant wish to bother with the substance. The changing role of women within the American Protestant foreign missionary movement of the nineteenth century illustrates these phenomena.

Nineteenth-century Protestantism shared the zeal for progress, the romantic optimism and heroic mythology, and the faith in manifest des-

---

[1] Olive Schreiner, *Women and Labour* (London: T. Fisher Unwin, 1911), 14.

tiny of other institutions. The theology and liturgy of most churches were softened and adorned, infused by ideals of love and service. The drama of the impending millennium impelled action since Biblical references required a converted world before the happy day of general resurrection could take place. Phillips Brooks called missionary activity "the apex to which all the lines of the pyramid lead up. The Christian life without it is a mangled and imperfect theory."[2] The "Spirit of the Age," a spirit of progress, heroism, and expansion, was identified as the "Missionary Spirit," and America's role was paramount and divinely ordained. The United States should export its religion, a Christianity untainted by Romanism, as it was exporting its goods, and with the same expectation of gain. America was that Christian candle which must shine far and wide. "It is selfish, it is inexcusable, it is wicked to hide that light at home. All Christendom would deplore it, and God would frown upon it."[3] The success of Protestantism abroad would, because of the principle of "reflex action," redound to the personal and economic good of the church at home. "We need the romance, the unworldliness, the heroism of foreign missions," wrote one observer, "to save us from . . . selfishness, narrowness of view, and all those pettinesses which, mosquito-like, are everlastingly buzzing and biting in the corridors of our churches."[4] The country must be up and doing and not allow other, less pure, nations to export their religion and their commodities. To that "all-important, God-ordained end," each member of the Church Militant must contribute.[5]

The Haystack Meeting at Williams College in 1806 and the founding of the American Board of Commissioners for Foreign Missions in 1810 signalled the beginning of a century of organization and action. By the time of the Columbian Exposition in Chicago in 1893, which was also the scene of a "Congress of Missions," the Americans had accomplished much, "although much more remained to be done, and the fields, white for the harvest, beckon those who wish to labor and serve in Christ's army."[6] Each Protestant denomination established machinery for popularizing the cause of missions, screening candidates, and administering work in the field, with a supportive network of publications, fund raising, and auxiliaries.

But while man created the organizations, at least in the early years, woman, as Harriet Beecher Stowe pointed out, "was left to follow with

---

[2] The Woman's Union Missionary Society of America, for Heathen Lands, *39th Annual Report* (New York, 1900), 19.

[3] S. C. Bartlett, "A Plea for Missions" (Boston, 1867), 10.

[4] Reuben Thomas, "Enlargement Through Service " (Boston: ABCFM, 1904).

[5] F. Wayland, "The Moral Dignity of the Missionary Enterprise" (Boston, 1824), 18.

[6] E. M. Wherry, ed., *Women in Missions: Papers and Addresses Presented at the Woman's Congress of the Missions* (New York, 1894), 3.

bleeding footsteps." The role of missionary wife, the only role within the missionary life that women were expected to fill in the first generation of service, was defined as important, self-denying, and subordinate.[7] Although from time to time Mission Boards debated the value of a celibate clergy, they invariably if unoriginally concluded that it was better to marry than to burn. Rufus Anderson, long Secretary of the ABCFM, wrote that "Wives are a protection among savages, and men cannot long there make a tolerable home without them. When well connected in respect to health, education, and piety, wives endure 'hardness' quite as well as their husbands, and sometimes with more faith and patience."[8] A Southern Presbyterian minister concurred: "A lady with a missionary spirit can be quite as useful as her husband—often more so." A woman was "even less trouble and expense than a man. Indeed I believe ladies are the cheapest missionaries the Board sends out."[9] Women were trained in submission, service, and love, all objects of the mission cause. Like women's work, the work of the conversion of nations was never done, until the last day. Christianity required submission of the will and intellect, and all for love. Love, "patient, self-denying, self-sacrificing," must, on the missions, be "the love of a mother for her children, however sickly, fretful, wayward, and self-conceited they might be." The object of this love was "the object of foreign missions . . . the conversion of the world by love, into an empire of love."[10] The ability of woman to love was the theme of many nineteenth-century novels; her search for a fitting love object was the theme of as many lives. The foreign missions provided a dramatic setting where that "perfect love, all other loves excelling" could be acted out to the final act of love, the laying down of life itself.[11]

If a woman had a call to this life of self-denying love it could, in the period before the Civil War, be fulfilled only by marriage to an appointed

[7] Harriet Beecher Stowe, *The Minister's Wooing* (Boston, 1868), 25.

[8] Rufus Anderson, *Memorial Volume of the First Fifty Years of the ABCFM* (Boston, 1863), 272. The ABCFM considered the question in its *Annual Report* (1842), 42–44, the Baptist Church in *The Helping Hand* (June 1890), 2, the Episcopal Church in *The Spirit of Missions* (Mar. 1844), 89–90.

[9] *The Missionary* (Nov. 1868), 117.

[10] Maria A. West, *The Romance of Missions: or, Inside Views of Life and Labor in the Land of Ararat* (New York, 1875), 91; Nehemiah Adams, "The Power of Chistian Gratitude" (Boston, 1855).

[11] The hymn "O Perfect Love," with lyrics by Dorothy Blomfield Gurney (1833), was a frequent wedding song, usually with the 1889 music. A popular hymn supplied the title chosen by Robert Pierce Beaver for his work, *All Loves Excelling: American Protestant Women in World Mission* (Grand Rapids: Eerdman, 1968).

missionary, with certain rare exceptions.[12] God who gave the vocation would provide the means, and the Mission Board sometimes played the role of marriage arranger or, more precisely, coordinator of marriages presumably already arranged in heaven. For the widower in the field an attempt was made to find a replacement of similar interests and, if requested, similar physical characteristics. In rare cases the Board gently but firmly suggested another prospective mate or refused one the missionary had proposed.[13] The missionary was a member of an elite corps and marriage to him provided an elevation in status, one function of marriage for nineteenth-century women. Lucy Lyons wrote of her intended husband, "I do not love him *only* because he is a missionary."[14] The ability of Adoniram Judson, aged 57 and twice a widower, to court and marry Fanny Forester, a best-selling author of 28, gives some idea of the persuasive power of the missionary adventure, and, of course, of Dr. Judson. "Dear Dr., only love me, do not see too many faults, censure gently, lead me to the enjoyment of higher religion, and to more extensive usefulness: *trust* me, and no place on earth is half so pleasant as 'grim Burmah.'" Fanny wrote a friend of her joy in resigning the "showy" pleasures of the world for something far more precious. "Did you ever feel as though all the things you were engaged in were so trivial, so aimless, that you fairly sickened of them, and longed to do something more worthy of your origin and destiny?" At last she was given the opportunity "of spending my short life in the way which would make me most happy—in doing real, permanent good." Their marriage, she finds, is discussed on every steamboat and in every hotel, but those who think she is throwing her life away are wrong; it is for sheer gain that she has accepted Dr. Judson's offer, the gain of heaven in the next world and "a dear little home in Burmah" in this one. She only hopes she will not be a "hindrance" to his work, with her "lack of the true missionary spirit," and she vows to "do all I can to make the autumn of your days brighter than their summer has been, that their winter may be glorious."[15]

Yet the young women who, like Fanny Forester, went off in an exalted state of piety to their chosen vocation as a missionary wife, found the reality fell short of their dreams. As children arrived, frequently in the

[12] Cynthia Farrar taught for the ABCFM in India from 1827 to 1837, returned home for two years, and returned to Ahmednugur to die there in 1862. R. Pierce Beaver, "Pioneer Single Women Missionaries," *Missionary Research Library: Occasional Bulletin*, Vol. 4, No. 2 (Sept. 30, 1953). Some ten other single women served in various mission fields before 1861.

[13] Correspondence Files, ABCFM, Houghton Library, Harvard University.

[14] William Dean, *Memoir of Mrs. Lucy T. Lord of the Chinese Baptist Missions* (Philadelphia, 1854), 123.

[15] "Fanny Forester" in real life was Emily Chubbuck. A. C. Kendrick, *The Life and Letters of Mrs. Emily C. Judson* (New York, 1860), 158–89.

middle of that arduous task of learning a difficult language, it became harder to function in the capacity of assistant missionary. The husband's time and energy were spent outside the home, with long hours in the study mastering the language that she was now too tired and too busy to master. Mrs. Fidelia Coan, in Hawaii, wrote to Laura Judd, "Do you not think that married ladies, mothers especially, in the multitude of their cares, are apt to lose sight of that constant improvement, that completeness of character to which we may attain? We have little time to ourselves; our spirits are often jaded; our bodies are weary; we are discouraged and believe what we have often been told, that the cares of a family leave no time or strength for intellectual efforts."[16] As one chronicler of women missionaries wrote cheerfully, "The unpretending labors of a female missionary are not of a nature to swell the historic page."[17] Emily Judson found that "This taking care of teething babies, and teaching darkies to darn stockings, and talking English back end foremost to teetotum John, in order to get an eatable dinner, is really very odd business for Fanny Forester . . . But I begin to get reconciled to my minute cares. I believe women were made for such things: though when I get settled, I hope to put in a mixture of higher and better things too."[18]

Yet these aspirations often met with little encouragement. Henrietta Shuck embarked on her adventure, the first American woman in the China field, carrying a note from her father entitled "A Few Private Thoughts for Henrietta." He might well have given her the same advice if she had married the boy next door. "*You must yield to the will of your husband.*" He hoped she would be happy and that her handwriting would improve ("It needs it"). Should anything happen to her husband, she must immediately get in touch with her father, who would tell her what to do.[19] Lucy Lord wrote home that "It is important to a missionary wife to have her worldly cares reduced as much as possible, that she may have the more time and strength for other and higher duties." But her biographer, William Dean, in his introduction to Mrs. Lord's memoirs, criticized her for this ambition. Dean asked why so many missionary females die young, a problem with which he had some acquaintance since two Mrs. Deans were buried in mission cemeteries. Too often the young women exceeded their wifely duties and tried to do outside work. "Thus attempting to do what they cannot perform, they sacrifice health and life

[16] Laura Fish Judd, *Honolulu: Sketches of Life Social, Political, and Religious, in the Hawaiian Islands from 1828 to 1861* (New York, 1880), 155–56.

[17] Rev. S. F. Smith, "Mrs. Sarah Davis Comstock," in Hamilton W. Pierson, ed., *American Missionary Memorial* (New York, 1853).

[18] Kendrick, *Life,* 247.

[19] J. B. Jeter, *A Memoir of Mrs. Henrietta Shuck: The First American Female Missionary to China* (Boston, 1850), 37–38.

in the vain endeavor, and what is more, neglect the duties of their sacred calling and domestic relations." Succumbing to a love for heroics and encouraged by zealots, they believed that "to leave the high and romantic sphere in which they had thought to move, and come down to common duties of the wife, was leaving the dignity of their calling, and that these domestic services would not be called 'missionary work.'" The woman dies, struck down by "the secret thought that she is not accomplishing what the public expect, though that expectation may be unreasonable, which is the worm at the root of her joys, and which withers her happiness and her health." The foolish girl thus "robs the missionary of the solace of domestic life, and the sympathy he needs in his public work." Women should remember that "their principal and usually only duty is to render their home a heaven, and their husband happy by lightening his cares, training his children, soothing his sorrows, sympathizing in his stresses, and lending their counsel and support to his duties. . . ." [20] This insistence on the proper role of a wife, most particularly a clergyman's wife, increased as the century extolled the idyll of the family hearth and as the cares of missionary life proliferated. As Eunice Beecher concluded in her novel about vicarage life, such ambitions would revolt the "strong minded females of this progressive age," but regardless of their horror, "It is, I am persuaded, just what God meant woman to do." [21]

Having relinquished active evangelical work, a married woman could teach in schools "when her home duties permitted." Fears for the moral and physical safety of her children further isolated her, since it was her duty to keep her child as pure "as if in the wholesome air of our own country." Since mission policy in most cases required the parents to send the child home for education at the age of ten, the mother's life was a series of tearful partings, the poetic expression of which was called "The Missionary's Farewell" and featured in every gift annual. One historian considered these leave-takings "the greatest trauma and sorrow of missionary life." But the Board, when taxed with the policy, pointed out that the number of committed Christians and second-generation missionaries among the children was sufficient proof of the wisdom of the ordeal. [22]

When married women are mentioned in missionary reports it is most often in connection with their cheerful and holy demise. No matter how

---

[20] Dean, *Memoir*, 8–11.

[21] [Eunice White Beecher], *From Dawn to Daylight; or, The Simple Story of a Western Home* (New York, 1859), 293–94.

[22] The problem of the "missionary child" is discussed in poetry by Mrs. Lydia Sigourney, "The Parting of Sarah Comstock with Her Children," in J. Dowling, ed., *The Judson Offering* (New York, 1848), 195, and in painfully remembered fact in Lucy G. Thurston, *Life and Times* (Ann Arbor, 1882), and Olive Jennie Bixby, *My Child-Life in Burma* (Boston, 1880), among many others.

brief her labors, or how unrewarding her time in missionary life, the woman could be counted on to expire with the hope that her passing would not discourage newcomers to the field, and with a heartfelt statement that she was glad that she had come to Africa, or Ceylon, or India, even if only to die there. In actual fact, insofar as we have any statistics, missionary women lived about as long as their counterparts who stayed home. If they were lucky enough to be sent to Hawaii, their actuarial prospects substantially increased.[23] But death had a value to the mission cause and was exploited and publicized as a vindication of it. Of course if a married woman had no children her career was likely to be more active, and even if she had children she might choose to leave them with servants and flout her "proper sphere," claiming that she followed a higher law. After children were grown many a woman labored long beside her husband, or even remained in the field after his death, to become a "matriarch" and symbol to the new generation of missionaries and converts.

Early attempts to encourage women to become missionaries, and to support the missionary venture at home, emphasized the depraved condition of women in heathen lands. Woman was urged to respond to the plea of her sister who, "suffering as a slave or beast, knows not the meaning of womanhood." Christianity was characterized as the liberator of women; only in Christian lands were women accorded respect and dignity.[24] Bishop Thoburn believed that "the actual status of any people can be discovered readily by ascertaining the position of womanhood in the country under review . . . the Hindu, Mohammedan, and Buddhist have failed to appreciate the dignity and worth of womanhood. . . ."[25] In their attempts to show the immensity of the difference between Christian and heathen women, ministers rose to eloquence; one went so far as to refer in 1854 to the enfranchisement of the one and not the other.[26] No one ever suggested that the differences between the heathen women and the Christian ones might be in degrees of bondage, and that "the hobbled feet and minds" which so disturbed the missionaries, the "hostility to education" for females that they found, the loveless marriage, the sense of inferiority, and the female subordination to male desires and laws which so affected

[23] The literature of female missionary death is vast and uniformly edifying. Although women in the field died more often than men before 1860, these statistics were sharply reversed after 1860. William G. Lennox, *The Health and Turnover of Missionaries* (New York: The Foreign Missions Conference, 1933). For Massachusetts statistics see *Historical Statistics of the United States,* I (Washington, D. C.: G.P.O., 1976), 56. Hawaii records from Mission Children Society Archives, Honolulu, Hawaii.

[24] Richard S. Storrs, "The Prospective Advance of Christian Missions," 75th Anniversary of the Founding of the ABCFM (Boston, 1885).

[25] Bishop James M. Thoburn, *The Christian Conquest of India* (New York: Young People's Missionary Movement, 1906), 92.

[26] Charles White, "Power Belongeth Unto God" (Boston, 1854).

their sensibilities might have a counterpart even in this "favored land," where women "owed all they had to One who loved them much."[27]

Having detailed the deplorable condition of the heathen woman and the contrast with the joyful lot of her American sisters, the Missionary Boards were forced to two somewhat contradictory conclusions: however degraded she might be, the pagan woman wielded great power, and these powerful women, because of local custom and taboos, were inaccessible to male missionaries. "Woman everywhere represents the stronger element in the religious faith of the community whether that faith be true or false," concluded the report of the Presbyterian Board in 1881.[28] The women of China were more "fierce and intractable" than the men; the women of India "controlled the home and home devotions"; the African woman "at birth and marriage and death" had charge of rituals and idols; the women of Persia "were able in subtle ways to influence their children and their husbands," so that no religious change took place against their will. But the Chinese "pavilions of women," the Indian zenanas, the women's quarters in Japan, Africa, and Persia, could not be entered by a male, whether missionary or doctor. And the married women missionaries were very busy being "the light and solace" of Christian homes. The answer to the dilemma was found in recruiting single women for the mission field.

To send single ladies to the foreign missions, the Woman's Union Missionary Society of America for Heathen Lands, a nondenominational organization, was formed in New York in 1861. By 1893, 65 missionaries were in the field in India, China, and Japan. The Woman's Union served as a model for the separate women's boards which the ABCFM and later the individual denominations set up between 1869 and 1888. It published a magazine, the *Missionary Link*, which exhorted the faithful to contribute money, to consider joining the force, or to "buy a substitute," supporting her as American males were doing during the Civil War. The women engaged in the work dutifully wrote long letters and developed a following as well as winning the support of prayers and money. Miss Marston's increasing deafness, "which made typhoons a hazard," and Miss Brittan's romantic story of a fiancé left behind in Africa because she refused to let him abandon the field just because the climate was killing her, captured the imagination and solidified support for the women's organization. The "girl," as she was called, no matter what her chronological age, was outfitted by her adoptive sisters and mothers, who continued to offer her their letters, gift boxes, prayers, and unsolicited advice.

[27] Lily Ryder Gracey, ed., *Gist: a Hand-Book of Missionary Information* (Cincinnati, 1893), 12.
[28] *Reports of the Board of Foreign Missions of the Presbyterian Church USA* (1881), 12.

The "Work of Women for Women" thus became the province of America's female churchgoers, whether at home or in the field. "From henceforth," said one history, "women's work for the welfare of women in non-Christian lands, whether physical, intellectual, or spiritual, was to be in women's hands, and was to be performed in women's way."[29] It would be more nearly the truth to say that henceforth women increased in absolute and proportionate representation in missionary life and began their struggle to translate these numbers into influence. In 1830 females made up 49 percent of the missionary force. In 1880 they constituted 57 percent of active missionaries, and the figure rose to slightly more than 60 percent in 1893.[30] Some commentators observed that the Civil War had trained women in administration, and made them aware of the superiority of organizations over individual attempts at change. The war had also dislocated the living patterns of American women, whether North or South, and drawn them into the Hallelujah Chorus of the missionary drama. One historian suggested it had demonstrated "new human fibres" which through the shared burden of grief predisposed women for the great service to their sisters.[31]

The churches embraced the idea of separate Boards for women, once it was demonstrated that they would raise money over and above what their husbands already pledged to their church. By 1893 the "systematic giving" and thousands of "mite boxes" were contributing about one and a half million dollars to the various mission boards.[32] Publications were edited and distributed. Children were organized and they too had magazines geared to their interests. The stories of contributions "from picking potato bugs" or from the dying bequest of a saintly "little friend of Missions" increased the popularity of the missions, and parishes held sprightly fund-raising entertainments. The American paterfamilias was besieged with propaganda: his wife enlivened the dinner table by making conversation gleaned from her Monthly Meetings, his children quizzed him unmercifully as part of their "committee" assignment, and his pastor insisted on his dollar and assigned a Mission hymn to be sung during the

---

[29] D. L. Leonard, *Missionary Annals of the Nineteenth Century* (Cleveland and New York, 1899), 178. Helen Barrett Montgomery, *Western Women in Eastern Lands: An Outline Study of Fifty Years of Woman's Work in Foreign Missions* (New York, 1911), identifies early Sewing and Dorcas Societies as forerunners of Women's Work groups.

[30] Leonard, *Missionary Annals*, Wherry, *Women in Missions*, and Lennox, *Health of Missionaries*.

[31] M. M. Underhill, "Woman's Work for Missions: Three Home Based Studies," *International Review of Missions*, 14 (July 1925), 379–99.

[32] Figures taken from Edwin Munsell Bliss, ed., *The Encyclopaedia of Missions*, 2 vols. (New York, 1895). Bliss accepted Board reports at face value.

Offering.[33] This saturation of the country's imagination carried out by women and children, the technique of the temperance societies, had even more dramatic results with the missionary cause. Popular novels—*Rebecca of Sunnybrook Farm, Anne of Green Gables,* and Fannie Macauley's *The Lady of the Decoration,* for example—dwelt on the missionary theme. In the sequel to Caroline Hentz's best-selling *Linda,* the heroine goes off to an Indian mission with her new husband. The rage for the exotic in home furnishing, from the Turkish Corner to the curio cabinet, reflected the influence of missionaries as well as other travelers.

The single woman who went to the missions might have been someone who had longed for this work since childhood but had been prevented from going by home responsibilities; the death of a parent or the improvement of her economic position freed her to fulfill her vocation belatedly. Another type of young woman left school and went to the missions as a temporary "first job," with a strong sense of vocation but no clear idea of her duty. The missionary wife had been irritated when she was regarded as the missionary's cook; the single woman missionary was horrified to be considered his polygamous second wife. Many unmarried women had further complaints of their isolation as constant boarders "who have no home, no real abiding-place in the land."[34] Some felt that married women and the more formidable and virginal of the single women regarded them as husband-hunters, ready to snatch the next man made available when a wife succumbed to cholera or dysentery. It took time for men to realize that single women could be missionaries in their own right. Isabella Thoburn dutifully copied out her brother's correspondence for some months until she insisted that he leave her free to accomplish her own work. Bishop Thoburn, writing his sister's autobiography, tells how her refusal raised his consciousness. He understood for the first time that "a Christian woman sent out to the field was a Christian missionary, and that her time was as precious, her work as important, and her rights as sacred as those of the more conventional missionaries of the other sex."[35]

Those more conventional missionaries were not always pleased at the increasing number of women. A single woman was sometimes refused by several stations because the resident missionaries feared she would cause tension. An article in the May 1882 *Missionary Review* dealt with the

[33] Louis A. Cattan, *Lamps Are for Lighting: The Story of Helen Barrett Montgomery and Lucy Waterbury Peabody* (Grand Rapids, 1972); Mrs. M. A. Miller, *History of the Woman's Foreign Missionary Society of the Methodist Protestant Church* (Pittsburgh, 1896); Augustus R. Buckland, *Women in the Mission Field* (New York, 1895); Mrs. J. Howard Smith, "Mrs. Thomas Doremus," *The Missionary Link,* 14 (March 1877); Mrs. Juliana Hayes (Nashville, n.d.).

[34] Maria West, *Romance,* 467.

[35] James M. Thoburn, *Life of Isabella Thoburn* (Cincinnati: Jennings and Pye, 1903).

unmarried woman as a disruptive force and the puppet of the Board. Women in missions were told to exercise no direct influence but to hold "the same relation to man in the mission fields of heathendom that she holds in the most happy homes and churches of christendom, where her work is accomplished with a grace that disarms opposition, her views and plans are adopted because none better can be devised, and her influence is all the more potent because unconscious." The nominal cause for this cautionary tone was the influx of women doctors to the field, potentially, because of their education and drive, a real threat to the men.[36]

Although they complained to the Board about their problems, and letters from missionary wives frequently complained about them, single women found in the missionary field a rare combination of church- and socially-sanctioned activity and freedom. The woman doctor found a far more interesting practice, an opportunity to perform operations, to study rare diseases, and to escape a professional life as a poorly paid listener to female complaints, her probable lot had she remained at home.[37] As Susan Hale once pointed out in a slightly different context, if you could "persuade any single woman that a pleasure is a duty . . . she is secured to it."[38]

Although women had been encouraged to enter the field largely so that they could work with women, some, like Lottie Moon, protested that the logic was wrong. She felt that to get "any tangible, visible results" she would have "in some way to reach the men of the community. How to do this was the problem." She solved it by scrupulously following the Biblical injunctions against female preaching. She could not help it if "the men crowded silently behind them [her female hearers] and studied along with them." Surely, she wrote, "even Paul would not have objected." But when asked to comply with a latter-day Pauline injunction that barred even single women from voting in missionary meetings, Miss Moon flatly

---

[36] "Lady Medical Missionaries," *The Missionary Review*, 5 (May 1882), 183–86.

[37] The best biographical information is found in "Notebooks of Women Medical Missionaries," Medical College of Pennsylvania, Historical Collection. See also Anna M. Fullerton, "The Woman Physician in India," *Transactions of the Alumnae Association of the Woman's Medical College of Pennsylvania*, 25 (1900), 55–58; Mary W. Griscom, "Medical Mission Work in China," ibid., 39 (1914), 86–89; Charlotte L. R. Hoskins, *Clara A. Swain, M.D.: First Medical Missionary to the Women of the Orient* (Boston, 1912); Ellen C. Potter, "The Woman Medical Missionary," *Bulletin of Woman's Medical College of Pennsylvania*, 65 (1914), 36; Bertha L. Selman, "Pioneer Women in Medicine: Early Service in Missions," *Medical Woman's Journal*, 54 (Apr., June, and Sept. 1947), 198–257; Mary H. Stinson, *Work of Women Physicians in Asia* (Norristown, Pa., 1884); and the work of several members of the Scudder dynasty, discussed in Dorothy Jealous Scudder, *A Thousand Years in Thy Sight: The Story of the Scudders in India*, typescript in Arthur and Elizabeth Schlesinger Library, Radcliffe College, Cambridge.

[38] E. E. Hale and Susan Hale, *A Family Flight through France, Germany, Norway and Switzerland* (Boston, 1881), 2.

refused. "To exclude the married women from the meetings might be unwise, but it could hardly be deemed unjust, as they could be represented by their husbands. To exclude the unmarried ladies would be a most glaring piece of injustice in my opinion. To such exclusion I could never submit and retain my self-respect." She asked for her return passage to Virginia since "It seems to be the purpose of the Committee to relegate me henceforth to the class of those women missionaries who must work in silence, without voice in any shaping of mission policies. I distinctly decline to be so relegated." The Board reconsidered.[39] But Miss Moon was an exception; the majority of women, even medical missionaries, had little to say in yearly meetings, even when they had the vote. According to one embittered child of Presbyterian missionaries, the "inevitable result" of this "religious subjection of women, was to breed in them an irrepressible independence and desire for self-expression, born of their innate and unconscious sense of injury and injustice."[40]

Perhaps equally inevitable was the attempt to find some compensatory form of solidarity and status. The "compound" of unmarried women sometimes filled this need, as did the isolated unit of two single women, either missionaries or a missionary and a native Bible woman who became a close friend. The "Deaconess" or "Protestant Sisterhood" associations, which gained prominence in the last years of the nineteenth century, although they had been in existence long before that, gave some women additional dignity and provided the visible bonds of habit and ritual. They were never widely popular, however, and the clergy had reservations about allowing them at all. "Sisterhoods should be under the general direction of wise *men*," was the firm advice of a British to an American bishop. "I have learned to fear female *rule*, unless it be itself under authority, able to know all and capable of controlling or overruling."[41] Lydia Fay stoutly denied her "need of a mother superior to accomplish something."[42] A better solution was to become the independent "Head of a Household," as Anna Safford did. "God has granted me the desire of my heart and given me a home of my own even in a foreign land and amongst an alien people." She added that besides her own pleasure in the arrangement, the Chinese, ever alert to status symbols,

[39] Irwin T. Hyatt, Jr., *Our Ordered Lives Confess: Three Nineteenth-Century American Missionaries in East Shantung* (Cambridge: Harvard Univ. Press, 1976), and Una Roberts Lawrence, *Lottie Moon* (Nashville: Sunday School Board of the Southern Baptist Convention, 1927), 135–37 and 141–42.

[40] Pearl S. Buck, *Fighting Angel: Portrait of a Soul* (New York: Reynal and Hitchcock, 1936), the fictional biography of her father, Presbyterian missionary Andrew Sydenstricker. Her mother, Carrie Sydenstricker, was the subject of *The Exile* (New York: Reynal and Hitchcock, 1936), 187–89.

[41] Henry C. Potter, *Sisterhoods and Deaconesses At Home and Abroad* (New York, 1873), 87.

[42] Lydia Fay to Dr. Denison, Secretary, Board of Missions of the Protestant Episcopal Church. April 28, 1877, Episcopal Church Archives, Austin, Texas.

instantly treated her with more deference when they saw she was the one who gave the orders.[43]

A recent history of American religion suggests that the missionary movement diverted American Protestantism from the problems it faced at home.[44] It might be that for American women a secondary diversion sent them to "the dark, the distant and the trying fields"[45] instead of facing up to the questions raised by the women's movement. The counsels to wives not to exceed their calling, to single women not to speak out of turn, to Sisterhoods not to act without consulting the Bishop, could be construed as warnings against the ungodly doctrine of women's rights. The *Woman's Evangel* wrote of women's work in missions as a "happy solution of the difficulty" when a woman found it hard to reconcile her religion and her rights, agitating her own and "the public mind, creating warm discussion and angry debate." In expanding her role and involving her energy and enthusiasm in the drama of foreign missions women could rejoice. "In God's work, our highest sphere—Our precious, our inalienable rights are to do His will and to show forth His light and love."[46] The potential problem and the vigilance with which it was monitored are revealed in a story, perhaps apocryphal but quoted in most histories of women's boards. A pastor in Michigan insisted on being present at all women's mission meetings, because "no one knew what they would pray for, if left alone."[47] At least one parent Board expressed the fear that some "mild form" of the "women's rights controversy" might be lurking in the proposed women's group.[48]

By the end of the century women were active missionaries, distinguished by their achievement as well as their supportive Christian homes and beautiful deaths. The "muscular Christianity" of the period had not passed them by and they gloried in their militancy. "I am glad the providence of God calls us there," wrote Loanza Benton during an uprising in Syria, "It is a place where we can feel that we are really in the midst of the battle."[49] The *Encyclopaedia of Missions* would have it that "The gospel

---

[43] Anna Cunningham Safford to her sister Janette Safford Thompson, January 1876, Soochow, Archives of the Southern Presbyterian Historical Society, Montreat, N. C.

[44] Sydney Ahlstrom, *A Religious History of the American People* (New Haven: Yale Univ. Press, 1972), 423–24.

[45] Beth Bradford Gilchrist, *The Life of Mary Lyon* (Boston: Houghton Mifflin Co., 1910), and Louise Porter Thomas, *Seminary Militant: An Account of the Missionary Movement at Mount Holyoke Seminary and College* (South Hadley, Mass., 1937), discuss in context this phrase often used by Mary Lyon in her "nursery of missionaries."

[46] *The Woman's Evangel*, 4 (May 1878), 2.

[47] For example in Ellen C. Parsons, "History of Women's Organized Missionary Work As Promoted by American Women," in Wherry, *Women in Missions*, 85.

[48] Mrs. M. A. Miller, *History of the Woman's Foreign Missionary Society*, 37.

[49] "A Diary and Some Reminiscences of Loanza Goulding Benton," Oct. 28, 1847. Typescript in Sophia Smith Collection, Smith College, Northampton, Mass.

had developed them and set them in honor; given them security and moral power; made them intellectually free, and queens of happy homes. . . . They undertook to carry the gospel where without them it could not go."[50] David Abeel's report of the piteous cry of the Chinese women, "O bring us some female men," had been more successful and more potentially upsetting than he realized.[51] When men abandoned the zenana, the harem and purdah to women they also abandoned much of their Biblical superiority. In everything but name women became full-fledged preachers. Mrs. Bishop Boone begged the Episcopal Board Secretary to "appreciate the fact that Miss Fay . . . has been doing a man's work, and that it will be next to impossible to find any woman to succeed to her work." In fact, "a young man should be her successor."[52] But male vocations were declining, just as women were becoming more numerous and prominent in the field.[53]

The logic of women influencing women did not bring about converts; nothing the missionaries did, with few exceptions, paid off numerically. But the recruiting of women for nineteenth-century Protestant missions created a new role and status for them within one of the most important movements of organized religion. Although women entered the missionary ranks largely in response to social change at home and the faulty strategy which made it seem desirable to replace men with women, they made valuable strides not only in professional but in personal growth. The cultural confrontation which was a necessary part of missionary life worked on both sides, and many missionaries were never quite the same afterwards. The ethnocentric attitude and national and religious absolutism of these men and women cannot be denied. In almost every case, however, if they remained in the field any length of time, there was identification with and sympathy for some aspects of the host culture. Missionaries were far more sensitive to the societies in which they worked than is generally believed. The ladies of the Chinese mission who stayed up all Christmas Eve replacing the blond hair on the dolls in the mission box with straight black wigs were making a small but affirmative statement. Sarah Smith wrote perceptively about the way in which mission life forced "a taking to pieces, if I may so speak, of all former habits

[50] "Woman's Work for Women," *The Encyclopaedia of Missions*, 2:479.

[51] David Abeel, *Journal of a Residence in China, and the Neighboring Countries* (New York, 1834). The philosophy and method was also open to criticism from another point of view. Flora Annie Steele, a bestselling author who lived in India 22 years and wrote about its customs and history, believed the "zenana mission" a great mistake, because without it India would have come out of purdah. *The Garden of Fidelity* (London, 1929).

[52] Henrietta Harris Boone to Denison, Nov. 22, 1875. Episcopal Archives.

[53] This was a matter of concern to the Boards. See, for example, "Where Are the Young Missionary Men of the Church?" *The Missionary Advocate* (June 1869), 220–24.

and associations, and modes of action and the constructing of new. . . . ''
The process was valuable both for work in the field and for personal
growth. ''This demolition and reconstruction, gives one the opportunity
to study his own character and attainments . . . not a little calculated to
produce humility and self-distrust.''[54] Like other expatriates the missionaries could see some aspects of their own country all the more clearly
once they left it. For women the experience provided a jolting examination of their vocation which carried with it a reassessment of their
nature and role.

The twentieth century offers similar examples of ways in which new
fields have been opened to women. Franz Boas encouraged his Barnard
students to enter anthropology largely because he needed access to certain rites available only to women. Women became dominant in elementary school education when it paid badly; when the pay increased, the
percentages of women in teaching began to decline. Women at universities may wonder at the workings of this social law which has given them
professional status just in time for a shrinking job market and numerous
academic and economic crises.

Even when men opened the doors for their own purposes, they could
not and cannot now control the consequences. The missionary woman of
the nineteenth century was indeed filling a role in a field abandoned to her
somewhat late and with many restrictions. She was achieving prominence
in an institution which was itself declining in prestige. She was keeping
alive a rhetoric, just as President McKinley and Senator Beveridge were,
at a time when the substance of American expansion was devoted to commerce and not to conversion. But for the individual woman the substance
was very much a part of her life. The doctor who treated 200 patients a
day (including five who were already dead) and the itinerant preacher
who spoke until midnight and was off in her jinrikisha at dawn, felt herself
necessary and important. Unlike many American women she defined herself in terms other than those of her husband and children. The historian
of the religious experience must always consider that, however much
religion involved the working out of social, political, and economic neces-
sities, it was also a matter of individual will and conscience. For the
nineteenth-century American woman, on the foreign mission field her life
had meaning and joy and was infused by a sense of privilege at being the
special recipient of God's grace. As they said on their gravestones, ''She
hath done what she could.''

---

[54] Edward W. Hooker, *Memoir of Mrs. Sarah L. Huntingdon Smith: Late of the American
Mission in Syria* (New York, 1840), 308.

Sr. Elizabeth Kolmer, A.S.C.

Catholic Women Religious and Women's History
A Survey of the Literature

*A*lthough Catholic sisters have been active on the American scene since the eighteenth century, the story of their life and work remains largely untold. In particular, we know little of their history in relation to that of women in general or to the cycles of feminist thinking and action. On first thought, one might suspect that few such connections existed. Catholic sisters of the nineteenth and much of the twentieth centuries lived in relative seclusion from society at large, their lives centering in the institutions they staffed and managed. In addition, the women's movement until recent times was almost exclusively Protestant and middle-class. Nevertheless significant opportunities exist for serious researchers in this untouched area of social history.

This essay will evaluate the existing literature on the history of Catholic nuns, identify bibliographical aids, and indicate the archival and other sources available for investigation of the history of women religious. First I will survey scholarly works on American religious history in general, histories of individual congregations and biographies of their foundresses, and unpublished dissertations on the role of sisters. Second, I will comment on materials available for the study of the relationship of Catholic sisters and their congregations to the women's movement of the 1960s and 1970s. In conclusion I will offer some recommendations for future study.

*G*eneral histories of religion in America say little if anything about Catholic sisters or sisterhoods. Sydney Ahlstrom's wide-ranging *Religious*

History of the American People mentions the work of women's orders and their contributions to Catholic education in America, citing very briefly the Ursulines, the Carmelites, and Elizabeth Seton and her Sisters of Charity. In the second edition of his *Religion in America*, Winthrop Hudson also mentions Seton and gives passing recognition to the "sacrificial devotion of the members of numerous sisterhoods" who became the backbone of parochial education in America. Otherwise Hudson gives space only to radical stances taken by some religious organizations of women in the 1960s vis-à-vis the authority of the Church.[1]

Lack of space might account for the brevity of coverage in the general religious histories, but publications centering on the Catholic Church in the United States similarly neglect women religious. John Gilmary Shea, the classic early historian of the American Church, touched upon the sisters in each of his four volumes, but mostly in passing reference to their work in the schools and other Catholic institutions. More recently, Thomas T. McAvoy wrote a *History of the Catholic Church in the United States* almost without mentioning the sisters, let alone their work in such an important Church institution as the parochial school. John Tracy Ellis in his short *American Catholicism* also gives them very little attention. While Theodore Roemer discusses the sisters' place in the history of the Church, his interpretation is limited and the book has other weaknesses.[2] Where these and others do discuss women, they treat the sisters by individual orders and in descriptive terms emphasizing their works. Only when recounting their service as nurses in the Civil War do these authors consider women in orders as a single sociohistorical group.

The researcher will find two bibliographies more helpful: Ellis' *Guide to American Catholic History* and Edward R. Vollmar's *The Catholic Church in America*.[3] Ellis' noteworthy second chapter describes manuscript repositories and his sixth chapter discusses some of the histories of the foundation of women's communities. Critics generally consider the Vollmar work (1956) the most complete bibliography on the Catholic Church in the United States; the second edition includes unpublished

---

[1] Sidney E. Ahlstrom, *A Religious History of the American People* (New Haven: Yale Univ. Press, 1972), chap. 32. Winthrop S. Hudson, *Religion in America*, 2d ed. (New York: Scribner's, 1973), 249–50, 420–21.

[2] John Gilmary Shea, *History of the Catholic Church in the United States* (New York: John G. Shea, 1886–1892). Thomas T. McAvoy, C.S.C., *A History of the Catholic Church in the United States* (Notre Dame: Univ. of Notre Dame Press, 1969). John Tracy Ellis, *American Catholicism* (Chicago: Univ. of Chicago Press, 1956). Theodore Roemer, O.F.M. Cap., *The Catholic Church in the United States* (St. Louis: B. Herder, 1950), 156, 192ff, 216ff, 235ff, 253, 258, 284, 339, 354.

[3] John Tracy Ellis, *Guide to American Catholic History* (Milwaukee: Bruce, 1959). Edward R. Vollmar, S.J., *The Catholic Church in America: An Historical Bibliography*, 2d ed. (New York: Scarecrow, 1963).

masters' theses and doctoral dissertations written at Catholic colleges and universities. Vollmar's entries are alphabetical, but the book contains an excellent topical index, as well as a 40-page historiographical essay. "A Selected Bibliography of the Religious Orders and Congregations of Women," by Joseph B. Code, published in the *Catholic Historical Review* (1937), lists the source material then available on orders of religious women founded in the United States before 1850. Though limited in its usefulness today, the article represents an early effort to assist in the study of religious women and their work.[4]

Most of the periodical literature published on the history of women religious has appeared in the Catholic press. One can readily locate these articles through the *Catholic Periodical Index*. Their concern has been either with the sisters' devotional lives or with the history of women's orders or provinces within the larger congregations. Essays in the scholarly journals, the *Catholic Historical Review*, published by the American Catholic Historical Association, and the *Records of the American Catholic Historical Society of Philadelphia* have the same limitations as the longer historical studies: they have not considered nuns from the viewpoint of their common identity or their relationship with other groups of women.

A large number of the some 450 orders of American sisters listed in the *Official Catholic Directory* for 1976 have provided a biography of their foundress or a history of their congregation. Many of these works have been privately printed, and are available primarily to members of the particular congregation or can be found in libraries of Catholic institutions. In quality they run the gamut from scholarly studies to popular episodic sketches. Most have drawn upon letters and papers relating to the congregation, but these are often used to poor advantage, either because of the writer's deficiencies or because of gaps in the congregation's archives. Often the book will not even list these sources.[5]

A few selected titles will suffice as a sample. Excellent both in scholarship and style is *The Society of the Sacred Heart in North America* by Louise Callan (1937). *With Lamps Burning* by Mary Grace McDonald

---

[4] Joseph B. Code, "A Selected Bibliography of the Religious Orders and Congregations of Women Founded Within the Present Boundaries of the United States (1727–1850)," *The Catholic Historical Review,* 23 (Oct. 1937), 331–51. An extended form of this bibliography is found in *CHR,* 26 (July 1940), 222–45.

[5] Titles of many of these works can be found in Vollmar's bibliography and Ewens' dissertation noted below. Ewens estimates that 45 percent of the books she examined (59 titles) were of scholarly value, with generous use of primary sources and good documentation; another 8 percent (11 titles) were diaries, letters, or journals; 20 percent (26 titles) used primary sources, but without documentation; and 27 percent made no use of scholarly technique.

(1957), a history of the Benedictines in Minnesota, and *Not With Silver or Gold* (1945), an account by the Dayton Precious Blood Sisters of their foundation in Ohio, are also works of distinction. In *We Came North* (1961), Julia Gilmore draws upon congregation archives, local newspapers, and personal interviews to recount the history of the Sisters of Charity of Leavenworth, Kansas.[6] Veronica McEntee's *The Sisters of Mercy of Harrisburg, 1869–1939*, gives evidence that there are ample resources in the houses of the Mercy Sisters, though the book is undocumented, as is *Mother Caroline and the School Sisters of Notre Dame in North America*. Other histories are written in a more popular style, among them Covelle Newcomb's *Running Waters* and *Builders by the Sea* by S. M. Johnston. One final example is Angela Hurley's *On Good Ground*, semipopular in style and written primarily from secondary works and newspaper sources.[7]

Biographies of such outstanding women as Elizabeth Seton and Philippine Duchesne are readily available. In addition, the pages of the histories mentioned above are full of other strong, fearless women who faced great odds and dangers in founding their convents and institutions. Poverty, the threat of starvation, overdemanding bishops, and hostile neighbors were some of their trials. Among the many "nameless" women in our pioneer history we should not forget the sisters who built not only schools but hospitals, foundling homes, and shelters for the sick and poor which served as the chief charitable resources of many nineteenth-century American communities.

Did the nineteenth- or early twentieth-century nun identify with the problems of women outside the cloister, or with secular women's movements of the time? Perhaps not. Her sequestered existence would make this unlikely, and in any case many congregations of that time were still in the building phase, struggling to establish themselves. In this effort they seem to have worked alone. We do not know if they recognized a need for bettering the position of women in society whether inside or outside convent walls; certainly there is little evidence that they looked to an or-

[6] Louise Callan, R.S.C.J., *The Society of the Sacred Heart in North America* (New York: Longmans, Green, 1937); Mary Grace McDonald, O.S.B., *With Lamps Burning* (St. Joseph, Minn.: St. Benedict's Priory Press, 1957); Dayton Precious Blood Sisters, *Not with Silver or Gold* (Dayton: Sisters of the Precious Blood, 1945); Julia Gilmore, S.C.L., *We Came North* (St. Meinrad: Abbey Press, 1961).

[7] Mary Veronica McEntee, R.S.M., *The Sisters of Mercy of Harrisburg, 1869–1939* (Philadelphia: Dolphin Press, 1939); School Sisters of Notre Dame, *Mother Caroline and the School Sisters of Notre Dame in North America* (St. Louis: Woodward and Tiernan, 1928), 2 vols.; Covelle Newcomb, *Running Waters* (New York: Dodd, Mead, 1947); S. M. Johnston, *Builders By the Sea: History of the Ursuline Sisters of Galveston, Texas* (New York: Exposition, 1971); Angela Hurley, *On Good Ground: History of the Sisters of St. Joseph* (Minneapolis: Univ. of Minnesota Press, 1951).

ganized women's movement for inspiration or aid in dealing with their own problems. If they refused to accept a bishop's categorization of them as weak, inexperienced, and ineffective, they worked, so far as we know, on a practical level as individuals or individual congregations to prove him wrong, rather than looking for intellectual or moral support in the broader society. It would be an interesting undertaking to determine whether a feeling of solidarity existed among the sisters earlier than the mid-twentieth century with contemporary secular women and, if so, with which classes of women they identified.

The availability of source material on this topic is an important consideration. The headquarters of most congregations have some archival material, but little of it has been catalogued. Furthermore, there has been no guide indicating how much and what kind of material is to be found in any given religious house such as that to the Canadian religious archives published by the Canadian Religious Conference, or Abbé Charles Molette's guide to religious women's archives in France.[8] Some of these needs, however, are soon to be met.

The Leadership Conference of Women Religious has initiated a program to promote the preservation and organization of the records of sisterhoods in the United States. As a first step, the Conference in 1977 and 1978 held six workshops in basic archival training for designated members of religious orders. Directed by Evangeline Thomas, C.S.J., the workshops were funded by the National Historical Publications and Records Commission. The Conference has now embarked upon a survey of some 650 convent archives in the United States, under a grant from the National Endowment for the Humanities. They expect to complete the survey by late 1980, and publish a *Guide to Source Materials in Repositories of Women Religious in the United States*. The *Guide* is designed as a research tool for scholars not only in women's history but also in related fields in the humanities and social sciences.

Meanwhile, a researcher would have to contact individual congregations for information. One can find the most readily available list of these houses in the annual *Official Catholic Directory*. A few other volumes might be helpful. Although certainly dated, *Religious Orders of Women in the United States* (1930) provides a brief historical and institutional account of many congregations. More up to date but less complete in information are Thomas P. McCarthy's *Guide to Catholic Sisterhoods in the*

---

[8] Canadian Religious Conference, *Abridged Guide to the Archives of Religious Communities of Canada* (Ottawa, Canada); Molette, *Guide des sources de l'histoire des congregations feminines francaises de vie active* (Paris: Editions de Paris, 1974).

United States (1952) and Joan Lexau's *Convent Life: Roman Catholic Religious Orders for Women in North America* (1964).[9]

Of great value and directly related to the topic of this essay is Mary Ewens' "The Role of the Nun in Nineteenth Century America," an American Studies dissertation from the University of Minnesota.[10] Ewens concludes that sisters were generally regarded with hostility in the early part of the nineteenth century, largely because the Protestant public's concept of them had come from European literature which portrayed a distorted image. Following the public's first hand experience with sister nurses in the Civil War, however, the nuns became highly regarded for their commitment to Christian living and humane concerns.[11] By the end of the century, they had moved to a stronger position in the sense that realistic questions were being asked about their cloistral practices and their adaptation to American society. Throughout her study Ewens examines the image of the nun in the serious literature of the times and compares it with the actual lives and work of the sisters. The bibliography contains a wealth of material about sisters in the profession of nursing and in popular and serious literature, as well as works of a broader scope on the Catholic Church in America. One section lists biographies and histories of individual religious congregations.

Limited material can be found in other dissertations in history, education, and sociology. Those in history are largely studies of the foundations of specific orders, although there is one on the Sisters of Mercy as nurses in the Crimean War.[12] Those in the second group deal with the education of sisters, the education of children by sisters, or the educational contributions of individual orders. The sociology dissertations have a special interest since they approach a religious situation from a different perspective, as part of a larger social structure. Some of the themes treated in these studies are the religious community as a social system; power, status, and institutionalization in the occupational milieu of the Catholic

[9] Elinor T. Dehey, *Religious Orders of Women in the United States* (Hammond, Ind.: W. B. Conkey, 1930); Thomas P. McCarthy, *Guide to the Catholic Sisterhoods in the United States* (Washington, D. C.: Catholic Univ. of America Press, 1952); Joan Lexau, *Convent Life: Roman Catholic Religious Orders for Women in North America* (New York: Dial, 1964).

[10] Mary Ewens, O.P., "The Role of the Nun in Nineteenth Century America: Variations on the International Theme" (1971), published by Arno Press in 1978.

[11] For example, when a statue of Abraham Lincoln was erected at Oak Ridge Cemetery in Springfield, Ill., President Grant, who himself was being honored by the citizens of Illinois on the same occasion, insisted that two nuns unveil the statue, in acknowledgment of the country's debt to sisters for their wartime services to the wounded. The story can be found in Sister Thomas Aquinas Winterbauer, O.P., *Lest We Forget . . .* (Chicago: Adams Press, 1973).

[12] Mary Gilgannon, R.S.M., "The Sisters of Mercy As Crimean War Nurses" (Diss. Univ. of Notre Dame, 1962).

sister; the process of socialization in a religious community; and the integration of dual professional roles in sisters.[13]

*T*he historian who seeks to record and interpret the effects of the women's movement in recent Catholic religious history will face several difficulties. So far there has been little written on the subject, and the literature that does exist tends to have a wider perspective. Sisters of today do not see themselves as set apart from other religious women, or even from other women generally. In the sixties and the seventies, in contrast to the past, there has been a pronounced expression by many Catholic sisters of feelings of solidarity with women in all walks of life, professional or otherwise, as well as with religious women of all faiths. Yet the impact of the feminist movement, in varying degrees, has been a common experience for the Catholic sisters in this country, 130,000 in number according to the 1978 *Official Catholic Directory* and constituting a more or less homogeneous group.

The inquiring student might begin with Sarah Bentley Doely's book entitled *Women's Liberation and the Church* (1970).[14] This deals with the question of women and religion on an interdenominational level, and from several different aspects. One essay discusses Catholic sisters, choosing as an example the Immaculate Heart Sisters of California, who wished to determine their own destiny in terms of lifestyle and apostolic work. When their male superiors in the Church disapproved of their plans, the group renounced their canonical status in the church and formed a lay association. Many sisters today are struggling for and gaining greater self-determination, but most strive to remain within the traditional structures of the religious congregation and Church authority. Study of these developments in the lives of women religious has hardly begun.

The subject of sisters and the women's movement is treated, but only briefly, in several books published in the late 1960s, such as Elsie Culver's *Women in the World of Religion*, *Women in Modern Life* by William Bier,

[13] Mary George O'Toole, *Sisters of Mercy of Maine—A Religious Community as a Social System* (Washington, D. C.: Catholic Univ. of America Press, 1964); Rosalma G. Wedhe, "The Occupational Milieu of the Catholic Sister" (Diss. St. John's Univ., 1966); Blake Hill, "Women and Religion: A Study of Socialization in a Community of Catholic Sisters" (Diss. Univ. of Kentucky, 1967); Mary Brigid Fitzpatrick, "The Sister Social Worker: An Integration of Two Professional Roles" (Diss. Univ. of Notre Dame, 1962).

[14] Sarah Bentley Doely, *Women's Liberation and the Church* (New York: Association Press, 1970).

and *Women of the Church* by Mary Lawrence McKenna.[15] Culver makes a case for the importance of the sister's role when she says that "within these orders women have an unusually good opportunity to develop special talents for religion, administration, the arts and professions, though they may not have the temporal power some did in earlier ages" (221). *Women in Modern Life,* dealing with women in general, discusses sisters only in connection with a survey of priests' attitudes toward them and another survey of attitudes of young girls toward sisters (55–96). McKenna, too, concentrates on the general topic of women in the Church, only briefly discussing the role of sisters. She concludes that active religious today perform real functions but no longer belong to the Church's hierarchic structure, only to her "life and holiness." She sees the present position of women in the Church as less than it was in the primitive Church, although the status of women in society at large has supposedly been bettered. "What is lacking today is the status of ecclesiastical order, and the attendant sense of having a definite place and function in the Church's official structure" (147).

Two other books represent the 1960s in still another way. *The New Nuns* and *New Works for New Nuns*[16] were written at the height of the renewal in the Catholic Church, when sisters were asking what they should be doing to meet the needs of present-day society. The informal essays in *New Works* discuss the ways of reaching those who need help—in education, social justice, or any other form. *The New Nuns* (1967) consists of essays gleaned from the "Sisters' Forum" of the *National Catholic Reporter,* which surveyed the sisters' life as it was a decade ago and their growing involvement in new areas of work. Both are now dated, but they do reflect the development of thought that women religious went through to come to renewal in the Church and greater participation in society. A final publication to mention is *The Role of Women in Society and in the Church* (1975), the work of the Canadian Religious Conference. Basically this is an extended annotated bibliography on several themes dealing with women; some twelve pages are devoted to the life of sisters.

Probably the most valuable source of material regarding nuns and the women's movement is the periodical literature of the recent past. Increasingly, magazines devoted to sisters are featuring articles that deal specifi-

[15] Elsie T. Culver, *Women in the World of Religion* (Garden City: Doubleday, 1967); William Bier, S.J., *Women in Modern Life* (New York: Fordham Univ. Press, 1968); Mary Lawrence McKenna, S.C.M.M., *Women of the Church: Role and Renewal* (New York, 1967).

[16] Mary Charles Muckenhirn, O.S.C., *The New Nuns* (New York: New American Library, 1967); Mary Peter Traxler, S.S.N.D., *New Works for New Nuns* (Saint Louis: B. Herder, 1968).

cally with the movement in one form or another. *Sisters Today*, a popular journal devoted chiefly to their religious lives, occasionally publishes personal reflections, such as Evelyn Mattern's "Woman—Holy and Free," or informative pieces like Angelita Fenker's "Sisters Uniting," which explains the function of the organization of that name, formed in 1974 as a forum for exchange of information.[17]

Review for Religious deals with feminist issues more frequently, and while its articles do not always relate specifically to religious women the implications are clear enough. Judith Vollbrecht's "The Role of Women in Social Change"[18] is of special interest for its anthropological approach to American social structure. She suggests a more radical living of the vows professed, through which the sister might be a voice that bespeaks values not totally accepted by her society. An article with a contrasting point of view is Rose Marie Larkin's article on "Religious Women and the Meaning of the Feminine" in *Communio*.[19] Larkin believes that radical feminism has obscured the true feminine and that faith is the most important element in its restoration. Surrender and the veil symbolize the essence of womanhood, the secret wisdom which the woman is to use through compassion, love, and sharing and in this way fulfill her vocation. Larkin's very nineteenth-century definition could have little appeal for today's feminists, religious or nonreligious. The literature on sisters and the women's movement does not usually take such a conservative position, except for some of the articles on the issue of the ordination of women in the Catholic Church.

Another periodical that deserves mention is *Benedictines*, which presents articles on Benedictine history and spirituality, as well as reporting on recent efforts of these sisters to redirect their lives and work. A look through the index discovers no articles on nuns and the women's movement, yet the periodical itself attests to women's independence. That these women have published a magazine of high quality for 30 years with almost no support from the male sections of the Church indicates some degree of liberation. The *Church Woman* is another kind of magazine, published by Church Women United, an international ecumenical group

---

[17] Evelyn Mattern, I.H.M., "Women—Holy and Free," *Sisters Today*, 47 (May 1976), 553–57; Angelita Fenker, "Sisters Uniting," *ST*, 45 (Apr. 1974), 465–73.

[18] Judith Vollbrecht, R.S.C.J., "The Role of Women in Social Change," *Review for Religious*, 35 (Mar. 1976), 265–71. One also finds in the periodical press bibliographies more or less complete; the same issue of *Review for Religious* prints a list of 30 books and 100 periodicals dealing with "every phase of womanhood." Though less than exhaustive in any of these areas, it gives some idea of what is available, particularly in the popular Catholic press, and could be a starting point for some types of research.

[19] Rose Marie Larkin, "Religious Women and the Meaning of the Feminine," *Communio, An International Catholic Review*, 3 (Spring 1976), 67–89.

of women united in faith who work to effect better participation of women in society through social action. Their 1971 pamphlet by Joan O'Brien entitled *Goal in Common* deals with the relation between Church Women United and Roman Catholic sisters. The magazine publishes many articles on social justice, and discusses aspects of the women's movement in all churches.

Newer periodicals are *Probe* and *Origins*, both started in the early 1970s. *Origins* is published by the National Catholic News Service (Washington, D. C.), and though it deals with a larger spectrum of religious considerations, articles by sisters on the women's movement are included from time to time—for instance, "The Role of Women in the Church" (July 3, 1975) by Margaret Farley, and Margaret Brennan's "Women's Liberation/Men's Liberation" (July 17, 1975). Lora Quinonez addresses herself to "The Women's Movement and Women Religious," (November 21, 1974). In her view the feminist movement and the renewal of life for Catholic sisters reflect some of the same concerns: for personal maturity, new ministries in the Church, and a new vision of celibacy. She says in conclusion: "I see affinities between our search and that of other women—a desire to experience ourselves and to be experienced as persons, not as symbols or mythic figures. . . ." *Probe* is the official magazine of the National Assembly of Women Religious (NAWR). This too deals largely with the social concerns of sisters in their work, but also from time to time publishes articles on feminism as it affects their lives.

Almost any of the general Catholic magazines carries articles on women's issues, women in the Church, and sisters in particular. These vary in depth and scholarship, the differences more often than not determined by the type of readership. One of the best has been the December 1975 issue of *Theological Studies*, devoted to women and religion. Though this is not confined to women religious, it presents some excellent scholarly essays by some of today's most prominent Catholic sisters. Particularly valuable is the bibliographical article on "Women and Religion: A Survey of Significant Literature, 1965-1974" by Anne E. Patrick, which includes books on historical analysis and works on selected issues such as canon law, ministry, and ordination, as well as some publications on constructive efforts and radical challenges. This is an insightful essay which makes a real contribution toward further research.[20]

Any discussion of sisters and the women's movement must include the issue of women's ordination, the debate over proposals that they be admitted into the traditionally male role of priest. Literature on this issue

---

[20] Anne E. Patrick, S.N.J.M., "Women and Religion: A Survey of Significant Literature, 1965-1974," *Theological Studies,* 36 (Dec. 1975), 737-65.

has been so abundant in the past few years that it is impossible to do justice even to part of it in this essay. At the conference on the ordination of women held in Detroit in November 1975, some of the speakers were among the most distinguished sisters in the country, who have written much on the issue of women in the Church. The meeting made available an eight-page bibliography, compiled by Donna Westly, of works since 1965 on the ordination of women. Related to this is the bibliography on women and ministry published in *Origins* in May 1972. The work of this initial conference was continued through an organized group, the Women's Ordination Conference, which held a second meeting in November 1978. Some 2,000 women and men attended from forty-three states and thirteen foreign countries. Following the conference a delegation of women proceeded to Washington, D. C. to attempt the beginnings of dialogue with the Bishops at their annual meeting. Since December 1976, WOC has sponsored a *Newsletter* which keeps interested parties abreast of developments, alerts them to needs for action, and informs them of happenings elsewhere. The objective of WOC is not simply the ordination of women in the traditional priest role. Rather it seeks to "explore how priesthood should and could be transformed in the twentieth century and how the ministry-style of women will help bring that about" (*Newsletter*, June 1978). Anyone interested in this aspect of sisters and the women's movement should contact this group, whose headquarters are in Rochester, New York.[21]

Finally we call attention to a production of a very different type, "Women of Promise," by Kay Schwerzler and Joyce Fey. This is a slide presentation available through the Leadership Conference of Women Religious which deals with sisters and the women's movement. It celebrates the great figures such as Frances Xavier Cabrini, Philippine Duchesne, and Elizabeth Seton, as well as the many nameless sisters who risked their lives caring for the sick and homeless and who "invented, administered, planned . . . who did 'men's' work without waiting to be permitted." The style of this presentation is visual and poetic; its scholarly base is inconspicuous. Most of the research was done in the Church History collection at the University of Notre Dame, a source which no researcher should overlook.[22]

[21] Women's Ordination Conference, 34 Monica Street, Rochester, N. Y. 14619.

[22] Because of the number and quality of manuscript collections housed in its University Archives, Notre Dame ranks second in importance to Baltimore as a research center for American Catholic history. The collection includes the early papers of the Archdioceses of Cincinnati, Detroit, Indianapolis, and New Orleans, as well as the personal papers of a number of leading Catholic laymen, and is well indexed and calendared. See Ellis, *Guide*, for descriptions of other depositories in the United States, 7–12.

Anyone seriously considering research in the areas discussed in this essay should contact some of the key organizations of sisters. Two are especially prominent. The Leadership Conference of Women Religious (LCWR) with headquarters in Washington, D. C. represents mostly those sisters who hold administrative positions in their congregations. More of a grass roots organization of the rank and file is the National Assembly of Women Religious, publishers of *Probe*. From its headquarters in Chicago, NAWR attempts to mobilize sisters for service to their Church and nation. Many of the religious active in these organizations are among the most competent and knowledgeable women leaders in the country and would be helpful to the researcher. Other organizations that could be contacted are the Black Sisters Conference, whose publication is *Signs of Soul*, and the National Coalition of American Nuns.[23]

*A*nyone interested in studying women and religion should find a rich mine in the American Catholic sisters, a group large and homogeneous enough to permit research to be carried on with some facility and valid conclusions to be drawn. It is well to remember in dealing with religious women of any faith that, if indeed they are interested in the women's movement, they also have another motivating force, namely their religious commitment. Also, in the natural order, their lives are probably less immediately dominated by men, although they too ultimately are subjected to some of the same discrimination suffered by other women. The following are some suggested areas for research.

1) One of the first that could be explored is the pioneer or founding experience. Just as colonial women performed many tasks and carried on businesses from sheer force of necessity, so did Catholic religious women in setting up their congregations and institutions. Most of these foundations were made in the nineteenth century, yet these women were apparently oblivious to concepts of "the Victorian lady" and "the cult of domesticity.". With or without the support of men of the Church, they did what needed to be done. As mentioned above, many of these stories are separately recorded but the Catholic woman religious as a type has not been studied. The question might well be asked how free were these women to determine their own existence and policy. Staffing hospitals, schools, colleges, asylums for children, and other kinds of institutions gave them a certain degree of autonomy; still we know that they often encountered difficulties in their relationships with Church authorities.

[23] Further information (addresses, officers, etc.) is available in the current issue of *The Catholic Almanac*.

2) Certainly an extension of Mary Ewens' work would be of value—to ascertain attitudes towards sisters in the twentieth century through experience and interviews with sisters and through the serious and popular literature of the times.

3) If the Roman Catholic girl always had the choice of a career in religion, does this explain why Catholic women were not attracted to the women's movement, especially in the nineteenth century? In a day when women were expected to marry, the life of the sister possibly constituted an appealing, respectable alternative. We know that, in the mid-twentieth century, many of the college presidents who were women were Catholic sisters. This seems to indicate that sisters enjoyed a freedom of movement, self-determination if you will, that other women did not have at that time.

4) Looking back a bit, and outside the confines of the United States, one might test McKenna's thesis that because the sister lacks an ecclesiastical order in the Church the status of women now is probably lower than it was in the early Church. Did religious life for women evolve in order to give those interested in working in the Church some kind of "status," but a status which at the same time removed them from such an official position as deaconess? In developing societies women frequently have roles that are later denied them when the society becomes more complex. Did this happen in the early Church, that once the primitive period passed and Church structure became more complex, the official position of deaconess was abandoned and women were relegated, so to speak, to the "life and holiness of the Church" (McKenna, 147)? Or in other words, were they given some "status" as sisters but, lacking an ecclesiastical order, no power of determining policy or making decisions?

5) It would also be interesting to ascertain what forces in the 1960s really brought about the change in the lives of sisters. Vatican II and the women's movement converged at some point, yet one wonders just how the motivating forces worked for individual sisters.[24] Accompanying this inquiry should be an assessment of attitudes towards feminism, not only the leaders' attitudes, but also those of the rank and file.

These topics and others could make a significant contribution not only to the religious history of the United States but to our knowledge of women and their roles in American society. The source material is available and abundant, a ready field for the interested researcher.

---

[24] This question is partially pursued in the Fitzpatrick dissertation noted above, in which she concludes that the role of the religious takes first place in the hierarchy of role obligations. Conflict is solved by making decisions in favor of the religious role. If an integration of the two is achieved, she says (as in this case, social work), a redefinition of the role of religion to include the occupational role is necessary.

Mary J. Oates

Organized Voluntarism
The Catholic Sisters in Massachusetts, 1870–1940

The labor force which historically has staffed most charitable and educational institutions of the Catholic Church in the United States has come from religious communities of women. Yet the sisters' role has rarely been studied. Literature dealing with them has ranged from anti-Catholic tracts of the nineteenth and early twentieth centuries to community histories and biographies of foundresses. Both have tended to reinforce the view of sisters as socially peripheral women, aloof from society, its needs and concerns.[1]

Official Catholic publications, while recording the activities and accomplishments of churchmen, have neglected full-time female church workers. For example, priests were enumerated by name, location, and work in every issue of the *Official Catholic Directory* over 1870–1940. In the case of sisters, the directory provided the name of the superior of the local convent and usually the number of sisters. Church histories remain

[1] See, for example, Maria Monk, *Awful Disclosures of Maria Monk* (New York: D.M. Bennett, 1878, originally written in 1836); Theodore Dwight, *Open Convents* (New York: Van Nostrand and Dwight, 1836); Edith O'Gorman, *Trials and Persecutions of Miss Edith O'Gorman* (Hartford: Connecticut Publishing, 1881); and Ford Hendrickson, *The "Black Convent" Slave or Nunnery Life Unveiled* (Toledo: Protestant Missionary Publishing, 1914); A Sister of St. Joseph, *Just Passing Through, 1873–1943* (Boston: The Sisters of St. Joseph, 1943); Sister Helen Nugent, *Sister Louise: American Foundress of the Sisters of Notre Dame* (Washington: Catholic Univ. of America Studies in American Church History, Vol. 10, Diss. 1931); and *Memoir of Rev. Mother Mary Teresa Comerford* (San Francisco: P.J. Thomas, 1882).

oriented toward the decisions of hierarchy and clergy.[2] Fortunately communities of women have preserved documents and annals of their members and work, although the quality and completeness of these records vary. This archival material, together with directory data and scattered contemporary sources, allows us to investigate the experience of the sisters in Massachusetts.

Though similar to that of their counterparts in other states, this experience is uniquely grounded in the history of the church in Boston. The Catholic Church remained a central social as well as religious institution in the lives of Massachusetts citizens between 1870 and 1940. In 1870, the diocese of Boston encompassed the state of Massachusetts. By 1880 and throughout the rest of the period, it included the counties of Essex, Middlesex, Suffolk, Norfolk, and Plymouth, with the exception of the towns of Mattapoisett, Marion, and Wareham. Our discussion of Massachusetts in this paper deals, unless otherwise noted, with the archdiocese of Boston. Although tensions between Irish Catholics and native New Englanders had eased in the years following the Civil War, they never disappeared, and church organizations served as supportive and unifying forces for a working-class population.[3]

*A*lthough in 1870 fewer Catholic women than men engaged in full-time church work in Massachusetts, the picture changed over succeeding decades. Table 1 indicates the extent of this change. By 1890 there were almost twice as many women as men, and in the twentieth century the female/male ratio climbed even higher, so that by 1940 more than two-thirds of church workers were women. (Included in the male totals are diocesan seminary students who, strictly speaking, were not actively engaged in church work; novices in religious communities of sisters in this era, on the other hand, were frequently working full-time.) This change in proportions is peculiar. Other things equal, one might expect the propensity for church service to be similar for both sexes. Or, if the higher prestige attached to church work for men is considered, the totals might be higher for them. If, as some have suggested, women's early socialization leads to their being more attracted than men to church work, it is difficult

---

[2] The most complete history of the Catholic church in Boston is a good example: Robert H. Lord, John E. Sexton, and Edward T. Harrington, *History of the Archdiocese of Boston, in the Various Stages of its Development, 1604 to 1943*, 3 vols. (New York: Sheed and Ward, 1944).

[3] Oscar Handlin, *Boston's Immigrants* (New York: Atheneum, 1968), 215–16; Barbara Miller Solomon, *Ancestors and Immigrants: A Changing New England Tradition* (Chicago: Univ. of Chicago Press, 1972).

to account for the near parity in numbers of men and women church workers before 1890.

Religious brothers (members of religious communities, but not ordained priests) never accounted for even one-fifth of churchmen throughout the period, and for the most part they taught boys in parochial schools and private academies. Most men belonged to the diocesan clergy and engaged in pastoral work in local parishes. Priests who belonged to religious orders taught men and boys, conducted retreats and missions, and assisted in parish work. Although an expanding Catholic population stimulated demand for more men to serve growing needs, the nature of the work they were expected to accomplish remained the same. In this sense the growth rate of male church workers may be considered natural. The difference between male and female growth rates suggests the presence of exogenous factors which affected the supply of women workers differently.

In 1870 Massachusetts sisters worked in the traditionally female professions, but within this category there was diversity: teaching, nursing, or

Table 1. DISTRIBUTION OF FULL-TIME CATHOLIC CHURCH WORKERS, BY OCCUPATION AND SEX, ARCHDIOCESE OF BOSTON, 1870–1940

A.   Members of Religious Communities of Women

Year	Hospital Work[a] (%)	Social Work[b] (%)	Academies and Boarding Schools[c] (%)	Parochial Schools[d] (%)	Other Work[e] (%)	Total Number of Sisters[f]	Female/ Male Ratio
1870	12.2	24.4	11.3	46.2	5.9	221	0.80
1880	10.0	28.4	4.9	42.4	14.3	370	1.19
1890	5.0	17.3	4.5	53.0	20.3	942	1.99
1900	5.1	14.0	6.2	54.7	20.0	1,457	1.98
1910	4.4	15.2	6.8	55.3	18.2	1,699	1.85
1920	4.0	11.6	7.8	59.6	16.9	2,649	2.48
1930	2.8	9.3	6.5	63.6	17.7	3,605	2.21
1940	3.1	9.2	8.2	62.6	16.9	4,164	2.16

[a] Nursing and administrative work.
[b] With women, orphans, the elderly, the handicapped, the poor in asylums and homes.
[c] Teaching and support services.
[d] Teaching and support services.
[e] This column includes sisters whose work is unspecified. Such work would include community administration, housekeeping, cooking, laundry work. Novices, postulants, sick and retired sisters who are not engaged in full-time work are included here. Also included are cloistered nuns, sisters in retreat work, missionaries.
[f] Includes professed sisters, novices, and postulants.

Table 1. Continued.

B. Members of Diocesan Clergy and Religious Communities of Men

Year	Religious Brothers[g] (%)	Religious Order Priests[h] (%)	Diocesan Priests and Clerical Students[i] (%)	Total Number of Churchmen
1870	none listed	n.a.[j]	n.a.[j]	278
1880	3.2	n.a.[j]	n.a.[j]	312
1890	9.1	14.8	76.1	473
1900	17.5	14.1	68.4	737
1910	17.0	14.9	68.1	918
1920	13.8	15.7	70.5	1,069
1930	16.8	23.3	59.9	1,628
1940	18.1	26.4	55.6	1,932

[g] Taught boys in parochial schools and tuition-charging boys' high schools. Did some orphanage work. Figures include novices and postulants.

[h] Taught men in colleges and boys in tuition-charging high schools. Gave missions and retreats. Did some pastoral work in parishes.

[i] Engaged in or preparing for pastoral work in diocesan parishes mainly.

[j] In 1870 and 1880, religious order priests and diocesan priests were not listed separately.

Sources: Compiled from data in *Official Catholic Directories: Sadliers' Catholic Directory, Almanac and Ordo, 1870* (New York: Sadlier, 1870); *Sadliers' Catholic Directory, 1880* (New York: D. & J. Sadlier, 1880); *Sadliers' Catholic Directory, Almanac and Ordo, 1890* (New York: D. &. J. Sadlier, 1890); *Official Directory, The Catholic Directory, Almanac and Clergy List, 1910* (n.p.: M.H. Wiltzius, 1910); *The Official Catholic Directory* (New York: P.J. Kenedy, 1920); *The Official Catholic Directory* (New York: P.J. Kenedy, 1930); *The Official Catholic Directory* (New York: P.J. Kenedy, 1940). An appendix discussing the Directory data is available upon request from the author.

social work with the poor, the handicapped, the elderly, or orphans. After 1880 (see Table 1) this variation disappeared as sisters moved into education, particularly into parochial school teaching. The parochial school, an elementary or high school owned and operated by an individual parish, was financed from general parish revenues and was "free" in the sense that students were charged no tuition. By 1940 two-thirds of all sisters in Boston were found in parochial schools. While in 1880 nearly 40 percent of all sisters undertook hospital and social work, by 1940 only 12 percent were found in these occupations. Instead of expanding, women's options narrowed.

Since women's communities specialized in a single occupation, it is unlikely that much of the increase of sisters in parochial schools can be accounted for by direct shifts of personnel out of nonteaching occupations into schools. Over the period, Catholic services expanded in all the areas in which sisters were involved. Table 2 indicates the growth by area in the number of institutions in which sisters worked. The number of sisters per thousand Catholics in the archdiocese increased more than six-fold over the 70-year period, allowing the sisters to staff these many institutions. Evidently the service which sisters elected to provide to the Catholic population was the education of their children in parochial schools. The growing numbers of young women interested in convent life selected the teaching orders.

The major explanation for this shift in sisters' occupational tastes is that after 1880 the development of a system of parochial schools was defined as the "critical need" of the church in Massachusetts. Young women entering church service were encouraged to join teaching communities in order to meet this need. These communities grew rapidly, and were remarkably youthful. Of the 536 living members of one diocesan teaching community in 1919, for example, more than 60 percent had not yet made perpetual vows. Most of these sisters would be well under 30 years of

Table 2. NUMBER OF INSTITUTIONS STAFFED WHOLLY OR IN PART BY SISTERS, 1870–1940, ARCHDIOCESE OF BOSTON

Year	Hospitals	Asylums and Homes	Academies, Boarding Schools and Colleges	Parochial Schools[a]	Sisters in All Activities Per 1000 Catholic Population[b]
1870	4	6	4	11	0.63
1880	3	9	3	15	1.19
1890	3	12	5	45	1.84
1900	4	17	8	59	2.39
1910	4	17	8	80	1.89
1920	5	21	11	108	2.75[b]
1930	5	25	17	142	3.54
1940	6	27	18	155	3.99

[a] If a parish school had high school as well as elementary grades, and sisters served in both, this was counted as one school.

[b] Catholic population for 1920 was arrived at by interpolation between 1910 and 1930 since the figure provided was based upon a 1909 census.

Sources: Official Catholic Directories, 1870–1940. The estimates for total Catholic population are not precise and are useful only to indicate a trend over time.

age.[4] Although communities outside Massachusetts were recruited for faculty (Canadian sisters were often invited to teach in parish schools in factory towns with French-speaking populations), the two major teaching groups, the Sisters of Notre Dame de Namur and the Sisters of St. Joseph, drew their members for the most part from the local population.

By 1870 parochial schools had become characteristic of many dioceses, but not in Massachusetts. In 1873, for example, 68 percent of parishes in the archdiocese of New York had schools attached; as late as 1900, the corresponding figure for the archdiocese of Boston was only 42 percent. In that year Boston ranked seventeenth among 20 chief dioceses in the country in this regard, only Portland, San Francisco, and Springfield ranking lower, although Boston was the third largest diocese in the nation.[5]

The concept of a large school system was never popular with Archbishop John J. Williams, leader of the Boston church from 1866 to 1907. Once a public school student himself, he was unconvinced of the need for separate schools for Catholic children. If parish priest and people proposed to build a school, he approved, but unlike many of his fellow bishops, he did not promote a school network. When questioned by Rome about the Boston school situation, Williams was casual in his reply. His 1879 report noted that "the schools are public. . . . Even in the smallest town they are set up according to law, and . . . this is defended as doing nothing contrary to the children's religion."[6] Not all his priests agreed with Williams' position, and the school issue occasioned some divisiveness within the diocese.[7]

In 1884 the situation changed. The Third Plenary Council of Baltimore, composed of the hierarchy of the United States, commanded that parochial school systems be developed in every diocese in the country. Increasing numbers of parish priests, viewing the schools as means of strengthening parish loyalties as well as the religious beliefs of the children, moved to comply. The decree was uncompromising:

We must multiply them, till every child in the land shall have the means of education within its reach. . . . No parish is complete till it has schools adequate to the needs of its children, and the pastor and people of such a parish should

[4] Archives, Sisters of St. Joseph, Brighton, Mass., *Motherhouse Annals*, Aug. 10, 1919.

[5] Jay P. Dolan, *The Immigrant Church* (Baltimore: Johns Hopkins Univ. Press, 1975), Table 3, 106; and Louis S. Walsh, *Historical Sketch of the Growth of Catholic Parochial Schools in the Archdiocese of Boston* (Newton: St. John's Industrial School, 1901), Appendix 6. It should be noted that parochial schools were rarely large enough to accommodate all the parish children.

[6] *Special Report of the Diocese to the Office of the Propaganda*, Jan. 11, 1879, in answer to a letter of June 1878. Cited by Donna Merwick, *Boston Priests, 1848–1910* (Cambridge: Harvard Univ. Press, 1973), 102.

[7] Merwick, *Boston Priests*, 111–16.

feel that they have not accomplished their entire duty until the want is supplied.[8]

Unlike John Williams, William O'Connell, who succeeded him in 1908 and led the diocese until his death in 1944, was a strong proponent of a school system. Throughout his career he espoused Catholic separatism, and the schools served as important means to this end. ". . .'Distinct Catholic lives'. . . were to be formed by strict rules of behavior, Catholic ideals, Catholic history and Catholic institutions."[9]

The decree of the Council of Baltimore brought about not only rapid construction of schools in Massachusetts, but also a demand for a teaching force. Sisters rather than priests, brothers, or laypersons became the group in demand. Their response was most evident in the increase in their numbers and in the slower expansion of their work in other areas, but the rise in demand for teachers had other effects on women. After 1884 the history of the Massachusetts sisters became linked to that of the parochial schools.

*T*he recruitment of female labor can be understood only in the context of the roles defined by church and society as acceptable for women. To have sisters for the schools, increasing numbers had to view membership in a religious community as a desirable lifestyle, and teaching as an attractive career. Throughout the period under study, long-term careers for women were the exception rather than the norm; their options remained centered around marriage and family. Liberal Catholic writers and intellectuals frequently argued for a wider choice, but official spokesmen did not.[10] Sermons, press editorials, and literature were consistent. In 1928 the leader of the Boston church stated unequivocally that "the home is woman's normal sphere—maidenhood, wifehood, motherhood and home. . . ." Such passive "virtues" as self-effacement and submission to authority he viewed as peculiarly female. "You must put yourselves in the background. . . . That is precisely the discipline which women even more than men need every day."[11] Ambition was not encouraged, and

---

[8] Pastoral Letter, Third Plenary Council of Baltimore, 1884. Cited in Patrick J. McCormick, "Church Law on Certification of Catholic Teachers," *Catholic Educational Review*, 20 (May 1922), 258. The decree itself (Decree 199) is cited on pp. 260–61.

[9] Merwick, *Boston Priests*, 183.

[10] Mary A. Dowd, "The Public Rights of Women," *Catholic World*, 59 (June 1894), 312–20.

[11] *Sermons and Addresses of His Eminence William Cardinal O'Connell* (Boston: Pilot Publishing, 1931), Vol. 10:226, and Vol. 5:126.

feminists advocating careers, independence, and equality for women were looked upon with suspicion and apprehension.

> And if, after graduating with highest honors, she insists on keeping up her study of—well, let us say astronomy, we doubt not but the telescope will not bother her husband half as much as it will the baby on her lap; and we venture to predict that she will find more delight in its twinkling eyes than in all the planets of the solar system.[12]

A 1910 survey found that nearly two-thirds (64 percent) of all females in Boston ten years of age and over were not employed. This figure does not include the 2 percent who were still enrolled in school. Only 34 percent were wage earners. Single women were in the labor force in this period but usually left it at marriage, and the average woman's working experience outside the home was short. The majority of Boston women were housewives, precluded from working outside their homes except in cases of necessity. Of females who were gainfully employed, 38 percent were engaged in domestic and personal service, work similar to that done in the home. Clerking in stores and office work occupied another 28 percent and factory work 24 percent. Only 9 percent were to be found in the professions. Within this category, teaching and nursing ranked first and second, accounting for 4 percent and 2 percent respectively of all employed women. The professions of women were fewer and less varied than those of Boston men.[13] Teaching had long provided attractive and accessible employment to women; a study of the period before 1860 found that 20 percent of Massachusetts women had been teachers at some time in their lives, even though in any given year the schools employed less than 2 percent of women in the 15–60 age bracket.[14]

Working-class or poor women had little prospect of acquiring the specialized training needed for most professions. Even the more accessible ones, such as teaching and nursing, may have appeared costly if the working life was expected to be but a few years before marriage. In 1920, 85 percent of American public school teachers were women and most of

---

[12] William Seton, "The Higher Education of Woman and Posterity," *Catholic World*, 73 (Apr. 1901), 149.

[13] Document No. 87, *Report of A Study of Certain Phases of the Public School System of Boston, Mass.* (Boston Finance Commission, 1916), from Table 2, 129, Table 3, 130–31, and Table 7, 137–38.

[14] Richard M. Bernard and Maris A. Vinovskis, "The Female School Teacher in Ante-Bellum Massachusetts," *Journal of Social History*, 10 (Spring 1977), 333.

them were single. This was hardly surprising, given the regulations concerning the hiring of married women. In Boston, the regulation read:

> The marriage of a woman teacher shall operate as a resignation of her position, and it shall be the duty of the principals to report the marriages of such teachers forthwith to the business agent, who shall remove the names of such teachers from the payrolls from the date of marriage. . . .[15]

The same regulation applied to school nurses.

For a number of Catholic women wishing to undertake socially important and professional work, a life of church service as a member of a religious community appeared at least competitive with its major alternative. Such a choice was socially acceptable; the sisters, drawn from and serving the Catholic population, were held in high regard. ". . . Woman was created to be a wife and mother; that is, after a special religious calling to the service of God."[16] Bound by vows of poverty, celibacy, and obedience, they were expected to epitomize the womanly virtues and to serve the church with little concern for recompense. We have seen that increasingly larger numbers of women than men undertook church work in the archdiocese of Boston between 1870 and 1940. Austere though convent life appeared, the prospect of banding together with other women to respond to pressing needs appealed to youthful idealism. The community would train the young woman for her life's work, and she could choose among a number of professions, expressing her preference through her selection of an order. Where several communities specialized in the same work, the choice was based on other distinguishing features, such as the order's rules and ethnic composition. (Cloistered life, where no social work was undertaken, was never popular. The first convent of cloistered nuns in the diocese was not established until 1890. In 1900, cloistered nuns accounted for only 1.2 percent of all sisters. By 1940, this figure had risen to 2.7 percent.) An observer commenting in the 1890s that "there is no observable drift of Catholic women to celibate professional careers . . ."[17] was overlooking the women in religious communities.

---

[15] School Document No. 11, 1910, *Rules of the School Committee and Regulations of the Public Schools of the City of Boston, 1910,* 62; David S. Tyack, "Pilgrim's Progress: Toward a Social History of the School Superintendency, 1860–1960," *History of Education Quarterly,* 16 (Fall 1976), 264.

[16] John Paul MacCorrie, "The War of the Sexes," *Catholic World,* 63 (Aug. 1896), 614.

[17] Katherine E. Conway, "Woman Has No Vocation to Public Life," *Catholic World,* 57 (Aug. 1893), 683.

It is often assumed that parents enrolled their sons as often as their daughters in the parochial schools, since this was true in public schools. Such was not the case in Massachusetts. Only in the later years of the period did the number of boys enrolled approach that of girls. In 1870 just two of every ten students were boys, and the ratio was slow to change.[18] (See Table 3.)

Table 3.

A. ENROLLMENT OF GIRLS IN PAROCHIAL SCHOOLS, 1870–1940

Year	Percent of Girls in Total Parochial School Enrollment	Total School Population
1870	79.9	6,110
1880	79.3	9,478
1890	65.6	24,966
1900	59.3	37,543
1910	56.4	51,237
1920	54.9	73,133
1930	53.1	95,346
1940	52.4	93,569

Source: Compiled from data in *Official Catholic Directories,* 1870–1940.

B. ENROLLMENT OF GIRLS BY GRADE LEVEL
IN PAROCHIAL SCHOOLS, 1900

Grade Level	Percent of Girls in Grade Enrollment
Ungraded[a]	52.8
Kindergarten	57.1
Primary (Grades 1-4)	56.0
Grammar (Grades 5-9)	59.0
High (Grades 10-12)	83.4

[a] These were students of several grade levels taught in one class by one teacher. See *Catholic Educational Review*, 1 (Mar. 1911), 266.
Source: Louis S. Walsh, *Historical Sketch of the Growth of the Catholic Schools in the Archdiocese of Boston* (Newton: St. John's Industrial School, 1901), Appendix 11. Data are for school year 1899–1900.

[18] Thernstrom, for example, in a study dealing exclusively with the social mobility of men, remarks that "large numbers of Boston's Irish and Italian Catholics attended parochial schools" and speculates that these schools may have ". . . muted rather than heightened aspirations and fostered a sense of alienation from the larger society." Stephan Thernstrom, *The Other Bostonians* (Cambridge: Harvard Univ. Press, 1973), 174. But Catholic girls were more affected by the schools than their brothers, and conclusions about parochial schools should be qualified by consideration of their sex composition.

One might suspect that the different proportions meant that boys left school earlier to take jobs. Since young girls had fewer work opportunities, they could stay in school longer. We can test this hypothesis for the year 1900. At that date, approximately three of every five parochial school children were girls. This contrasts with the enrollment figures for Boston public schools in 1902, where boys comprised 51 percent.[19] If boys were leaving parochial schools more often than girls, we should observe similar proportions in kindergarten and primary grades, and a lower representation of boys at the grammar and high school levels. Table 3 shows the percentages of girl students by grade level in 1900. High school enrollments were heavily female, but fewer than two percent of all parochial school children were found in these grades. In both kindergarten and primary grades, the proportion of girls is above 50 percent, and the enrollment of boys in grammar grades is not notably lower than that in kindergartens. If boys were not leaving school earlier, we must conclude that parents were enrolling daughters more often than sons in these schools.

During the nineteenth century, Massachusetts sisters were identified with the education of girls. A large number of parochial schools in the state were staffed by a single community, the Sisters of Notre Dame de Namur, whose work was the education of girls and whose rule forbade the teaching of boys. In 1872 "there were thirteen Catholic Parochial Schools [in the Boston diocese] eleven for girls. . . . The Sisters of Notre Dame . . . did not wish to teach the larger boys."[20] If a parish were to undertake the education of boys, additional costs could be expected since brothers or laypersons had to be found to instruct them. A number of parishes did open boys' schools, but these were usually opened latest and closed first if costs proved prohibitive. In a Chicopee parish, for example, the Christian Brothers were dismissed after 25 years of teaching in the school ". . . as the expense of two communities was too heavy on our little parish. . . ."[21] In public school systems, separate schools for girls and boys were not uncommon; of 23 Boston grammar schools in 1866, nine were solely for boys and eight for girls.[22] The problem peculiar to the parochial schools at this time was that, unlike women teachers in public schools, the sisters available to teach would not instruct boys.

---

[19] School Document No. 14, *Annual Report of the School Committee of the City of Boston, 1903*, 4.

[20] Walsh, *Historical Sketch*, 3–4.

[21] A Member of the Congregation, *The American Foundations of the Sisters of Notre Dame de Namur, Compiled from the Annals of Their Convents* (Philadelphia: Dolphin, 1928), 363.

[22] *General Regulations of the Public Schools*, Boston, Jan. 1869, 61.

Two changes brought about the greater enrollment of boys in the Catholic schools of the twentieth century. The Sisters of Notre Dame, in response to pressure, agreed by the 1880s to teach boys through the second grade, or up to about age eight.[23] This concession alleviated the problem somewhat. In 1873, however, an economy-minded pastor, eager to enroll both boys and girls in his school in Jamaica Plain, had invited Sisters of St. Joseph from Brooklyn, New York, to staff it. The rule of this community did not prohibit the teaching of boys at any grade level, and the Jamaica Plain school became the first in New England to have both boys and girls taught by sisters through the elementary grades. Nevertheless, since there was then no pressure to enroll every child in a parochial school, parishes often maintained schools for girls if sisters were available to teach them, while the boys attended public schools.

It was not until the school campaign of the 1880s and 1890s that the Sisters of St. Joseph, by then the diocesan teaching community, became important. Since the Council of Baltimore had mandated schools for every child, the education of boys had to be undertaken, but the supply of brothers for teaching was dwindling. Young men were being encouraged to become priests in order to do that work in the church which only men could do. The status of the priest was high in the Catholic community, whereas the teaching of young children had come to be viewed as "women's work."[24] Brothers moved toward teaching in private high schools for boys which, unlike the parish schools, were under their control. The education of young men and boys had higher status than elementary school teaching and was considered more appropriate work for brothers. Teaching the young children, both boys and girls, became the work of women, a trend paralleling developments in the local public schools half a century earlier.[25] For the most part the sisters worked under the supervision of pastors and bishops.

In this period the parochial schools were distinctive in their heavier enrollments of younger children. Table 4 compares them with public schools in Boston and suburban Brookline by grade levels. Since new school openings may have biased parochial enrollments toward lower grades, eight schools opened between 1895 and 1900 are omitted. Fifty-seven percent of public school students in both systems were enrolled in grammar and high school grades, in contrast to only 44 percent of parochial school students registered at these levels.

---

[23] Nugent, *Sister Louise*, 193.

[24] For the school year 1866–67, 90 percent of regular teachers in all Boston public schools were women (*Annual Report of the School Committee of the City of Boston, 1867*, 301).

[25] Bernard and Vinovskis, "Female School Teacher," 337.

The Sisters of Notre Dame, who held to their work of teaching girls and young boys, were replaced in a number of schools by more flexible communities. By the 1920s these sisters had agreed to teach boys through the elementary grades, but by then the question had become their willingness to teach high school boys. A coeducational high school was opened in St. Mary's Parish in Brookline in 1924, staffed by the Sisters of St. Joseph. At the same time, this community replaced the Sisters of Notre Dame in the elementary school where they had taught for many years.[26] The parish thereby avoided the need to provide separate residences. The Sisters of

Table 4. DISTRIBUTION OF STUDENTS BY GRADE LEVELS: PAROCHIAL SCHOOLS, 1900, BROOKLINE PUBLIC SCHOOLS, 1900, AND BOSTON PUBLIC SCHOOLS, 1903

Grade Levels	Brookline Public Schools 1899–1900 (%)	Parochial Schools 1899–1900 (%)
Ungraded[a]	—	3.0
High School (grades 10–12)	10.6	1.7
Kindergarten	10.7	7.2
Primary (grades 1–3)	32.5	46.3
Grammar (grades 4–9)	46.1	41.8

Grade Levels	Boston Public Schools Jan. 1, 1903 (%)	Parochial Schools 1899–1900 (%)
Ungraded[a]	—	3.0
High School (grades 9–12)	7.6	5.1
Kindergarten	5.6	7.2
Primary (grades 1–3)	37.5	46.3
Grammar (grades 4–8)	49.4	38.4

[a] See note (a), Table 3.

Sources: The School Committee, *Educational Survey of the Public Schools of Brookline, Mass., 1917,* from Table 1, 177; *Superintendent's Report, Documents of the School Committee of the City of Boston, 1903* (Boston: Municipal Printing Office, 1903), 130; and Louis S. Walsh, *Historical Sketch of the Growth of the Catholic Schools in the Archdiocese of Boston* (Newton: St. John's Industrial School, 1901), Appendix I.

[26] Sister Juliana O'Hara, *Educational Contribution of the Sisters of St. Joseph in the Archdiocese of Boston from 1873 to 1939* (Masters thesis, Catholic Univ. of America, 1941), 61–62.

St. Joseph, responsible by their rule to the Bishop of Boston, now became the major community in the system. Even though 17 different communities of women had been represented in the system as early as 1900, the Sisters of Notre Dame and Sisters of St. Joseph were the dominant groups, nearly half of all sisters then being members of one of these communities. Because of their size, their experience was typical of sisterhoods employed in Massachusetts.

In maintaining a parochial school system financed by working class parishes the cost of teaching services was paramount. In local public schools in late nineteenth- and early twentieth-century Massachusetts, instructional expenses averaged 60 percent of annual school expenditures.[27] Paying a faculty at public school scales was out of the question, and the teaching communities of men and women were identified as an attractive source of low cost labor. These groups were willing to subsidize the schools by contributing their services, receiving only a salary for living expenses. Soon sisters were sought in preference to brothers since their salary levels were lower.

As in the public schools, reimbursing women less than men for the same work appears to have been a long-standing practice. This was so despite the fact that male and female religious workers were equally bound by the vow of poverty and benefited similarly from any efficiencies resulting from communal living. And, unlike many women teaching in public schools, sisters worked full-time in the schools until retirement. Yet the salaries paid brothers to meet their living expenses were roughly double those paid sisters. Maintenance of differentials approaching 100 percent in payments for the same work was justified by the argument that women "could live more cheaply and consequently with a lower salary" since "the living expenses of women are not so high as those of men. . . ."[28] The fact that no effort was made to reduce the total wage bill by paying brothers the same salaries offered sisters, thus retaining their services in the schools, indicates acceptance of the claim that men and women faced different expenses.

Actual salaries paid sisters for full-time work over the 1870–1940 period varied little over time, location, or occupation. A comparison of the sis-

---

[27] Charles Phillips Huse, *The Financial History of Boston, 1822–1909* (Cambridge: Harvard Univ. Press, 1916), Appendix 1, 365; and School Document No. 1, 1920, *Annual Report for the Financial Year Ending January 31, 1920,* School Committee of the City of Boston, 60–61.

[28] J. A. Burns, *The Growth and Development of the Catholic School System in the United States* (New York: Benziger Bros., 1912), 23, 100, 282.

ter's salary with the salary of the woman teaching in a Boston public school can be made by examining Tables 5 and 6. Public school salaries were not adjusted annually. In fact, they were practically unchanged between 1866 and 1877 and between 1889 and 1896. Adjustments, when made, were not always favorable to the teachers. In 1877, for example,

Table 5. MAXIMUM ANNUAL SALARIES OF WOMEN TEACHERS IN PUBLIC ELEMENTARY SCHOOLS, BOSTON, MASSACHUSETTS, SELECTED YEARS, 1867–1919

Year	Salaries of Regular Teachers[a]	Salaries after Adjusting for Cost of Living (1913 = 100)[f]
1867	$ 650	$ 628
1873	800[b]	945
1878	1,080[c]	1,552
1880	1,080	1,515
1896	1,146[d]	1,822
1899	936	1,416
1911	936	1,023
1916	1,176[e]	1,037
1919	1,368	725

[a] Teachers without executive or administrative duties.

[b] Primary grades only.

[c] Grammar grades only.

[d] Average of maximum primary ($1,080) and maximum grammar ($1,212) salaries. After 1906, the distinction between grammar and primary grades was eliminated.

[e] Median salary.

[f] Burgess Cost-of-Living Index, Series E 184, *Historical Statistics of the United States, Colonial Times to 1970* (Washington: U.S. Department of Commerce, 1975), Part I, 212.

Sources:

1867: *Annual Report of the School Committee of the City of Boston, 1867,* 20–21.

1873: Charles P. Huse, *The Financial History of Boston* (Cambridge: Harvard Univ. Press, 1916), 140.

1878 and 1896: *School Document No. 15, Annual Report of the School Committee of the City of Boston, 1909,* 58.

1880: *School Document No. 6, Report of the Committee on Salaries, Boston Public Schools, 1880,* 4–5.

1899: *School Document No. 5, Report of the Committee on Salaries, Boston Public Schools, 1899,* 5.

1911: Boston Finance Commission, *Report on the Boston School System, 1911,* 216.

1916: Boston Finance Commission, *City Document No. 87, Report of a Study of Certain Phases of the Public School System of Boston, Mass., 1916,* from Table 2, 174.

1919: *School Document No. 19, Salaries of Public School Teachers, November, 1919,* 18.

Table 6. ANNUAL SALARIES PAID TO SISTERS WORKING FULL-TIME IN CHURCH INSTITUTIONS, SELECTED YEARS, 1860–1937

Year	Cash Payment per Sister	Payment in Kind per Sister	Type of Work	Location
1860	no fixed sum	housing,[a] board	teaching	elementary school, South Boston[1]
1898	$ 50	housing, board	nursing	hospital, Springfield, Mass.[2]
1902	325	housing	teaching	school for deaf,[b] Jamaica Plain, Mass.[3]
1908	300	housing probably	teaching	parochial school, New York City[4]
1910	300	housing	teaching	parish high school, U.S. average[5]
1912	200	housing	teaching	elementary school, U.S. average[6]
1912	250	none	teaching	elementary school, U.S. average[6]
1919	300	housing probably	teaching	parochial school, Chicago[7]
1924	under $300	housing	teaching	parochial school, Boston[8]
1937	335	housing	teaching	parochial school, U.S. average[9]

[a] Utilities, simple furnishings, and maintenance were included in all cases.

[b] This school, opened in 1899 by the Sisters of St. Joseph, received state aid a year later. It remained under Catholic auspices, but was open to all and inspected by the state. The state aid explains the relatively higher reimbursement of the sisters teaching there.

Sources: (1) A Member of the Congregation, *The American Foundations of the Sisters of Notre Dame de Namur, Compiled from the Annals of Their Convents* (Philadelphia: Dolphin. 1928). 339; (2) Rev. John J. McCoy, *History of the Catholic Church in the Diocese of Springfield* (n.p.: Hurd and Everts, 1900), 27–28; (3) Letter of Rev. Thomas Magennis to Mother Genevieve, Feb. 15, 1902 (Archives, Sisters of St. Joseph, Brighton, Mass.); (4) J. A. Burns, *The Growth and Development of the Catholic School System in the United States* (New York: Benziger, 1912), 280. In 1909, this salary was raised to $400 for the diocesan teaching order; (5) "Report of the Committee on High Schools," *Catholic Educational Review*, 2 (June 1911), 605–26; (6) Burns, *The Growth and Development*, 280; (7) James W. Sanders, *The Education of an Urban Minority, Catholics in Chicago, 1833–1965* (New York: Oxford Univ. Press, 1977), 159; (8) *Motherhouse Annals*, Sept. 4, 1924, Archives, Sisters of St. Joseph; (9) Clarence Elwell, "The Financing of Teacher Education," *Catholic Educational Review*, 38 (Feb. 1940), 152–53. This figure is the average salary per year per sister for 53 communities.

salaries were cut 7½ percent.[29] Nevertheless, salaries did increase, and a Boston Public School Teachers' Retirement Fund was established in 1900.

This comparison indicates how women were subsidizing the parochial schools. But another question remains: Was the salary paid the sister-teacher sufficient for her to live on? A 1911 study of 450 wage-earning women in Boston concluded that "annual earnings of approximately $500 a year, or $10 a week, may be taken as the amount of a living wage for women workers in Boston."[30] Using the data presented in Table 6, let us estimate the sister's average income for 1911 as $300, a cash stipend of $250 plus a $50 payment in kind in the form of housing. If we view the sister as a single working woman, then it is clear she was not receiving a salary even approaching the minimum standard. Her income was only 43 percent of the average income received by other professional women, and 32 percent of the salary paid public elementary school teachers.

Even though the sisters received only about three-fifths of the estimated living wage, their salaries did allow them to subsist, although not in any degree of comfort. (See Table 7.) Since they lived communally their situation resembled that of a family more than a number of independent single women. Funds were held in common, with all stipends paid to the local superior. After deducting the local group's contribution to central community expenses, the superior had discretion over the remaining funds. The sisters cooked for themselves, so their food expenditures were lower than if they had had to purchase meals in restaurants, cafeterias, or lodging houses. Similarly, in 1915, the estimated cost of rent, light, and heat for an individual in a normal family was $44.72 for a year. The $50 per sister per year for housing is consistent with this interpretation. "Living costs more for a woman 'adrift' than for a member of a family group."[31]

Clothing for sisters was not so great an expense as for the average working woman. With the exception of such items as shoes or gloves, sisters rarely purchased ready-made clothing. Cloth for their habits was purchased in bulk and the clothing was made by the sisters themselves. These habits never varied and were not replaced until worn out. Ordinary health costs may have been lower than might be expected since physicians and dentists often cared for the sisters at little or no charge. Ex-

---

[29] School Document No. 7, 1929, *Annual Report of the Superintendent, 1929,* 86; School Document No. 15, 1909, *Annual Report of the School Committee of the City of Boston, 1909,* 39; and John Koren, *Boston, 1822 to 1922* (Boston: Printing Dept., 1922), 107.

[30] Louise Marion Bosworth, *The Living Wage of Women Workers,* Supplement to the *Annals of the American Academy of Political and Social Science* (May 1911), 11. A similar estimate was provided for 1915 by Lucile Eaves, *The Food of Working Women in Boston,* Massachusetts State Department of Health (Boston: Wright and Potter, 1917), 99.

[31] Eaves, *Food of Working Women,* 80.

Table 7. AVERAGE ANNUAL EXPENDITURES OF WOMEN WORKERS BY OCCUPATION, 1911

Occupation	Average Net Income	Food	Rent	Clothing	Health	Savings	Miscellaneous
(1) Professional Workers	$695.41[a]	$192.18	$80.33	$112.27	$26.38	$130.41	$142.13
(2) Kitchen Workers	342.30[a]	156.65	82.17	28.22	8.64	61.67	40.28
(3) Sisters in Parish Schools	300.00	82.84	50.00	28.22	8.64	100.00	30.30
(4) "Living Wage" Recipients	504.28	169.70	74.81	88.99	22.09	31.63	117.06

[a] For (1) and (2), each entry is an average for the women in the group. The expense categories do not necessarily sum to average net income. *Sources:* (1), (2), and (4): Louise Marion Bosworth, *The Living Wage of Women Workers*, Supplement to the *Annals of the American Academy of Political and Social Science* (May 1911), 11, 16; (3): *Average Net Income, 1911*: is estimated at about $300, based on Table 6. *Food*: the estimate of the cost of food for one individual in a normal family in 1915, Lucile Eaves, *The Food of Working Women in Boston*, Massachusetts State Department of Health (Boston: Wright and Potter, 1917), 80. *Rent*: estimate is taken from Table 6 for 1912. *Clothing*: roughly estimated as equal to the clothing expenditure of a kitchen worker. *Health*: estimated as same as that of a kitchen worker. *Savings*: amount of assessment from cash stipend allocated for central needs. Estimated at 40 percent of cash stipend. *Miscellaneous*: a residual calculation.

traordinary or lengthy medical care was paid for by the motherhouse from central funds.

The proportion of sisters' salaries allocated to "savings" was higher than that of other working women. These salaries were the major source of revenue for central community needs, including the provision of food, housing, clothing, and all personal needs of the novices and postulants, the retired, and sick sisters. All educational costs incurred in preparing the young sisters for their work in the schools had to be borne by the communities, since no regular assistance in this area was given by either the diocese or the parish. The communities also met retirement and long-term medical costs. Land had to be purchased and buildings erected to house and maintain the young, the sick, and the elderly. With such limited income, substantial debt was often incurred. Although sympathetic pastors and wealthy Catholics helped in meeting these costs, for the most part they were assumed by the communities. For example, an 1893 land purchase by one teaching community was financed through a generous interest-free loan from a local pastor who took a mortgage on the land, two smaller interest-free loans from relatives of sisters, a small cash gift from the Archbishop, and borrowing by the community "at the lowest possible rate." And for the construction of a novitiate in 1901, although a sizable gift was received from a Cambridge pastor, most of the necessary money had to be borrowed at interest.[32]

Sisters supplemented the stipends from the schools by giving art and music lessons and, when possible, by opening tuition-charging academies for girls. Although the number of such schools increased from four to eighteen between 1870 and 1940, the proportion of all sisters teaching in academies, boarding schools, and colleges remained constant. (See Table 1.) The communities in demand for parochial school work opened the smallest number of academies, since the permission of the bishop had to be obtained. But these sources of income remained minor, and pressures on the stipends from the parishes increased as payments remained stable while the communities expanded and matured. At the turn of the century, about 40 percent of the cash stipend was needed for central expenses.[33] This proportion varied over time and among communities, according to

[32] Archives of the Sisters of St. Joseph, Brighton, Massachusetts, *Motherhouse Annals*, May 2, 1893, and Feb. 14, 1901.

[33] In 1902, 54 percent of each sister's salary at the School for the Deaf in Jamaica Plain was sent to the motherhouse. (Letter of Father Magennis to Mother Genevieve, Feb. 15, 1902, Archives of the Sisters of St. Joseph.) This meant that $150 per sister was left for local needs for the year. If a typical cash salary was $250 in parish schools, and if about $150 was retained at the local convent, then the assessment for central needs would be about 40 percent.

their degree of involvement in the parochial schools, but it remained substantial.

Despite increasing costs, requests by women's communities for larger stipends were sometimes considered unreasonable. One community appealed for a salary of at least $300 for the sisters in 1924, since "they can hardly live on the present one. . . ." Ironically, a local pastor refused to consider it because he was building a school.[34] Others expected the sisters to contribute toward parish expenses, and diocesan officials had to assure the sisters that the "pastor is to supply whatever is necessary for school and convent."[35]

Early arrangements for financial support made by the sisters in Massachusetts, as elsewhere, had been loose, with little money requested. In 1860, for example, South Boston sisters remarked that "all that was said about our support was the proposition of dear Sister Superior that Father Lyndon would procure us bread and butter."[36] Sisters relied upon the generosity of priests and parishioners to supplement their stipends with gifts in kind. This arrangement may have contributed to the inflexibility of the cash payments. The subsistence of sisters in local houses required considerable skill on the part of the superior; even with excellent management, there were no funds available for discretionary purposes. So casual a system of reimbursement became entirely inadequate as the years passed, with growth bringing heavy educational, medical, and institutional costs, none of which came under the direct observation of parishioners or their pastors.

The movement of men away from parish school teaching and the increasing concentration of Massachusetts sisters in education strengthened the already substantial segregation by sex in church work. The teaching of parish school students was left to the sisters, who had no real control over either the schools or the convents attached to them. The degree to which women's communities subsidized the parochial school system makes all the more surprising the dearth of literature on this aspect of the schools' financing.

*S*ince historians have given much attention to Protestant disapproval of parochial schools in Massachusetts, especially after 1884,[37] it is some-

---

[34] Archives of the Sisters of St. Joseph, *Motherhouse Annals*, Sept. 4 and Sept. 16, 1924. This was an appeal for a *cash* stipend of $300.

[35] Archives of the Sisters of St. Joseph, *Motherhouse Annals*, June 15, 1929.

[36] *The American Foundations of the Sisters of Notre Dame de Namur*, 339.

[37] Solomon, *Ancestors and Immigrants*, 48–55, provides a good survey of the varied reactions of Protestants to the schools. See also *Address of Archbishop Williams to the Catholic Union of Boston*, Mar. 12, 1891.

times assumed that local Catholics received the Council decree of a school in every parish with unanimous enthusiasm. On the contrary, there is evidence of "great lukewarmness" among the laity. Although reminded that support of parochial schools was a duty, parishioners were not convinced of the dangers of the public schools. In Haverhill in 1887 and in Cambridge in 1889 schools opened over significant opposition by parish members. *The Sacred Heart Review* editorialized that "the hearts of many Catholics are more with the opposition to parochial schools than with their own co-religionists. . . ."[38]

The objection of Catholics to parochial schools was not their cost but their inferiority to public schools. "Now what is the motive that prompts these disobedient Catholics in preferring the public to their parish schools? Why it is that their children will be better taught in the former. . . ."[39]

> The present generation have nearly all been educated in the public schools and we have become so accustomed to consider them better than any other, that now that Catholic schools are being established in many parishes, there is found a strange reluctance on the part of many to send their children to them.[40]

Pressures on parents in the post-1884 period to enroll their sons as well as their daughters in schools taught by sisters raised questions about the kind of education the boys would receive. Although public school faculties had long been female, the public had never associated them primarily with the education of girls. Contemporary descriptions of parochial schools suggest that they emphasized moral development and manners. "In the heart, we . . . cultivate piety and the domestic virtues; . . . in the mind, a knowledge of the branches deemed necessary or useful to a woman."[41] Another commentator spells out more precisely the special features of the parochial school:

> The parochial school is a reflection from the convent mirror, and the good nuns, besides teaching and enforcing the domestic virtues, especially correct whatever is rude or unbecoming in the manners of their scholars. Hence, even to the smallest points, such as the position of the feet in standing and walking, etc., they pay strict attention. . . .[42]

---

[38] O'Hara, *Educational Contribution,* 15–17; *The Sacred Heart Review,* Jan. 5, 1889, 1; Mar. 29, 1890, 9.

[39] *The Sacred Heart Review,* Sept. 6, 1890, 1.

[40] *The Sacred Heart Review,* Sept. 3, 1892, 9.

[41] Sisters of Notre Dame de Namur, "Course of Studies," cited in *The Sacred Heart Review,* Oct. 12, 1889, 1.

[42] Ibid., Feb. 22, 1890, 5.

Not all Catholic parents approved of such training for daughters, many of whom were attending public schools. An editor chastised "those misguided Catholic parents and guardians who keep their girls out of the sisters' schools, asserting that they learn more in other schools."[43] Under such criticism and with enrollments, of boys rising after 1884, parochial schools were soon searching for more stimulating curricula. In 1890, the Sisters of Charity of Halifax, at St. Patrick's School in Roxbury, "did not hesitate to adopt the general system, which they found established in the public schools, which have obtained such a reputation for general excellence throughout the country."[44] The schools of the Sisters of St. Joseph were described as "graded after the plan of the public schools . . . and their textbooks, save in studies involving religious references, are the same."[45]

Inadequate facilities and large class size also supported the view that the burgeoning schools were inferior. A not uncommon situation prevailed in St. Thomas School in Jamaica Plain, where classes were conducted in the basement of the church for 17 years before a school building was erected.[46] An average class size of 48.6 pupils in parochial schools in 1899 compares favorably with 51.5 in Boston elementary schools. If all classes (kindergarten, elementary, high, Latin, and normal) are included, the Boston figure would be 44 for 1897. The grades for this comparison, however, are the elementary ones, since few parochial schools went beyond this level. Educators of the day considered the Boston averages and quotas too high and every effort was being made to reduce them. Table 8 indicates the progress made. The Boston quota of 50 for elementary classes above grade one in 1899 had been lowered by 1910 to 44, and in the more affluent and less congested suburbs of Boston, public schools had much smaller classes. In these towns new parochial schools were opening, making the disparity in class size more evident. In 1899 George A. Aldrich, Superintendent of the Newton Public Schools, evaluated a Boston parochial school for girls with an average class size of 47. His report, based on a five-day visit, praised the sisters but noted that their work was hampered not only by physical deficiencies in plant, but by the size of classes. "Forty-five is the largest number which should be assigned to one pupil-teacher."[47] In the public schools of suburban Brookline average class size, only 30.7 in 1911, had fallen to 28.8 by 1915.[48]

[43] Ibid., Oct. 4, 1890, 14.

[44] Ibid., Dec. 20, 1890, 1.

[45] Katherine E. Conway, *The Pilot*, Oct. 1, 1898.

[46] O'Hara, *Educational Contribution*, 8. Walsh, *Historical Sketch*, Appendix 4, 11, reports that in 1900, 17 percent of parochial schools were located in convents and church basements.

[47] Letter of George A. Aldrich to Rev. J. J. Johnson, Oct. 25, 1899, Archives of the Sisters of St. Joseph.

[48] Weighted average of grammar and primary figures. The School Committee, *Educational Survey of the Public Schools of Brookline, Mass., 1917*, 48.

The average class size for the parochial schools obscures the diversity among schools by sex of teacher and ethnic composition of the parish. Table 8 shows that sisters, on average, were teaching larger classes than were either brothers or lay teachers. The prospect of having one's child in a class taught by brothers or lay teachers was dim since, by 1899, 85 percent of all parish teachers were sisters. And the likelihood of seeing a falling student/teacher ratio appeared slight to many Catholic parents. Schools in French-speaking parishes in particular had large classes and enrolled a sizable proportion of the total school population. The seven French schools considered in Table 8 accounted for 14 percent of total enrollments in 1899.

Another concern was the training of parochial school teachers. Young sisters, without normal school preparation, were expected to acquire their skills on the job. In average level of schooling these young women were like their contemporaries in the nation's normal schools, 88 percent of whose students as late as 1890 were not yet high school graduates.[49] In this era, the small number of sisters who had graduated from high school before joining a community were assigned to teach older students.[50] The bishops at the Council of Baltimore, sensitive to criticism on this point, sought to ensure a minimum training for sisters by requiring an examination of all new teachers. They urged the women's communities to open normal schools for their members and also requested that sufficient time be allotted for teacher training.[51] But the mandate of a school in every parish slowed progress toward better preparation. The local parish was more concerned about the number of sisters available than their quality.

Religious superiors of the women's communities had little choice but to acquiesce in the wishes of bishops and pastors, many of whom were not convinced of the necessity of pre-job training for elementary teaching. Mother Mary Regis, first superior of the Sisters of St. Joseph, wished to delay opening a school in 1879 until the sisters were better trained. The bishop's representative informed her that novices, with no pre-service training, could learn by apprenticeship. The superiors provided what assistance they could to their new teachers, but this was necessarily sporadic and informal. "For a few months we have had Professor Dunton of the training school in the city, to give the sisters instruction in the

---

[49] W. W. Parsons, "The Normal School Curriculum," *National Educational Association Proceedings, 1890* (Topeka: Kansas Publishing, 1890), 718–24.

[50] For example, an 1899 graduate of Mt. St. Joseph Academy in Brighton returned to her alma mater as a sister and a faculty member two years later. Sister Mary Catherine, *History of the Sisters of St. Joseph*, unpublished manuscript, Archives of the Sisters of St. Joseph, no date, 102, 118. The period covered by this manuscript is 1873–1914.

[51] The new teachers who were, in fact, subject to the examination requirement included only lay teachers and sisters in diocesan communities. James A. Burns, "The Development of Parish School Organization," *Catholic Educational Review*, 3 (May 1912), 424.

Table 8.

A. AVERAGE CLASS SIZE, PAROCHIAL SCHOOLS, ARCHDIOCESE OF BOSTON, 1899–1900

Teaching Group	Percent of All Teachers	Student/Teacher Ratio	Number of Schools
14 communities of sisters	77	47.5	54
3 communities of French sisters[a]	7	68.2	5
3 communities of brothers	7	39.8	7
1 community of French brothers[b]	3	56.9	2
lay teachers	6	42.9	6
	100.0	48.6 overall average	74

Sources: Compiled from data in Louis S. Walsh, *Historical Sketch of the Growth of Catholic Parochial Schools in the Archdiocese of Boston* (Newton: St. John's Industrial School, 1901), Appendix III.

B. AVERAGE CLASS SIZE, BOSTON PUBLIC SCHOOLS, ELEMENTARY GRADES, SELECTED YEARS, 1867–1939

Year	Students/Teacher, Elementary Grades
1867	45.1[c]
1899	51.5[c]
1910	43.6
1919	41.2
1929	38.1
1939	38.3[d]

[a] Grey Nuns of the Cross, Grey Nuns of Montreal, Sisters of the Good Shepherd, Quebec.
[b] Marist Brothers.
[c] Weighted average, grades 1–8.
[d] Weighted average, grades 1–9.

Sources:
1867: *Annual Report of the School Committee of the City of Boston, 1867,* 198.
1899: Boston Finance Commission, *Document 87, 1916, Report of Certain Phases of the Public School System of Boston, Mass., 1916,* 212.
1910: *School Document No. 11, 1930, Annual Statistics of the Boston Public Schools, 1929–1930,* 30.
1919, 1929, and 1939: *School Document No. 5, 1940, Annual Statistics of the Boston Public Schools, 1939–1949,* 23.

methods of teaching."[52] During the school year, better educated sisters were sent from convent to convent to instruct the others. Young, inexperienced teachers were assigned to the lower grades.

Apologists for parochial schools minimized the disparity in background between public and parochial school faculties. But in Massachusetts, where the public schools were highly regarded, their arguments were not always accepted.[53] The Commonwealth's teacher training standards had never typified national norms. Shortly after 1872, the Boston Normal School began requiring a diploma from a four-year high school for admission. An entrance examination was added in 1901, with the requirement that students be at least 18 years old. The regular course took two years,[54] and graduates had little difficulty being placed in local public schools. The Boston school superintendent reported in 1903 that, for the past five years, "out of 617 places technically opened to Boston Normal graduates, 426 were given to them, and 191 were given to others, that is, to older and more experienced teachers."[55]

As the number of parish schools increased late in the century, Archbishop Williams lent support to the women's communities in their efforts to reconcile conflicting pressures from pastors and parents. In 1889 he ordered them not to send novices into the schools. Again in 1901, they were instructed to refuse pastors seeking teachers for new schools "unless the number of Sisters who have made their novitiate is sufficient to supply the demand."[56] That the communities welcomed such support is demonstrated by the diocesan teaching community's refusal to accept any new schools during 13 of the 17 years between 1893 and 1910.[57] But the training that could be provided to young women in a brief novitiate was unsatisfactory. It was supplemented by lectures and summer study, but not by any program that would reduce the movement of sisters into the schools. The novitiate in many communities lasted only a year, and religious training occupied much of this time. The Constitutions of the Sisters of St. Joseph prescribed a two-year novitiate, after which the sisters took

---

[52] Letter of Sister M. Regis to Rt. Rev. J. Laughlin, Dec. 31, 1879, Archives of the Sisters of St. Joseph. The instructor referred to was Professor Larkin Dunton, Headmaster of the Boston Normal School. See also *Just Passing Through*, 34–35.

[53] See, for example, McCormick, "Church Law on Certification," 261.

[54] School Document No. 10, 1903, *Catalogue of the Boston Normal School for the Year, 1903* (Boston: Municipal Printing Office, 1903), 7.

[55] School Document No. 3, 1903, *Annual Report of the Superintendent of Public Schools of the City of Boston, 1903*, 65.

[56] Letter of Rev. William Byrne, Vicar General, to Mother M. Regis, Nov. 30, 1889, and Letter of Father Magennis to Mother Mary Genevieve, Aug. 24, 1901, Archives of the Sisters of St. Joseph.

[57] *Just Passing Through*, 76, 81, 86.

perpetual vows.[58] In 1921 the first two sisters in this major community received bachelor's degrees, although the community had been teaching in parochial schools since 1873. Thereafter the community opened a formal summer school, and patronized an extension school begun at Boston College in 1924 which offered courses that did not conflict with teaching programs. Acquisition of degrees, although delayed, became more common.[59]

Despite lack of formal training, especially in the pre-1920 period, the sisters had an advantage not shared by many public school colleagues in their commitment to a lifetime career. The young teacher started out "learning by doing," but she had the guidance and counsel of older, more experienced sisters. Her own experience in the teaching of young children became an increasing asset. Given the restrictions on the hiring of married women, the average public school teacher's experience was short. The expansion of the parochial schools after 1880 obscured this potential advantage of the sister-teacher in the eyes of parents concerned with the short-run impact of the situation on their children. When comparing two young women, the sister-teacher and public school teacher, both without classroom experience, parents observed that the sisters tended to be younger and were less likely to have completed normal school.

Though the inability of women's communities to give their members professional education was related to the demand after 1884 for sisters in the classroom, there was little recognition of the cost either to sisters or to their students. Sometimes it was acknowledged obliquely; Cardinal O'Connell, for example, in 1923 ordered that one community omit some daily prayers "so as to give the Sisters more time for study."[60] But assistance was not provided at the expense of the sisters' presence in the schools, and short normal training in novitiates and extension courses remained the ordinary means of educating parochial school faculties.

Another obstacle in the way of professional training was its expense. Even if it were possible to withdraw a few sisters from classrooms for college study, their tuitions and expenses would not be insignificant, and the community would feel the loss of even their small salaries. Under prevailing financial arrangements, it was all but impossible for many communities to fund full-time study.

[58] Chapter 2, *The Constitutions of the Congregation of the Sisters of St. Joseph, 1827,* Translation of the Constitutions of Lyons (New York: O'Shea and Co., n.d.). These constitutions were in effect from 1873–1937. A code of canon law revision in 1917 required the introduction of a period of annual vows before perpetual vows were taken. See also Burns, "The Development of Parish School Organization," 431.

[59] *Motherhouse Annals,* June 15, 1921, Archives of the Sisters of St. Joseph.

[60] *Motherhouse Annals,* Jan. 29, 1923, Archives of the Sisters of St. Joseph.

A related issue is the effect of low incomes on the sisters' professional and social lives. Extra-convent activities permitted to sisters had traditionally been fewer than those considered acceptable for priests and brothers. In this, church authorities reflected, in a more extreme way, society's strictures on women's activities and behavior, always more circumscribed than men's. But in the 70 years between 1870 and 1940 social and professional options for American women had broadened. Higher education and economic independence were becoming realities for many, and the goals of countless others. At the same time, the sphere of action allowed to members of women's communities not only did not widen, but in some areas appears to have become more restricted.

Limitation of extra-convent activities served to minimize the financial needs of sisters above subsistence, and the greater scope of action viewed as appropriate for male church workers was used to justify wage differentials between men and women. The economic constraints facing women's communities no doubt contributed to the stringency of the rules regulating their members' behavior. Aware of increasing costs, inflexible salary scales, and falling real incomes, community superiors were unable to press for modification of regulations inhibiting sisters' activities. Thus occurred a widening of differences between norms of behavior acceptable for sisters and laywomen. The clearest evidence of the importance of financial considerations is the imposition by Church authorities from without of many regulations with little observable "religious" significance. In the early years of the period, to take but one example, travel among convents and to the homes of relatives was not uncommon in some communities. But by 1890, an ecclesiastical authority was on record as disapproving of sisters' leaving the convent for visiting or shopping. A decade later, social visiting and visits to the sick were curtailed. By the close of the period, social visits of any kind by sisters were enjoined by the cardinal unless specific permission were obtained for each visit.[61] By 1940, therefore, sisters were limited in mobility to convent, church, and school, while their lay counterparts were moving into new arenas.

In their professional activities, sisters were even more restricted. Anonymity and self-effacement, rarely demanded of their male colleagues in church service, were carried to extremes. At the July 1909 convention of the Catholic Education Association in Boston, for example, a paper written by a Sister of Notre Dame was read for her by a priest.[62] Such restrictions abounded and discouraged professional participation.

[61] *Motherhouse Annals,* various years in the 1880s; July 21, 1890; Apr. 10, 1903; Sept. 21, 1935, Archives of the Sisters of St. Joseph.
[62] *The American Foundations of the Sisters of Notre Dame de Namur,* 218.

Although the activities of sisters were generally restricted, Massachusetts sisters were particularly affected after 1907. William O'Connell's views on women's place, set forth earlier, were evident in his dealings with communities of sisters. In his analysis, their financial straits resulted from inept and inefficient management by women. As an example of the problems these groups presented for him on his arrival in Boston, he cited the motherhouse and convents of the Sisters of St. Joseph which, he maintained, were "floundering about in a very precarious moral and financial condition."[63] Yet most members of this community were employed in parochial schools, lived in parish-owned convents, and had no control over their salaries. O'Connell never conceded that low salaries might have occasioned some of the financial difficulties faced by sisters. Rather, the charge of incompetence was used repeatedly to justify tighter control over communities of women. Consultation was required on minor as well as major matters throughout his 36-year tenure. His approach was described with pride in his autobiography:

> After removal of the old Superior, the new one who took her place received the clearest and minutest instructions which to this day she has carefully and docilely executed. . . . The whole management and control . . . was put under close supervision and direction, with the result that the institution today, once nearly swamped in debt, is financially perfectly sound, while the real work of the institution . . . is incomparably more capably and efficiently accomplished.[64]

While there were instances of mismanagement in women's as in other communities, the methods of rectifying it showed little regard for the sisters. Under canon law, the bishop had the right to intervene in a range of areas affecting women. But the exercise of heavy control over their internal as well as external affairs prevented any steps toward self-determination for decades. Although churchmen did not escape his paternalistic approach,[65] O'Connell viewed women's communities as especially needing clerical supervision and direction.

*   *   *

The expansion of the parochial schools in Boston after the Council of 1884 had little effect on the numbers of churchmen, their rate of increase, or their choice of work. But it had dramatic implications for the lives of

[63] William Cardinal O'Connell, *Recollections of Seventy Years* (Boston: Houghton Mifflin, 1934), 270.

[64] O'Connell, *Recollections,* 279, referring to the Sisters of the Good Shepherd, Roxbury, Mass.

[65] See O'Connell, *Recollections,* 273, and Merwick, *Boston Priests,* 188–96.

the labor force that staffed the schools. After that date, the control of women's communities over their work and the institutions in which they worked eroded. The sudden and exogenously ordered expansion in a major occupation of sisters created serious problems, especially in Massachusetts, a state which prior to 1884 had moved slowly in response to directives in the matter of church schools. Responding to a special need of the church, young women joined teaching communities. At the same time, these communities were gradually losing much of the moderate control they possessed over the professional and social lives of their members.

If the school campaign had not occurred, parishes wanting church schools for their children would have opened them when they could afford them, and sisters could have expected to receive reasonable recompense. With adequate salary levels and enlightened leadership the communities would presumably have allowed their members to take advantage of professional opportunities and to move, as laywomen and male members of religious communities were doing, into a wider range of activities. Altogether, the quality of the sisters' work would have been enhanced.

The 1870–1940 period ended with Massachusetts sisters still concentrated in "women's work." Occupational segregation had even deepened in these years. While women in full-time church work in 1870 were well distributed over a range of occupations, by 1940 that variation and flexibility of choice were gone. Within women's occupations, the majority of sisters by 1940 were engaged in the teaching of young children.*

* This study was undertaken with the support of a grant from the American Philosophical Society.

Virginia Lieson Brereton and Christa Ressmeyer Klein

American Women in Ministry
A History of Protestant
Beginning Points

*I*n 1970 the Lutheran Church in America and the American Lutheran Church voted to ordain women. In 1976 the Episcopalians followed. By these actions the ministry had become a possible life's work for women in all the "mainline" Protestant churches.[1] The general acceptance of women's ordination appeared to be a high point in a long history of expanding female leadership in the American Protestant churches.

A glance back to antebellum America reveals that the church has indeed come a long way in accepting women in roles of authority. Until the Civil War social prohibitions bolstered by certain Biblical injunctions kept churchwomen from speaking or praying aloud in religious assemblies. Literal interpretation of such passages as I Timothy 2:11–12 made most women uneasy even about speaking before their sisters in women's church societies—or leading them in prayer, if indeed they were permitted to at all. Women seldom appeared at congregational or denominational deliberations, and could neither vote nor speak. Nor could they venture forth as missionaries except under the protection and counsel of their husbands. Most colleges and theological seminaries were closed to them.

---

[1] This chapter treats the issue of women's ordination in the context of the Christian (Disciples of Christ), Baptist, Congregational and Reformed, Methodist, Presbyterian, and Lutheran denominations. For the Disciples, at one end of this spectrum, ordination is a matter of practicality and not doctrine. For Lutherans, at the other end of the spectrum, ministry is a mediating agency for the imparting of faith through the Gospel and the sacraments.

By taking the initiative in home and foreign missions and in religious education, to mention two arenas of female activity in the latter part of the nineteenth century, women proved that they could serve the church in significant ways. Slowly ordination opened up to them. Yet women's victory has somehow been a hollow one. Equal access to the ordained ministry has not resulted in equal access to positions of leadership traditionally available to the clergy. Everywhere women ministers face longer periods of unemployment, lower salaries, less opportunity to shoulder full responsibility for parishes—especially larger ones—and less likelihood of appointment or election to leadership positions within ecclesiastical structures. As a result, feminist groups have emerged within most denominations to expose these inequities and to propose solutions whose minimum demands are for affirmative-action goals in the churches. Not infrequently these groups question a denomination's entire heritage for insensitivity to women in its polity, theology and piety.

Hence, the unfulfilled possibilities of women's ministry have served to keep the basic question of women's status and service in churches in the forefront. Ordination, far from being the culmination of women's expanding participation, is another beginning point in a history of beginning points. Here we attempt to consider women's ordination within the broad historical context of women's quest for leadership in service within the American Protestant denominations, highlighting outstanding movements and eras and perhaps prodding others to explore them more carefully.

In putting together this essay we have encountered still another kind of beginning which needs mention: the task of reconstructing the history of women in the church has gotten under way only in the last few years. Our attempt to take a broad view across denominational lines has therefore been hindered at many points by the dearth of writing on women by denominational chroniclers. Historians of American Methodism almost alone have turned their attention to the story of women in that denomination.[2] In some of the otherwise thorough histories women hardly appear at all. Fine work has appeared on women in the foreign missions movement.[3] Historian Eliza-

---

[2] E.g., Theodore Agnew, "Reflections on the Woman's Foreign Missionary Movement in Late 19th Century American Methodism," *Methodist History*, 6 (Jan. 1968), 3–14; Norma Taylor Mitchell, "From Social to Radical Feminism: A Survey of Emerging Diversity in Methodist Women's Organizations, 1869–1974," ibid., 13 (Apr. 1975), 21–44; Kenneth E. Rowe, ed., "Discovery. My Ordination: Anna Howard Shaw," by Nancy N. Bahmueller, ibid., 14 (Jan. 1976), 125–31; Elaine Magalis, *Conduct Becoming to a Woman* (Women's Division, Board of Global Ministries, United Methodist Church, 1973).

[3] R. Pierce Beaver, *All Loves Excelling: American Protestant Women in World Missions* (Grand Rapids: Eerdman, 1968); Irwin T. Hyatt, Jr., *Our Ordered Lives Confess: Three Nineteenth-Century American Missionaries in East Shantung* (Cambridge, Mass.: Harvard Univ. Press, 1976); also very helpful is Helen Barrett Montgomery, *Western Women in Eastern Lands* (New York: Macmillan, 1911).

beth H. Verdesi has completed a valuable thesis on Northern Presbyterian women, focusing on the missions and the religious education movement.[4] Short historical sketches have appeared in denominational periodicals and reports.[5] Since the 1920s, periodic denominational and interdenominational surveys have explored the status of women in the church.[6] Otherwise, we have had to rely on commemorative histories of various women's societies and of the deaconess movement, and on scattered biographies and autobiographies of churchwomen.[7]

[4] Elizabeth Howell Verdesi, "The Professionally-Trained Woman in the Presbyterian Church: The Role of Power in the Achievement of Status and Equality" (Diss. Teachers College, Columbia University, 1975; also published as *In But Still Out: Women in the Church* [Philadelphia: Westminster Press, 1976]).

[5] E.g., "Two Goodly Heritages; Presbyterian Women: How Does Our Past Inform Our Future?" *Concern*, 19, no. 3 (Feb. 1977). The popular histories of women in the church also provided some leads for historical scholarship: Elsie Culver, *Women in the World of Religion* (Garden City, N.Y.: Doubleday, 1967); Georgia Harkness, *Women in Church and Society* (Nashville: Abingdon Press, 1972).

[6] M. Katharine Bennett, "Status of Women in the Presbyterian Church in the U.S.A., with References to Other Denominations" (Philadelphia: General Council of the Presbyterian Church in the U.S.A., 1929); Conference on Women's Status and Service in the Church, "Reports Relating to the Status of Women in the Church" (Philadelphia: Office of the General Assembly, 1929); Joint Committee to Study the Place of Women's Organized Work in the Church, "The Relative Place of Women in the Church," New York City, 1927; Inez Cavert, "Women in American Church Life," mimeographed, Federal Council of Churches of Christ in America, 1948; Kathleen Bliss, *The Service and Status of Women in the Churches* (London: SCM Press Ltd., 1952); Elsie Gibson, *When the Minister Is a Woman* (New York: Holt, Rinehart & Winston, 1970).

[7] Margaret Gibson Hummel, *The Amazing Heritage* (Philadelphia: Geneva Press, 1970); Alma Hunt, *History of Woman's Missionary Union* (Nashville: Convention Press, 1964); Lorraine Lollis, *The Shape of Adam's Rib: A Lively History of Woman's Work in the Christian Church* (St. Louis: Bethany Press, 1970); Ruth Esther Meeker, *Six Decades of Service, 1880–1940: A History of the Woman's Home Missionary Society of the Methodist Episcopal Church* (Cincinnati: Steinhauser, 1969); Ruth Fritz Meyer, *Women on a Mission: The Role of Women in the Church . . . Including a History of the LWML During Its First Twenty-five Years* (St. Louis: Concordia Publishing House, 1967); Audrie E. Reber, *Women United for Mission: A History of the Women's Society of World Service of the Evangelical United Brethren Church, 1946–1968* (Dayton: Otterbein, 1969); Patricia Houck Sprinkle, *The Birthday Book* (Atlanta: Board of Women's Work, Presbyterian Church in the U.S., 1972); Noreen Dunn Tatum, *A Crown of Service: A Story of Woman's Work in the Methodist Episcopal Church South, 1878–1940* (1960); *These Fifty Years* (Chicago: Woman's Missionary Society, 1942)—Augustana Lutheran Church; Robert G. Torbet, *Venture of Faith: The Story of the American Baptist Foreign Mission Society and the Woman's American Baptist Foreign Mission Society* (Philadelphia: Judson Press, 1955); Elizabeth Meredith Lee, *As Among the Methodists: Deaconesses Yesterday, Today, and Tomorrow* (New York: Woman's Division of Christian Service, Board of Missions, Methodist Church, 1963); Frederick S. Weiser, *Love's Response: A Story of Lutheran Deaconesses in America* (Philadelphia Board of Publication of the United Lutheran Church in America, 1962); Lucy Rider Meyer, *Deaconesses, Biblical, Early Church, European, American* (Chicago: Message Publishing Co., 1889); Margaret Blair Johnstone, *When God Says "No": Faith's Starting Point* (New York: Simon and Schuster, 1954); Margaret Henrichsen, *Seven Steeples* (Boston: Houghton Mifflin, 1953); Hilda Libby Ives, *All in One Day* (Portland: Bond Wheelwright, 1955).

Women Alongside the Churches:
The Great Missionary Societies, 1861–1925

Despite the many obstacles to full participation in their churches before the Civil War, women organized themselves into numerous local mission-ary societies, financing their efforts out of their household budgets. One early interdenominational attempt by women in 1834 to organize more broadly and systematically collapsed before opposition from the secretary of the American Board of Commissioners for Foreign Missions.[8]

Nevertheless, by the 1860s and 1870s, neither the fears of men on the general missionary boards nor the misgivings of the women themselves could halt the momentum of women's entry into large-scale and well-coordinated missionary activity. Women widely separated geographically joined forces to forge regional and national societies, beginning with the interdenominational Woman's Union Missionary Society of America in 1861. The principal early groups and their founding dates were:

Woman's Board of Missions (Congregational), 1868.
Woman's Foreign Missionary Society (Methodist Episcopal), 1869.
Woman's Foreign Missionary Societies of the Presbyterian Church, U.S.A., 1870.
Woman's Auxiliary (Protestant Episcopal), 1871.
Woman's Baptist Foreign Missionary Society, 1873.
Woman's Parent Mite Missionary Society of the African Methodist Episcopal Church, 1874.
Christian Woman's Board of Missions (Disciples), 1874.
Woman's Board of Foreign Missions of the Reformed Church in America, 1875.
Woman's American Baptist Home Missionary Society, 1877.
Woman's Executive Committee for Home Missions (Presbyterian), 1878.
Woman's Missionary Society of the Evangelical Lutheran Church, 1879.
Congregational Women's Home Missionary Association, 1880.
Woman's Home Missionary Society (Methodist Episcopal), 1884.

Southern women, despite being hindered by conservative ideas about the place of the "Southern lady" and by the general devastation resulting from the war, followed suit shortly after: Woman's Board of Foreign Missions, Methodist Episcopal Church South, 1878; Woman's Missionary Union, Aux-iliary to the Southern Baptist Convention, 1888; and Woman's Auxiliary, Presbyterian Church in the U.S., 1912.[9]

---

[8] Beaver, *All Loves Excelling*, 88.
[9] For a complete and helpful list of women's foreign missionary societies organized be-fore 1911, see Montgomery, *Western Women in Eastern Lands*, foldout page following p.

By 1882 the sixteen existing women's missionary societies had raised almost six million dollars and had sent out 694 single women missionaries. By 1900 the women's societies were supporting 389 wives, 856 single women missionaries, and 96 doctors. They were responsible for numerous orphanages, hospitals, schools and dispensaries around the world.[10] In home missions, the accomplishments of the women were impressive also, although we do not possess the summary statistics we have for foreign missions. In 1889 and 1890, for instance, the Woman's Executive Committee for Home Missions of the Presbyterian Church in the U.S.A. raised more money than did the main home missions board of that denomination.[11]

Such remarkable efforts and achievements call for an explanation which must begin with an understanding of the deep sense of Christian responsibility for the unconverted in an age of millennial fervor. American Protestant women were also responding to the social condition of women and children—particularly in the Far East, but also among the immigrants in American cities—in other cultures. Reports from missionaries in the Orient, which documented such religiously sanctioned practices as the binding of Chinese women's feet and the confinement of Indian women in close dark zenanas, deeply unsettled prosperous American women. Surely, they thought, Christianity would transform mores even as it made converts.[12] In addition, two generations of missionaries reported little progress in their work with men; perhaps Oriental women provided the key to opening foreign cultures to Christianization. American Protestants took the idealized Victorian view of women to heart, believing that female converts might wield all manner of moral and religious influence. But clearly male missionaries could not approach Eastern women; rather, this was uniquely a task for Western women.

Women's initiative in mission work, ripening in the postwar era, bore the marks of the emerging social order. In building their work on a national scale, women were paralleling similar developments in the rest of the church and also, of course, in American industry.[13] If Theodore Agnew's findings on the Woman's Foreign Missionary Society of the Methodist Episcopal Church

---

286. National missionary societies developed among immigrant Lutheran women somewhat later. One of the first, the Women's Missionary Society of the Augustana (Swedish) Lutheran Church, was founded in 1892 (Burnice Fjellmen, "Women in the Church," *Centennial Essays* [Rock Island, Ill.: Augustana Press, 1960], 210–12). One of the last, the Lutheran Women's Missionary League of the Missouri Synod, was not founded until 1941 (Alan Graebner, *Uncertain Saints: The Laity in the Lutheran Church–Missouri Synod* [Westport, Conn.: Greenwood Press, 1975], 133–40).

[10] Beaver, *All Loves Excelling*, 107–8.

[11] Verdesi, *In But Still Out*, 61.

[12] See Montgomery, *Western Women in Eastern Lands*, 45–75.

[13] Allen R. Bartholomew, "Mission Boards Fifty Years Ago: A Half Century of Changes in Missionary Administration and Organization in the Home Boards," *The Missionary Review of the World*, 50 (Dec. 1927), 899–905.

hold true for other societies—and we believe that they will—women missionary leaders represented an emerging elite within the denominations.[14] Since these women were frequently the wives and relatives of male denominational leaders, the missionary societies created a virtual "interlocking directorate" of prosperous families. Such women could engage in travel and other time-consuming activities outside their homes, and frequented such Protestant watering holes as Chautauqua Lake, Ocean Grove, and Martha's Vineyard. They shared the assurances of cultural and racial superiority characteristic of the age, amply illustrated in the Methodist Episcopal Society's periodical *The Heathen Woman's Friend*.

But firm belief in the goals of late-nineteenth-century American Protestantism and ties to the emerging social and religious leadership do not in themselves explain the accomplishments of the women's missionary societies. Above all, those societies must be credited with recognizing the existence and value of huge reserves of untapped volunteer labor among women of the middle and upper classes. Missionary leader Helen Barrett Montgomery noted in 1911 that women "have one tenth of the work in the home that their grandmothers bore. We must work for the life of the world."[15] Women missionary leaders displayed ingenuity in channeling the energy of these women, encouraging the multiplication of auxiliary and branch missionary societies. They further perceived that women would become most deeply involved if each of these local societies took special responsibility for a particular project or missionary field or the support of a certain missionary. Fund-raising followed this pattern of massive involvement also. Since church policies generally prohibited women from raising money in congregational or other general church meetings (lest they compete with the general missionary boards), the societies had to be well enough organized to collect "large sums in small gifts."[16]

Behind the success of the fund-raising lay broad efforts to disseminate missions information, activities in which the women had no peers. According

[14] Theodore Agnew, "Reflections on the Woman's Foreign Missionary Movement in Late 19th Century American Methodism," 3–14. We know, for instance, that Helen Barrett Montgomery, a leader in Baptist women's missionary societies and first woman to be president of the Northern Baptist Convention, graduated from one of the early classes at Wellesley College and later became a trustee of the college. Her husband, a Rochester, N.Y., businessman, made a fortune supplying the new automobile industry and was also chairman of the board of Colgate Rochester Divinity School. Lucy Waterbury Peabody, another Baptist missionary leader, was related to Andrew Jackson and Grover Cleveland. Her second husband, a rich businessman, was a member and president of the Board of Managers of the Baptist Missionary Union. See Louise Armstrong Cattan, *Lamps Are for Lighting: The Story of Helen Barrett Montgomery and Lucy Waterbury Peabody* (Grand Rapids: Eerdmans, 1972).

[15] Cattan, *Lamps Are for Lighting*, 57–58.

[16] Lucy W. Peabody, "Woman's Place in Missions Fifty Years Ago and Now," *The Missionary Review of the World*, 50, no. 12 (Dec. 1927), 907.

to missions historian R. Pierce Beaver, the women's societies taught the general missionary boards the value of publicity.[17] Women provided the first easily readable and widely available missions information—"The light infantry of missionary literature."[18] Besides holding regular conventions, women developed summer schools for missions which served as opportunities for vacationing as well as learning. At other times of the year, institutes, study conferences, missionary exhibits and jubilees enlarged women's familiarity with missions. Not content with educating adult women only, the female societies cultivated enthusiasm in the next generations through societies for young people and children and through their contributions to Sunday school curricula.

By enabling single women to work in the mission fields at home and abroad, these societies freed an extremely valuable resource for the missionary cause. Until the women's societies showed the way, the general denominational boards had resisted appointing single women, unless they agreed to live safely in the household of married missionaries and to confine themselves to roles which would not expose them to danger or undue exertion.[19] But single women were eager to perform the same tasks as male missionaries. At a time when American society offered few vocational opportunities for women besides teaching, the mission fields promised exciting challenges for single women. Many restless, ambitious and devout women from small American towns and farms escaped the tedium of a confined existence by sailing to the mission fields or by venturing to the American frontiers, both Western and urban.[20] A Methodist missionary to India, Isabella Thoburn, spoke for all her sister missionaries when she said:

> We have found sickness and poverty to relieve, widows to protect, advice to be given in every possible difficulty or emergency, teachers and Bible women to be trained, houses to be built, horses and cattle to be bought, gardens to be planted, and accounts to be kept and rendered. We have found use for every faculty, natural and acquired, that we possessed, and have coveted all that we lacked.[21]

[17] Beaver, *All Loves Excelling*, 177.

[18] Montgomery, *Western Women in Eastern Lands*, 38.

[19] R. Pierce Beaver, "Pioneer Single Women Missionaries," *Occasional Bulletin of the Missionary Research Library*, 4, no. 2 (Sept. 30, 1953), 1–7; and Beaver, *All Loves Excelling*.

[20] One of these adventurous women was Lottie Moon, a Southern Baptist from Virginia who arrived in north China in 1873. Overeducated by Southern standards, Moon did not see many prospects in the war-torn South of the late sixties, and the schoolteaching which she tried for a time did not wholly satisfy her. In China she was not content with a town life of sedate teaching; she embarked upon extensive preaching tours in the back country and settled for a number of years in one of the interior towns by herself, living a style of life as close to that of the Chinese as any Western woman up to that time. See Hyatt, *Our Ordered Lives Confess*, 65–136.

[21] Montgomery, *Western Women in Eastern Lands*, 175.

The desire for "all the faculties that we lacked"—on the part of the women missionaries and their sponsors alike—helped nurture a new educational form, the religious or missionary training school.[22] This school, while not exclusively for women, was particularly attractive to prospective female missionaries and other female religious workers because most of the theological seminaries were closed to them (and did not in any case offer many "practical" courses in missions). The earliest training school, the Woman's Baptist Missionary Training School in Chicago, was established in 1881 by the Woman's American Baptist Home Mission Society. By 1916 a survey listed about sixty religious training schools, the majority of which were for women or primarily for women.[23] Like the Chicago school, many of the women's missionary training schools were started by denominational women's missionary societies or by deaconess organizations or had a close connection with such bodies. In the early years, the only educational prerequisite of most of the training schools for women was the possession of a basic literacy. The intensely practical curriculum, generally spanning one or two years and taught mostly by women, consisted of such subjects as the Bible, religious pedagogy, the history of missions, and practical work in city missions or other agencies. Supplementing the formal curriculum was a schooling in piety, with frequent meetings for prayer, visits and letters from missionaries, and the inspiring example of women like Lucy Rider Meyer at the Methodist women's Chicago Training School.[24]

Women involved in missions shared in that "respectable" or pragmatic feminism emerging at the end of the nineteenth century. Eagerness to espouse the missionary cause may have prompted them to avoid confrontation over women's-rights issues in their own denominations.[25] Nevertheless, more "radical" feminist concerns were inherently close to the surface. The missionary societies served as a training ground for lay leadership, and the women's cause and the leaders' developing skills were bound to make them seek out regular denominational forums. The few lay and clergy delegates who dissented from the 1880 refusal of the Methodist Episcopal General Conference to sanction the admission of women to the office of deacon (or

[22] The first, mostly informal preparation of women for missions had taken place in new schools for women like Mount Holyoke. Hardly any woman who came under the tutelage of Mary Lyon at Holyoke graduated unconverted, and many of her alumnae became missionaries and wives of missionaries or were prominent in the organization of the missionary societies of the 1860s and 1870s. See, e.g., Montgomery, *Western Women in Eastern Lands*, 8.

[23] Walter Palmer Behan, "An Introductory Survey of the Lay Training School Field," *Religious Education*, 11 (1916), 47–52.

[24] The writers of this chapter are currently engaged with others in a study of Protestant theological education in America, which will include a section on women's missionary training schools.

[25] See Mitchell, "From Social to Radical Feminism," pp. 21–44.

elder) were aware of a certain irony in the fact that women were unofficially performing some of the functions of these offices in their missionary societies anyway. In their minority report these delegates called for the application of all offices of the laity to women "in the same sense and to the same extent as men" precisely because missionary society leaders were already engaged in "hortatory and didactic practices" and "official duties."[26]

The diaconate was another form of organization for channeling women's service in the nineteenth century, but it did not have the same critical importance as the missionary movement in the development of female leadership. The American deaconess movement grew out of the German effort to reintroduce an early Christian practice at Kaiserswerth, in 1883. Although the concept of consecrating Protestant women for church work was imported to the United States by Lutherans in 1849, it failed to take hold among them until 1884. The Methodist General Conference recognized its own order of deaconesses in 1888, shortly after Lucy Rider Meyer opened the Chicago Training School. Episcopalians also established orders. American deaconesses served the church primarily as nurses, but also pioneered as social workers.

Nevertheless, the movement never flourished in America as it had in Europe. The Kaiserswerth Conference in Europe in 1910 drew twenty thousand deaconesses.[27] There were never more than two thousand deaconesses among all the American denominations at any one time.[28] Few American women found deaconess work a satisfying option, perhaps because other forms of lay activity were available, which was not the case in Europe. The strain of anti-Catholicism among American Protestants also worked against a concept which set women apart by special garb, living stipends instead of salaries, and, for Lutherans, highly disciplined life within motherhouses. Among the Methodists, after the initial period of organization, women who chose the work failed to emerge as leaders, deferring instead to the oversight of ministers and district superintendents.[29] Among the Lutherans, the movement rarely appealed to middle-class women interested in higher education, be-

---

[26] "Minority Report on the Status of Women," quoted by Kenneth E. Rowe, ed., "The Ordination of Women: Round One: Anna Oliver and the General Conference of 1880," *Methodist History*, 12 (Apr. 1974), 70–71. Anna Howard Shaw and Anna Oliver were the two seminary graduates seeking ordination.

[27] Emilie G. Briggs, "The Restoration of the Order of Deaconesses," *Biblical World*, 41 (June 1913), 382.

[28] This 2,000 figure is an educated guess. The highest total reached in American Lutheranism, one of the denominations in which the deaconess movement succeeded best, was only 487 in 1938 (see Weiser, *Love's Response*, 70). In 1950, the first time for which we have clear figures, the Methodist Church had 488 active and 261 retired deaconesses (Lee, *As Among the Methodists*, 76).

[29] Amy Blanche Greene, "Woman's Work in the Church," *Labors of Love*, 25 (Jan. 1924), 15.

cause of the minimal educational requirements and the close association with tedious work in hospitals.[30] Clearly, the movement failed to attract enough women of talent or to employ the full talents of women. After World War I up through the 1970s there were attempts to upgrade the image, the status and the educational requirements of the position, sure evidence that the consecration and sacrifice associated with it had all too easily led to subordination and subservience.[31]

Those few women who were not content to accept "supplementary" leadership roles in home and foreign missions or in deaconess work but hoped instead for ordination faced a lonely and often futile struggle.[32] Unlike women in the mission movement or the diaconates, they did not benefit from the buffer of supportive organizations. Unlike male seminarians, they could not receive scholarship aid or free room and board in those seminaries which did accept them. Moreover, the academic credentials which they painstakingly earned—and which were not considered essential for most male ministerial candidates of the day—were insufficient to assure either ordination or a parish position.

Such years of effort took their toll, as illustrated by the careers of two Methodist seminary graduates. Anna Oliver and Anna Howard Shaw both sought permission for ordination from the Methodist Episcopal Church Conference in 1880. After the conference refused to act on the issue, only Oliver continued her struggle. By the time her financially weak congregation collapsed in 1883, her health was broken, and she died nine years later.[33] Shaw, who had successfully sought ordination in the smaller Methodist Protestant Church, was so embittered that she soon ceased to care about the churches and turned her attention to the suffrage movement.[34] The founding of the interdenominational Women's Ministerial Conference in 1882 (after annual meetings since 1873) reflected the effort of women to create a supportive— if powerless—agency where none existed.[35]

Women Within the Churches:
Organizational Mergers, Lay Status, and Professional Church Workers, 1920–1945

"Our place and contribution seem to be at this moment in question," wrote Lucy Waterbury Peabody, a leader of the Woman's American Baptist Mis-

[30] Weiser, *Love's Response*, 74–92.

[31] Ibid., 67–92; Margaret Sittler Ermath, *Adam's Fractured Rib* (Philadelphia: Fortress Press, 1970), 142–46.

[32] Dorothy Bass Fraser, "Women with a Past: A New Look at the History of Theological Education," *Theological Education* (Summer 1972), 213–24.

[33] Rowe, "Anna Oliver and the General Conference," 60–72.

[34] Rowe, "Discovery. My Ordination: Anna Howard Shaw," 126–31; Ralph W. Spencer, "Anna Howard Shaw," *Methodist History*, 13 (Jan. 1975), 41–45.

[35] Harkness, *Women in Church and Society*, 127.

sionary Society, speaking in 1927 of the women's missionary movement.[36] What threw the women into confusion about their place and contribution were several events that took place in the first quarter of the twentieth
century. In 1906 the Methodist Episcopal Church South reorganized the
women's missionary societies under the control of the denominational Board
of Missions.[37] In 1919 the Christian (Disciples) Woman's Board of Missions
and the American Christian Missionary Society were united.[38] The Presbyterian Church in the U.S.A. merged its women's missionary societies into
the main missionary boards in 1923, after little consultation with the
women.[39] In 1925 the Congregational Women's Home Missionary Federation
disappeared into one vast denominational missionary organization.[40] As early
as 1927 (if not before) some leaders in Peabody's own denomination, the
Northern Baptist Convention, were suggesting that the women's missionary
organizations be combined with the main ones.[41] (This was not actually accomplished until 1955.)

On the face of it, the consolidations seemed to herald a new era of "full
cooperation between men and women," and many women accepted them in
that spirit.[42] After all, women received positions of leadership on the new
combined missionary boards, and some provision was usually made to preserve the integrity of the women's work, though budgets were no longer
separate. Moreover, the popular wisdom of the time advocated greater "efficiency" and less waste through combined societies, and the women's organizations were not the only ones affected by the enthusiasm for consolidation.

In a parallel development, almost every one of the women's missionary
training schools closed or was absorbed into a denominational theological
seminary in the decades after World War I. There were many reasons for this.
In an educational world that was increasingly moving toward a system of
four-year colleges, followed by graduate study, the training schools became
an anomaly. The Great Depression dried up extra educational funds and lessened the demand for graduates of the training schools. But also the theological seminaries had learned from the example of the training schools and had
begun to incorporate their emphases on religious pedagogy (which became
religious education), on missions and on practical experience (which turned

[36] Peabody, "Woman's Place," 909.
[37] Anne Firor Scott, *The Southern Lady: From Pedestal to Politics 1830–1930* (Chicago/
London: Univ. of Chicago Press, 1970), 141.
[38] Lollis, *The Shape of Adam's Rib*, 99–124.
[39] Verdesi, *In But Still Out*, 70–78.
[40] Horton, *The United Church of Christ*, 227. The writers have found no information on
the circumstances of this consolidation.
[41] "Report of the Committee of Nine of the Northern Baptist Convention," *The Baptist*, 8
(April 2, 1927), 436.
[42] Mrs. W. C. Winnsborough, "Woman's Part in Home Missions," *The Missionary Review
of the World*, 50 (Feb. 1927), 97.

into field education). At long last they admitted women, primarily to non-ministerial programs. But in so doing they deprived the missionary training schools of their formerly unique function. And seminaries never allowed women theological educators a place among the trustees, the faculty, and the student body comparable to the one they had enjoyed in the training schools.

Despite certain gains from the mergers, some women were uneasy, and not a few grew angry over the new developments. Helen Barrett Montgomery predicted in 1911 that consolidation would work only if women truly received equal status in the integrated bodies, but she doubted that men would be "emancipated from the caste of sex so that they [could] work easily with women, unless they be head and women clearly subordinate."[43] While hoping for the best, Lucy Peabody wondered whether a new generation of women leaders would be able to develop out of the consolidated boards.[44] The disaffection of Presbyterian women was so apparent, partly in reduced female contributions to missions, that alarmed denominational leaders asked Katharine Bennett and Margaret Hodge to do a study of "Causes of Unrest Among Women of the Church." Not surprisingly, Bennett and Hodge noted that

> among thinking women there arose a serious question as to whether their place of service could longer be found in the church when a great organization which they had built could be autocratically destroyed by vote of male members of the church without there seeming to arise in the mind of the latter any question as to the justice, wisdom and fairness of their actions.[45]

The supposition that women gave up power in each denomination as a result of such mergers is strong but awaits further documentation.[46] Though these mergers apparently destroyed much that missionary women had created, it is possible that they also conferred an indirect and unexpected side benefit. Out of the anger and turmoil which resulted, some women (and men) of the church were jolted into greater awareness of the issue of women's place in the church. Bennett and Hodge declared firmly that

---

[43] Montgomery, *Western Women in Eastern Lands*, 269.

[44] Peabody, "Woman's Place," 909.

[45] Report of the Special Committee to the General Council of the Presbyterian Church in the U.S.A., "Causes of Unrest Among the Women of the Church" (1927), 11.

[46] Elizabeth J. Miller has documented the loss which occurred for Baptist women after the 1955 integration of the women's foreign and home missionary societies into the American Baptist Foreign Mission Society and the American Baptist Home Mission Society. She argues that upon merger of the women's societies into the larger bodies, the women received significant positions of leadership in the new societies. However, as each of these women retired or resigned, her place was filled by a man. The number of women in executive positions, never large, declined steadily to 1970. Miller's study might serve as a model for studies of the results of earlier consolidations. (Elizabeth J. Miller, "Retreat to Tokenism: A Study of the Status of Women on the Executive Staff of the American Baptist Convention," mimeographed, October 1970, 10–11.)

So long as there was a service into which they could put their strength and affection, the women were willing to ignore the disabilities that faced them in general church work. . . . But when the church, by action taken by the men of the church with but the slightest consultation with the women . . . decided to absorb these agencies which had been built up by the women, the by-product of such a decision was to open the whole question of the status of women in the church.[47]

It is even conceivable that, upset by the reaction of some of their loyal women, male denominational leaders settled on a half-conscious "trade-off." If women were to be deprived of their independent organizations, they would have to be granted some enhanced status in the regular denominational organization.

Other factors encouraged the reevaluation of women's position in the churches. A triumphant feminism which had just accomplished the passage of the Nineteenth Amendment had simultaneously served to educate church people. Women's success in staffing critical institutions on the home front during World War I convinced the skeptical of their ability to take on larger responsibility outside the home. The widespread acceptance of higher criticism in many denominations made it possible to interpret the Biblical "prohibitions" against women's speaking in the churches as culturally conditioned and as having limited authority for the present.[48]

Thus, the number of women who were ordained during the twenties and thirties increased by a slight but significant amount. An American Association of Women Preachers, organized in 1919 by two Methodist women, was a hopeful omen for the twenties, as was the publication of the Association's organ, *Woman's Pulpit*, beginning in 1921.[49] In another sign of the times the Congregational Hartford Theological Seminary declared in 1920: "In view of the changed attitude toward the ordination of women, we no longer require women to state on entering the seminary that they do not expect to enter the ministry."[50] Ordination had long been a theoretical possibility for Congregational, Baptist and Disciples women if they could only convince a local congregation to accede. Few congregations had proved willing in the past; in the new climate, however, ordination of women took place with slightly greater frequency. Congregationalists counted one hundred women ministers by 1927, whereas they had listed fewer than forty in 1900.[51] The Methodist

[47] "Causes of Unrest," 10.

[48] Aileen S. Kraditor, *The Ideas of the Woman Suffrage Movement, 1890–1920* (Garden City, N.Y.: Anchor Books, 1971), 64–81.

[49] Gibson, *When the Minister Is a Woman*, 21.

[50] Ibid.

[51] Charles E. Raven, *Women and the Ministry* (Garden City, N.Y.: Doubleday, Doran, 1929), 22; and *Congregational Year-Book 1900* (Boston: Congregational Sunday School and Publishing Co., 1900), 489–524. See also Joint Committee, "The Relative Place of Women in the Church," 52.

Episcopal Church in 1924 began allowing ordination of women as local preachers, but without granting them full membership in the General Conference.[52] Despite the admonitions in the document "Causes of Unrest Among Women of the Church," the presbyteries constituting the Presbyterian Church in the U.S.A. voted down ordination of women as ministers in 1930, but in the same ballot allowed them to become ordained elders.

Even denominations which did not ordain women were becoming more tolerant of women speaking, and in some instances preaching, in church assemblies. In 1918 two Baptist laywomen, advocates for the Woman's Baptist Missionary Union Training School, were the first women to address the Southern Baptist Convention.[53] There were also advances in lay status. In 1920 the Methodist Episcopal Church South granted women lay rights.[54] Southern Presbyterian women began serving on national boards in 1924.[55] And, for the first time, in the 1930s some Lutheran synods allowed women to speak at synodical meetings and in some cases to hold church offices.[56]

Only a handful of women were able to take advantage of the right to ordination, and even those few had to endure attempts to discourage them. One seminarian, Margaret Blair Johnstone, was examined before the Chicago Congregational Advisory Board in the early 1930s. After attempting to persuade her to become a pastor's assistant or a religious educator, the board admonished:

We are your friends. It is because we know so well the frustration awaiting any woman in the ministry that we are urging you to enter related work. We are trying to protect you not only from heartbreak, but also from ridicule. Think of the sensationalism of women evangelists. No matter how earnest you would be, no one would believe your sincerity. And consider our obligation to protect the dignity of the profession. . . . There's only a slight chance you'd get a church and little promotion or professional advancement for you if you did.[57]

[52] Magalis, *Conduct Becoming*, 138.

[53] Juliette Mather, "Women, Convention Privileges of," *Encyclopedia of Southern Baptists* (Nashville: Broadman Press, 1958), 1543.

[54] Magalis, *Conduct Becoming*, 120.

[55] Bliss, *Service and Status of Women*, 173.

[56] Augustana (Swedish Synod) allowed women delegates at synodical meetings in 1930. In 1934 the United Lutheran Church granted women rights to elected lay offices. Many other Lutheran bodies did not act until after World War II. (*The Ordination of Women*, condensed by Raymond Tiemeyer, a report distributed by authorization of the church body presidents as a contribution to further study, based on materials produced through the division of theological studies of the Lutheran Council in the U.S. [Minneapolis: Augsburg, 1970], 36.)

[57] Johnstone, *When God Says "No,"* 37.

One of the very few ways for a woman to acquire a parish was to succeed to the pulpit upon the death of her minister husband.[58]

If women still did not find numerous positions as ordained ministers and denominational leaders in this period, the creation of new professional positions in the church in the teens and the twenties gave them new opportunities to serve the church full time in exchange for a salary and a degree of dignity. These roles grew out of a society which was becoming increasingly preoccupied by the idea of professionalization and also out of an enlarged conception of the church as "the social center of the community."[59] To perform in this way, the church, it was argued, needed paid and specially trained religious educators, social workers, youth workers and others—no longer lay volunteers as in the past. The "expert," the specialist, the "professional" appeared in the church as in most areas of American social, economic and educational life.

Church leaders who observed that other professional roles for women were opening up in society warned that gifted women would desert the church if not given proper recognition for their talents. They called for certain minimal levels of training; for professional associations—denominational, national and local; and for standard hours, clearly defined functions, and salaries commensurate with those for similar roles in the society at large.[60]

Doubtless women gained increased recognition through their participation in the emerging corps of paid, specialized church workers. But theirs was very much a limited victory. Professionalization cut two ways: it was just as likely to exclude women as to give them access to positions in the church world. First, the number of churches which could afford to hire an expert in education or youth work or social work was limited. The new positions doubtless caught on in the church press much sooner than in the local churches. Second, women almost universally received lower salaries than men in the same positions. Third, precise delineation of roles was difficult, and it varied from church to church. The title "church assistant," for instance, seemed to have a number of other rough equivalents: director of religious education, director of young people's work, church secretary, church visitor, church missionary, deaconess, social worker, and pastor's assistant. Church journalists tried gropingly but without success to define precisely the func-

---

[58] Hazel E. Foster, "The Ecclesiastical Status of Women," *The Woman's Pulpit*, 30 (Jan.–March 1952), 2.

[59] Mrs. Henry W. Hunter, "The Work of the Church Assistant," *Religious Education*, 12 (Feb. 1917), 26.

[60] See, e.g., ibid.; also, Agnes Mabel Taylor, "Standards of Preparation of Women Church Assistants," *Religious Education*, 12 (Dec. 1917), 438–46; Henry F. Cope, "The Professional Organization of Workers in Religious Education," *Religious Education*, 16 (1921), 162–67.

tions of various positions.[61] Many women "professionals" became merely glorified errand girls who found themselves saddled with the detail work of the parish. Fourth, often when "professional" associations were attempted, men came to dominate them. For instance, the Association of Church Directors of Religious Education, organized in the early teens, required college graduation plus two years of specialized training in graduate school for membership at a time when many women workers in religious education could not claim this kind of background.[62] Finally, job security was not high; these new specialists were the first to go when budgets grew tight, as they did with the onset of the Depression.

Women in the Pulpit:
Ordination, 1945–1970

If the social ferment of the twenties and the thirties helped women to gain new positions and rights in the churches, the events of World War II helped to consolidate these advances. Wartime disruptions in gender roles especially affected the European churches. There women with university theological training were ordained and assumed pastoral office in the absence of men. Moreover, the attempt by the Nazis to exploit the traditional arenas of women's work—*Kinder, Kirche und Küche*—for the benefit of the state had provoked an adverse reaction.[63] For the first time, events in in the international church prompted advances in status in the American churches. The first meeting of the World Council of Churches in Amsterdam in 1948 provided the forum for an international discussion of the "Life and Work of Women in the Church."

Events surrounding that meeting evoked a self-consciousness about the role of women at a time when secular feminism was quiescent. In preparation for the meeting, Inez Cavert of the Federal Council of Churches in America compiled the study "Women in American Church Life."[64] Following the meeting, Kathleen Bliss interpreted the various national reports prepared for the conference in a volume entitled *The Service and Status of Women in the Churches*, which appeared in 1952.[65] In the same year *The Christian Century*, editorializing on Bliss's work and the 1948 meeting, called for women's ordination and produced a series of articles "intended to make better known to the American public women who are playing conspicuous parts in the

[61] See, e.g., Taylor, "Standards of Preparation of Women Church Assistants."

[62] E.g., most of the membership appointments announced in 1920 for this association were male. See *Religious Education*, 15 (Oct. 1920), 293.

[63] First Assembly of the World Council of Churches, "Interim Report of the Study on the Life and Work of Women in the Church" (Amsterdam, 1948), 5–6.

[64] Mimeographed report, Dept. of Research and Education, Federal Council of Churches of Christ in America, 1948.

[65] London: SCM Press, 1952.

church life of this country."[66] In 1952 also the United Church Women of the National Council of Churches urged member denominations to continue to study the role of women.[67]

Indeed, the ferment produced new wine. In 1953 the Disciples Committee on the Service and Status of Women in the Churches published a report calling for full and equal participation of women in all leadership positions at all levels of the denomination.[68] The Presbyterian Church in the U.S.A. voted to ordain women in 1956, and the Methodist Church granted full Conference privileges to ordained women in the same year. Interdenominational seminaries were also impelled to action. Harvard Divinity School, long inhospitable to women, began to accept them on equal terms with men in a new divinity program, while Yale Divinity School built a new dormitory for women.[69]

There were other pressures on the American churches which contributed to these changes. Church bodies which had granted women lay status earlier were increasingly aware of their dependence on women's leadership. In addition, there were shortages of clergy and professional church workers in a period of growing church membership. Theological seminaries began admitting women to their Bachelor (now Master) of Divinity programs. Ordination of women came as a natural outgrowth of these developments. No major struggle accompanied discussion of the issue; no fanfare greeted the outcome.[70] Apparently, clergymen did not imagine that many women would seek ordination, nor did they expect them to alter the office in any significant way.

Ordination of women did not come as easily in American Lutheranism as in the other denominations. While some Lutheran bodies participated in the World Council of Churches from its founding, the Lutheran churches, as immigrant churches bound to orthodoxy, were generally isolated from the broad front of American Protestantism. They were also separated from the wartime experiences of their sister churches in Germany and Scandinavia.

---

[66] "Women in the Churches," *The Christian Century*, 69 (May 1952), 606–7.

[67] An account of one such denominational study can be found in "Women in the Church: A Symposium on the Service and Status of Women Among the Disciples of Christ" (Lexington: College of the Bible, 1953), 23–32. Apparently in reaction to such positive responses, the official publishing house of the Lutheran Church–Missouri Synod (not a member of the WCC) published a translation of a German work opposing ordination for women (Fritz Zerbst, *The Office of Woman in the Church*, trans. Albert G. Merkens [St. Louis: Concordia Publishing House, 1955]).

[68] Howard Elmo Short, "The Service and Status of Women Among the Disciples of Christ," in "Women in the Church."

[69] Hazel E. Foster, "The Ecclesiastical Status of Women," *The Woman's Pulpit*, 23 (1955), 3; 25 (1957), 8.

[70] Doris Moreland Jones of the Board of Higher Education and Ministry, United Methodist Church, noted these reactions in the Methodist Church General Conference in 1956 (telephone interview with Rev. Doris Moreland Jones, June 29, 1977).

The question of women's ordination for Lutherans at midcentury was different from the question of equal access, the core issue by then among most other Protestants. Until the seventies most Lutherans would have found women in the pastorate an inconceivable breach of the Biblical "orders of creation" as interpreted in Lutheran doctrine. In addition, American Lutherans still revered the authority of the clergy in ways corresponding more to European than to American practice. When most European Lutheran churches adopted the practice in the sixties—after nearly two decades of study—American Lutherans were suddenly in the minority among world Lutherans.[71] The action of the European churches, based as it was on new hermeneutical principles and acceptance of the changing role of women in society, probably had as much to do with the breakup of traditional opposition in America as did American feminism.

Nevertheless, vestiges of the earlier viewpoint still remain in American Lutheranism. The Missouri Synod, long recognized for its concern with orthodoxy, has balked on the issue entirely, although some member synods of its breakaway body, the Association of Evangelical Lutheran Churches, have voted to ordain women. The Synod opposed national lay organizations for men or women until well into the twentieth century, refused to grant women teachers equal status with men in its parochial school system, and advised congregations to grant only limited lay rights to women in 1969.[72]

Epilogue

In the process of reaching a decision for ordination, Lutherans had joined with other denominations in the late sixties and early seventies in examining anew the question of the place and status of women in the churches. Spurred on by the secular women's movement, church leaders and others marshaled a host of disappointing statistics. They found that women's participation in the church at almost all levels had declined in the decade of the sixties. For instance, among the United Presbyterians women constituted only 16 percent of all the elders in 1974.[73] In 1967 only one quarter of American Baptist Convention directors of religious education were women, although religious education was traditionally a feminine field.[74] The proportion of single women foreign missionaries in that denomination had

---

[71] Christine Bourbeck, "Women as Clergymen in Germany," *Lutheran Quarterly*, 18 (May 1966), 168–72; Erika Reichle, "The Ordained Woman in the Parish and in Other Ministries," *Lutheran World*, 22 (1975), 49–53; *The Ordination of Women*, condensed by Raymond Tiemeyer, 34–35.

[72] Graebner, *Uncertain Saints*, 129–40, 184–86.

[73] Sarah Frances Anders, "The Role of Women in American Religion," *Southwestern Journal of Theology*, 17 (Spring 1976), 56.

[74] American Baptist Executive Staff Women, "Fact or Fallacy: Equal Employment Opportunity in the American Baptist Convention," n.d.

also declined.[75] Almost all denominational reports noted an erosion of the participation of women in all church agencies in the decade of the sixties, even in those which had customarily been associated with women, such as the mission boards.

The number of women in the ordained ministry gave the greatest reason for concern. In 1972 less than one percent of the clergy in the American Baptist Convention, the United Methodist Church, and the Presbyterian and Disciples of Christ denominations were women.[76] The number serving parishes was even smaller, and smaller yet the number serving as sole or senior pastor.

In response, advocates for women in almost every denomination set up task forces and committees, surveys and newsletters, all designed to produce a new awareness of women in the church. Biblical arguments were rehearsed once again. Feminists urged quotas or goals upon denominational agencies and deliberative bodies, and denominations began to monitor the number of women in lay and ordained positions.

To all appearances this concentrated focus on women bore fruit. By 1976 there were about 240 ordained women in the United Presbyterian Church, an increase of nearly 80 percent over the 1973 figure of 131.[77] Among the United Methodists, there were 373 women in 1970 and 620 in 1975 in all ministerial categories (deacons and elders).[78] In most denominations the number of women employed in denominational agencies began to rise. And the enrollment of women in seminary ministerial-degree programs had sharply increased.[79]

For the first time in the history of each of the major denominations, the number of ordained women is large enough for them to project a "presence." As women in every denomination assess their experiences, common themes surface.[80] There is a quest for jobs. At a time when church bodies and their budgets are contracting, a shortage of job opportunities plagues both women and men. Many advocate new styles of ministry such as shared positions and

[75] Board of Managers, American Baptist Women, "Women in Church-Related Vocations," mimeographed, 1968. Comments of Richard Beers during symposium on "Opportunities for Women in Church-Related Vocations," 17.

[76] Anders, "The Role of Women in American Religion," 55.

[77] "Forces Affecting the Employment of Women in the Church," n.d., mimeographed (United Presbyterian Church in the U.S.A.).

[78] "Commission on the Status and Role of Women in the United Methodist Church" (pamphlet issued for the General Conference, 1976), Figure 5.

[79] Marvin J. Taylor, ed., *Fact Book on Theological Education 1976–1977* (Association of Theological Schools, 1977), 8. For the most recent statistics on women ministers see Constant H. Jacquet, Jr., "Woman Ministers in 1977" (study issued by Office of Research, Evaluation and Planning, National Council of Churches, 1978).

[80] For a review of some of these issues, see Linda J. Hanson, "A Survey of Interests and Agendas of Women in U.S. Church Denominations," *Theological Education*, 11 (Winter 1975), 82–95.

alternative sources of income. There is a quest for collegiality. Women feel excluded from established modes of interaction among the male clergy and seek to alter these patterns and also create new networks of support for themselves. Such networks may have their drawbacks. Some women may fear that they cause a diminution of independence, leadership, and assertiveness that may hamper their work. There is a quest to make the churches more responsive to the experience and outlook of women in general by arguing that ordained women bring unique gifts to ministry that will enhance the churches' sensitivity to all their members. This argument is reminiscent of the overly optimistic one advanced by suffragists claiming the moral superiority of women and their potential reforming effect on the nation. Finally, there is a quest to redefine the exercise of authority in the churches. As with those other questions, this is not a "women's issue" alone. It is part of a more generalized discomfort with "directive" leadership and a preference for non-directive styles. A decisive move toward nondirective styles of thought and leadership would doubtless have radical effects on theology and ethics.

Emerging feminist groups in all denominations will continue to pose answers to these and other questions. They occupy center stage in current discussions of women in the church because they often comprise the most articulate, well-organized and politically minded of church women and because many denominational leaders, having experienced a certain measure of guilt because of their past stance toward women, are eager to redress grievances quickly. Yet, even the most ardent of their supporters will admit that the feminists wield an influence that is out of proportion to their numbers in the churches and that introduces viewpoints from outside denominational traditions.

Denominational and feminist leaders face an awesome responsibility. Together they are in a position to reshape the conception of ministry in all its manifestations—pastoral, theological, liturgical, educational. Agendas and programs will have to be weighed critically in this fluid situation. It needs to be asked whether the cultural viewpoint of the feminists in the seventies is large enough and mature enough to do justice both to centuries of Christian tradition and to the need to integrate women more fully into the life of the church. Decisions that would be unmindful of the history of the church or of the diversity of its membership might well diminish the richness of Christian life and mute the witness of women who worked so energetically alongside of and within the churches for more than a century.

James J. Kenneally

Eve, Mary, and the Historians
American Catholicism and Women

Nineteenth-century Americans enshrined women on a pedestal whose base was the four ladylike virtues of piety, purity, submissiveness, and domesticity. It was assumed that females, naturally religious and inherently modest, would strive to maintain these attributes against the assaults of inferior, sensual men. Once married, as a mark of love and femininity they would subordinate their entire being to that of their husbands, continuing to be submissive, passive responders. However, in affairs solely domestic they would reign supreme, for women were uniquely qualified to rule as queens in their own domain, the home.[1]

To many American Catholics this was not only an acceptable model but a familiar one, resting in part on a Christian tradition that held that such a pattern was designed by God, exemplified by the Virgin Mary, and revealed by a Pauline interpretation of scripture and natural law. Furthermore, it was reenforced by biological differences and supported by a historical tradition proclaiming the supremacy of man. Consequently numerous Catholics believed in distinct spheres of activity for each sex. Woman's centered around her position as perpetuator of the race and nucleus of the family. If she moved from that orbit, critics claimed the action would be abnormal and thus endanger universal order and jeopardize society.[2]

Obviously such sentiments did not end with the nineteenth century. In 1930

Reprinted from *Horizons* 3/2 (1976), by permission of the publisher.

[1] Barbara Welter, "The Cult of True Womanhood: 1820–1860," *American Quarterly*, 18 (Summer 1966), 151–74.

[2] James J. Kenneally, "Catholicism and Woman Suffrage in Massachusetts," *Catholic Historical Review*, 53 (Apr. 1967), 43–44.

Pope Pius XI described women's efforts for social, economic, and physiological equality as debasing and unnatural. Over a decade later Pius XII asserted that: "The heroism of motherhood is the pride and glory of the Christian wife" and that "every woman is called to be a mother, mother in the physical sense; or mother in a sense more spiritual and more exalted, yet real, nonetheless." Furthermore, he cautioned wives to be submissive to their husbands' authority: "Many voices will suggest rather a proud autonomy; they will repeat that you are in every respect the equal of your husband, and in many respects his superior. Do not react like Eve to these lying, tempting, deceitful voices."[3]

Such pronouncements served to reenforce those contemporary American Catholic thinkers who proclaimed motherhood a God-given, privileged destiny and attributed many societal problems to women's failure to acquit themselves properly in the home.[4] Many post–World War II Catholic college students studied from an ethics textbook affirming that woman was "more religious, more moral, more God-fearing" than man but that "modern woman, somewhat after the fashion of the dog in Aesop's fable who saw in the water the reflection of himself carrying a bone is snapping after a delusive emancipation; and if she completely descends from the regal throne she once enjoyed, to go down into the hurly-burly of everyday life to contend with man for a false equality, she will get hurt. And badly."[5] In 1964 Bishop Fulton J. Sheen (Rochester) wrote that as purity, protection of the weak, sacrifice, procreation and sustaining and caring for human nature were qualities proper to a woman, every woman without exception was then morally obligated to realize either an actual or potential motherhood.[6]

Despite the new era ushered in by Pope John XXIII and the Second Vatican Council, these views were not unorthodox. The pope's 1963 encyclical, *Pacem in Terris*, proclaiming the human rights of women, was circumscribed by traditional caution, as were the Council decrees declaring female entitlement to cultural and educational opportunities and a state of life equal to that of males. John announced that women's right to work was only in accordance with their requirements and duties as wives and mothers, while the Vatican

---

[3] Pius XI, *Casti Connubi*, 1930, as in Benedictine Monks of Solesmes, eds., *The Woman in the Modern World: Papal Teachings* (Boston: St. Paul Editions, 1959), 37–38; and in the same collection Pius XII, *To All Italian Women*, October 1945, 131; *To All Newly Weds*, September 1941, 68–69; *To Newly Weds*, February 1942, 83.

[4] Grace H. Sherwood, "The Church and the Dignity of Woman," *Catholic Action*, 14 (July 1932), 11–12; W. B. Faherty, "American Feminism: a Century After," *America*, 80 (Dec. 4, 1948), 235; Frederick W. Fries, "Should Women Work," *Catholic Digest*, 2 (May 1938), 29–31; Lydwine V. Kersbergen, "Toward a Christian Concept of Woman," *New Catholic World* (Oct. 1955), 9–11; John B. Sheerin, "Mary Most Gracious Advocate," *Homiletic and Pastoral Review*, 52 (May 1952), 681.

[5] Thomas Higgins, *Man as Man* (Milwaukee: Bruce Publishing Co., 1949), 421.

[6] Quoted in George Tavard, *Women in the Christian Tradition* (Notre Dame, Ind.: Univ. of Notre Dame Press, 1973), 129.

"Fathers," although teaching that the legitimate social progress of women should not be "underrated," reasserted the conviction that the domestic role must be preserved and that children need their mothers at home.[7] A more recent pontiff also has perceived women's role myopically: after extolling the uniqueness of her nature, psychology, and vocation, Paul VI declared in 1974 that "as we see her, woman is a vision of virginal purity . . . she is for man in his loneliness, the companion whose life is one of unreserved loving dedication, resourceful collaboration and help, courageous fidelity and toil, and habitual heroic sacrifice . . . she is the Mother—let us bow in reverence before her."[8] Obviously sexual equality is impossible from such a perspective. In an address to a Committee for the International Women's Year in April 1975, the pope pronounced that "nothing is accomplished by talking of equalization of rights, since the problem goes far deeper. The aim must be a complementarity in which men and women contribute their respective energies to the building of a world which is not leveled into uniformity but is harmoniously organized."[9]

As a result of these concepts many Catholics, male and female, have worked to preserve society and its values by defending woman's traditional role from those who would change it. One of the greatest threats came from suffragists, who would wrest females from the pedestal and thrust them into the sordid and debased world of politics. Catholic journals, newspapers, and leaders, lay as well as clerical, assailed this alleged reform that would usurp male prerogatives and rights. As early as 1869, the prominent Catholic convert Orestes Brownson claimed the ballot would bring harm to man and woman, destroy the family, and hasten the dissolution of society. A few years later Joseph Macheboeuf, bishop of Colorado, contemptuously dismissed suffragists as "old maids, disappointed in love."[10] Addressing the first national antisuffrage convention, James Cardinal Gibbons (Baltimore) warned that the vote would rob woman of her character, and he declared that its opponents were the real upholders of the dignity of women. Archbishop Henry Moeller (Cincinnati) implored females to stand fast against this un-Christian assault and to sign antisuffrage petitions. In a classic example of

[7] John XXIII, *Peace on Earth* (Boston: St. Paul Editions, n.d.), 10–11, 17; "Pastoral Constitution of the Church in the Modern World," in Walter M. Abbott, ed., *The Documents of Vatican II* (New York: Guild Press, 1966), 257, 227, 228.

[8] "The Role of Women in Contemporary Society: Address of Pope Paul VI to the Convention of the Union of Italian Catholic Jurists, December 8, 1974," *Pope Speaks*, 19 (Spring 1975), 316.

[9] Paul VI, "Women in the Life and Mission of the Church: an Address to the Committee for the International Women's Year, April 18, 1975," ibid., 20 (Summer 1975), 39.

[10] Orestes Brownson, "The Woman Question," *Catholic World*, 9 (May, 1869), 147, 150; Elizabeth C. Stanton, et al., eds., *History of Woman Suffrage*, 6 vols. (1881–1922; reprint ed., New York: Arno and the *New York Times*, 1967), 3, 720; also see Arlene Swidler, "Brownson and the 'Woman Question,'" *American Benedictine Review*, 19 (June 1968), 211–19.

circuitous reasoning, Archbishop Sebastian G. Messmer proclaimed to the State Federation of Catholic Societies that suffrage could not be sanctioned "because of the essential inequality of man and woman." Essayist, poet, and reformer John Boyle O'Reilly, who has been hailed as the most distinguished Irishman in America, seemed to represent a generation of Catholic thought when he wrote:

> Woman suffrage is an unjust, unreasonable, unspiritual abnormality. It is a hard, undigested, tasteless, devitalized proposition. It is a half-fledged unmusical, Promethian abomination. It is a quack bolus to reduce masculinity even by the obliteration of femininity. . . . It is the sediment, not the wave of sex. It is the antithesis of that highest and sweetest mystery— conviction by submission, and conquest by sacrifice.[11]

Dangers inherent in this reform were apparent to the entire Catholic community. In the only nineteenth-century test of popular sentiment, Catholic areas voted overwhelmingly against woman suffrage in the Massachusetts referendum of 1895.[12] In 1900 the National American Woman Suffrage Association was able to list only six Catholic clergymen who supported woman suffrage (Revs. J. W. Dalton, Thomas Scully, Edward McGlynn and Bishops John Ireland, Bernard McQuaid, and John Spalding). The Church Work Committee of that organization as late as 1915 singled out as one of the suffragists' most important tasks "the organization of Catholic women, that they will make their demands so emphatic the church will see the wisdom of supporting the movement."[13]

More subtle than suffrage but equally threatening to traditional concepts were demands for female education. Bishop William Stang (Fall River) dismissed this movement as a luxury, because women whose proper sphere was the home did not have to be as well educated as their husbands. Furthermore, they should eschew newspapers and novels, for "smartness is not becoming to a woman."[14] According to the *Sacred Heart Review* (Cambridge, Massa-

---

[11] Kenneally, "Catholicism and Woman Suffrage," 47; Katherine E. Conway, ed., *Watchwords from John Boyle O'Reilly* (Boston: Joseph George Cupples, 1891), 20. Catholic opposition was also based on suffrage's alleged and actual association with socialism and nativism, see: Lois Bannister Merk, "Boston's Historic Public School Crisis," *New England Quarterly*, 31 (June 1958), 194, 199; Alan P. Grimes, *The Puritan Ethic and Woman Suffrage* (New York: Oxford Univ. Press, 1967), 11, 89, 125, 140; David Goldstein and Martha M. Avery, *Socialism: the Nation of Fatherless Children* (Boston: T. J. Flynn & Co., 1911), 21–22, 211, 223, 251, 298; Joseph W. McKee, "Shall Women Vote," *Catholic World*, 102 (Oct. 1915), 53; and *New York Times*, Nov. 8, 1917.

[12] James J. Kenneally, "Woman Suffrage and the Massachusetts 'Referendum' of 1895," *Historian*, 30 (Aug. 1968), 630–31.

[13] Stanton, *History of Woman Suffrage*, 4, 1079–80 and 5, 448.

[14] William Stang, *Socialism and Christianity* (New York: Benziger Bros., 1905), 78–80. For an excellent summary of American opposition to women's education see Barbara Welter, "Anti-Intellectualism and the American Woman," *Mid-America*, 48 (1966), 258–70.

chusetts) if girls became more intelligent and read more, the role of the father would become one of helpless bewilderment in a matriarchy.[15]

These positions were logical developments of Catholic moral theology, which subordinated the "housewife" to the husband. Conservatives taught that women should emulate Mary and prepare for their roles as wives and mothers, for complete fulfillment was to be found in the home.[16]

However, other Catholics believed that education could and should reenforce feminine subordination to men. Brownson contended that Protestants needed Catholic schools "to teach maidens modesty and reserve, and wives and mothers due submission to their husbands . . . to train them to be contented to be women, and not to aspire to be men, or to usurp the functions of men and to bid them to stay at home and not be gadding abroad, running over the country and spouting nonsense, free love, infidelity, and blasphemy at suffrage conventions."[17] Fifty years later the perceptions of Catholic intellectuals had changed but little. Thomas Shields, professor of psychology and education at Catholic University, who was considered the leading Catholic educator in the first quarter of the twentieth century, contended in his widely used text, *Philosophy of Education* (1917), that the education of women should be determined by their nature and the work that awaited them; consequently the ultimate aim of female schooling was to develop future mothers and homemakers. In his article on education in the *Catholic Encyclopedia*, Shields was more direct. Here he asserted not only that woman's learning must be limited to those things belonging to her calling, but that any influence making her duties less sacred is a menace to society. Decades later, during the 1940s, these values were reflected by listing in the *Religious Bulletin* of Notre Dame University qualities that educated Catholic young men should look for when courting. Education and intelligence were ignored; however, the "boys" were advised: "Try out her cooking. . . . She may never have to soil her hands with dishwater; but if she doesn't you will. There'll come a time! Don't wait until after marriage to domesticate her. If she doesn't know how to run a home, you won't have a home."[18]

Similar views were promulgated even in 1961 by a Catholic female educator who advocated that women college students major in home economics to insure that they "will not be disillusioned by the monotony of daily chores because such tasks have assumed deeper meaning in the broader context of human existence. They no longer spell drudgery but are a challenge to inves-

---

[15] Donna Merwick, *Boston Priests 1848–1910: a Study of Social and Intellectual Change* (Cambridge: Harvard Univ. Press, 1973), 135.

[16] Robert D. Cross, *The Emergence of Liberal Catholicism in America* (Cambridge: Harvard Univ. Press, 1958), 133.

[17] Quoted in Swidler, "Brownson and 'Woman Question,'" 218; also ibid., 157.

[18] Quoted in John A. O'Brien, *Courtship and Marriage* (Paterson, N.J.: St. Anthony Guild Press, 1949), 41–42.

tigate more fully the significance of the particular to the general, the transient to the permanent, and the temporal to the eternal." A 1963 marriage manual advised that "Wives are in some instances actually superior in mentality or in character to their husbands; their role in marriage arises not from personal qualities but rather from status. Accordingly such wives even though superior in person remain obligated to a subordinate position." (The index of this work, Alphonse Clemens, *Design for a Successful Marriage*, under the heading "Wives" states, "see Home Economics, Housewives.")

Education may have been a danger to the traditional family role but working women represented a transgression of divine planning so serious as to menace all of society. Leonora M. Barry, the first full-time female labor organizer in the nation, campaigned indefatigably to get working women to join the Knights of Labor. A devoted Catholic and widow, she believed that women belonged at home and that marriage and adequate wages for males should make it unnecessary for females to work. However, if compelled to seek employment, women should join unions, for these organizations would create favorable working conditions for potential mothers and protect their "honor" and "purity." Practicing what she preached, when Barry remarried in 1890 she resigned as an organizer and pursued more "ladylike" activities. Yet despite her traditional views, she had been attacked by a priest as a "Lady Tramp," and the Knights had been denounced as a "vulgar immoral society" for encouraging the unionization of women. Even the members of the Knights, many of them Catholic, found Barry's labors unnatural. Women refused to join due to "religious scruples," and to the chagrin of the leadership, men tended to ignore or impede her efforts.[20]

Other Catholics in addition to Barry attempted to reconcile the church's precepts with economic realities forcing women to work under dehumanizing conditions. It was advocated, naively, that women avoid occupations leading to overly free association with men and instead strive for positions consistent with their delicacy and modesty. Furthermore, single women were exhorted to raise conditions of employment by driving married females from the work force into their natural vocation of child rearing. But above all, working women were implored to cling to their faith as succor in the face of hardship and temptation.[21] By the turn of the century, however, the prominent proponent of social justice for the worker, Monsignor John Ryan, found a different solution to the problem by championing equal pay and minimum wage leg-

[19] Sister M. Leonita Smith, "Catholic Viewpoints About the Psychology, Social Role and Higher Education of Women" (Diss. Ohio State Univ., 1961), 144.

[20] James J. Kenneally, "Women and Trade Unions, 1870–1920: the Quandary of the Reformer," *Labor History*, 14 (Winter 1973), 43–44. Also see Leonora M. Lake, "Economic Wrongs as a Woman Sees Them," *Donahoes*, 31 (Jan. 1899), 17.

[21] B. Murphy, "Women as Bread Winners," *Catholic World*, 17 (May 1873), 230, 232; Mary B. O'Sullivan, "The Sacrifice of the Shop-Girl," *Donahoes*, 29 (May 1893), 532; "Should Married Women Work?" *Donahoes*, 29 (May 1893), 632.

islation. Competition with men for employment, which was detrimental to women's health,. preparation for marriage, and the entire race, would be sharply reduced as these laws would remove females from the cheaper labor category, thus eliminating the major incentive for hiring them.[22]

During World War II Catholic spokesmen continued to warn that working mothers endangered society and that "we shall have lost the war, if we lose the home."[23] Enlistments in the Women's Auxiliary Army Corps (WAAC) were attacked by James Cassidy, bishop of Fall River, who claimed that the organization contravened the teachings and principles of the Church.[24] Urging that the hiring of mothers be kept to a minimum, the bishops of the United States expressed anxiety over the moral atmosphere where females worked (needless to say they ignored the moral climate where men were employed) and cautioned against turning the "mind and heart [of women] away from the home, thereby depriving the family, State, and Church of her proper contributions to the common welfare."[25] Admonishments similar to these continued in the postwar years. One writer in 1964 implored women not to work and maintained that instead they should be prepared to offer their lives to the home, the training of children, and obedience to husbands, and a leading Catholic marriage manual asserted that employment might foster undesirable traits in a wife by making her less willing to sacrifice and adjust emotionally in order to keep her husband happy. Contentment ordinarily achieved by giving herself to him thus would be endangered by a new-found aggressiveness and egotism.[26]

Readily embraced by American Catholics, the "pedestal-Mary" concept contained the seeds of its own destruction, for if women were inherently so pious and pure, so "superior" to men, it was only logical to ennoble society by having them extend their good influence to the larger world family about them. Catholicism had a long tradition of this type of service in its women's religious institutions. Ladylike qualities, nurtured and fostered by the institutional Church, made nuns ideal for teaching children, blacks, and Indians, for running orphanages and nursing the infirm and aged. On the other hand,

[22] Francis L. Broderick, *Right Reverend New Dealer: John A. Ryan* (New York: Macmillan, 1963), 58–59.

[23] "Bishop Duffy Deplores Mothers' Wartime Jobs," *Catholic Action,* 24 (July 1942), 6; Joseph B. Schuyler, "Women at Work," *Catholic World,* 157 (Apr. 1943), 27–30; Editorial, *Boston Pilot,* May 30, 1942.

[24] *Fall River Herald News,* May 18, 1942.

[25] "Statements Issued by the Archbishops and Bishops of the United States on Victory and Peace, November 14, 1942," 112 and "Statement on International Order of the Hierarchy of the United States, November 16, 1944," 119, both documents in Raphael Huber, ed., *Our Bishops Speak, National Pastorals* (Milwaukee: Bruce Publishing Co., 1952).

[26] Solange Hertz, "The Two Faces of Eve," *Ave Maria,* 94 (Feb. 29, 1964), 6–9; Editorial, "Women at Work," *America,* 80 (Jan. 8, 1949), 364; George A. Kelly, *The Catholic Marriage Manual* (New York: Random House, 1958), 116–18.

these activities wherein sisters performed as administrators and superiors, natural "male roles," sometimes led to clashes with hierarchy. (Of the twelve nuns listed in *Notable American Women*, six had difficulties with male superiors.)

The notion of extending the influence of virtuous women encouraged Bishop John Spalding (Peoria) to proclaim as early as 1884 that he could see no harm in experimental suffrage for women because these "Natural educators of the Race" were the most religious, most moral, most sober portion of the people and might succeed in elevating American society, a task men had failed to do.[27] This same rationale was offered by the handful of clergymen and eminent laity who endorsed that reform.[28] In the same spirit Catholic women's suffrage groups were organized around 1915 to offset the radical, unladylike suffragists who advocated using the ballot for changes jeopardizing the sacred family.

When the Nineteenth Amendment was finally ratified, Cardinal Gibbons and many Catholic journals, previously opposed to the ballot, entreated Catholic women to vote and thereby check those females who would use the ballot as a tool to legislate "unladylike reforms" menacing the family and the home. The presiding officer at the 1920 National Conference of Catholic Charities exhorted women to join political parties and "in response to the urge of mother love that is experienced by every normal woman" to become involved with those issues affecting the home, such as inflation, schools, and child labor.[29] Even the Bishops' Pastoral Letter of 1919 proclaimed that the franchise might prove an advantage, gentle women may purify and elevate the political life as they can "reach the hearts of men and take away their bitterness . . . this is woman's vocation in respect to public affairs." Voting was still not viewed as a woman citizen's *right* in 1931, as *America* magazine pleaded with Catholic females to sacrifice and vote in order to offset "narrow, bigoted women."[30] Forty years after the ratification of the Nineteenth Amendment some were still unable to reconcile the women's ballot with Mary-like virtues. Dominic M. Prummer in *Handbook of Moral Theology* (1957) stated that since woman came from Adam's rib and was excluded from the priesthood by God, it was clearly "never God's intention for complete equality,"

---

[27] John L. Spalding, "Basis of Popular Government," *North American Review*, 134 (Sept. 1884), 199–208.

[28] Edward McSweeny, "Das Ewige Weiblich," *Catholic World*, 49 (June 1889), 331; Thomas M. Murray, "Municipal Suffrage for Women," *Donahoes*, 21 (May 1889), 451; Katherine Conway, "Present Aspect of Woman Suffrage," *Donahoes*, 35 (Apr. 1896), 394; *New York Times*, Apr. 12, 1915. Also see Margaret H. Rorke, *Letters and Addresses on Woman Suffrage by Catholic Ecclesiastics* (New York: Devin-Adair Co., 1914).

[29] *New York Times*, Sept. 13, Oct. 12, 1920; *America*, 22 (1920), 448; *Catholic World*, 112 (1920), 152; *America*, 44 (1931), 553–54.

[30] "Pastoral Letter, 1919," in Huber, *Our Bishops Speak*, 46.

her chief duty is "care for the home," and although there is nothing to prevent capable women from having the right to vote, it is questionable whether any useful purpose is served the state or the Church in granting it. ⌉

In the same way that belief in a uniquely feminine moral excellence enabled many Catholics to support suffrage, others were convinced of societal advantages resulting from women's education. When the Third Plenary Council of Baltimore in 1884 required parishes to build parochial schools and bishops to provide teachers, higher education of Catholic women became a practical necessity. The leading proponent of female schooling, Bishop Spalding, claiming education would enable the "beauty and charm" of woman's nature to "be brought more effectively into play," also contended that a learned woman would be better able to fill the duties of wife and mother, for an ignorant mind would dull the intellects of husband and child. Advocating a curriculum to develop further women's glories of "pure mindedness, modesty, patience, piety, reverence, gentleness, amiability and helpfulness," the bishop of Peoria concluded that "since it is our duty to educate, it is our duty to give the best education to woman, for she, as mother, is the aboriginal God-appointed educator."[31]

In order to realize these ladylike objectives, several girls' academies were converted into four-year colleges. Since the Catholic University of America refused to admit females, a new woman's college, Trinity, was established in 1900 in Washington, D.C., the first institution designed as a school of higher education for Catholic women. A curriculum "deemed useful in fitting a woman for her proper sphere in the Home and Society" was developed to insure that Trinity students increased in Christian womanliness, gentility, sweet voice, feminine piety, and fear of God.[32]

As Rosemary Ruether so well points out, there was a sharp contrast in the founding of Catholic and non-Catholic women's colleges. Institutions such as Vassar, Smith, and Wellesley were established to combat the restrictive myth of women's incapacities and therefore they developed curricula and standards rivaling male institutions. However, the rationale of Catholic colleges was the distinct nature of women and the need for a specific feminine education.[33] As a result, well into the twentieth century

---

[31] John L. Spalding, "Woman is the God-Appointed Educator," *Donahoes*, 95 (Feb. 1901), 176; John L. Spalding, *Means and Ends in Education* (Chicago: A. C. McClurg and Co., 1895), 100–130; John L. Spalding, "Women and the Higher Education: an Address Delivered Under the Auspices of the Auxiliary Board of Trinity College, at the Columbian University, Washington, D.C., January 16, 1899," in *Opportunity and Other Essays and Addresses*, 3d ed. (Chicago: A. C. McClurg and Co., 1903), 57–60, 64–65.

[32] Sarah W. Howe, "Trinity College," *Donahoes*, 45 (Feb. 1901), 319; William Seton, "The Higher Education of Women and Posterity," *Catholic World*, 73 (May 1901), 148–49.

[33] Rosemary Ruether, "Are Women's Colleges Obsolete," *Critic*, 27 (Oct.–Nov. 1968), 61–63.

many Catholic educators have maintained that the purpose of higher education for women was to foster feminine attributes including submissiveness,
and to prepare females for marriage and a career in the home. Instruction,
discipline, and rules of dress frequently have revolved around these ends.[34]
As recently as 1961 a survey of 109 presidents of Catholic colleges and
universities that admitted women revealed that the vast majority of administrators, believing that females had a unique social role and differed psychologically from males, advocated a special curriculum in keeping with
women's nature. Over two-thirds of these presidents contended that the "essential role" of women is motherhood. More surprising was the conclusion
of the female educator who completed the survey: "Surely we do not want
education to be the great leveler of the sexes. If this comes to pass, neither
would excel in the particular gifts with which nature has endowed it."[35]

Many Catholics advocated the Mary ideal, removing in part restraints on
freedom and opportunity for women, but others maintained another ideal—
one more directly repressive. Based on Old Testament traditions of Eve, and
Paul's apparent misogyny, it viewed woman as a temptress, a source of sin
for helpless and easily aroused males, as Cardinal Leon Suenens wrote in
1963: "Woman has the awe-ful choice of being Eve or Mary . . . either she
ennobles and raises man up by her presence, by creating a climate of beauty
and human nobility, or she drags him down with her in her own fall."[36]

Consequently young women were cautioned that to tempt men by dressing
provocatively was a sin, so easily committed that even striking colors and
designs were considered lascivious. Churchmen frequently railed against immodest dress, defined by the Sacred Congregation of Religion in 1929 as that
"which is cut deeper than two fingers breadth under the pit of the throat,
which does not cover the arms at least to the elbow, and scarce reaches below
the knee." Calling for each diocese to form "special councils of vigilance to
watch over the modesty of women's dress" was the Sacred Congregation of

---

[34] I. J. Semper, "The Church and Higher Education for Girls," *Catholic Education Review*, 29 (Apr. 1931), 215–22; Mary M. Bowler, *History of Catholic Colleges for Women
in the United States of America* (Washington: Catholic Univ. of America, 1933), 85–88;
Edgar Schmiedeler, "Near Equality with Men—So What," *Homiletic and Pastoral Review*,
45 (Oct. 1944), 17–22; Sister Mary Brennan, "Marriage is a Career," *Catholic Educator*,
29 (May 1959), 666; Faherty, "American Feminism," 235. For a particularly offensive
expression of these notions see the 1940 commencement address at Notre Dame College,
Md., where the speaker stated, "Once again the quality which I exhort you to give back to
the world is a quality which peculiarly befits woman. I speak of the proper role of suffering." He claimed this would refine and temper women's qualities and that mortification and
purification of the flesh, in an acceptance of God's will, would liberate the spirit; see Hunter
Guthrie, "Woman's Role in the Modern World," *Catholic Mind*, 38 (Dec. 8, 1940), 497. A
similar approach to women and suffering is found in C. J. Woolen, "Failure of Feminism,"
Homiletic and Pastoral Review, 48 (Oct. 1947), 30–39.

[35] Smith, *Catholic Viewpoints*, 118, 169–70, 183, 193, 203.

[36] Leon Suenens, *The Nun in the World* (Westminster, Md.: Newman Press, 1963), 15.

Councils, but American bishops were fully capable of acting alone.[37] In one of the oldest and largest dioceses in Illinois the bishop, Henry Althoff of Belleville, forbade the distribution of communion to women in sleeveless or low-necked dresses, or to those who used rouge, lipstick, or other facial cosmetics. George A. Quertin, bishop of Manchester, New Hampshire, avowed women's dress was directly responsible for much of the world's turmoil. Both sexes, reminded that virginity was a more noble and perfect state of life than marriage, were taught that one of the sacrament's chief ends was a remedy for concupiscence. Nonetheless, failure to abstain voluntarily from married conjugal relations was nothing other than "un-Christian hedonism."[38] Conservative perceptions of women's baser nature were clearly revealed in the 1913 *Catholic Encyclopedia* article proclaiming that "the female sex is in some respects inferior to the male sex, both as regards body and soul," and in Bishop William Hickey's (Providence) 1927 entreaty that pastors, in keeping with the teachings of Pius X, eliminate women from choirs. (In *Motu Propino*, issued in 1903, the pope had affirmed that church singers filled a "real liturgical office" and that "women, being incapable of exercising such office, cannot be admitted to form part of the choir"; soprano and contralto parts must be sung by boys.)[39]

To protect priests against the unconscious snares of American "Eves" Bishop Stang (Fall River) warned clerics that "a dangerous rock which the priest encounters in the stormy sea of the world is the hearing of women's confessions. . . . Guard your eyes. . . . The eyes are the windows of the soul; close them to keep sensuality aloof. Do not look at a female penitent either before, during, or after confession. It would be injurious to you and others for several reasons. . . . Guard your tongue; never use expressions of friendship and familiarity; but the fewest possible questions. . . . Speak to the woman in the confessional as if you were addressing her spirit, separated from the body and standing before the judgement-seat of God. . . . Do not permit them to tell more than their sins, and check garrulity. . . . Be not deceived by tears: they may be sincere, but women's tears are always cheap and handy. Frequently raise your heart to Mary Immaculate that it may not be moved by human sentiment."[40]

Although the major effect of this "seductive" model was on interpersonal relationships and the perceptions of women by men and by themselves, it

---

[37] "Immodest Women's Dress," *Homiletic and Pastoral Review*, 30 (Nov. 1929), 171–73; *Boston Pilot*, Apr. 30, 1938; *New York Times*, Apr. 24, 1922, July 18, 21, 1924, Nov. 19, 1925, May 27, July 18, Nov. 1, 1927, June 24, 1929, Feb. 15, 1930.

[38] John C. Ford and Gerald Kelly, *Marriage Questions* (Westminster, Md.: Newman Press, 1963), 201; Pius XII, *Sacra Virgenitus*, Mar. 1954, in Benedictine Monks, *Woman in the Modern World*, 13–17, 24.

[39] *New York Times*, Nov. 17, 1927; *Providence Journal*, Nov. 17, 1927; Pius X, *Motu Propino*, 1903 (n.p. 1928), 12.

[40] William Stang, *Pastoral Theology* (Boston: Benziger Bros., 1897), 178–79.

had wider repercussions in the realm of education. Warning the bishops of the United States that in the majority of public schools "good morals" were endangered as adolescents of both sexes were grouped together in the same classrooms, the Holy Office pointed out in 1875 that "boys and girls must sit together on the same benches [a condition that] exposes them to corruption to a certain extent."[41] Similar trepidations extended to higher education. When liberals proposed that a women's college be located in Washington, D.C., conservatives berated the plan, fearing that proximity to Catholic University and faculty sharing was not only a step toward coeducation but would have a deleterious affect on the morals and minds of the males enrolled at the bishops' university. Accordingly Cardinal Gibbons and the Catholic University's rector were obliged to get approval from Rome, but still found it necessary to caution Sister Julia McGroarty, Trinity's founder: "Do not exult too loud, but proceed joyfully in secret, grateful that the difficulty has been overcome."[42]

As a result of the "Eve" mentality and the conviction that women were psychologically different from men, male Catholic colleges admitted women only reluctantly and as a matter of financial necessity. The first to do so, Marquette University, planned to admit nuns to its eight-week summer school for religious in 1909, and was shocked when laywomen applied. A badly divided Jesuit community ignored the provincial's recommendation that the program be canceled and instead appealed to the General, who granted permission for coeducation in 1912.[43] After two decades coeducational university education was still assailed in an article in the *Catholic Educational Review*. Asserting that it was an impediment to the development of a Christian gentlewoman, the author charged that coeducation obstructed the training of women in virtue and home management.[44]

The conservatism of Catholic educators was reenforced by Pius XI's encyclical *Christian Education of Youth* (1929), condemning "false and harmful" coeducation, which "mistakes a leveling promiscuity and equality for the legitimate association of the sexes." Additional support was rendered in 1951 when the Sacred Congregation of Religion pronounced that no Catholic can defend coeducation on principle.[45] Consequently, many Americans fought the proposal, especially on the secondary level, assured that their

---

[41] Benedictine Monks of Solesmes, *Papal Teachings: Education* (Boston: St. Paul Editions, 1960), 67.

[42] Cross, *Liberal Catholicism*, 79; *American Foundations of Notre Dame de Namur Compiled from Annals by a Member of the Congregation* (Philadelphia: Dolphin Press, 1928), 552; Sister M. P., "Trinity College," *Catholic Historical Review*, 5 (Jan. 1926), 661–64.

[43] Edward J. Power, *Catholic Higher Education in America* (Milwaukee: Bruce Publishing Co., 1940), 185–88.

[44] Semper, "Church and Higher Education," 220–22.

[45] William F. Cunningham, *Pivotal Problems of Education* (St. Louis: B. Herder Book Co., 1940), 185–88.

convictions that females play, work, feel, and think differently than males were in keeping with Catholic tradition.

Needless to say these perceptions of women were antagonistic to the feminist movement and to the equal rights amendment first introduced in 1923. To many Catholic leaders, clerical as well as lay, and to organizations such as the National Council of Catholic Women and the National Catholic Welfare Conference, these unnatural reforms obscured the differences between the sexes, undermined the stability of the home, usurped the natural position of man, and imperiled the moral leadership of women.[46] In order to combat them more effectively the Capuchin Franciscan Fathers established a magazine, *The Catholic Home Journal: the National Voice of Catholic Women*, and Cardinal William O'Connell of Boston founded the League of Catholic Women.

Stereotypes of women as either "Eves" or "Marys" were not unique to Catholicism. American Protestants shared these concepts. However, an examination of nineteenth- and early twentieth-century religious literature reveals that antifeminism was probably more deeply ingrained in the Catholic community than the Protestant, and, more significantly, is currently reflected in Catholic historical scholarship.

Most historians have tended to ignore the role of women in American history, and in so doing they failed to reveal alternative paths and female heroes in the struggle for social justice and human dignity. Refusing to acknowledge misogynistic elements of our culture and value system, they have populated our past with chimerical stereotyped females such as Betsy Ross and Pocahontas, rather than using it to liberate men and women. In this respect historians of American Catholicism are as guilty as their colleagues in other areas, if not more so, for they have denied Catholic women a respectable past. Only one of the leading histories of the American Church treats women specifically, and that work, published in 1923, does little more

---

[46] For an example of these contentions through the years see the *New York Times*, Mar. 9, 1920, Nov. 3, 1922, Nov. 21, 1925; *Boston Pilot*, Mar. 13, 1920; Mrs. Francis Slattery, "The Catholic Woman in Modern Times," *Catholic Mind* 28 (Mar. 22, 1930), 124–31; "N.C.C.W. Protests Passage of Equal Rights Amendment," *Catholic Action*, 15 (July 1933), 30; "Opposition to Bill Explained by Miss Regan Speaking for N.C.C.W.," *Catholic Action*, 20 (March 1938), 5; "Perils of Equal Rights Measure Cited by N.C.W.C. Representative," *Catholic Action*, 26 (Aug. 1944), 8, 23; "Face Equal Rights Amendment Realistically," *Catholic Action*, 27 (Nov. 1945), 18; "Equal Rights Amendment," *Ave Maria*, 65 (Feb. 1, 1947), 133; C. J. Woolen, "Failure of Feminism," *Homiletic and Pastoral Review*, 48 (Oct. 1947), 30–39; Elizabeth Morrissy, "The Status of Women: an Address before the National Council of Catholic Women, New Orleans, September 12, 1948," *Vital Speeches*, 15 (Nov. 1948), 55–60; John B. Sheerin, "May, Mary and Mothers," *Homiletic and Pastoral Review*, 49 (May 1949), 601–5; Mrs. Norma Folda, President National Council of Catholic Women, "Statement for the Record, May 13, 1970," *The Equal Rights Amendment, Hearings before the Subcommittee on the Judiciary*, United States Senate, 91st Congress, 2d session on S. J. Res. 61, May 5, 6, 7, 1970 (Washington: Government Printing Office 1970), 662.

than list the names of Catholic women of accomplishment. Even this token compilation is undermined in its section on "Social Action," where the author regretfully notes the employment of women in occupations that interfere with motherhood and marriage.[47] One study, published in 1964, has only a single line on women, and that in a paragraph entitled "Social Hysteria." "A Century of Struggle" to correct injustices against women is dismissed by the male clerical author as follows: "Emancipation of women in some instances was a pretext for excesses in feminine freedom: abandonment of restraints in modesty and decorum, birth prevention, and divorce."[48] Of 70 eminent Catholics included in the recently published three-volume reference work *Notable American Women*, most are not mentioned in any of the histories of American Catholicism; yet obviously they contributed significantly to many facets of American life.

Equally as deplorable as the omission of women is the failure of historians to examine whether antifeminist traditions imposed restraints on Catholic liberalism. Arthur Mann in *Yankee Reformers in an Urban Age*[49] affirms, almost casually, that this was true of John Boyle O'Reilly, but there has been no substantial effort to investigate this Catholic dilemma. More important would be an examination of Catholic antifeminism as it affected Catholic women. How significant was the experience of Martha Moore Avery? A Unitarian of Yankee heritage, she became a Socialist in the 1890s, ran for the Boston School Committee in 1901, and testified for woman suffrage before the state legislature on several occasions. However, after her conversion to Catholicism she fought the women's movement. Avery debated at Faneuil Hall with Anna Howard Shaw, president of the National American Woman Suffrage Association, testified against suffrage before the Massachusetts General Court, and claimed in her essays that enfranchisement "was an up-to-date temptation suggested by the prince of devils and intended to destroy the unit of Christian civilization."[50]

Aileen Kraditor in her *Ideas of the Woman Suffrage Movement*[51] analyzed the lives of suffrage leaders in the period from 1890 to 1918. Of the 26 women, officers of the National American Woman Suffrage Association and the Woman's Party, only one—Lucy Burns, the youngest—was a Catholic. Absence of Catholic women could be a reflection of class distinction, since the suffrage movement was primarily middle class and Kraditor's study included only the leadership. Nevertheless, it still appears that there is a direct

[47] Constantine McGuire, *Catholic Builders of the Nation*, 5 vols. (Boston: Continental Press, 1923), 2, 218.

[48] Newman C. Eberhardt, *Survey of American Church History* (St. Louis: Herder, 1964), 145.

[49] (Cambridge: Belknap Press of Harvard Univ. Press, 1954.)

[50] *America*, 4 (1916), 276–77; *Catholic Mind*, 13 (1915), 625–55; Kenneally, "Catholicism and Woman Suffrage," 53.

[51] (New York: Columbia Univ. Press, 1956.)

relationship between religion and women's rights. Of the 60 subjects classified as feminists in *Notable American Women*,[52] only three were born Catholic (two of these apostatized), and only one was a convert to that faith. On the other hand, eight of 40 prominent antisuffrage women were Catholic.[53]

Religion may have been an impediment to feminism, yet many Catholic women were able to reconcile their faith with energetic careers and societal contributions. Despite the limitations of Spalding's feminism, he still recognized that marriage was no longer the only proper objective of woman and that her "sphere" was "wherever she can live nobly and do useful work."[54] Katherine Conway, who liked and admired suffragettes, was unable to support them, for their reform fostered "disesteem" for the "Divine Plan," and consequently she was an active member of the Massachusetts Association Opposed to Woman Suffrage. Yet adhering to these traditional norms did not preclude Conway's service as editor of the *Boston Pilot* and the *Republic*, and as an officer in the New England Press Association.[55] Poet and essayist Mary Elizabeth (Mrs. John) Blake was the mother of eleven children. A leading Boston Catholic intellectual, she advocated that every woman, through education, be prepared to be self-supporting and self-reliant so that she would be "rid of that haunting fear of the future which obliged her to seek marriage as a necessity, and often made her ready to submit inclination, feeling, and principle to the wretchedness of union without congeniality or respect."[56] Her rather radical views were not very different from those of the essayist Mary B. O'Sullivan, who, in the pages of a leading Catholic journal, proclaimed that "the time has gone by when a girl was born to no higher destiny than humiliating dependence on father and brothers, or a sordid, loveless marriage." It was probably she who, before the turn of the century, defended the prerogative of married women to work, on the basis that they were entitled to the same rights as men and that outside employment was necessary to the happiness and development of every human.[57] An analysis of the careers of activists such as these coupled with a study of the 70 Catho-

[52] 3 vols. (Cambridge: Belknap Press of Harvard Univ. Press, 1971.)

[53] The three Catholic "feminists" were Hortense Ward, Mathilde Anneke, and Kate Kennedy; the latter two abandoned Catholicism; the convert was Mary Nichols. Over one-third of the women identified as feminists by the editors of this work left the church in which they were born for a more liberally structured one, or abandoned religion altogether, a trend not noticeable in analyzing leading antisuffragists.

[54] Spalding, "Women and Higher Education," 58–59.

[55] Katherine Conway, *The Christian Gentlewoman and the Social Apostolate* (Boston: T. J. Flynn & Co. 1904), 13–14, 25; Katherine Conway, "Woman Has No Vocation to Public Life," *Catholic World*, 57 (Aug. 1893), 681–84; Katherine Conway, "Present Aspect of Woman Suffrage," 394.

[56] Mary E. Blake, "True Solution of the Woman Question," *Donahoes*, 29 (Apr. 1893), 418; for Blake's career see her obituary in the *Boston Pilot*, Mar. 2, 1907, by Conway; Merwick, *Boston Priests*, 58, 167–68; McGuire, *Catholic Builders*, 4, 393.

[57] Mary B. O'Sullivan, "Are Girls a Burden?" *Donahoes*, 29 (Mar. 1893), 359; "Should Married Women Work: a Symposium," *Donahoes*, 29 (May 1893), 633.

lic subjects in *Notable American Women*, should pose many questions for the historians of American Catholicism, the answers to which might encourage modern feminists in their efforts to reconcile their convictions with their faith.

In 1922 Arthur M. Schlesinger, Sr., made an appeal to historians to break from their sexist interpretations and analyze and include the role of women in their research, an appeal just now being answered. One hopes that it does not take 50 years more for the historian of American Catholicism to meet this responsibility.

Norma Fain Pratt

Transitions in Judaism
The Jewish American Woman
Through the 1930s

"To be a Jew in the twentieth century is to be offered a gift," wrote Muriel Rukeyser, the New York–born Jewish poet. "If you refuse, wishing to be invisible, you choose death of the spirit. . . ."[1] Most American Jewish women accepted this gift, even though the tenets of Judaism circumscribed the role of women in worship and community activity. Women had never been encouraged to examine the nature of their own religious beliefs, nor had the traditional assumptions about their inferiority and subservience to men been challenged. In the late nineteenth and early twentieth centuries, however, a minority of women began to redefine their place within Jewish life, and in the 1920s and 1930s patterns perceptibly changed for the majority. Women became participants in the synagogue, the schools, and the social institutions which expressed the new culture of American Jewry. Nevertheless they continued to face limitations and intolerance; by the 1940s, a new pattern had been established with its own forms of inclusion and exclusion.

In order to distinguish the ways in which women altered their role, it is important to consider the nature of American Judaism and its course of development. American Jews never centralized their religious institutions. What could be termed "organized" Judaism was congregational. Essentially, public rituals were practiced in local synagogues whose con-

[1] Muriel Rukeyser, "To Be a Jew in the Twentieth Century," in Abraham Chapman, ed., *Jewish-American Literature* (New York: New American Library, 1974), 342–43.

gregations selected a mode of worship and expressed their preference for certain Jewish theological interpretations. In popular parlance, the types of worship came to be categorized as Orthodox, Conservative, and Reform. National synagogue unions were formed at the turn of the present century.[2]

In the seventeenth century, Sephardic Jews brought to British America from Spain and the Middle East a variation of the ritual and theology of medieval Judaism practiced by their co-religionists in Western and Eastern Europe. A few Sephardic women took an active part in business and in the high cultural life of American urban centers. German Jews arrived in considerable number just before the middle of the nineteenth century. Between 1840 and 1880 some 250,000 settled in the eastern and midwestern United States, mainly in the cities. Many had already been influenced by secular European culture and in America they created their own version of Reform Judaism. The Reform synagogues, now called temples, eliminated some of the ancient ritual, substituted English for Hebrew, altered the theological emphasis of the liturgical literature, and departed substantially from the traditional orthodox service.

Reform Jews initiated radical innovation in the position of women. The temples permitted the desegregation of the sexes; women and men now sat together in the family pews. Women were allowed to sing in the choir. Girls were confirmed. The Reform prayerbook eliminated the male benediction thanking God "that I am not a woman." Women were counted as part of the *minyan* (the ten-person quorum necessary to hold services). Through the temple "sisterhood" organizations women participated in the administration of charitable and other social services; they were granted the privileges of tending to temple upkeep and to the religious education of children.[3] These changes did not come without opposition. One dissenter posed the argument familiar in the Judaeo-Christian tradition in his article "God's Curse on Womanhood," published in 1864 in the popular Philadelphia German-Jewish English-language periodical, *The Occident*:

Now when Eve was created she was made equal to Adam in every respect, and by no means had he any power or authority over her whatever. . . . But after she had induced him to break the commandment of God, and he was cursed to labor and to toil for his living, and to support her, to supply all their wants through hard work, she was also cursed by losing her right to be equal

[2] Maurice J. Karpf, *Jewish Community Organization in the United States* (New York: Block Publishing, 1938), 51–56.
[3] Charlotte Baum, Paula Hyman, and Sonya Michel, *The Jewish Woman in America* (New York: Dial Press, 1976), 17–53, deals with German Jewish Reform Judaism.

to him. . . . Now this was the curse pronounced against her, that she should always remember and repent of what she had done. She shall always desire to be equal with him, as before she sinned, but he shall rule over her. . . .[4]

By 1900, many middle-class Jewish American women of German descent had assumed responsibilities in the work of their Reform temples. A National Federation of Temple Sisterhoods was founded in 1913 with a membership of 5,000, representing 52 local groups.[5] Sisterhoods met both for recreation and for temple and community work. Contemporary feminist thought has variously interpreted such voluntarism as a cult of the leisured woman; as an aspect of middle-class conspicuous consumption; as an outlet for female energies which did not conflict with home duties and which in fact translated women's work in the home into social terms; as an expression of a feminist consciousness; or as a factor of labor division in a developing capitalist economy.[6] While all these theories might be applied to the women of the Reform movement, as well as to the voluntary work of American women of other faiths, the leadership of the Federation understood their own purpose in specifically Jewish terms. "The increased power which has come to the modern American Jewess ought to be exercised in congregational life," stated the NFTS constitution.[7] Another motif, the future of Judaism, pervaded their ideology. "Woman is the bearer, the guardian and the preserver of the nation," the feminist Bertha Pappenheim proclaimed. This is her "primary function—on which depends the welfare and continued existence of the people, Israel. . . ."[8] But guardianship was not enough. By the 1890s German Jewish American women also defended the faith. The founding convention of the National Council of Jewish Women in 1893 stood aggressively against anti-Semitism. Along with religious understanding, philanthropy, and education, the purpose of the NCJW was "to secure the interest and aid of influential persons in arousing the general sentiment

---

[4] January 21, 1864.

[5] XXIV Biennial Assembly of the National Federation of Temple Sisterhoods, *The Days of Our Years* (Chicago, Ill., Nov. 1963), 24.

[6] See, for example, Doris B. Gold, "Women and Voluntarism," in Vivian Gornick and Barbara K. Moran, eds., *Woman in Sexist Society* (New York: New American Library, 1971), 533–54.

[7] *The Days of Our Years*, 24. Joseph Leiser, *American Judaism* (New York: Block Publishing, 1925), 174–203, discusses the "modern American Jewess."

[8] Bertha Pappenheim, "The Jewish Woman in Religious Life," pamphlet reprinted from *The Jewish Review* (Jan. 1913) by the Jewish League for Woman Suffrage. For biographic studies of Pappenheim see Marion Kaplan, "Bertha Pappenheim: Founder of German-Jewish Feminism," in Elizabeth Koltun, ed., *The Jewish Woman* (New York: Shocken Books, 1976), 149–63.

against religious persecutions whenever and by whomever shown, and in finding means to prevent such persecutions."[9]

German Jewish women also defended the faith by taking measures to prevent assimilation. Although, like the men, they responded to the temptations of Americanization by adopting aspects of the dominant culture, they also wanted to retain their individuality as Jews. Zionism served this purpose. Hadassah, the women's division of the Zionist Organization of America, founded in 1912, planned to foster Judaism at home through the propagation of Zionist ideals. Books for young women explained that the chief problem for Jews in America was "finding a way back to the original Jewish National life and thereby defeating assimilation."[10] The solution was "a return to the sources of Jewish culture, to the Bible and to the study of Hebrew and by contact with the living Jewry of the East."[11] Ida Adlerblum, the head of Hadassah's Cultural Committee, boasted in 1930 (when the organization had the largest membership of any Zionist group in the United States) that "The future historian of the twentieth century will reckon Hadassah among the forces which operate in creating Judaism anew. . . . From a mere organization, Hadassah has become a spiritual historical movement knitted with the life of Palestine as well as with Jewish life in America."[12]

The migration of Eastern European Jews began in 1880; by the early 1920s more than 2½ million had immigrated.[13] The place of Eastern European immigrant women in Judaism was far different from that of their American German-Jewish co-religionists. Some inequalities, explicit and implicit, still existed in the Reform community (for example, women could not join the rabbinate or hold administrative posts in their temples), but in the orthodox system segregation and subordination of women was the rule.

Orthodox men and women were responsible for different spheres of religious behavior. Men were obligated to say prayers at three specific times during the day, to participate in synagogue worship and maintenance, and to study not only the Bible in Hebrew but also the Talmud.

[9] Rebekah Kohut, "Jewish Women's Organizations in the United States," *American Jewish Year Book*, 1931–1932 (Philadelphia: Jewish Publication Society, 1931), 33:175, hereafter referred to as *AJYB*.

[10] *Junior Hadassah Yearbook*, 1924–1925 (New York: Junior Hadassah, 1925), 24.

[11] Ibid.

[12] Ida S. Adlerblum, "Cultural Committee," in *Reports* of the National Board, Standing Committee and Regional Units to the Sixteenth Annual Convention of Hadassah, Buffalo, N. Y., Oct. 26–28, 1930, p. 19.

[13] Karpf, *Jewish Community Organization*, 1–8. The most recent study, Irving Howe, *World of Our Fathers* (New York: Harcourt, Brace, Jovanovich, 1976), gives limited attention to the woman immigrant.

Unlike men, orthodox women were not required to pray at appointed times or to attend the synagogue regularly. When women did attend, they were segregated from men by a specially constructed partition. Of course, an orthodox woman could not become a rabbi nor could she sing in the synagogue, since the ancient rabbis considered the female voice to be profane in a holy place. Women did not count as part of a *minyan*. Male children were given a religious education by male teachers after the age of five or six, but girls were not obligated to study. One could find in the Talmud adages which warned: "Whoever teaches his daughter Torah is as though he taught her folly," or "Let the words of the Torah rather be destroyed by fire than imparted to women."[14] Orthodox women were restricted to observing only particular rituals. They were permitted to light Sabbath and holiday candles, to separate the *hallah* portion from the bread dough in preparation for the Sabbath, and to bathe in the *mikva* (ritual bath). Interestingly, orthodox women were encouraged to become involved in the business enterprises of the marketplace, and they often supported their Talmudic scholar husbands who tended the sacred sphere.[15]

Orthodox Judaism encompassed civil as well as religious life. Thus marriage, divorce, inheritance, and the administration and execution of justice were all regulated within the jurisdiction of *halakah* (Jewish law) as expressed in the *Talmud* and interpreted by the rabbis. The *halakah* regarding women were the dictates of a patriarchal society. Woman's role in life was defined as caring for her husband, children, and home. For satisfaction of her needs she depended upon father, husband, or son. "It says in the Torah," wrote the immigrant novelist Anzia Yezierska in her novel *Bread Givers* (1925), "only through a man has a woman an existence. Only through a man can a woman enter Heaven."[16]

Women's spiritual sphere was the moral purity of the household, and this was assured by observing dietary laws of *kashruth* and by keeping to a strict system of bodily cleansing. A woman's word regarding *kashruth* of her home or her attendance at the *mikva* was sufficient but the testimony of a woman in court was not acceptable. Legal dicta regulated sexual behavior by defining a close relationship between sexual performance and the so-called cleanliness of the female body. For example, the *Shulchan*

[14] For a discussion of women in the Talmud see Judith Hauptman, "Images of Women in the Talmud," in Rosemary Radford Ruether, ed., *Religion and Sexism* (New York: Simon and Schuster, 1974), 184–212.

[15] See Charlotte Baum, "What Made Yetta Work? The Economic Role of Eastern European Jewish Women in the Family," *Response*, No. 18 (Summer 1973).

[16] Quoted by Alice Kessler-Harris in her introduction to Anzia Yezierska, *Bread Givers* (New York: George Braziller, 1975), vi.

Aruch, a code book of laws culled from the Talmud for daily use as a guide to behavior, contains numerous chapters dealing specifically with sexual cleanliness, "Laws concerning Chastity," "Laws forbidding the being alone with Women and other familiarities with them," "Laws concerning a woman menstrually unclean," "Laws concerning the regulation of the Menses and the examination before and after cohabitation."[17] Often, however, crucial aspects of women's lives were not celebrated. As a feminist recently remarked, "There are blessings in Judaism for almost everything including going to the bathroom, but there isn't one for menstruation or for a healthy pregnancy."[18]

Not all Eastern European immigrant women remained orthodox Jews. A minority had rejected some or all of the ancient practices even before coming to America. Many young women became "enlightened" when their parents enrolled them in Eastern European non-Jewish state schools.[19] In the United States the degree of strict religious observance varied. With the desire to Americanize, some of the more foreign-appearing practices were eliminated. For example, orthodox married women shed the traditional headcover *(shaytl)*; *kashruth* and the Sabbath might not be strictly observed. The prestige of the rabbis as interpreters and executors of the rabbinic law was undermined; for women, American civil law often appeared more efficient and more fair. Katya Govsky recalled her discovery that her husband was a bigamist. "I went to the criminal court and the man said, 'In twenty-four hours, you can get a divorce.' And that's what happened; but Pa says, 'You have to get a Jewish divorce.'" It took her more than a year to obtain a rabbinic decree. Furthermore, Govsky remembered, "I wanted to adopt my son (you know, a child belongs to the father). Pa had to take the rabbi to New York and talk to my husband, fill out all kinds of papers. And I had to go to four rabbis. . . ."[20]

Despite the greater freedom for women within the Reform movement, very few Eastern European women joined the Reform temples. To them as well as to the men, Reform seemed too Christian in style, and the wealth of German Jews appeared to place them in a higher social class. It was not until the 1930s that any significant number of Eastern European

[17] Rabbi Solomon Ganzfried, *Shulchan Aruch* (Code of Jewish Law), Hyman E. Goldin, trans. (New York: Hebrew Publishing, 1927), 13–42.

[18] K. S., "Judaism is not for men only," *Brown Alumni Monthly*, 19, cited in Anne Lapidus Lerner, "'Who Has Not Made Me a Woman': The Movement for Equal Rights for Women in American Jewry," *AJYB*, 1977, 8.

[19] Patterns of education for Jewish girls in Eastern Europe are discussed in Celia Heller, *On the Edge of Destruction* (New York: Columbia Univ. Press, 1977), 157–58.

[20] Sydelle Kramer and Jenny Masur, eds., *Jewish Grandmothers* (Boston: Beacon, 1976), 70–71.

Jews joined in worship with those of German ancestry,[21] and then they often were accused of social climbing. Esther Bengis, a young orthodox *rebetsn* (rabbi's wife) in a small town in Connecticut in the early 1930s, complained that some members of her husband's congregation held "dual membership"—in the Orthodox *shul* and in the Reform temple.[22] German and Eastern European Jewish women, however, began in the 1920s to work together in areas not directly religious, such Zionist or social service organizations, contributing to a growing homogeneity in American Jewish life.

For nearly 40 years after 1880, Jews who were no longer orthodox and yet could not accept Reform Judaism had no form of Judaism through which to express their changing mode of behavior. Conservative Judaism, a movement attracting mainly second- and third-generation American Jews of Eastern European background, was still in its formative stages. The majority of Conservative congregations were established during or soon after World War I, their synagogues located in the newer non-ghetto neighborhoods where the Jewish population was in the minority and where living conditions expressed middle-class tastes. Marshall Sklare has described Conservatism as a mediation "between the demands of the Jewish tradition . . . and the norms of middle class worship."[23] The new patterns altered the liturgy, showed tolerance toward personal deviation from traditional practices like *kashruth* or rest on the Sabbath, and created social clubs as part of the function of the synagogue. Following somewhat the practice of Reform Judaism, Conservatives adjusted the status of women. Men and women were seated together. Women's synagogue organizations participated in the upkeep of the synagogue and in the religious education of the children. Women, however, still were excluded from significant parts of the worship, for instance the rituals surrounding the handling and reading of the Torah. In the 1920s and 1930s Conservative women wrestled with a felt dichotomy between the new position in synagogue life and the traditional home. Some thought that things had gone too far. "At the risk of being declared a reactionary, a menace to women's freedom," wrote Rose Goldstein in the Conservative Women's League paper *Outlook*, "I maintain that the

---

[21] Author's interview with Jane Evans, Executive Director of the National Federation of Temple Sisterhoods, New York, June 30, 1977.

[22] Esther Bengis, *I am a Rabbi's Wife* (Moodus, Conn.: Esther Bengis, 1934), 14.

[23] Marshall Sklare, *Conservative Judaism: An American Religious Movement* (New York: Shocken, 1972), 75.

greatest part the Jewish woman can play in the future of a healthy American Judaism is through the conduct of her own household."[24]

Beside the Orthodox, Conservative, and Reform modes, a secular form of Judaism developed in the late nineteenth century which offered women a different place in Jewish society. While secular Jews rejected most theological values, they retained *Yidishkayt*, a sense of Jewishness embracing a respect for the Yiddish language and traditions and for the contemporary common Jewish fate. One could observe secular Judaism without prayer and without joining a special group. The *veltlekhe* (secular) Jews did organize, since they not only accepted a Jewish identity in theory but put this into practice by creating a cultural life for themselves and their children. The study of Jewish history, appreciation of Yiddish and Hebrew literature, celebration of Jewish holidays, and support of a Yiddish theatre were characteristic expressions.

A vital part of the secular movement, which divided along sectarian lines, was radical political ideology in such forms as socialism, Zionist-socialism, and anarchism. Actually, the roots of secular Judaism were found in Eastern European Jewish radical and labor movements that provided doors through which working-class men and women entered the secular world. Some radical groups like the Marxist Jewish Labor Bund discouraged workers from following religious customs since religion was held to reflect the Jewish bourgeois power structure. Bund ideology transformed the special Jewish religious identity into a national one, urging Bundists to work for a socialist revolution in which Jews would obtain cultural autonomy.[25]

Radical Jewish movements accepted equality between the sexes and this made political radicalism attractive to women. Because Jewish women had been excluded from those male sanctuaries, the orthodox synagogues, women intellectuals and workers joined radical organizations expecting to find equality within the movement. For these women, a nonreligious mode of life within a Jewish community became bound with socialism and equality. When an increasing number of Eastern European radicals emigrated to America after the unsuccessful Russian revolution of 1905, many of the politically conscious women began participating,

[24] Rose B. Goldstein, "Women's Share in the Responsibility for the Future of Judaism," *Outlook* (May 1938), 3. For a more recent statement of a woman's ambivalence regarding inclusion of women in the synagogue see the historian Lucy Davidowicz, "On Being a Woman in Shul," *Commentary* (July 1968), 71–74.

[25] Ezra Mendelsohn, *Class Struggle in the Pale: The Formative Years of the Jewish Workers' Movement in Tsarist Russia* (London: Cambridge Univ. Press, 1970), 107. For the Bund see also Henry Tobias, *The Jewish Bund in Russia From Its Origins to 1905* (Stanford, Cal.: Stanford Univ. Press, 1972).

soon after their arrival, in the feminist and suffrage movements. Esther Luria, a Bundist who in Europe had engaged in revolutionary activities, played a role in the suffrage and labor movements among Jewish immigrant women in New York. Far less known than Emma Goldman, Luria tried to provide Jewish women with role models through her writings and the example of her own life. Her biography had the romantic ring of that first generation of immigrant radical intellectuals. Born in Warsaw in 1877, Luria completed the Russian gymnasium and studied at the University of Bern in Switzerland, where she received the degree of doctor of humanistic studies. In Bern she joined the socialist movement, and she returned to Russia as an active member of the Bund. Arrested there several times, she was sent to Siberia in 1906. She escaped in 1912 and came to New York City. Luria made her debut in the Yiddish-language socialist literary and political monthly *Zukunft* (Future). She wrote more than sixty articles about Jewish and non-Jewish women who broke out of traditional molds, including "Famous Jewish Women in America and England," "Marx's Wife and Daughter," "The Russian Women and the Revolution," and the "Life and Works of Liebknecht and Luxemburg." Her contributions to the International Ladies Garment Workers' Union Yiddish weekly *Glaykhhayt* (Equality) advocated political activism for women in America. Without a family, impoverished, and in poor health, Luria disappeared in the early 1920s and her fate is unknown.[26]

Women in these Jewish circles had more equality with men than their sisters in the Orthodox, Conservative, and even Reform movements. In theory, at least, they were unencumbered by religious traditions, restrictions, and ancient prejudices. As a consequence, working-class women joined trade unions and occasionally were trade organizers;[27] literary women wrote fiction or poetry and were employed on the staff of the Yiddish press and in the Yiddish theatre; women were active within political groups. Nevertheless there were inequalities. Ambivalent or negative attitudes toward the "emancipated" Jewish woman existed in subtle, perhaps unconscious form, and the contradiction between the ideal and the real would become more apparent by the 1920s. Such attitudes could be found in the literature of the time. The novel *Worshippers* (1906) by Henry Berman (who was sympathetic to socialism and thus to the rights of women) centers upon Katherine Bronski, the creatively frus-

---

[26] Biographic information in *Leksikon fun der nayer yidisher literatur*, 7 vols. (New York: Congress for Jewish Culture, 1956), 5:30. Khaim L. Fuks, "Vegn eynegste shriber fun der *Zukunft*," *Zukunft*, 11–12 (Nov.–Dec. 1962), 494–95.

[27] Alice Kessler-Harris, "Organizing the Unorganizable: Three Jewish Women and Their Union." *Labor History*, 17 (Winter 1976).

trated and sexually unsatisfied wife of a Philadelphia pharmacist. Katherine leaves her husband to follow a stage career and to engage in an extramarital affair with a New York Yiddish socialist poet. According to Berman, Katherine's emancipation illustrates the fallacy of the socialist aspiration for sexual equality. Katherine's freedom is merely a mask for her egotism, her desire to dominate males, and her inability to understand political commitment. Berman assigns all the affirmative values to her lover, whose virtues include intelligence, idealism, compassion, and a sense of responsibility. In the end Katherine, a failure on the stage, deserts her lover to return to Philadelphia and the pharmacist.[28] Berman's novel focused some of the traditionally negative attitudes upon the so-called emancipated woman: her intellectual inferiority, the superficiality of her political and artistic purpose, and her destructive sexual powers.

*B*y the early 1920s Jews had ceased to be an immigrant nation in America. Increasing numbers left immigrant work to enter business and the professions. Jewish women and men moved out of the old ghetto-like neighborhoods into newer, more middle-class parts of town. Although occasional anti-Semitism created feelings of insecurity, social mores in the United States permitted Jews to retain their religion, sacred or secular, and still become American. In fact the American partiality for religious affiliation encouraged Jews to identify themselves in religious terms. Concurrently, most became convinced that an American style of life was appropriate for all citizens.[29]

Far from merging into their surroundings, however, the Jews developed a particular culture during the years between the two world wars. A myriad network of institutions demonstrated this adherence to what Horace Kallen called "cultural pluralism":[30] Jewish congregations (3,118 in 1927),[31] theological seminaries, religious schools and secular Yiddish culture schools, local and national philanthropic agencies, and social and recreational groups. At least four organizations dealt with the problem of

---

[28] Berman's book is discussed in Carole S. Kessner, "Ghetto Intellectuals and the 'New Woman,'" *Yiddish*, 2:2–3 (Winter–Spring 1976), 23–31. Kessner accepts Berman's view of the emancipated woman uncritically.

[29] For a recent study of problems of assimilation see Deborah Dash Moore, "Jewish Ethnicity and Acculturation in the 1920s: Public Education in New York City," *Jewish Journal of Sociology*, 18 (Dec. 1976), 96–104.

[30] Horace Meyer Kallen, *Cultural Pluralism and the American Idea: An Essay in Social Philosophy* (Philadelphia: Univ. of Pennsylvania Press, 1956).

[31] Karpf, *Jewish Community Organization*, 54. For statistics on religious and community organizations see the annual *AJYB*.

Jewish rights in America and abroad. The Jewish socialists and communists ran their own political sections, children's schools, camps, and cultural and social groups, and published books and periodical literature.

Within this structure the functions women performed expanded. The status of all American women had been enhanced by their enfranchisement in 1920. Jewish women had benefited both economically and educationally during the movement into the middle class and were now capable of shouldering the burdens and privileges of community life;[32] many accepted civic duties. One slogan of a girl's youth organization in 1930 declared: "Every member of Junior Hadassah is an American, a Jew and a Zionist. She is not one time one, another time another; she is all three in one."[33]

Changes in the practice of Judaism itself contributed to the new involvement of women. Orthodox Judaism, regulating all daily life (secular and sacred) by religious law, made heavy demands upon the male. The Reform movement of the nineteenth century and the new Conservative movement, by separating the sacred and secular, left only the actual religious service in the realm of the sacred. The male was no longer required to uphold the faith of his fathers by daily worship, religious study, and synagogue attendance. Jewish education, philanthropy, social services, and sociocultural expression had moved out from under Talmudic-rabbinic regulation. Under these circumstances, women became more participant in all areas of Jewish life while men became less so.[34]

Women in some numbers also began writing about their feelings toward Judaism in general and about being an American Jew in particular. The articles, memoirs, novels, and poems were the first candid disclosure of distinctly female religious sentiment since the *tkhines* (devotional prayers) written by women for women in the late Middle Ages.

One women's vehicle for the ideas of Jewish women was a mixed Yiddish-English emulation of the *Ladies' Home Journal: Der yidisher froyen zhurnal,* published in New York, which lasted from May 1922 to October 1923. It was intended for a first-generation immigrant audience of middle-class status. The *froyen zhurnal* printed sentimental poetry but

---

[32] The columns of *Who's Who in American Jewry*, 3 vols. (New York: National News Association, 1927, 1928, 1938) show the increasing number of Jewish women who received college educations and went on to participate in community and professional affairs. Also see "Professional Tendencies Among Jewish Students in Colleges, Universities and Professional Schools," *AJYB*, 1920–1921, 22:383–86, which describes the educational pattern of women students.

[33] *The Story of Junior Hadassah on its Twentieth Anniversary* (n.p., 1940), 22. This pamphlet is in the collection of the Jewish Division of the New York Public Library.

[34] Sklare, *Conservative Judaism*, 87.

also ran articles about marriage, infant care, women's organizations, mother-daughter generational conflicts, college girls and their careers, achievements of outstanding American Jewish women, and women in politics. Each number included at least one article about women and religion, almost all of which lauded the woman's role in Jewish holiday celebrations. In the first issue, Ella Blum's "Pesakh un di yidishe froy " (Passover and the Jewish woman) reminded the reader that Moses' mother and sister and the Pharaoh's daughter all played active roles in the Jewish struggle for freedom from Egyptian slavery.[35] Ethel Judensen, writing about Chanukah, explained that "The highest pinnacle of success in life is achieved by consecration of one's self to an ideal and the readiness to make sacrifices for it. In the possession of this particular virtue, we feel sure, the Jewish woman excelled."[36]

In poetry and memoirs women expressed their intimate feelings about their Jewishness. One of the finest Yiddish poets, Anna Margolin, wrote about her ambivalence toward the past in "Mein shtam redt" (My Ancestry Speaks). She described her female forebears, "a few of whom I am ashamed," tramping through her "like through a dark house" so that she could not recognize her own voice.[37] In "A mentsh" (A Human Being) published in the experimental magazine *In zich* (Introspection) in 1923, Margolin sardonically chided God as she forgave Him for creating an imperfect human being and for creating a Jew. Describing the *mentsh* she wrote:

> Er iz a nit farendikter eksperiment
> In groyse laydnshaftn, emes, poze,
> A nit derbakene metamorfoze
> Fun hoykhn glutikn gedank
> In orem fleysh un blut,
> Mit milyonen andere halb-rizn un halb gnomen
> A shpotisher umnitslekher bavayz
> Az der almekhtiker ken shvakh
> Zayn fakh.
>
> He is an unfinished experiment
> In great passion, truth, pose,
> A half-baked metamorphosis
> Of glowing thoughts

[35] *Der yidishe froyen zhurnal*, I (May 1922), 3.
[36] "A Miracle of Chanukah," ibid., I (Dec. 1922), 3.
[37] Anna Margolin, "My Ancestry Speaks," in Joseph Leftwich, ed. and trans., *The Golden Treasury: A Worldwide Treasury of Yiddish Poetry* (New York and London: Thomas Yoseloff, 1961), 668–69.

In paltry flesh and blood,
Along with millions of other half-giants and half-gnomes
A scornful unnecessary proof
That the Almightly did not know
His trade.[38]

Margolin's chastisement of God gave voice to an ancient strain in the Jewish tradition as well as to her own private revolt.

Leah Morton, a social worker and author, published her memoir, *I am a Woman—and a Jew,* in 1926. In the tradition of prodigals, she described her odyssey from the total rejection of her immigrant parents' orthodox Judaism, through her marriage to a non-observant Christian and years of indifference to religion, to her renewed interest in organized Jewish practices when, in her late thirties, she returned to a personal identification with Jewishness. She wrote: "As a Jewess, I had found a creed not mine to believe, and I had put it aside, but I had not been able to put my Jewishness aside. . . . I am a Jewess, though I do not belong to any church, nor has my world enclosed my people. The divisions are in my memories, in my heart."[39]

What did ordinary women think and feel about religion—apart from professional writers? One glimpse into their thoughts is given in a master's essay written at the New York School of Social Work in 1937 by Sadie Josephson. The author examined how six New York women understood the influence of Jewishness in their lives. The "subjects" were between the ages of 26 and 46; two were Eastern European immigrants and four the children of immigrants. Josephson's information suggests interesting patterns. All the subjects believed that their Jewish identity was of central importance in determining their lives. Josephson noted in her summary, "The tendency . . . was to feel that they had made their own adjustment through their own thinking, yet none of them had thought through very clearly ideas and feelings about religion or Jewishness." Each woman had decided points of view. Subject "E" felt that she had been unsuccessful in her career and personal relationships because she was born a Jew. Yet she would not change her religion. Subject "D," an ardent Yiddishist, said she was not religious and was interested in Judaism only as a cultural expression. As a child she had spoken Yiddish but had been unaware of Jewish religion until five years before the interview, when her grandparents had come to America. Subject "S" remained orthodox and, as Josephson commented, "carried out in her ways

[38] Margolin, "A mentsh," *In zich,* 3 (Mar. 1923), 5.
[39] Leah Morton (pseud. Elizabeth Stern), *I am a Woman—and a Jew* (New York: J. H. Sears, 1926), 361–62.

of living as many customs as she finds convenient." Subject "J" claimed indifference to religion but expressed guilt about not keeping the traditional customs and so observed the Sabbath and High Holy Days. Subject "R" had married a Catholic but stated that "since her marriage she feels more Jewish than before." Subject "G," the only woman in this group to emigrate to the United States in her late teens and to work at a menial job was critical of Jews. She felt persecuted by her Jewish employers and she made anti-Semitic comments about them. Except for the Yiddishist, who taught at a Sholom Aleichem Folkschule, none of the subjects appeared to be active in organized Judaism.[40]

Such lack of formal ties—the problem of the unaffiliated Jew—was a source of anxiety among leaders of this era, apprehensive that Judaism might not survive in America because of the changes that already had taken place. Women often were blamed by rabbis and other male writers for their share in this so-called decline of Judaism. David Goldberg took the mother to task in 1921 in an article in the *Jewish Forum*: "There is no time for the Sabbath . . . as her boys 'must' attend one or the other of the mediocre social 'events,' a musicale or a dance which, counting on the lack of backbone of the modern Jewish mother, her gentile friends invariably arrange for Friday evening."[41]

Adopting a more analytic but equally patronizing tone, Rabbi Mordecai M. Kaplan of the Jewish Theological Seminary echoed Goldberg's admonition. "[T]he Jewish Emancipation, or the change in the civic status of the Jews, has alienated the Jewish woman from Judaism far more than the Jewish man," he lectured the annual convention of the Hadassah in 1932. Kaplan contended that men had managed to deal with Emancipation without loss of their Jewish identity. "There are very few women who can claim the credit," he said. The rabbi attributed this female failure to resist assimilation to "the fact that she had been ill-prepared to play an active part in the process of Jewish adjustment." Passive and conforming to man's guidance, "she did not know how to make even a single stroke to save her Jewish selfhood." Culturally neglected, "she had turned to other cultures. . . ." Hungry for acknowledgement, she had given "undue significance to social advancement. . . . To the Jewish woman, therefore, the Jewish Emancipation has meant not freedom for her people from bondage of fear and oppression, but rather the chance to win a place for herself and

[40] Sadie Josephson, "Adjustment Histories of Six Jewish Women: A Study of Life History Material with Special Emphasis on the Problems of Jewish Adjustment," manuscript in the Jewish Division of the New York Public Library, 370, 36a, 94–97, 129, 182, 223, 360.

[41] David Goldberg, "Woman's Part in Religious Decline," *Jewish Forum* (May 1921), 871–75, cited in Rudolph Glanz, *The Jewish Woman in America* (New York: Ktav, 1976), 187.

her family in the so-called higher circles of Gentile society." Rabbi Kaplan urged the Hadassah to amend for their failures through Zionism. "Hadassah," he preached, "will save the soul of the American Jewish woman. . . ." She "needs Zionism if her personality is to achieve that normal and complete growth which living up to one's historic heritage makes possible."[42]

To the contrary, Jewish women had not lost their souls, had not abandoned Judaism. If, for example, intermarriage was an indication of assimilation, then statistics for the period suggested that far fewer women than men married outside their faith.[43] The predominance of male over female intermarriage was even more striking when one realized that in accordance with *halakah* a child's religion in a mixed marriage was determined by the religion of the mother. The child of a Jewish mother and a non-Jewish father was still considered a Jew. The popular literature of the 1920s and 1930s was replete with novels dealing with intermarriage between Jewish men and non-Jewish women. Sholem Asch, Ludwig Lewisohn, Ben Hecht, and others worried the question. Elmer Rice's Broadway play *Counsellor at Law*, about a Jewish lawyer and his gentile wife, came to the silver screen with John Barrymore as the romantic lead.[44] The literary critic Leslie Fiedler has suggested that these Jewish writers were investigating the ramifications of assimilation through the male-female relationship. In fiction and perhaps in life, the *shiksa* (non-Jewish woman) represented the aspirations and conflicts inherent in the blending of two different cultures.[45]

The literature dealing with marriage between a Jewish woman and a non-Jewish man was meager. An anonymous autobiographical statement published in the *Menorah Journal* in 1929 offered the testimony of a "Nordic" biology professor who married an Eastern European immigrant

---

[42] Mordecai M. Kaplan, "What the American Jewish Woman Can Do For Adult Education," *Jewish Education*, 4 (Oct.–Dec. 1932), 139, 140, 146.

[43] *AJYB*, 1972–73, 295. The following sources are helpful: Julius Drachsler, *Intermarriage in New York City* (New York: Columbia Univ. Press, 1921); Reuben B. Resnick, "Some Sociological Aspects of Intermarriage of Jews and Non-Jews," *Social Forces* (Oct. 1933), 94–102; Milton L. Barron, "The Incidence of Jewish Intermarriage in Europe and America," *American Sociological Review*, 11 (Feb. 1946), 6–13; Erich Rosenthal, "Some Recent Studies About the Extent of Out-Marriages in the U.S.A.," in *Intermarriage and Jewish Life: A Symposium* (New York: Herzl Press and Jewish Reconstructionist Press, 1963), 84–89.

[44] For novels that deal with intermarriage see Sholem Asch, *East River* (1938); Ludwig Lewisohn, *The Island Within* (1940); and Ben Hecht, *A Jew in Love* (1931). There is an interesting discussion of intermarriage and the Jewish male in Bernard Cohen, *Sociocultural Changes in American Jewish Life as Reflected in Selected Jewish Literature* (New Jersey: Fairleigh Dickinson Univ. Press, 1972), 129–34. See comments about Barrymore in *Counsellor at Law* in Axel Madsen, *William Wyler* (New York: Thomas Y. Crowell, 1973), 90–93.

[45] Leslie Fiedler, "Genesis: The American Jewish Novel through the Twenties," in *Jewish-American Literature*, 570–86.

Jew. In the academic community where the couple lived, anti-Semitic sentiments were expressed on social occasions. He described their plight in this way:

> My wife has no desire to pass as Nordic. Whenever she is due to meet people, it is my duty to let such people know that she is Jewish. She regards it a duty to tell all new acquaintances thus to disarm them or to warn them. . . . Telling people in advance often avoids embarrassment. Once we sat at a table where the guest of honor regaled the party with Jewish jokes. I have learned that Jews prefer to have Jewish jokes told by Jews; at least my wife feels that way. The guest of honor was greatly mortified when someone warned him. . . .[46]

It seems that a mixed marriage could painfully increase the woman's sense of Jewishness.

The number of national women's organizations founded in the 1920s and 1930s testified to the vitality of Jewish women and to their interest in religion and community affairs, as well as to the strength of the separatist tradition. The list includes Junior Hadassah (1921); Conference Committee of National Jewish Women's Organizations (1923); Women's Branch of the Union of Orthodox Jewish Congregations of America (1924); Women's Division of the Communist Workers' Order (1924); Women's Organization of the Pioneer Women of Palestine (1925); Women's American ORT (1927); Women's League for Palestine (1927); American Beth Jacob Committee (1928); Mizrachi Women's Organization of America (1930); and the Menorah League (1935).[47]

Along with the older groups like the National Council of Jewish Women, the National Federation of Temple Sisterhoods, or the Women's League of the United Synagogues of America (1918), all these associations provided a complex Jewish "woman's world." She could choose to work at several levels—congregational or civic, national or international. The range of her activities might encompass personal study of history, politics, and religion; mundane social events; teaching children; social work in the community with the poor, with recent Eastern European immigrants or, in the 1930s, with refugees from Germany; programs to aid impoverished Eastern European girls or to settle Jews in Palestine; assistance to universities and Jewish libraries; or the publication of periodical

[46] Anonymous, "My Jewish Wife," *Menorah Journal*, 16 (May 1929), 460–61. For a Jewish father's response to his daughter's marrying an Italian Catholic see New York *Jewish Daily Forward*, Jan. 22, 1921.
[47] The women's organizations and their purposes are listed in the *AJYB*. For the Women's Division of the Communist Workers' Order see Yiddish-language *Almanac* (New York: International Workers' Order Cooperative, 1934), 461; for the Women's Organization for the Pioneer Women of Palestine see "Constitution," *The Pioneer Women*, 1 (Mar. 1927), 7.

literature. Not all commitments were alike: some women contributed money to their favorite cause, while others joined the rank and file or took active leadership roles. These positions were exacting and prestigious, and women like Henrietta Szold emerged as heroic role-model figures.[48] Nor were all workers volunteers. Jewish social services were becoming professionalized; the Graduate School of Jewish Social Work was organized in 1925 and attracted young women in search of socially approved careers.

Trends in Jewish education generally reinforced women's interest in perpetuating their religious, social, and cultural life. By the 1920s, the example of American coeducational public schooling, the increased number of organized Jewish women, and changes in rituals like the introduction of a *bas mitzvah* or female confirmation ceremony in the Conservative synagogues all encouraged the inclusion of girls in Jewish educational programs. These were held after regular school hours or on Sunday. Hebrew or Yiddish and Jewish rituals, holidays, and history were the major subjects. The Conservative schools, however, emphasized the male *bar mitzvah* and offered girls a less intensive and hence less socially important program. By the 1930s one-third of the pupils enrolled in Jewish schools were girls. The Reform Sunday schools and the secular Yiddish schools had still higher female enrollments, mainly because their programs were not *bar mitzvah* oriented.[49]

Orthodox Jews, whose sons attended daily religious schools and received a more rigorous theological training than the children of their coreligionists, included girls in their Talmud Torah or yeshivas only with reluctance. They did, however, voice concern about the preservation of their faith; as a pamphlet of the Agudath Israel read: "While the Jewish boy was relatively safe from the onslaughts of assimilation in the yeshivas . . . the girls were easier prey for the Enlightenment."[50] By the late 1930s, a few schools for girls were in operation in New York City and girls were occasionally accepted as students in the traditionally all-male orthodox schools. Nevertheless the study of the Talmud remained a male privilege, girls being restricted to studying Hebrew, Jewish history, and the literature of the Bible. A new concept of educating orthodox women, the Beth Jacob schools, originating in Poland during the 1920s,[51] combined the

[48] See, for example, Susan Dworkin, "Henrietta Szold—Liberated Woman," in *The Jewish Woman*, 164–70.

[49] *AJYB*, 1936–37, 40–41. Also see Azriel L. Eisenberg, "A Study of 4473 Pupils Who Left Hebrew School in 1932–33," *Jewish Education*, 7 (April–June 1935), 91–96.

[50] Joseph Friedenson, *A History of Agudath Israel* (New York: Agudath Israel, 1970), 22.

[51] For a discussion of the education of girls among the Orthodox see Zvi H. Harris, "A Study of Trends in Jewish Education for Girls in New York City" (Diss. Yeshiva University, 1956).

study of religion with the training for a vocation. These schools attracted the interest of American Jewish women's organizations, which raised funds to assist the experiment. Dora Edinger, visiting Cracow in 1937 as a representative of the Conservative Women's League, was favorably impressed by the religiosity of the Beth Jacob students. "I heard two of these girls give marvelous sermons on the Sedra," she observed.[52]

In America, female students and teachers were involved in experimental programs to improve education in the part-time Reform, Conservative, and secular Jewish schools which supplemented regular public school. Since the boys' teachers were wary of tampering with the traditional curriculum and methods, innovative approaches to learning languages or new subjects were tried out on the girls. In this way, as one historian noted about the Orthodox and Conservative schools, though "Jewish education for girls generally lagged behind that of boys, girls . . . strangely enough made a unique contribution to Jewish education."[53]

Women teachers, who by 1935 made up about one-third of the teaching force, were in the forefront of developing not only new methods but a new philosophy for Jewish education. For example, Fannie R. Neumann, an articulate educational theoretician at the Brooklyn Jewish Center, hoped to create a method of rearing Jewish children which would offer them a "cultural synthesis." She envisioned a way to educate "a new type of Jew—steeped in Jewish culture, yet thoroughly at home in . . . [the] American milieu, disciplined yet free, adjusted to the machine age but saved from its serfdom by a critical eye and a sentient heart."[54]

In the 1930s, girls seemed to respond more enthusiastically than boys to Jewish education. This was especially true in the secular Jewish schools, where preparation for the *bar* or *bas mitzvah* was not the final goal and where girls were taught the same curriculum as boys. In fact, Leibush Lehrer, a leading educator in the Yiddishist Sholom Aleichem Folkschule, was struck by the differences in male and female reactions to Jewish interests. Interviewing former students, Lehrer found young women to have a more tenacious identification with Yiddish. Many more women than men continued to read Yiddish fiction and poetry and to attend Yiddish theatre after they had ceased their formal education. Discussing the possible reasons for the differences, Lehrer suggested that the female students were more intellectually mature than the males during the ages from 8 to 14 when they were studying Yiddish culture. He attributed

[52] Dora Edinger, "A Visit to Beth Jacob," *Outlook*, 7 (May 1937), 1.
[53] Zvi Harris, "Trends in Jewish Education," 66.
[54] Fannie R. Neumann, "A Modern Jewish Experimental School—in Quest of a Synthesis," *Jewish Education*, 4 (Jan.–Mar. 1932), 27.

the male students' lack of interest to an overemphasis on sports in American culture. Not being involved in sports, the girls had time for languages and literature.[55] It was likely, too, although Lehrer did not state this, that Jewish girls were encouraged to study humanistic subjects as part of the feminine ideal of a "cultured lady," while the boys rejected these subjects for that very reason.

Although by the end of the 1930s women were thus taking a prominent part in public aspects of American Jewish life, the extent of their exclusion and segregation continued to be profound. In fact the changes tended to mask the remaining inequalities. The unresolved problems in the most "progressive" Jewish sectors illustrate the biases that operated throughout the community. Reform Judaism, for instance, had integrated women into the temple and into the religious service for almost a hundred years. Reform women were lawyers, judges, and doctors. Nevertheless, in 1922 when Martha Neumark, a student at the Reform seminary, Hebrew Union College, expressed her intention to seek ordination as a rabbi, her request was denied. The lay members of the Board of Governors who opposed her ordination argued that such a departure from tradition was too radical and might alienate the Conservative and Orthodox co-religionists. The calling of rabbi required strenuous full-time activities and complete devotion; the essential role of the Jewish woman was to cultivate a Jewish home life and family. The board could not encompass the thought of combining the two. Dr. Jacob Z. Lauterbach, one of the more articulate members, assured the rejected candidate that there was "no injustice done to woman by excluding her for this office. There are many avenues open to her if she chooses to do religious and educational work."[56]

But women who were active in the "work" of the Jewish community discovered that a male bureaucratic hierarchy firmly controlled finances, policies, and plans. In Jewish schools male principals directed female teachers who were often paid less than their male counterparts. Female membership in the B'nai Brith, the mutual aid society, rose in the 1930s as did their financial contribution to the organization; at the end of the decade about a third of the B'nai Brith members were women. But, as in most other Jewish organizations, the B'nai Brith women were relegated to auxiliary sections and had no representation on the national executive board, which controlled finances and policy. At the 1938 B'nai Brith convention, as a historian of this organization has noted, "the rapid

[55] Leibush Lehrer, "Di tsey yidishe doyres in amerike " (The Two Jewish Generations in America), *Zukunft*, 36 (Sept. 1931), 593–99.
[56] Jacob Z. Lauterbach, "Responsum on Question 'Shall Women Be Ordained Rabbis? '" *Central Conference of American Rabbis Yearbook* (Cape May, N. J., 1922), 32:162.

growth of women's activities emboldened them to seek representation at Supreme Lodge conventions. But the best the delegates . . . could do for them was—conveniently without changing the Constitution—to permit each women's District at the next triennial convention to designate one representative to attend, with voice but no vote, and at her own District's expense."[57]

Radical secular groups upheld sexual equality in theory throughout this period, but the socialist and communist organizations in particular followed in the footsteps of their bourgeois brethren by encouraging women's auxiliaries[58] and by allowing males to dominate party bureaucracies. The woman's voice was heard mainly on the woman's page of the Sunday edition of the paper. In the socialistic *Jewish Daily Forward* or in the more feminist-conscious communist *Freiheit*, women were not on the editorial boards and only rarely wrote on political or economic issues. Occasionally an individual, especially a poet, would question aspects of Jewish tradition. Lily Bes made an open call in *Freiheit* in 1929 for rebellion against *tsnies* (modesty), a supposed female virtue incorporating the traditional notion of discreet behavior.[59] Writing in Yiddish the poet said:

> Es hot geplatst in mir di tsnies fun mayn bobe
> Es brent in mir revolt vi zummerdiger vayn
> Zol gute layt mikh shultn oder hasn
> Ikh ken shoyn ander nit zayn.

> Within me has burst my grandmother's sense of modesty
> Revolt burns in me like effervescent wine
> Let good folk curse and hate me
> I can no longer be otherwise.[59]

Rebellion, however, did not extend to criticism of the position of women in the radical movement. For the most part, social relationships within the Jewish movement were similar to those outside radical circles.

*   *   *

Jewish women in the 1920–1940 period lived within a pattern of seeming acceptance combined with implicit exclusion that remained characteristic of American Judaism until the 1970s, when Jewish feminists pressed for

---

[57] Edward E. Grusd, *B'nai Brith: The Story of a Covenant* (New York: Appleton-Century, 1966), 217–18.

[58] The development of female auxiliaries in the *Arbeiter Ring* (Workmen Circle) is discussed in Maximilian Hurwitz, *The Workmen Circle: Its History, Ideals, Organization and Institutions* (New York: The Workmen's Circle, 1936), 212–14.

[59] Lily Bes, "Fun eygene vegn" (On My Own Path), New York *Freiheit,* Jan. 20, 1929.

new changes. Obviously they were not unique. Women were socially and organizationally segregated for the most part in American Protestant and Catholic society as well. But American Judaism did not merely imitate American culture, although imitation was an aspect of Jewish historical development. The perspective which Jewish women faced in the 1920s was complex. For most Jewish women secularization was of recent origin. The traditions of orthodox Judaism explicitly, even legally, maintained separate worlds for women and men. The meeting of these worlds within a secular frame of reference had brought about a radical change. Comparing their own position with that of their grandmothers, most women believed themselves to be already living a revolution; few developed much insight into the contradictions of their situation.

It was difficult, too, for women to form a common ground upon which to base criticism of their role within Judaism. The myriad women's organizations reflected the structural decentralization of the faith. Identification as a Reform, Orthodox, Conservative, Yiddishist, or Socialist Jew obfuscated the sense of being a Jewish woman at odds with a set of common limitations. Furthermore, since the Jewish education of women was not grounded in theological literature, they did not feel qualified to muster arguments in their own defense.

Despite their many successful adjustments, Jews additionally did not feel secure in their newfound homeland in the 1920s and 1930s. The sense of existing as foreigners, as immigrants, was still a part of Jewish thinking. The threat of anti-Semitism combined with the apprehensions regarding assimilation had marked ramifications for women. Anti-Jewish sentiments were commonly expressed during the First World War, and immediately following the war restrictions were placed upon Jewish immigration to the United States. In the 1930s the rise of Nazism and echoes of fascism in the Coughlinites, Pelley's Silver Shirts, and others intensified Jewish anxiety. Anti-Semitism acted as a centripetal force exacting solidarity. In the face of external hostility, Jewish women were not able to begin their own crusade as women.

Concurrently, the perceived threat of assimilation kept Jewish women in their place. Since Biblical times Judaism had been inherited genetically through the mother. In America women had increasingly shouldered the responsibility of preserving a faith which men often found burdensome. The school and the social institutions became part of the domain of women—even if men controlled the upper reaches of power. Thus as newly installed defenders of the faith, it seemed contradictory for women also to be critics of that faith.

In the early 1970s Jewish feminists began to battle these contradictions. They questioned power relationships in Jewish institutions, religious inequality in Judaic practices, and anti-female bias expressed in some traditional Jewish literature. Concurrently, feminists sought Jewish precedent to legitimize the concept of equality of the sexes in Judaism. Like many religious reformers in the past, feminists have turned to a reinterpretation of the Bible. Rabbi Laura Geller, one of several women ordained in Reform Judaism, noted during a recent interview that Jewish feminists can look to another creation story than that of a masculine God creating in male terms. The first chapter of Genesis reads, "in the image of God created He them, male and female . . . , and he called their name 'adam' (human beings)." thus all human beings are created in the image of God. "Just as God is the father, God is also the mother," said the Rabbi.[60]*

[60] There are two good bibliographies on Jewish women related to the contemporary women's movement: Aviva Zuckoff, *Bibliography on the Jewish Woman*, 2d rev. ed. (New York: Jewish Liberation Project, 1972) and *The Jewish Woman in the Community: A Selected Annotated Bibliography* (pamphlet prepared by the Blaustein Library for the American Jewish Committee, 1976). The interview with Rabbi Laura Geller is by Tova Feder in the Los Angeles *Jewish Federation Council Bulletin*, Aug. 15, 1977.

*The author wishes to thank Marsie Scharlatt, Hillel Kempinski, Janet Hadda, Ariela Erhlich, Kenneth Pratt, and the library staff of YIVO Institute for Jewish Research for their kind assistance.

Alan Graebner

Birth Control and the Lutherans
The Missouri Synod as a Case Study

$\mathbf{D}$espite the familiarity with which Americans now speak of The Pill (nobody has to inquire *which* pill), general public acceptance of contraception is of comparatively recent origin, and its endorsement by some Protestant groups more recent still. Ironically, while in the present ecumenical age Protestant disenchantment with papal intransigence on contraception strikes a discordant note, in earlier decades of bitter interdenominational polemic much of Protestantism wholeheartedly agreed with Rome in denouncing birth control as contrary to God's will. Most Protestants of course subsequently reversed their position. How the shift was accomplished bears study because it illustrates the interplay between church and society in the definition of religious attitudes on social questions. The Lutheran Church–Missouri Synod, the most conservative and homogeneous of the three major Lutheran bodies in this country, serves admirably here as a case study.[1] Through its eventual acceptance of contraception it may demonstrate, in slow motion as it were, the Protestant progression. And in the painful hesitation with which it surrendered on this issue, the Synod may help illumine through parallel and contrast the still unresolved controversy within Roman Catholicism.

An earlier version of this essay was published in the *Journal of Social History*, vol. 2, no. 4 (Summer 1969), 303–32. Copyright © 1969 by the Regents of the University of California. Portions are reprinted by permission of the publisher.

[1] In this case, continuity seems to hold more fascination than change. Perhaps attracted by the problem of explaining that church's continued opposition, historians have focused on Roman Catholic attitudes, most notably in John T. Noonan, Jr.'s monumental *Contraception: A History of Its Treatment by the Catholic Theologians and Canonists* (Cambridge: Harvard Univ. Press, 1965). But what is to the contemporary mind so sensible, the Protestant reappraisal of birth control, has received short shrift from historians.

From the nineteenth century through the 1930s, Missouri Synod spokesmen flatly opposed all forms of contraception. They did so because of their views of sex and women. These perceptions were determined, Missourian theologians asserted, by the divine *Schoepfungsordnung*, the order of nature God established at Creation. Man was to subdue the earth; woman, to people it.[2] Although in the most judicious statements within the Synod the purposes of marriage were threefold—"legitimate sexual intercourse, the procreation of children, and cohabitation for mutual care and assistance"—many of the clergy reverted to a position closer to Augustine and perhaps Luther, stipulating procreation as the sole or at least the chief end of matrimony.[3] When pleasure in sex was thus either denigrated or ignored in favor of its utility, Missouri Synod Lutherans could speak of "perverting" or "subverting" the purpose of marriage through contraception; birth control made matrimony

---

The Lutheran Church–Missouri Synod, despite its name a national denomination, is the eighth largest religious body in the United States. Of nineteenth-century German immigrant origin (*Die Deutsche Evangelisch-Lutherische Synode von Missouri, Ohio und anderen Staaten*), it was founded in 1847. Its headquarters, main seminary, and publishing house are located in St. Louis. Particularly after World War II it gained considerable notice for its emphasis on doctrinal purity and its rapid growth. More recently it was the object of attention in the news media because of a bitter and debilitating division occasioned by a conservative takeover (led by J. A. O. Preüs) of the Synodical machinery. For access to Synodical history and historiography, see *The Lutherans in North America*, ed. E. Clifford Nelson (Philadelphia: Fortress Press, 1975); *Moving Frontiers: Readings in the History of The Lutheran Church–Missouri Synod*, ed. Carl S. Meyer (St. Louis: Concordia Publishing House, 1964); Alan Graebner, *Uncertain Saints: The Laity in the Lutheran Church–Missouri Synod, 1900–1970* (Westport, Conn.: Greenwood Press, 1975); and issues of *Concordia Historical Institute Quarterly*.

[2] See, for example, Francis Pieper, *Christian Dogmatics*, trans. Theodore Engelder (St. Louis: Concordia Publishing House, 1950), 1:523–26 (the original, German edition was published in 1924); August L. Graebner, *Theological Quarterly*, 3 (1899), 134, 412, 421; W.P.S., *Concordia Magazine*, 1 (1896), 33. When positive of identification, I have inserted the full name of contributors and editors without use of brackets to isolate the initials customarily employed to indicate authorship. When in doubt, I have simply given the initials. Absence of either denotes an anonymous contribution. Books published by Concordia Publishing House are so identified to signify their official standing in the Synod.

[3] August L. Graebner, *Outlines of Doctrinal Theology* (St. Louis: Concordia Publishing House, 1910), 94; A. L. Graebner, *Theological Quarterly*, 3 (1899), 406. Interestingly enough in light of later theological justification for a new position, in his proof-texts Graebner twice placed the comment of Genesis 2, with its emphasis on the unitive aspect of marital sex, over Genesis 1, with its emphasis on propagation (*Doctrinal Theology*, 59, 95). For Augustine, see Noonan, *Contraception*, 107–39; several different and not always reconcilable Luthers may be quoted on this point. See, however, his exposition of the sixth commandment in his Large Catechism.

Representative Missourian comment is in Carl Manthey-Zorn, *Der Lutheraner*, 50 (1894), 120; Manthey-Zorn, *Questions on Christian Topics Answered from the Word of God*, trans. J. A. Rimbach (Milwaukee, 1918), 153; O. H. W. Hornbostel, "*Die Christliche Familienleben*," *Sechsundzwandzigster Synodal-Bericht des Kansas-Distrikts, 1925*, 20; A. L. Graebner, "*Lehrverhandlungen ueber das sechste Gebot*," *Achter Synodal-Bericht des Minnesota- und Dakota-Distrikts*, 1892, 46.

"legal adultery" or "legal prostitution." Such "abominable doings," wrote one pastor, "make marriage far filthier than a pigsty."[4]

But it was the place of women which provoked the most urgent words. For the Synod's theologians, God placed women in a subordinate position at Creation and reaffirmed this at the Fall: he created Eve second and she became the agent for the introduction of sin. St. Paul made it clear this was not changed in the New Testament.[5] To the dismay of Lutheran churchmen, all this was under attack in the late nineteenth century, and they responded vigorously. For the Synod's most important German organ, *Der Lutheraner*, the feminist movement was a *Zeitkrankheit* and female suffrage an *Unordnung*, to be voted down by good Lutherans wherever it appeared on a ballot. Missouri's official English newspaper, the *Lutheran Witness*, described the catastrophe female suffrage would produce. "Many women," it predicted, "will be so busy about voting and political office that the home and children will have no attraction for them, and American mothers and children, like Christian charity, will be a rarity."[6]

Men wedded to such a definition of women and so convinced of the fragility of the home could hardly respond favorably to something which promised to accomplish the very revolution they feared. Birth control not only diminished at least the quantitative importance of the woman's sphere, but even provided women the means to escape the home entirely. Sympathetic discourse on birth control alone would have been difficult; it was impossible, as the *Witness* demonstrated, when feminism became involved. "The new woman has cast the church aside, because it teaches subordination of the wife to the husband, and enjoins domestic duties from which the 'taste' of the new woman revolts. The new woman hates children, and is madly exerting her ingenuity in frustrating the ends of matrimony." An editor attacked women active in public life who "gave speeches and essays and high moral instruction to the world instead of giving children."[7]

---

[4] A. W. Meyer, *Lutheran Witness*, 24 (1905), 157. Richard Jesse, *Lutheran Witness*, 44 (1925), 337. Quoted in *Lutheran Witness*, 20 (1901), 55. M. H. Coyner, "The Christian Home," *Proceedings of the Nineteenth Convention of the Central Illinois District, 1936*, 24. Manthey-Zorn, *Questions*, 180.

[5] The most extensive discussion is W. H. T. Dau, *Woman Suffrage in the Church* (St. Louis: Concordia Publishing House Print, n.d. [c. 1916]).

[6] A. L. Graebner, *Der Lutheraner*, 50 (1894), 71–72, 91. J. Frederic Wenchel, *Lutheran Witness*, 39 (1920), 330. See also Alan Graebner, *Uncertain Saints*, 17–19.

[7] *Lutheran Witness*, 17 (1898), 55. Luecke, *Lutheran Witness*, 19 (1900), 14. For similar polemical linking of feminism, female suffrage, and birth control, see James Kenneally, "Catholicism and Woman Suffrage in Massachusetts," *Catholic Historical Review*, 53 (Apr. 1967), 43–57. On the relationship between feminism and family planning, see Joseph A. and Olive Banks, *Feminism and Family Planning in Victorian England* (New York: Schocken, 1964); Linda Gordon, *Woman's Body, Woman's Right: A Social History of Birth Control in America* (New York: Grossman, 1976); James Reed, *From Private Vice to Public*

Biblical witness was, as we have seen, called upon to support the natural order thesis. In addition, Holy Writ provided one concrete episode which speaks directly of birth control. This is the peculiar case of Onan, an obscure Old Testament figure ordered to produce children by his brother's widow. He disobeyed by deliberately spilling his semen on the ground and was thereupon killed by God (Genesis 38:8–10).[8] The basic argument against birth control, then, went something like this: according to the natural order, woman's place is in the home; according to divine injunction her role is to bear children; to this end marriage was instituted; to interfere in any way with the process is to frustrate a/the purpose of marriage, and to violate the moral order established by God.

The Missouri Synod condemnation of birth control in the nineteenth century was unequivocal, but two further characteristics require mention. First, the practice was usually not specified as entrenched within Lutheran circles. Instead, German immigrant girls working as maids in upper-class, American homes or economically successful, more Americanized laity were said to come into contact with this otherwise unknown sin.[9] Such statements are reminders that for the Missouri Synod, contraception originated among outsiders—in homiletical parlance, it was "of the world." This had particular import in a denomination with Missouri's immigrant ghetto ethos; in addition, the Synod tended to place unusual emphasis on the wall between the Christian and the world and, by insisting upon extensive doctrinal agreement as a prerequisite for association, to remain aloof even from most other Lutherans. Birth control would have been denounced in any case, but in this denomination its origin discredited its advocates and was further cause for censure.

A second important characteristic is the infrequency of the Synod's nineteenth-century comment on birth control, especially when compared to the attention given it after 1900. An anonymous tract in 1868 and scattered, brief references during following decades are all one can produce until the late 1890s.[10] This may well indicate still limited incidence of rigorous con-

Virtue: The Birth Control Movement and American Society Since 1830 (New York: Basic Books, 1978).

[8] See, e.g., A. L. Graebner, _"Lehrverhandlungen,"_ 47. The passage had been cited for centuries by early Jewish and Christian writers against contraception. Noonan, _Contraception_, 34 _passim_.

[9] Anon., _Das Kindermord_ (St. Louis, 1868); J.F.S.H., _Der Lutheraner_, 51 (1895), 138; A. L. Graebner, _Theological Quarterly_, 2 (1898), 349; A. M., _Lutheran Witness_, 13 (1894), 78; H. B. Hemmeter, _Lutheran Witness_, 16 (1897), 110; _Lutheran Witness_, 18 (1899), 67.

[10] C. F. W. Walther (1811–87), the patriarch of the Synod, mentioned birth control in a condemnatory way a number of times, but his remarks were few and scattered. See _Der Lutheraner_, 28 (1871), 4; he was quoted in _Der Lutheraner_, 57 (1906), 241, without source and I have been unable to locate the original reference. He does not recognize the subject in his influential _Amerikanisch-Lutherische Pastoraltheologie_, first published in St. Louis in 1872, and frequently reissued thereafter by Concordia Publishing House.

traceptive practice in what was yet a heavily rural denomination. The uncharacteristic reticence may also reflect the failure of some clergy to detect at first what was going on; others perhaps saw the practice, but hesitated to say anything in print. To account for this hesitation as well as for the increased incidence of comment after 1900, one must examine the broader American scene. Missouri Lutheran spokesmen could—and did—quote Luther and their favorite seventeenth-century orthodox theologians for support, but they were still men of the late nineteenth century. It is hardly remarkable that the results (though not always the processes) of their reasoning on most questions connected with sex usually coincided closely with general conservative opinion in the decades around the turn of the century.

The view of sex then held in common by this immigrant church and by middle-class America was the congeries of silence, repulsion, disdain, innocence, and repression often loosely labeled Victorian. In that age, according to a reminiscing Henry Seidel Canby, "sex, as they say of poultry in the market, was steady and quiet. Old roosters were lively, young broilers up and down, but fowls kept their price and their counsel."[11] At least the reticence was challenged well before World War I. The Progressives' successors were repelled by their negativism about sex. But the Progressives' predecessors were more impressed by their frankness. Between the turn of the century and the war, Americans engaged in or at least frequently read about energetic campaigns against prostitution, white slavery, pornography, divorce, and contraception. William Marion Reedy may have been hasty in diagnosing the new American malady as coprolalia, but the extent of the campaigns and the publicity given them was undeniably unprecedented.[12]

The attack on birth control took a peculiar turn under presidential leadership. Theodore Roosevelt shared some of the northeastern patrician's racist fears, but, refusing to accept immigrant restriction, he adopted E. A. Ross's phrase, "race suicide," and exhorted patriotic fecundity in letters from the White House and even in a message to Congress. When the president thus sounded the trumpet, other voices need remain muted no longer; indeed, preservation of the republic required further description of the peril. As a result, from 1905 through 1909, more than thirty-five articles dealing with race suicide appeared in general publications.[13]

[11] "Sex and Marriage in the Nineties," *Harper's Magazine*, 169 (Sept. 1934), 431.
[12] Henry F. May, *The End of American Innocence: A Study of the First Years of Our Time, 1912–1917* (New York: Knopf, 1959); James R. McGovern, "The American Woman's Pre–World War I Freedom in Manners and Morals," *Journal of American History*, 55 (1968), 315–33; John Burnham, "The Progressive Era Revolution in American Attitudes Toward Sex," *Journal of American History*, 59 (1973), 885–908. Reedy was quoted in *Current Opinion*, 55 (1913), 113–14.
[13] Ross, "The Causes of Race Superiority," *Annals of the American Academy of Political and Social Science*, 18 (1901), 67–89; Roosevelt to Mrs. Bessie Van Vorst, Oct. 18, 1902, *Presidential Addresses and State Papers*, 2 (New York: P. F. Collier and Son, 1904),

Though in other respects still far from Americanization, the Missouri Synod shared this national preoccupation. In 1905 the *Lutheran Witness* reprinted the text of Roosevelt's address before a convention of mothers and in the following decade spoke more frequently and openly on the subject than at any other time before the 1960s.[14] To evaluate this rhetoric, one must be clear on the precise object of condemnation. A wide variety of birth control methods existed by the turn of the century. Advances in rubber technology permitted improved condoms and the vaginal diaphragm; pessaries and suppositories of one form or another and douching were also known and utilized. The crudest form was early-term abortion or, for the timorous, unusual exertion to induce miscarriage. As would be expected, both were indicted by Lutherans as murder and menaces to maternal health, "a suttee of a different form."[15] Abortion's status, if predictable, is nevertheless noteworthy, because it tended to color thinking on birth control by contraception. Many clergy extended the physical effects of repeated, clandestine abortion and the supposed psychic effects of coitus interruptus to all forms of birth control, painting a dark picture indeed. Eighty-five percent of all woman in Chicago hospitals were said to be there as a result of birth control. "All forms of contraceptives," announced one cleric, "are more or less injurious to the health, both of husband and wife, but particularly of the latter, as every reputable physician will testify."[16]

Some of such pious fraudulence may be attributed to credulity. Circumlocutions for contraception may represent either discretion or ignorance. Probably many pastors were typified by the minister who privately confessed in 1925, "I know next to nothing about it." Yet, though contraception suffered by association with abortion, its condemnation was not always out of ignorance. Quite early in the century, Lutherans mentioned the existence of a contraceptive industry and supplies of all kinds of medicines and instruments—"rubber goods" appears as an English phrase in a German article—which agents peddled from house to house.[17] Such writers made a differen-

---

508–10; "Message of the President . . . to . . . Congress . . . Dec. 6, 1904," *Presidential Addresses and State Papers*, 3 (New York: P. F. Collier and Son, 1910), 137; "Address before the National Congress of Mothers," March 13, 1905, *Presidential Addresses and State Papers*, 3: 282–99; *Review of Reviews*, 35 (1907), 551.

[14] 24 (1905), 51–53.

[15] James Reed, *From Private Vice*; James C. Mohr, *Abortion in America: The Origins and Evolution of National Policy, 1800–1900* (New York: Oxford Univ. Press, 1978). The quotation is from Otto C. A. Boecler, *Lutheran Witness*, 27 (1908), 77. See also C. A. Weiss, *Lutheran Witness*, 28 (1909), 217; *Kindermord*, 6–7; Luecke, *Lutheran Witness*, 20 (1901), 47, 55; Luecke, *"Be Fruitful and Multiply": Earnest Words to Married People* (n.p., n.d. [1914]), 6.

[16] *Lutheran Witness*, 36 (1917), 196. Luecke, *Be Fruitful*, 7. Arguments based on the sexually unsatisfactory nature of withdrawal appear to be inadvertent clerical testimony sanctioning the female orgasm, an aspect of woman's nature not otherwise discussed.

[17] J. H. Lindemeyer to Theodore Graebner, Sept. 15, 1925, Theo. Graebner Papers, Box 101, Concordia Historical Institute, St. Louis. R.v.N., *Der Lutheraner*, 60 (1904), 242;

tiation between abortion and contraception, but they treated it only as a technical nicety. Ethics were not to be influenced here by a different means to an end, for ends were as much at issue as means.

Early twentieth-century Lutheran birth control pronouncements not only increased in frequency, but they diverged somewhat in content. For example, the marked, early decline in the French birth rate occasioned frequent and dolorous comment in the church press—something probably not uncongenial for a denomination both German and Lutheran and opposed to birth control as well. Typical was the clergyman who identified St. Paul's Corinth as the Paris of the ancient world.[18] But increasingly appended to remarks on France were admissions of Lutheran guilt. After a look at parochial school enrollments in 1908, the *Witness* observed sadly that the tendency toward small families "is no longer confined to the 'Yankees'; it has already invaded every class of the population, and also the Lutheran portion, German and otherwise, is no longer exempt."[19]

The changes during the early twentieth century in the type of argumentation employed against family limitation also reflect this conviction. Writers did not suddenly desert the classic brief, but they did modify it. They still referred to the natural order, but once the Nineteenth Amendment had settled the political status of woman, her place was stressed much less than the basic position and role of the family.[20] Onan's example was still cited, though especially after World War I the clergy was likelier to quote the more affirmative verses of Psalm 127.[21] Most important, after 1900 the church's leaders began to consider specific arguments for birth restriction in order to refute them.

Walther, *Der Lutheraner*, 62 (1906), 241; Alb. H. Brauer, *"Die Schaeden der Korinthischen Gemeinde und Pauli Weisung diese abzutun und zu ueberwinden, eine Lehre auch fuer unsere Gemeinden,"* *Dritter Synodal-Bericht des Nord-Illinois-Distrikts, 1912*, 52. Before the turn of the century, A. L. Graebner had in his library several works by John Humphrey Noyes, explaining the pecularities of birth control (coitus reservatus) at Oneida. Copies of *Essay on Scientific Propagation* and *Male Continence* with Graebner's autograph are now in the Ludwig Fuerbringer Library at Concordia Seminary, St. Louis.

[18] Brauer, *"Die Schaeden,"* 47. For a sampling of additional references. see Luecke, *Be Fruitful*, 9; W.D., *Lutheran Witness*, 19 (1901), 190, Fritz, *Lutheran Witness*, 21 (1902), 166.

[19] Luecke, *Lutheran Witness*, 27 (1908), 17. *Der Lutheraner* corroboration is in R.v.N., 60 (1904), 242; and Fuerbringer, 61 (1905), 24. The only exception to such prewar dating I have located is Carl Eissfeldt's 1921 opinion that birth control was not quite yet rampant in Lutheran circles. His use of archaic phraseology, however, does not lead to confidence in his perspicacity. *Magazin fuer Ev.-Luth. Homiletik und Pastoraltheologie*, 45 (1921), 118–20.

[20] It should be noted, however, that synodical spokesmen did not quickly change their opinion about either suffrage or woman's place.

[21] Verse 3–5: "Lo, sons are a heritage from the Lord, the fruit of the womb a reward. Like arrows in the hand of a warrior are the sons of one's youth. Happy is the man who has his quiver full of them! He shall not be put to shame when he speaks with his enemies in the gate."

Why do people limit the size of their families? denominational spokesmen asked rhetorically. Many, they answered, try birth control because they believe they cannot financially support a large family. This however is gross materialism and displays a lack of trust in God; it is assuredly grounds for alarm when even Lutheran congregations refuse to call ministerial candidates with large families because of the high cost of support.[22] Still others practice birth control, wrote Synodical observers, because large families are not fashionable. It is true, they complained, that landlords of fine apartments specify "no children." "It requires no expert sociologist to note how 'race suicide' and the ubiquitous 'divorce' seem to flourish with the modern 'apartment' house"; neighbors and friends even of a Christian woman who is pregnant deplore that there must be another childbirth in that home, and parents of large families are subject to all kinds of sly innuendo.[23]

Some married couples limit the number of children, churchmen stated, because they fear for the health of the mother. On this point the clergy came down hard. The plea of health, Lutherans were assured, is in nine cases out of ten a mere subterfuge to mask female selfishness. The most uncompromising authors maintained that even if experience demonstrated that childbirth did shorten a mother's life, one could not rightfully interfere with God's natural order. Fortunately, childbearing does not have a deleterious effect, they insisted; in fact, a mother's health is preserved by it. Seminarians studying pastoral theology in the 1920s and 30s read that "women with many children are in middle age much more beautiful than those who have few children. . . ."[24]

Concentrating their fire upon agitation for fewer, but better, children, Synodical writers frequently reminded their readers that fertility and genius are not incompatible. In fact, "genius is rarely found where there is one child." Often included were impressive compilations of famous people from large families. Thus Franklin was fifteenth of seventeen children; Caruso was a nineteenth child, while Schubert was a fourteenth, though presumably no less talented for it. The fact was, one author contended, "that the oldest children are often weaker than the younger. If the latter remain unborn, and if only the oldest children continue the family trunk, degeneration is not to

[22] Theo. Wuggazer, *Lutheran Witness*, 28 (1909), 591 (in part this article is an unacknowledged paraphrase of *Das Kindermord* of a half-century earlier); R.v.N., *Der Lutheraner*, 60 (1904), 242–43; R. Piehler, *"Das Leben der sichtbaren Kirche unserer Zeit, ein Zeichen der Nache des Juengsten Tages,"* *Zwoelfter Synodal-Bericht des Nord-Illinois-Distrikts, 1925*, 36.

[23] Brauer, *"Die Schaeden,"* 53. H. B. Hemmeter, *Lutheran Witness*, 24 (1905), 30. J. T. Mueller, *Der Lutheraner*, 81 (1925), 129; Manthey-Zorn, *Questions*, 179.

[24] "Wayfarer," *Lutheran Witness*, 36 (1917), 82. R.v.N., *Der Lutheraner*, 60 (1904), 242–43. Fritz, *Walther League Messenger*, 38 (April 1925), 462. Quoted by Fritz, *Pastoral Theology* (St. Louis: Concordia Publishing House, 1932), 178.

be avoided."[25] Even the financial difficulties incurred in attempts to breed genius are not disadvantageous; "in families . . . where constant frugality is demanded in the distribution of the family income, there seems to be a rugged independence for which wealth can offer no compensation." If nothing else, Lutherans contended, family limitation promoted the already alarming rate of divorce. Couples with children were more likely to stay together than those without. And upon the home and family rest the fortunes of the nation.[26]

Clerical spokesmen were caught in a difficult dilemma—though it is not clear they recognized this. To strengthen the anti–birth control argument was an admission of weakness, for appeals to lay self-interest implied the inadequacy of an argument from divine mandate. To introduce a prudential ethic was a step toward capitulation. But the clergy failed to see that their non-theological contentions were susceptible to test by any lay person, and if disproved, the Biblical base lost credibility by association.

In a shorter perspective, such arguments were tacit acknowledgment of the effectiveness of the increasingly open advocacy of birth control. Though there was a long and generally unhappy history of agitation for family limitation, no American received—or had the talent for gaining—the publicity given Margaret Sanger after her dramatic emergence in 1914.[27] Religious freethinker, divorcee, radical feminist, intimate of English and American literati, possessed of a vigorous social conscience, Margaret Sanger was everything the Missouri Synod was not, and Lutherans responded in vituperative terms. The *Witness* complained in 1923 that the *Nation* was aiding Mrs. Sanger's organization "to spatter the country with its slime." Describing Margaret Sanger's latest speech, one pastor reported, "this she-devil has again opened her trap."[28] As in the past, opposition to birth control and antipathy to its advocates reinforced each other. When in 1925 birth control advocates

[25] Quoted in *Lutheran Witness*, 36 (1917), 196. Quoted by Fritz, *Pastoral Theology*, 179.
[26] Walter A. Maier, *For Better, Not for Worse*, 3d ed. (St. Louis: Concordia Publishing House, 1939), 389. For the connection between birth control and divorce, see Luecke, *Lutheran Witness*, 20 (1901), 110; M. Brueggemann, *Lutheran Witness*, 35 (1916), 174; "Wayfarer," *Lutheran Witness*, 36 (1917), 83; M. H. Coyner, "The Christian Home," 25; Maier, *Walther League Messenger*, 46 (1938), 603.
[27] James Reed, *From Private Vice*; David M. Kennedy, *Birth Control in America: The Career of Margaret Sanger* (New Haven: Yale Univ. Press, 1970).
[28] Theo. Graebner, *Lutheran Witness*, 42 (1923), 173. Piehler, *"Das Leben der sicht-baren Kirche,"* p. 35. The original reads, *"Dieses Teufelsweib hat auch wieder ihr Maul gross aufgerissen."* Later switching to irony, the author characterized the movement as one run by rich people who prefer pets to children and who desire to "help" the poor and foreigners because their many children pose the same danger to the 100 percent Americanists as the Israelites did for the Egyptians. To throw children into the water is indelicate, so birth control became the solution. The 1927 *Concordia Cyclopedia* entry for birth control was equally condemnatory (ed. Ludwig Fuerbringer, Theodore Engelder, Paul E. Kretzmann [St. Louis: Concordia Publishing House], 84).

were able to bring to Congressional committee investigation their proposals for eliminating the ban on mailing items associated with contraception, the Synod's president delegated a Washington pastor to join those successfully lobbying against repeal.

Much sterner trials were in store, however, during the Depression, when public opinion became explicitly favorable toward family limitation. Probably most indicative was the Sears-Roebuck catalog, which in 1925 had not even dared recognize the existence of contraceptives, but devoted a whole page in 1935 and two pages by 1939 to what were thinly disguised as "feminine hygiene needs."[29] Reflecting and aiding this shift were defections within church circles. In 1930 the Lambeth Conference of Anglican bishops passed resolutions supporting birth control in principle. The following year a Federal Council of Churches of Christ report defended family limitation and called for the repeal of laws restricting dissemination of information on contraceptives.[30]

Outside pressure on the Synod thus increased substantially. Contraceptives were more readily available to the laity. And within Protestantism at least, the Synod was being left in an increasingly isolated position. Missouri, however, was not unaccustomed to such a situation and outwardly made no accommodation. A "lapse into paganism" was one editor's verdict on the Federal Council's carefully reasoned statement with its emphasis on the beauties and responsibilities of parenthood. Congressional hearings on contraceptive legislation in 1931 again brought a Synodical representative, J. Frederick Wenchel.[31]

Deepening economic malaise produced in the church press no concession on family limitation; in fact, one correspondent was of the opinion that "more babies would solve a lot of our economic problems."[32] The most comprehen-

---

[29] David L. Cohn, *The Good Old Days: A History of American Morals and Manners as Seen through the Sears, Roebuck Catalogs, 1905 to the Present* (New York: Simon and Schuster, 1940), 254. For a convenient summary of the major polls on contraceptives, Hazel Gaudet Erskine, "The Polls: The Population Explosion, Birth Control, and Sex Education," *Public Opinion Quarterly*, 30 (Fall 1966), 490–501 and "The Polls: More on the Population Explosion and Birth Control," *Public Opinion Quarterly*, 31 (Summer 1967), 303–13.

[30] A brief review of religious attitudes in the twenties is in Mary Patrice Thaman, *Manners and Morals of the 1920's: A Survey of the Religious Press* (New York: Bookman Assoc., 1954), 143–52. The text of the Federal Council's report is in *Current History*, 34 (April 1931), 97–100. See Richard M. Fagley, *The Population Explosion and Christian Responsibility* (New York: Oxford Univ. Press, 1960), 195–208, for a summary of subsequent Protestant positions on contraception.

[31] Walter A. Maier, *Walther League Messenger*, 39 (1931), 552. Wenchel later reported on the large attendance and enthusiasm of Mrs. Sanger's "camp followers" at the hearings, describing them further as unmarried and largely Jewish (*Lutheran Witness*, 50 [1931], 174).

[32] R. P. Young, *Lutheran Witness*, 58 (1939), 306; for further Depression comment, see Martin Sommer, *Lutheran Witness*, 55 (1936), 52; Theo. Graebner, *Lutheran Witness*, 50 (1931), 119–20; Maier, *Walther League Messenger*, 46 (1938), 603.

sive statement to appear in the 1930s was in Professor John H. C. Fritz's *Pastoral Theology*. Fritz did state that procreation is not the only purpose of marriage, but left the impression that it is the primary one; he advised that healthy, young people might have intercourse once or twice a week without injury and warned that even in marriage sexual desire should be curbed. Certainly, he wrote, an *"artificial* sexual appetite should not be created." Fritz quoted an early nineteenth-century physician's statement that "the act of copulation is to be regarded as the beginning of the existence of the future being."[33] With such a rigorous view of sexual pleasure and such a primitive view of sexual physiology, it is understandable that Fritz did little trailblazing in attitudes toward birth control.

By the 1930s, however, the denomination did not merely repeat the old argument on family restriction. In the Depression decade a number of cracks appeared in the wall reared against birth control. One came in 1935 in the first full-length marriage manual published within Synodical circles, *For Better, Not for Worse*, written by Walter A. Maier, one of Fritz's colleagues at Concordia Seminary, St. Louis, and soon to become a famous radio preacher. Maier's attitude toward family limitation seems obvious in the chapter title, "The Blight of Birth Control," and indeed, he ran through the familiar sequence. However, at the end of his discussion, Maier made an extraordinary concession when he referred sympathetically to young couples "disquieted by the thought of abnormally large families and the resultant inability to provide adequate means and cultural growth for their children." Such people should know, wrote Maier, that the church neither required families of ten or more children, nor insisted that pregnancies follow in rapid succession without regard to the mother's health. In other words, some type of birth limitation was acceptable. But on the now separate question of *means* for family restriction, Maier was less venturesome. "Artificial methods" were not permitted the Christian. Instead, seizing upon the recent popularization of studies on the ovulation cycle, Maier stated that the church "has never protested against the employment of those means which the course of nature itself seems to provide, unless their employment is a selfish attempt to evade the responsibilities of parenthood."[34]

Without resort to the proof-text style so dear to Missourian writers, without appreciable supporting argument, Maier thus blandly announced a crucial shift in his church's position. Politically the rhythm method was an ideal way

---

[33] Pp. 174–78. Just what an artificial appetite was Fritz did not explain. He was, however, by no means alone in the Synod. A *Witness* editor in 1921 had advised young men not to wait for marriage until infatuated with a girl, but to make a choice before affected by passion. And a respected pastor warned married couples "not [to] recklessly abandon themselves to sensual passion or even to the natural stimulation of it" (Sommer, *Lutheran Witness*, 40 [1921], 101; H. M. Zorn, *Lutheran Witness*, 43 [1924], 244).

[34] Pp. 361–62.

station. It demonstrated the concern of the church for hard-pressed laity. Yet the required abstinence might reassure conservatives concerned about uxo- riousness. Of course Maier did not intend this to be a way station. He betrays little awareness of being the first Synodical author to separate publicly the issue of birth control into two questions: is family limitation justifiable? and, what methods are permissible? But as it was to turn out, he had divided to surrender.[35]

In making the distinction he did, Maier was not alone; he was unique mostly in stating the matter so openly.[36] Curiously, those who concurred here were deceptively offhand about opposition on the matter of family restriction itself. As Theodore Graebner, professor at the St. Louis seminary and an editor of the *Lutheran Witness*, asked rhetorically in 1934, "who denies that there is a proper limitation of birth control?" Graebner's correspondent, a parish pastor questioning his stand, was not so easily put off. His answer was a prompt "a great many deny it. . . . I have heard quite a number of Pastors argue, that since God gives children, any act tending to take the control out of His hands is sinful. They advocate hewing to the line and letting the chips fall where they may."[37] The metaphor was striking, and the observation correct. The line of thinking was clear already in *Das Kindermord* of 1868— children are a blessing; therefore, "the more children, the more blessing"— and in A. L. Graebner's attacks on the "three-children-system." As A. W. Meyer put it in 1905, "if God designs to bless them [a married couple] with children, *they have not the right to refuse that blessing*." John Fritz still agreed when in his revised *Pastoral Theology* of 1945 he mentioned the sterile period as a divine provision against too frequent conception; nevertheless, he warned, God did not intend that this should "permit parents to determine for themselves how many or how few children they will have."[38]

With this position men such as Maier and Graebner did not argue; they simply failed to recognize it in public. A glimpse of their thinking is con-

[35] Luecke, writing in 1914, had allowed limitation (by continence only) when imperative for the health of the mother or for demonstrated genetic reasons. The context, however, makes it clear that he had in mind unusual instances, not the typical couples Maier was writing for (*Be Fruitful*, 10). The entry under "birth control" in the *Concordia Cyclopedia* of 1927 allowed total continence only in case of illness. In stating his views Maier seemed blissfully unaware of ominous historical precedent. In statements of 1908, 1914, and 1930, the Anglican bishops went from prohibition of birth control, to approval of natural means only, to leaving the whole matter to private judgment. Joseph A. Banks, *Prosperity and Parenthood: A Study of Family Planning among the Victorian Middle Classes* (London: Routledge and Kegan Paul, 1954), 160–61.

[36] See, e.g., John T. Mueller, *Concordia Theological Monthly*, 2 (1931), 627.

[37] Graebner to Egbert Schaller, June 5, 1934; Schaller to Graebner, June 7, 1934, Theo. Graebner Papers, Box 101.

[38] *Kindermord*, 8; Graebner, *Theological Quarterly*, 2 (1898), 350. *Lutheran Witness*, 24 (1905), 157. Fritz, *Pastoral Theology*, 165. For similar examples see Boecler, *Lutheran Witness*, 27 (1908), 76, and Louis Nuechterlein, "Series on the Christian Marriage Relation," *Concordia Pulpit for 1940*, 11 (St. Louis: Concordia Publishing House, 1939), 392.

tained in a letter Theodore Graebner wrote in 1931. Responding to an inquiry whether family limitation by abstinence, formerly "condemned," was now permissible, Graebner began a bit disingenuously. "I am not aware of any official statement condemning abstinence as a means of keeping down the number of children." Finding no mandate in Holy Writ that births be as frequent as biologically possible, Graebner agreed that parents may "practice abstinence if they do not desire to have, say, one child a year." This would be sinful only if done for selfish reasons. But, he concluded,

> . . . the use of contraceptives . . . is to be condemned, when they are used for selfish reasons and *also per se*. On this latter point, I realize that I am at variance with some Christian physicians and also theologians, who condone such practices when a woman is able to bear children only with abnormal suffering. . . . With this I cannot agree, but must admit also my inability to prove my negative position in such a manner as to compel the agreement of others.[39]

Graebner was virtually admitting that on the issue of contraceptives he was operating with emotion rather than logic. The emotion was the common anxiety and fear that American moral standards were collapsing. Looking about him at the family and home in 1925, one commentator observed that the "unit of the nation is going to pieces like the battered hulk of some ancient schooner."[40] In such an emergency, with women and children aboard, it would be tantamount to desertion for the crew to relax its efforts. Conservatism regarding the status of women and anxiety that contraceptives would contribute to promiscuity helped keep opposition to birth control emotionally alive well after it was intellectually dead.[41]

As an argument, though, emotion has its limits, as Graebner tacitly admitted in his 1931 letter. Interestingly enough, *Witness* editorials were remarkably reticent on birth control after 1931. Despite repeated urgings that the paper should reply to continuing birth control propaganda, Graebner steadfastly refused. Professional journals for pastors, not a general church paper, should deal with such sexual questions, he replied. Though he was probably not insincere in this response, Graebner was probably also not quite

---

[39] To correspondent, Aug. 15, 1932. Theo. Graebner Papers, Box 101.

[40] P. E. Kretzmann, *Lutheran Witness*, 44 (1925), 334. Of course, such viewing with alarm is to be expected from any professional custodian of morality. But the sense of foreboding seems perceptibly deeper in the generation which came of age in the 1890s. Maier, though a younger man, expressed the feeling well in 1938 when he reviewed fifty years of the *Ladies Home Journal* and anxiously questioned, "what changes in public and domestic morals will the next fifty years bring if the past five decades have leaped from questioning the parasol to favoring divorce?" *For Better*, 3d ed., 428.

[41] See Theo. Graebner to Egbert Schaller, June 5, 1934, Theo. Graebner Papers, Box 101; Theo. Graebner, *Lutheran Witness*, 43 (1924), 199; *Lutheran Witness*, 53 (1934), 59.

candid, for the reason he gave served as a convenient pretext to avoid occupying what he recognized as a vulnerable battlement.[42]

Whatever the motives, the *Witness*, once a stalwart in the ranks against family limitation, had during the 1930s less and less to say to the laity on contraceptives. Moreover, as depression gave way to war, this was the pattern for nearly all Missourian publications.[43] In other words, sometime during the 1930s the Missouri Synod entered the second stage in the metamorphosis of opposition–silence–advocacy which characterized the development of its thought on birth control. Except perhaps in retrospect, there was nothing very dramatic about the process. Silence is usually deafening only in history books. There was no public confrontation, no highly controversial book to mark the passage. Instead, construction of a new edifice proceeded very slowly and rather hidden behind the decaying walls once presented against the world and now shored up but rarely.[44]

How early the traditional stand was subjected to searching criticism by the clergy is impossible to say, but this was much advanced by the Depression. Sometimes the critique came from an obscure pastor willing and able to think for himself; writing in 1934 Egbert Schaller was impatient with hairsplitting: "for me methods are not at issue. If the intent itself is right, if, in other words, birth control is ever permissible, it is immaterial what method is used. I hold birth control can be practiced." Occasionally the questioning came from troubled ministers who could not square what they observed with what they had been taught: "in my experience these cases [of divorce] do not turn up in the childless families, or in homes with one child, but in homes with quite large families. . . . From my experience I could not say that the large family is, of itself, a blessing, or the small family a curse." Or questions were forced by observation of contemporary conditions; every urban pastor, wrote O. A. Geiseman, knows young couples who could not survive financially without the wife's wages, and that means birth control. There were cases in which a clergyman was led to think through the matter "when well-meaning

---

[42] Albert F. L. Schroeder to M. S. Sommer, April 10, 1934; Graebner to correspondent, March 8, 1934; to Schroeder, April 20, and July 26, 1934, Theo. Graebner Papers, Box 101. Significantly, Graebner did not pursue the matter in the Synod's pastoral journal, nor mention it in books where it would have been in order. *Pastor and People: Letters to a Young Preacher* (St. Louis: Concordia Publishing House, 1932); *Borderline of Right and Wrong* (St. Louis: Concordia Publishing House, 1938).

[43] This generalization includes the proceedings of the Associated Lutheran Charities, an organization which brought together those in various forms of Lutheran social work. Not even papers on the pathology of family life during the 1930s considered the subject of family limitation.

[44] Irregular and rather uninspired jibes at contraceptives appeared in some of the sermons printed in the *Concordia Pulpit*, an annual homiletical compendium published by Concordia Publishing House. Louis Nuechterlein, "Series on the Christian Marriage Relation," 11 (1939), 392; W. F. Troeger, "Marriage a Divine Institution," 14 (1942), 484; Henry J. Eggold, Jr., "Sermon for Mother's Day," 22 (1950), 386.

Christian mothers hand birth control literature . . . to the pastor's wife and ask what should be done in the matter." At least a few seminary students rebelled sufficiently to ask pointed questions: "If there is a valid reason for preventing conception why is it wrong to interfere with nature? . . . We do interfere . . . in many ways: medicine, operations, delivery by instruments, etc. . . . Even the 'rhythm method' (which we allow in certain cases) would in the final analysis *interfere with the natural process*, because man does *not naturally* have intercourse *only* at *certain* times of the month."[45]

Dissatisfaction with the distinction driven between natural (permissible) and artificial (forbidden) means of family limitation is apparent, but an exposition of a new position was very slow in coming. A leading figure in producing it was Alfred Rehwinkel, professor of ethics and church history at the seminary in St. Louis. By no means a theological radical, Rehwinkel was nevertheless by temperament free in expressing his convictions and often ready to stride boldly into controversial areas where most churchmen feared to tread. In this case an important factor was a woman's perspective, for Rehwinkel was much influenced by his wife, a remarkable woman trained as a physician who was practicing medicine and homesteading in Wyoming when she met Rehwinkel. She had grown up a Methodist; thus, "when you told her something was wrong, she wanted to know why, and you couldn't just quote Walther [the Synod's patriarch] to her." Impatience with ultraconservative standards of woman's role, inquiring skepticism, and professional medical competence were highly corrosive; by the early 1940s Alfred Rehwinkel was exploring a new position before groups of pastors and occasionally laymen.[46] In such sessions, Rehwinkel provided a sympathetic history of family restriction, explicitly defending the much maligned Margaret Sanger. To dispel intimations that contraception was murder, he explained the mechanics of conception and tried to vitiate the simplistic equating of race suicide and birth control.

The most critical part of Rehwinkel's presentation was his development of a supportive theological rationale. To refute the divine order thesis, Rehwinkel separated the natural order and basic moral law. The latter is admittedly immutable, but man's relation to nature is different; though subject to it, he is at the same time able to modify and limit nature. Thus anesthetics are used in the otherwise naturally painful process of childbirth without causing Christians concern. Only a clear scriptural word could prohibit contraceptives, Rehwinkel insisted, and this he could not find. Onan's punishment, so

[45] Egbert Schaller to Theo. Graebner, June 7, 1934, Theo. Graebner Papers, Box 101. Quoted in J. W. Behnken to I. C. Heinicke, Dec. 31, 1938, Graebner Papers, Box 55. Geiseman, *American Lutheran*, 18 (1935), 2308. Single, typed sheet, with handwritten identification, "Student, Nov. 1936," Theo. Graebner Papers, Box 101.

[46] Alfred M. Rehwinkel, *Dr. Bessie* (St. Louis: Concordia Publishing House, 1963); interview, Alfred Rehwinkel, June 21, 1967. For a report of one appearance before laymen, see *Lutheran Layman*, 18 (1947), 25.

often cited, was not for coitus interruptus but for refusing an order based on levirate law. And "Be fruitful and multiply," so often quoted, was not a command but a blessing. In a denomination formally committed to *sola Scriptura*, Biblical authority for all doctrine, such a survey was devastating because it left the opposition no place to stand other than a hermeneutical debate.

For Rehwinkel the Bible assigns matrimony three purposes: intimate companionship, procreation, and moral prophylactic. Thus the author was close to the most judicious definition of marriage stated at the turn of the century. But with a different perspective he could see fuller implications for marital sex in the same Genesis 2 passages which had been cited then. Freed of the natural order argument and of a repressive view of sex, he could do what was impossible in 1900: be as enthusiastic as any Lutheran author about the joys and benefits of parenthood and yet agree to the use of contraceptives.[47]

Here then in the 1940s was limned the essential argument which justified the use of contraceptives. However, Rehwinkel's view was not to be fully articulated in print until 1959. In the meantime the most that may be said for official Synodical publications is that they realized the impossibility of repeating the threadbare arguments of the 1920s and before. For example, to contend that birth control "logically and inevitably leads to deliberate childless marriages" would have been ludicrous after 1945 when surveys indicated a rise in the number of children Americans considered ideal; contraceptives had not killed the family.[48] Nevertheless, counsel more positive than silence was rare. Arthur E. Graf's "any form of family limitation is sinful when prompted by selfishness" was as direct a statement on contraceptives as appeared in the *Lutheran Witness* through the 1950s.[49]

The first to move publicly beyond such timidity was Pastor Walter G. Hansen, author of a regular column in the young people's *Walther League Messenger*. Hansen found the Bible silent as to methods of birth control and recommended family planning to all couples.[50] His opinions were of more than routine interest, for he was a member of the Synod's Family Life Com-

[47] "Planned Parenthood or Birth Control" (mimeographed, n.d. [late 1940s]); *Planned Parenthood and Birth Control in the Light of Christian Ethics* (St. Louis: Concordia Publishing House, 1959).

[48] Quoted in *Lutheran Witness* 36 (1917), 196.

[49] *Lutheran Witness*, 76 (1957), 306. The whole issue was avoided through silence in both O. A. Geiseman, *Make Yours a Happy Marriage* (St. Louis: Concordia Publishing House, 1946), and the *Lutheran Cyclopedia*, ed. Erwin L. Lueker (St. Louis: Concordia Publishing House, 1954). For the views of a professional sociologist, see Frederick K. Kruger, *American Lutheran* 31 (1948), 8. None of the most important official journals even reviewed Rehwinkel's book when it appeared in 1959, although it was later cited approvingly. W. J. Fields, *Unity in Marriage* (St. Louis: Concordia Publishing House, 1962), 118; Keith Kiihne, *Lutheran Witness*, 81 (1962), 371.

[50] 62 (Dec. 1953), 14–17; 63 (April 1955), 32; 64 (March 1956), 4; 65 (Nov. 1956), 4, 6.

mittee. Established in 1947, the committee's duty was to formulate statements on sex and marriage. Tellingly, the committee presented a view of sex that was affirmative and illuminated by historical study.[51] Such historical consciousness does not automatically induce ethical relativism, but it does have an impact. Exegetically it helps produce a different reading of the Biblical record.[52] And it facilitates a less embarrassed revision of position because earlier attitudes and polemic now rejected may be legitimately traced to the peculiar context out of which they came.

At the beginning of the twentieth century, fears of depopulation were common coin and "race suicide" the popular term. Sixty years later, overpopulation was the subject of endless discussion in which the term "population explosion" was nearly mandatory.[53] The loss of Lutheran consensus on this issue produced a less positive and less uniform reaction than in 1905. But finally by 1964, nearly sixty years after reprinting Theodore Roosevelt's exhortation to aid the state through fecundity, the *Lutheran Witness* was ready to state editorially that world poverty and the population explosion had to be included in Christian thinking on parenthood.[54] In the early 1960s too, the Family Life Committee remarked briefly that procreation is not the sole purpose of intercourse, but is tied to the unitive function of sex. "The use of contraceptives does not change this fact; on the contrary, contraceptives are a recognition of this fact." Once convinced that God tolerated no interference in human reproduction, many in the Synod had come to the belief that "God has given His Children a great deal of freedom in certain areas. This is one of them."[55]

Describing the steps by which the Missouri Synod lumbered from resistance to such advocacy on birth control is not the same as accounting for why

[51] See, e.g., *Sex and the Church*, ed. Oscar E. Feucht and others (St. Louis: Concordia Publishing House, 1963). Greater affirmation of sex becomes visible after World War II—Geiseman in 1946 was the first to stress in print the importance of the female orgasm—and is noteworthy because a theologian who accepts sexual pleasure per se is more likely to accept contraceptives.

[52] See Victor Bartling, *Concordia Theological Monthly*, 39 (1968), 355–65.

[53] According to the Population Reference Bureau, Robert C. Cook was the first to apply the term "population explosion" to human fertility. See his "Latin America: Area of Population Explosion," *Population Bulletin*, 9 (Oct. 1953), 65–75. *Time* magazine was prompt to pick up the phrase (Oct. 19, 1953, p. 48).

Entries in *Readers' Guide to Periodical Literature* under "overpopulation" and "increase of population" serve as a crude index of heightened concern. In 1953–55, there were but five such entries. During 1959–61, there were 55, and interest was sustained thereafter at more or less the same level.

[54] 83 (1964), 420–21. In 1957 the *Witness* categorically denied that world population would ever outstrip natural resources, but within three years Richard M. Fagley's *The Population Explosion and Christian Responsibility* produced reviews with a soberer view of the future. 76 (1957), 443; David S. Schuller, 79 (1960), 285. On Fagley, see also John Klotz, *Lutheran Education*, 79 (1961), 129.

[55] *Sex and the Church*, 216–17. Otto W. Toelke, *In the Presence of God: Devotions for the Newly Married* (St. Louis: Concordia Publishing House, 1962), p. 23.

it did so. Probably the equation for the latter is one which cannot be factored out, but some components may be isolated. The most important force producing change was the behavior of the laity. In 1925 John Fritz put matters bluntly when he asked rhetorically, "do you not believe that the Lord who gives you the children will also provide for them food and shelter?"[56] Had they been compelled to answer, many of the laity would have responded negatively. There is no way to determine precisely their behavior, that is, the Missouri Lutheran birth rate. But a crude index which permits at least internal comparisons may be constructed by use of baptismal totals reported annually in the Synod's *Statistical Yearbook*.[57] This baptismal rate fell astonishingly, dropping from about 58 per 1,000 baptized membership in 1885 to approximately 37 in 1913.[58] As shown in Figure 1, the decline continued through the Depression. The baptismal rate did not recover until World War II, but fell once more beginning in the late 1950s. The Lutheran baptismal rate was always above the national birth rate (the lower line on Figure 1), but

[56] *Walther League Messenger*, 33 (1925), 462.

[57] As a sacrament in Lutheran theology, baptism is a prerequisite for membership and is performed soon after birth for practically all children in Lutheran families. Fortunately, figures permitting discrimination between infant baptism and those of adult converts are available after 1919, about the time the latter became appreciable (3 percent).

[58] The drop should not automatically be attributed entirely to the introduction of birth control practices. Because of its immigrant origin, the Synod may in 1885 have had a disproportionate percentage of child-bearing couples. As these aged and as immigration declined, the birth rate would necessarily fall without a decrease in family size. It must be said, however, that if this was in fact the case, one would expect the burial rate temporarily to rise or at least hold steady after 1885. Instead, this rate, too, fell after 1885. The 1885 figure is arrived at by subtracting 25 percent from the total reported because in 1883—the last year separate statistics were reported—about one-fourth of all baptisms were of children whose parents were not members of a Synodical congregation. The *Reiseprediger*, or circuit rider, who ranged over the frontier searching out German Lutherans, inevitably performed many baptisms among those he found long before a congregation was formed and the family was included in other parish statistics. And in the ethnic ghetto, an apparently large number of German immigrants, baptized and confirmed Lutheran in the old country, disdained the American pattern of denominational affiliation, but did come to the Lutheran pastor for at least the baptism of their children. Ernst Eckhardt, *Statistical Yearbook, 1937*, 155. The percentage of "nonmember" children baptized declined from nearly 40 percent in 1865 to 25 percent in the early 1880s, and it seems reasonable to believe that as the Synod matured and as the average age of the general immigrant community rose, the baptism of such children declined still further. Of course, at some point in the Americanization process, Synodical pastors began to baptize children of native American stock whose parents were not members. There is no hard evidence for the dating of such a transition, other than time-consuming parish reconstitution studies, the possibility of which is severely curtailed because of high mobility. But from a study of the Americanization process in the Synod, I think it probable that the baptism of immigrant nonmember children was of a fairly low order of magnitude by about 1910, and that the baptisms of American-stock, nonmember children did not reach substantial proportions in much of the Synod until the marked post–World War II expansion. In any case, it should be pointed out that, were it possible, the accurate reduction after 1885 of the baptismal rate to reflect only children of members would only contribute to my central point—a falling birth rate. The chief disappointment in the early years is that the data available mask the timing of the decline after 1885. But a study of birth rates in clerical families (below) indicates that the decline may have been most precipitous just after the turn of the century.

Figure 1. LUTHERAN BAPTISMAL RATE AND UNITED STATES BIRTH RATE

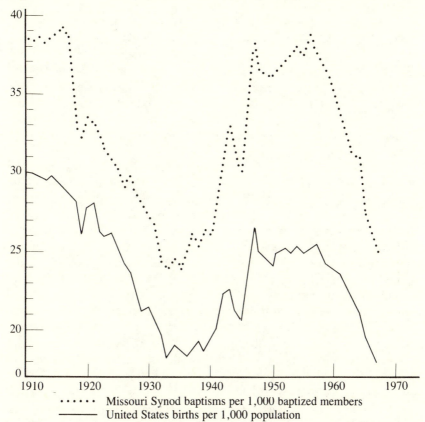

•••••• Missouri Synod baptisms per 1,000 baptized members
——— United States births per 1,000 population

especially after 1915 moved up and down in uncanny concert with it.[59] When juxtaposed with contemporary observation, the baptismal rate leaves no doubt that large numbers of the laity practiced one or another means of birth restriction.[60]

[59] That the gap between the two expanded between about 1945 and 1965 is difficult to explain satisfactorily. This may be due to a rise in numbers of nonmember children baptized in a fast-growing and increasingly open Synod. Or it may reflect a disproportionate expansion into middle-class suburbs with a high percentage of membership in the child-bearing years.

The national rate used in the graph is from U.S. Bureau of the Census, *Vital Statistics of the United States, 1965,* I—Natality (Washington: Government Printing Office, 1967), 1–4. There are, of course, more sophisticated indices than the gross birth rate, as well as differing estimates of that rate. However, the baptismal rate is itself hardly a refined instrument, so that the figures used seem sufficient for comparative purposes.

[60] The marriage rate in the Synod follows reasonably closely the undulations of the national rate, thus seeming to rule out any anomaly in first-marriage pattern to account for fewer births.

Save for the Lutheran antagonism to birth control, such a development would hardly be surprising. The twentieth century saw important improvements in contraceptive technology as well as a startling reversal in public discussion of it. Within the Missouri Synod, the former immigrant enclave dissolved into the broader American community, particularly after World War I; and after the next war large accessions from outside the Synod diluted still further the original character of the constituency. In the decades after 1890, the degree of urbanization, educational expectations, income level, and occupational prestige of the laity all rose more or less steadily.[61] For the American population at large all these trends were associated with declining birth rates.

It would be precipitous, however, to conclude that religious affiliation was entirely ineffectual in controlling Lutheran belief and practice. The Lutheran baptismal rate does follow the course of the national birth rate, but it is always appreciably above it. Furthermore, as late as 1953 a large minority still was uncertain about or rejected contraception, according to a survey conducted by Walter G. Hansen for the Family Life Committee. Twenty-two percent in the representative sample of laity and clergy disapproved of the enjoyment of marital intercourse without intention of conception. Approximately one-third of those polled were either unsure or opposed on the question of contraceptives to space or limit children. This figure dropped to about one-quarter if natural means such as abstention or rhythm were used. Outright disapproval declined with college education (20 percent to 11 percent on natural means) and with urban residence (27 percent to 19 percent on contraceptives; 19 percent to 17 percent on natural means). Those the survey defined as religiously inactive were much likelier than active laity to approve birth control (70 percent versus 56 percent on contraceptives; 75 percent versus 67 percent on natural means). Whether active or inactive, however, about two-thirds of the Synod's laity admitted having used contraceptives.[62] Obviously then,

[61] For more extensive discussion of these trends, see Alan Graebner, *Uncertain Saints*.

[62] Other questions focused upon attitudes if means were used to avoid all children (disapproval rose sharply to 86 percent for contraceptives and 81 percent for natural means) and for reasons of health (in which case the proportions were reversed and disapproval sank to 8 percent for both contraceptives and natural means). "Parenthood," Section VI of "The Lutheran Family" (mimeographed working papers of the Family Life Committee, n.d.), 20–36; *Sex and the Church*, 245.

In 1961 the Lutheran Academy for Scholarship, an intersynodical organization to further Lutheran intellectual endeavor, mailed a questionnaire on medical ethics to 2,000 Lutheran physicians, pastors, professors, and laymen. Unfortunately the response was only about 20 percent. Of those who replied, about 37 percent did not believe right the use of contraceptives to space or limit children solely for economic reasons. Of the physicians who responded (96), 21 percent concurred in such a negative judgment. Questions on the permissibility of marital intercourse for pleasure only and on the ethics of oral contraceptives in themselves drew negative judgment only from 13 percent and 15 percent respectively of those polled. The low rate of return as well as concentration upon leaders makes it difficult

Synodical rhetoric was not completely without effect. And just as obviously, that effect was limited.

The behavior and opinion of the laity should probably be termed a necessary but not sufficient cause for a change in the church's position. An important link between the official publications from St. Louis and the individual layman was the parish pastor. The laity's idea of what the pastor should tell them—and what he was not to tell them—as well as the clergy's concept of pastoral prerogatives were not the same in a suburban congregation of 1960 as they were in an immigrant parish of 1890. Decreasing disparity between the educational attainments of laity and clergy, the increasing availability of secular sources of help and guidance, lessened physical contact because of greater mobility and dispersion, and declining social prestige acceded to clergy in America all eroded clerical authority.

Even without such attrition, the early twentieth-century minister faced a delicate problem in birth control. Church-paper editors might fume over pastoral inactivity in this matter, but what was the conscientious minister to do?[63] Significantly, a precise answer to this question is virtually impossible to find. When Carl Eissfeldt attempted it in 1921 he emphasized repeatedly the need for tact and wisdom.[64] In public discourse, he advised, one dare not be too specific for fear of giving the weak useful information or of making a sin sound attractive. In private conversation, if the guilt is clear the pastor should not hesitate to act in a determined fashion. But when the pastor has only rumor or suspicion to go on, as is usually the case, he should not ask a direct question about the practice nor make a direct accusation, but instead should proceed indirectly, seeking to sensitize the conscience if the burden of birth control lies upon it. How delicate the matter was Eissfeldt indicated by recommending the ultimate in circumspection: the use of some tract which, he specified, must mention birth control only among other topics. On the question whether the practice of family limitation should ever lead to excommunication, Eissfeldt seemed negatively inclined. It depends in part, he said, upon how public the sin is. Furthermore, he continued, we must be aware that contemporary city living leads to a natural decline in fertility; birth control is not the only reason for smaller families and it would be un-Christian automatically to attribute sin when there are few children in a marriage.

The counsel to suspect no couple unjustly was as sound as it was frequently

---

to say whether the increase in percentage of permissiveness represents a chronological or a selectivity factor. "Proceedings of the Colloquium on Medical Ethics, 1961" (St. Louis: The Lutheran Academy for Scholarship, mimeographed, 1962), appendices C and D.

[63] Theo. Graebner, *Magazin fuer Ev.-Luth. Homiletik und Pastoraltheologie*, 43 (1919), 5.

[64] *Magazin*, 45 (1921), 116–21. In 1898, A. L. Graebner, capable of stern counsel in the other matters, pondered the subject briefly and decided that practices of birth control "are of such a nature as to render special pastoral treatment of the evil extremely difficult and in most cases impossible." *Theological Quarterly*, 2 (1898), 350.

given, but it vitiated a rigorous position in guidance and discipline of the laity.[65] Without an institutionalized, individual confessional, the Missouri Synod pastor faced a difficult dilemma. He would only rarely acquire the information to speak openly to an erring couple, but dared take no action without it. And it would require a dedicated—and thick-skinned—pastor, indeed, to gratuitously hint at forbidden topics over a cup of coffee during a pastoral call upon the good Christian mother of a fine young boy already enrolled in the parochial school. Even a prosaic soul could imagine the agonies of rehearsal and of fumbling for words such a conversation would entail. No, better to emphasize the simple joys of motherhood and let well enough alone.

Furthermore, unlike the celibate Catholic priest giving instruction to married people, the Missouri pastor had a wife and children of his own. His words would be measured by his example. Put in another way, the Lutheran pastor was subject to the same pressures and temptations as his flock. And to a greater or lesser degree, he, too, succumbed to them. The birth rate among the clergy fell along with that of the laity. Figure 2 displays the mean number of children in the families of clergy by the year of marriage. Quite obviously, in the years before World War I there was a substantial drop in the birth rate among Missourian clergy. The decline continued after 1920, though considerably lessened.[66]

One may infer from these statistics that for the generation married after about 1920 the matter of family limitation itself was a closed one. If a question remained it was about the means to this end. On that issue important reservations continued for some time. The Family Life Committee's survey of the early 1950s found strong adherence to the distinction between natural and artificial means articulated in the 1930s and early 1940s—the most recent dates of seminary attendance for the majority of the clergy in 1953. To cite the extremes, 85 percent of the clergy polled approved of natural means to control births for reasons of health, but only 30 percent could agree to space or limit children by contraceptives for reasons other than health.[67]

How is it then that within a decade contraceptives were explicitly sanctioned in Synodical publications? Aside from factors already mentioned, nor-

[65] A. L. Graebner, *Theological Quarterly*, 2 (1898), 349; Brauer, *"Die Schaeden,"* 54; Luecke, *Be Fruitful*, 9; Hornsbostel, *"Die Christliche Familienleben,"* 23; Fritz, *Pastoral Theology* (1945 ed.), 166.

[66] From 1890 (about the first year in which data exist for sufficient numbers) until 1919, statistics are based on all pastors for whom this information was on file at Concordia Historical Institute, St. Louis. Beginning in 1920, a sample of approximately 20 percent was employed. Figures are thus computed on nearly 2,300 cases.

[67] Of those who responded to the 1961 Lutheran Academy poll, the percentage of clergy approving contraceptives to limit children for solely economic reasons had risen to 45 percent. More importantly, 80 percent of the St. Louis seminary faculty responding approved of such a practice.

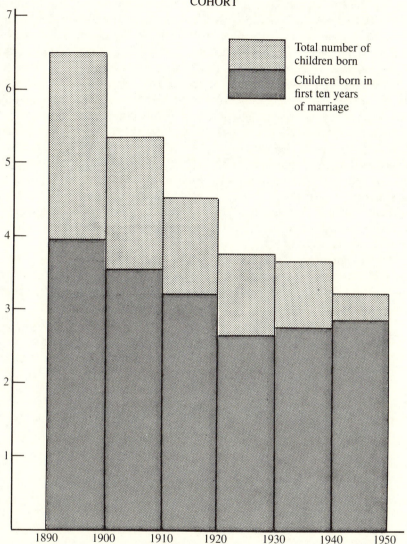

Figure 2.　MEAN NUMBER OF CHILDREN BY DECENNIAL MARRIAGE COHORT

Total number of children born

Children born in first ten years of marriage

mal turnover within the clergy must be taken into account. By 1953 men such as Fritz, Graebner, and Maier were dead. Perhaps fortuitously, no one came forward then to lead a fight for the old position.[68] In addition, the structure of authority and decision-making certainly played a role. The Prot-

[68] The 1953 Family Life survey documented a significant difference by age on matters of family limitation.

estant emphasis upon individual conscience facilitated arriving at independent conclusions by clergy and laity alike. Affected by the changes within
the Synod and by the pressures of the environment, Missouri Lutherans
turned to scripture. Given the secular context and the indecisive nature of
Biblical statement on this point, it was almost inevitable that a widespread
reappraisal would take place.[69] Politically there was no ready-made bureaucratic machinery by which conservatively inclined clergy could block this
process or silence new spokesmen. With sufficient determination the Family
Life Committee might have been packed to produce traditional answers, but
by the time it was finally clear what the committee was up to, matters had
gone too far.[70] Above all, there was no central authority in the Synod to insist
doggedly on the maintenance of the status quo. When clergy disagree irre-
concilably on social issues, the laity has to think for itself, and in doing so
the majority is likely to be attracted to the less demanding norm.[71] The result,
especially when combined with the ubiquity of family limitation and the pervasive American optimism about birth control, was virtually to silence all but
the hardiest dissenter.

With this the process was complete. From opposition to silence to acceptance, it was not a very graceful, or even courageous, encounter with an
important social question, but the sequence demonstrates how significant
change could occur in a highly conservative American denomination.

[69] What would have happened had Biblical statements seemed more explicit to Missourian exegetes is difficult to say, though the case of female suffrage in the church—not approved by the Synod until 1969—would indicate that the process of change would have been
slowed, not stopped.

[70] An attack on the committee at the 1959 Synodical convention was successfully defeated. *Proceedings of the Forty-fourth Regular Convention*, 220–21.

[71] Gerhard Lenski, *The Religious Factor: A Sociological Study of Religion's Impact on
Politics, Economics and Family Life* (Garden City, N.Y.: Doubleday, 1963), 194–95.

Paul Boyer

Minister's Wife, Widow, Reluctant Feminist
Catherine Marshall in the 1950s

In the early morning hours of January 25, 1949, the Rev. Peter Marshall, pastor of the New York Avenue Presbyterian Church in Washington, D.C., and chaplain of the United States Senate, awoke with severe pains in his chest. Five hours later he lay dead of a heart attack, at age forty-six. Although Marshall had already won a considerable reputation as a preacher, his greatest fame was still to come. That fall, Fleming H. Revell and Co. published *Mr. Jones, Meet the Master*, a collection of his sermons edited and introduced by his widow, Catherine Marshall. The book sold well, and soon Mrs. Marshall was approached by McGraw-Hill with the suggestion that she prepare a second volume of Peter Marshall sermons. Instead, she proposed to write his biography. The result was *A Man Called Peter*, one of the spectacular publishing successes of the 1950s. Issued in October 1951, the book climbed to the nonfiction bestseller lists within ten days and remained there for three years, for a time at the top. *Reader's Digest* published a condensation, and in 1955–with over a million copies of the book in print—a movie version appeared. Starring Richard Todd and Jean Peters, *A Man Called Peter* was 20th Century-Fox's biggest moneymaker that year. *To Live Again*, a 1957 book in which Mrs. Marshall related her emotional and spiritual development since her husband's death, also became a bestseller.[1]

---

[1] Biographical information in this article has been drawn primarily from Catherine Marshall's *A Man Called Peter* (New York: McGraw-Hill, 1951) and *To Live Again* (New York: McGraw-Hill, 1957). See also entries on Mrs. Marshall in *Contemporary Authors*, 17–20 (revised and published in a single volume, Detroit: Gale Research Co., 1976), 477–78, and *Current Biography* (1955), 403–5.

Catherine Marshall was not, of course, the first widow of a famous minister to write about her husband. Mrs. Henry Ward Beecher produced a ten-part series entitled "Mr. Beecher as I Knew Him" for the *Ladies' Home Journal* in 1891–92, and in 1907 the bereaved wife of a colorful Georgia revivalist took pen in hand to record *The Life and Sayings of Sam P. Jones.*[2] But no earlier work in this genre achieved anything like the success of Mrs. Marshall's books.

Reading *A Man Called Peter* and *To Live Again,* one may recapture something of the climate of the 1950s as it shaped attitudes toward women and women's attitudes toward themselves. From them, too, one can get a sense of the ambiguous relationship between modern American Protestantism and the "feminine mystique"—an aspect of women's history that has been somewhat neglected.[3] Above all, these books open a window on the consciousness of an intelligent, articulate, and conservative woman forced to reexamine and redefine her status in society. If Catherine Marshall ultimately reaffirmed a traditionalist view of woman's role, it was not without questions, soul searching, and many revealing observations about the toll which conformity to that role could exact.

S arah Catherine Wood was born in 1914 in Johnson City, Tennessee, the daughter of a Presbyterian minister. She spent her later girlhood in Keyser, West Virginia, where her father was assigned a parish. A bookish girl, she later recalled being influenced by L. M. Montgomery's *Emily of the New Moon* (1923), a romantic account of a young girl's dreams of becoming a writer, and by Annie Fellows Johnston's *Little Colonel* series, books on the Old Confederacy "replete with the beautiful woman reigning supreme over the domestic concerns of her own domain . . . , a Southern mansion." As a preacher's daughter she frequently delivered impromptu talks before church gatherings; indeed, her forensic skills were such that in her high school years she won local and even statewide competitions.[4]

In 1932 she enrolled in Agnes Scott College, a Presbyterian woman's college in Decatur, Georgia, an Atlanta suburb. Here her aspirations toward authorship ripened. She composed poetry in the style of Edna St. Vincent Millay, devoured Katherine Mansfield's short stories and jour-

---

[2] Mrs. Henry Ward Beecher [Eunice Bullard Beecher], "Mr. Beecher as I Knew Him," *Ladies' Home Journal,* 8–9 (Oct. 1891–Aug. 1892); Laura M. Jones, *The Life and Sayings of Sam P. Jones* (Atlanta, 1907).

[3] In *The Feminine Mystique* (1963), Betty Friedan devoted only two pages to the relationship between religion and woman's role (pp. 399–400 of the Dell paperback edition) and in this brief space discussed only Catholicism and Judaism.

[4] *To Live Again,* 64, 98, 102 (quoted passage).

nals, and began to keep a self-consciously "literary" journal in preparation for a future career as a writer. She continued to pursue public speaking, joining the college debating society and participating in prohibition rallies throughout north-central Georgia. She dreamed, too, of establishing a school in the West Virginia mountains.[5]

These aspirations were sidetracked when the twenty-year-old sophomore, full of "girlish romanticism," met and fell in love with Peter Marshall, a Scottish immigrant twelve years her senior. Marshall had attended a Presbyterian theological seminary in Decatur, and in the early 1930s was pastor of Atlanta's Westminster Presbyterian Church. They were married in November 1936, a few months after Catherine's graduation from college. This turn of events she later described as "one of God's nicest miracles and the first big evidence of God's hand on my life."[6]

A handsome bachelor whose brogue, charm, and pulpit eloquence attracted crowds wherever he preached, Marshall was a great "catch" for the young college girl. He was also a man whose ideas about women were indistinguishable from the early nineteenth-century ideology Barbara Welter has called "The Cult of True Womanhood."[7] Those ideas are formulated most fully in "Keepers of the Springs," a sermon which he delivered in pulpits throughout the country. It bears quotation (in the form Marshall favored) for beneath the flowery prose one finds defined the terms of the Marshall marriage:

> When women in this country achieved equality with men,
> it was accomplished only by stepping down from the pedestal
> on which Christianity, chivalry, and idealism
> had placed her . . . .
>
> So she copied the vices of men—in the name of progress!
> But it is not progress to go in a downward direction.
> It is not progress to lower moral standards and to lose ideals!
> No woman ever became lovelier by losing her essential femininity.
>
> There is no substitute for goodness . . .
>   nothing can take the place of purity.
> To be sweet is far better than to be sophisticated.
> America needs young women who will build true homes

---

[5] Ibid., 65–66, 98; *A Man Called Peter*, 50, 51, 65, 116.

[6] *A Man Called Peter*, 51, 53. On Peter Marshall's career, see *A Man Called Peter* and also the entry in *Who Was Who*, 2 (Chicago, 1950), 347.

[7] Barbara Welter, "The Cult of True Womanhood, 1820–1860," *American Quarterly*, 18 (Summer 1966), 151–74.

> . . . [H] omes where harassed husbands may find peace
> understanding
> refreshment of body and soul . . .
> where children may find the warmth of love . . .
>
> The average woman, if she gives her full time to her home
> her husband
> her children . . . .
> If she tries to understand her husband's work . . .
> to curb his egotism while, at the same time, building up his
> self-esteem
> to kill his masculine conceit while encouraging all his hopes
> to establish around the family a circle of true friends . . . .
>
> If she provides in the home a proper atmosphere of culture
> of love of music
> of beautiful furniture
> and of a garden . . . .
>
> If she can do all this, she will be engaged in a life work
> that will demand
> every ounce of her strength
> every bit of her patience
> every talent God has given her
> the utmost sacrifice of her love.
>
> It will demand everything she has and more.
> And she will find that for which she was created.
> She will know that she is carrying out the plan of God.
> She will be a partner with the Sovereign Ruler of the universe.
>
> And so, today's daughters need to think twice before they
> seek to make
> a place for themselves
> by themselves
> in our world today . . . .[8]

Marshall never shrank from expounding his opinions on the woman question. He expressed them freely to a *Washington Post* reporter in 1938 and as a government witness in the federal obscenity prosecution of *Esquire* magazine in 1943.[9] Nor were such views merely for public consump-

---

[8] Peter Marshall, "Keepers of the Springs," excerpted in *A Man Called Peter*, 54–55, and *To Live Again*, 95–96. The version of this sermon in *Mr. Jones, Meet the Master* (New York: Fleming H. Revell, 1949; rev. 1950), 147–58, differs in phrasing.

[9] *A Man Called Peter*, 115, 144.

tion. In letters to Catherine during their courtship he made plain that he expected their own relationship to measure up to the ideal of his sermons:

> Our life together will be a poem, a song, a monument to Love, and a memorial to the Holy Spirit who brought us together . . . . Life can hold nothing more satisfying or more glorious than this—the joy of building with you, a home that will be a temple of God, a haven and a sanctuary, a place of peace and love . . . .[10]

As well as being a man with exalted ideas about woman's sphere, Marshall was also a minister whose already heavy commitments were soon to grow heavier. On the first morning of his honeymoon he had to rise early to meet a visiting pastoral committee from Washington's New York Avenue Presbyterian Church, and the following year he and his wife made the move from Atlanta to the nation's capital. From the first day of her marriage to the last, Catherine Marshall's identity was shaped by her role as a minister's wife.

Though she could hardly have grasped the full implications of the fact, the constricted, highly spiritualized feminine ideal that Peter Marshall so seductively painted in his sermons had for generations been imposed with particular insistence upon ministers' wives as a social group. Ever since the question of woman's role had emerged as a social issue in the wake of Jacksonian urbanization, the minister's wife had been assigned a special mission: not only to accept with grace that role as it was taking shape— economic and political subordination, moral and spiritual superiority— but to embody it publicly. As the author of an 1832 book of advice to the minister's wife put it, she was expected to view herself as "wedded . . . to her husband's parish, and to the best interests of his flock."[11]

At a time when middle-class American women were being subtly pressured to conform to a conventionalized image of their nature, needs, and sphere, the constraints imposed on ministers' wives, in their capacity as social models and spiritual exemplars, were doubly exacting. While a few did manage to carve out distinctive careers for themselves within those limits—as moral reformers, religious leaders, inspirational writers, or missionaries—most led lives of pious self-denial, rewarded at the end

---

[10] Ibid., 60, 63.

[11] [Anon.], *Hints for a Clergyman's Wife; or, Female Parochial Duties* (London: Holdworth and Ball, 1832), quoted in William Douglas, *Ministers' Wives* (New York: Harper and Row, 1965), 2.

by stilted tombstone tributes and by the hope of reward in the hereafter. This 1832 work continued:

> Happy, thrice happy the Christian female, who is permitted to consecrate her life, her time, and her talents to the service of her God and Saviour! He will not forget her work and labor of love. She shall receive a crown of glory.[12]

Whatever frustrations were involved in adapting to the conventional role were either borne silently or confined to the privacy of family letters, such as the one written by the wife of a Maine minister to her parents in the late nineteenth century:

> It is drive, drive, drive, with the callers and meetings and a vain attempt to sandwich in reading, letter writing, or anything else. . . . I sometimes long for a desert isle; I get so tired of seeing people and talking to people.[13]

By the late 1930s, just as Catherine Marshall was beginning her twelve years as a minister's wife, American Protestantism was itself on the threshold of a period when that tradition-bound role would no longer be taken for granted but would become an object of much anxious attention. From 1939 to 1963, no fewer than *twelve* books offering encouragement and counsel to ministers' wives were published, in contrast to only three or four in the entire century preceding. Bearing titles like *The Care and Feeding of Ministers* and *How to Be a Preacher's Wife and Like It,* these books reinforced the traditional model. The minister's wife, they urged with disarming humorous asides ruefully noting the difficulties involved, must live up to her calling: supporting her spouse in his labors; striving for a radiant and contagious personal faith; and denying self to create a model Christian home.[14]

Yet the very proliferation of such books offered unmistakable advance warning that the social group they sought to reassure was experiencing strain. This conclusion is supported by a number of sociological studies of ministers' wives undertaken in the 1950s, culminating in a major one at Boston University in 1959 by William Douglas (a Presbyterian minister with a Harvard Ph.D. in psychology) on a grant from the Lilly Endowment. Surveying some 5,000 ministers' wives representing the Protestant spectrum, this study found striking evidence of a pervasive malaise. For example, while 85 percent of those surveyed professed themselves "satis-

---

[12] Ibid., 2.

[13] Ibid., 5. From a letter of Harriet Angell Anthony, as quoted by her daughter, Mrs. R. C. Dexter, in a paper read at a Radcliffe College Women's Archives workshop, Mar. 17, 1954.

[14] Douglas, *Ministers' Wives,* 7–12, 253–55; Kathleen N. Nyberg, *The Care and Feeding of Ministers* (New York: Abingdon Press, 1961); Lora L. Parrott, *How to Be a Preacher's Wife and Like It* (Grand Rapids: Zondervan, 1956).

fied'' (in varying degrees of enthusiasm) with their role in life, and only 14 percent said they felt ''so-so'' or ''frustrated'' about it, a more probing questionnaire revealed that many of these women, especially the younger ones, felt a ''constant sense of falling short'' as they tried to live up to their image of the ideal minister's wife.[15] The typical mistress of an American parsonage, concluded Douglas, summing up his findings,

> aspires to *give* (to God, to family, to others), yet finds herself constantly yearning to *receive*. She has a mental picture of the MW [Douglas's abbreviation for "minister's wife"] as calm, cool and collected, poised, gracious and radiant. But she perceives herself as harried and distraught, overwhelmed and underpowered.[16]

So steadily did this erosion of the traditional ideal proceed—hastened, of course, by the impetus of the women's movement—that by the mid-1970s even so conservative a journal as *Christianity Today* could publish a bitter if pseudonymous diatribe in which a minister's wife mocked the ''self-help'' literature of the 1950s and lamented ''all those barren years when I did all the right things with such a wrong sense of uselessness.'' Having rejected the conventional model, this MW reported that the locus of her intellectual, social, and even spiritual life now lay outside the constricting confines of her husband's congregation, toward which she maintained an attitude of cool detachment. ''[T]he only way I can be a minister's wife,'' she ringingly if tritely concluded, ''is by being me.''[17]

In joining the ranks of ministers' wives in 1936, Catherine Marshall thus assumed a social role shaped by the Victorian feminine ideal, but one that in succeeding decades would be challenged, investigated, defended, and—in some quarters—repudiated. Writing of her experience in *A Man Called Peter* and *To Live Again*, she graphically conveyed the kinds of pressures that later studies would document, and that a spate of reassuring books would soon seek to ease. The elders of Peter Marshall's new parish in Washington—a venerable and very ''social'' church where eight Presidents, including Abraham Lincoln, had worshiped—lost no time in making plain to her that ''New York Avenue expected a great deal of its minister's wife,'' and she soon learned what ''a great deal'' meant:

> To say that the pastor's helpmate was expected to be gracious, charming, poised, equal to every occasion, would be a gross understatement. . . . There is

[15] Douglas, *Ministers' Wives*, ix-xii (author's background); 19–31 (description of research project and methodology); 70 (quoted phrase); 90.

[16] Ibid., 70.

[17] Meredith Wells [pseud.], ''Thrice I Cried, Or, How to be a Minister's Wife If You Loathe It,'' *Christianity Today*, Jan. 18, 1974, 7–10, quoted passage, 8.

a very real sense in which a church feels that its minister and his wife belong to *them*, and they want to be proud of their possession."[18]

For a young woman fresh from the ambience of the college dormitory, the strain of living up to this exacting standard was intense. Even her taste in dresses and hats was scrutinized and discreetly discussed each Sunday. As she would later observe, "The package a minister's wife comes in is important."[19]

From the first, Marshall found herself chafing against the role history and chance (God, she would have said) had decreed for her. Not even the blush of young love could blind her to the reactionary quality of her suitor's notions about her sex. "He still places women on such a pedestal, much as my father's generation did," she wrote in her journal, "and he seems quite old-fashioned in some ways—especially toward marriage and the home. . . ."[20] But she acquiesced and adapted, accepting his assumption that his interests must now take precedence over her own inchoate aspirations. Turning over the larger decisions to him, she concentrated on household affairs. When their son was born, she soon realized that her husband would not be "one of those fathers who mixed the formula or bathed the baby. . . . [He] considered such things my province." So totally did she efface herself that many of her husband's admirers, even some who regularly attended his church, did not even realize that he was married![21]

She at first felt "inadequate" to the expectations growing out of her role and found that she had to make "many painful changes," but in this area, too, she eventually conformed. Her future mother-in-law back in Scotland, congratulating her son upon his engagement, had expressed satisfaction that Catherine's background as a "daughter of the manse" would likely "make her just what you need in a life partner," and this prediction proved accurate. Catherine Marshall dressed and lived the part expected of her; she "attended women's meetings, led Bible studies, made talks, called on parishioners, and took part in program-committee meetings."[22] Beyond this, she "shared" in her husband's career only in the sense that she occasionally fed him sermon ideas and tried to create a supportive domestic environment to which he could retreat from the stresses of his public life: "His job was constantly to pour himself out for the hungry hearts of men and women. My job was to try to feed him

[18] *A Man Called Peter*, 72, 101 (quoted passages).
[19] Ibid., 79–81, 101 (quoted passage).
[20] Ibid., 55.
[21] Ibid., 153 (quoted passage), 155.
[22] Ibid., 101, 67; Catherine Marshall, *Beyond Ourselves* (New York: Mc Graw-Hill, 1961), 37.

spiritually, to strengthen him, to supply understanding and encouragement, so that he would always have something to give to others.''[23]

*T*his was the life that fell apart for Catherine Marshall on January 25, 1949. Her decisions within the next few months first to edit her husband's sermons and then to write his biography had complex sources—the need to find an anodyne for grief, the sense of divine guidance, the resurgence of old literary ambitions—but the most immediate was simple economic necessity. Like Sarah Josepha Hale, who had turned to writing after being left a widow with five children in 1822 (eventually to become editor of *Godey's Lady's Book*), Catherine Marshall did not seek a career: she had it thrust upon her. Her husband had saved little from his modest salary, the life-insurance payments were small, her parents had no money, and the problem of where to live was an urgent one. (She and her son stayed on in the parsonage for a time, but when a new minister was appointed they moved into a cramped apartment.)[24]

But however compelling the need for money, the fact remained that Mrs. Marshall's decision for a career involved a sharp break with her sheltered past. As she wrote in *To Live Again*, ''. . . Peter's death and the publication of his sermons thrust me into the public eye. It was no wonder that I found the reversal of my position with my husband somewhat difficult. . . . Peter was now the one in the background; I, the one forced to the forefront.''[25] It also involved an apparent repudiation of the idealized role upon which her husband had expended so much eloquence, and to which she herself had given tacit support.

Faithful to her heritage, she resolved this awkward fact theologically. The same belief in God's direct intervention in everyday affairs that had earlier led her to give up her career ambitions for marriage was now invoked by Mrs. Marshall to justify her career. God had a new mission for her: to carry on her husband's work, to bring his message to a larger public. ''[T]he book project about to be undertaken was God's venture—not mine,'' she later wrote. God was guiding her pen, and any merit her work possessed redounded to His glory, not her own: ''Out of my helplessness, a book had been written through me.''[26] Even the sexual frustrations of widowhood (a subject Mrs. Marshall discussed obliquely but with sensitivity in *To Live Again*) served the divine plan: they could

[23] *A Man Called Peter*, 227.
[24] *To Live Again*, 38–41, 74–76, 125–27; Paul S. Boyer, ''Hale, Sarah Josepha,'' in *Notable American Women*, 2:110–14.
[25] *To Live Again*, 97.
[26] Ibid., 60, 151.

be redirected into literary effort. "For this particular period of your life," God told her, "use the creative energy that I've given you for My purposes for the book. Allow me to channel it in a steady stream into your writing."[27]

So long as she remained subject to God's guidance, her career would represent a divinely sanctioned *extension* of the duties of the Christian wife, not a repudiation of those duties. (Though such details should not be overinterpreted, it is interesting to note that much of *A Man Called Peter* was written in the bed she and her husband had shared, and that when she mailed off the manuscript, her thoughts were of childbirth: "Writing a book is so much like having a baby. No wonder I had wanted the man at the post office to handle my precious bundle with gentleness!")[28] When thousands of readers responded by sharing with her their own problems and sorrows, her conviction that she was remaining faithful to the supportive, maternal role was confirmed: "As these letters poured in," she wrote, "the world began to seem like one big family."[29]

In keeping with this view of her career, Mrs. Marshall used her books of the 1950s to publicize her husband's views on marriage and women's proper role. She selected "Keepers of the Springs" for inclusion in *Mr. Jones, Meet the Master*, and reprinted long extracts from it in *A Man Called Peter*, recalling the impact the sermon had had on the young women of Atlanta in the 1930s: "Like the rest of young America, I would never have taken the philosophy of marriage Peter advocated from any of the older generation, but we took it from him, liked it, and came back for more. . . . Apparently even the most modern young women found something refreshing and appealing in this sermon."[30] Insisting that her husband had not been antifeminist but only "an idealist and a romantic," she went still further—though not quite all the way—in identifying herself with his views:

Was it possible, I wondered, under the stimulus of his thinking, that women in seeking careers of their own, were seeking emancipation from their own God-given natures, and so were merely reaping inner conflict? . . . Could God have created us so that, ideally, we achieve greatest happiness and greatest character development as our husband's career becomes our own, and as we give our selves unstintingly to it and to our homes? I was not sure, but it was worth pondering deeply.[31]

---

[27] Ibid., 144, 102–23 (chap. 7, "They Walk in Wistfulness").
[28] Ibid., 134, 147 (quoted passage).
[29] Ibid., 174.
[30] *A Man Called Peter*, 55, 116.
[31] Ibid., 55–56, 116.

There was "clear common sense," she concluded, in his assertion that women "become progressively less attractive as they desert their essential femininity, and seek either to copy or to compete with men."[32]

In at least some passages of her next book, *To Live Again*, she committed herself even more unqualifiedly to her husband's ideas. Early in her marriage, she reported, she had discovered that "putting these ideas into practice brought . . . joy and satisfaction at a deep level."

> All the talents I possessed, all energy, all creativeness, were poured into the marriage partnership, and no effort was made to channel any part of it in other directions. . . . [I]n giving all of myself to our marriage, with no reservations . . . I found . . . fulfillment of every shred of femininity in me.[33]

The message came through, too, in the accounts of other women's experiences which Marshall interspersed throughout these books. For example, she tells of the time in 1943 when she was ordered to bed by her doctor (having developed some symptoms of incipient TB) and a young female newspaper reporter in her husband's congregation impetuously decided to respond to Marshall's need for domestic help. Though warned by her editor that she was committing "professional suicide," she was convinced that this was God's will for her, and in 1944 she came to live as the Marshalls' housekeeper. As a result of this decision, Catherine Marshall reported, the young woman's personality was transformed:

> Before our eyes, all the potentialities of beauty and character which had been lying dormant in her came to fruition. She became a poised and delightful person. Even her looks changed; she developed a flair for wearing clothes. She acquired an artistry for homemaking, as well as rare qualities of leadership.[34]

The story had a happy ending as well: when this recruit to domesticity left the Marshall household after four years of service, she "stepped into a fine position in the National Red Cross, at more than twice the salary of her old job. . . ."[35]

A similar note is struck in the story of "Babs," a young minister's wife from Iowa, in *To Live Again*. Babs had married Dennis while she was still in college and he a successful industrial engineer. For a time she was "deliriously happy," but then disaster struck: Dennis announced a call to the ministry. Resentfully Babs acquiesced, even helping put Dennis through divinity school by working as a secretary. But then he took his

---

[32] Ibid., 116.
[33] *To Live Again*, 96.
[34] *A Man Called Peter*, 174–78, quoted passages 177.
[35] Ibid., 178.

first pastorate, and Babs found him increasingly inaccessible as his church duties piled up. Lacking any comparable outside interest, she withdrew into bitterness and despondency. Matters came to a head one New Year's Eve when Dennis went off to a party while Babs, let down by a babysitter at the last minute, sulked at home. But that evening she began *A Man Called Peter,* and soon was weeping over her failure to sustain her husband in his God-ordained calling. "[R]eading your book," she wrote Mrs. Marshall, "something in me melted."

> I felt so ashamed when I thought what I could be and haven't been. All at once I saw myself clearly. The demand in me, the pettiness, the self-centeredness. In those hours, I grew up. That night Dennis and I knelt down together and with unashamed tears turned it all over to God and started a fresh chapter in our marriage. I have never known such serenity. . . .[36]

*   *   *

Read hastily or selectively, Catherine Marshall's books of the 1950s may seem little more than a grieving widow's reaffirmation of the traditional role of the minister's wife and a paean to domesticity and female subordination—quintessential expressions of the "togetherness" we have come to think of as the all-pervasive marital ideal in that decade. But there are other themes in these books—muted, perhaps, but important—which deepen our understanding of Marshall's experience and that of her generation of women.

In the autobiographical sections of these books she conveyed the excitement and sense of fulfillment which came with her emergence as a writer. The decision for a career may have been made with trepidation, but once made, Marshall plunged ahead with enthusiasm. The practical, activist side of her upbringing as a "daughter of the manse" and the *de facto* sexual egalitarianism of many aspects of her early experience—the extemporaneous church talks, the assumption that she would go on to college even in the depths of the Depression, the college debate competitions and prohibition rallies, the never-failing Protestant confidence that her experiences and feelings were meaningful and interesting—now stood her in good stead as she found herself dealing with publishers, negotiating contracts, appearing on TV, giving lectures and newspaper interviews, and starring in bookstore autograph parties.[37]

The introduction she wrote for *Mr. Jones, Meet the Master* may have been a tribute to Peter Marshall's memory, but it was also, as she recognized, her "foot in the door of the publishing world," and she did not

[36] *To Live Again*, 163–66, quoted passages 164, 165–66.
[37] Ibid., 59–63, 87–94.

intend to withdraw that foot. "If we can handle this book right," she wrote her publisher briskly, "I believe that it is going to hit the country like a ton of bricks. . . ."[38] She avidly followed her fortunes in the bestseller charts, and by 1955 she had acquired sufficient mastery of the ways of the world that her lawyers spent nine months negotiating an acceptable movie contract for *A Man Called Peter*. In *To Live Again*, she wrote—at variance with her more characteristic hymns to feminine self-effacement—"[A]s the editing work on the sermons progressed, I began to experience the deep satisfaction and inner contentment known only to those who have found the right vocational spot. . . . [I]t was as if I had come home to my own element."[39]

Occasionally, too, in these books she suggested a more complex marital reality than that conveyed in the more rose-tinted passages. *A Man Called Peter,* for example, described her husband's frequent withdrawal into silence when they were alone together. This man who held forth so eloquently in the pulpit often found it impossible to express his feelings to his wife. She wrote, too, of her nagging doubts as to whether he really *needed* the sermon suggestions and spiritual ministrations that figured so importantly in her assessments of her role. And she hinted at her resentment over his work habits—six days a week, all day, at the church—and trips for guest appearances in other cities.[40] Even a lighthearted chapter on "The Perils of a Young Preacher" describing the infatuated women who had sent him flowers and anonymous poems, pestered him in his office, and called him to their bedsides during vague illnesses led to a rather bleak and possibly self-revelatory conclusion: "Every congregation contains women whose hearts cry out for something life has denied them. Inevitably, they see the minister through a romantic haze."[41]

The resentment and frustration surfaced openly in her 1957 book, *To Live Again,* especially when she described her experiences as a widow. Her husband's checking account and safe deposit box had been sealed at his death, and only through complicated legal procedures was she able to gain access to them. Since he had died intestate (after urging any number of his male parishioners to draw up their wills!), two-thirds of the estate went to their minor offspring under District of Columbia law, necessitating further red tape to establish herself as legal guardian of her own son.[42]

---

[38] Ibid., 60, 62.
[39] Ibid., 63 (quoted passage), 229.
[40] *A Man Called Peter*, 117, 118.
[41] Ibid., 47.
[42] *To Live Again*, 74–76.

Even the minutiae of life endlessly reminded her of how totally she had turned such matters over to her husband:

> In many ways, I was still a little girl. . . . Like many a sheltered woman who has married young, I had never once figured out an income tax blank, had a car inspected, consulted a lawyer, or tried to read an insurance policy. Railroad timetables and plane schedules were enigmas to me. My household checking account rarely balanced. I had never invested any money; I had been driving a car for only three months. I would never even have considered braving a trip alone to New York.[43]

Under the spur of such reminders of her inability to function as an autonomous adult, she reflected more critically on the marital ideal her husband had "spread all over the landscape" in his sermons, and wrote much more candidly of the bitterness she had felt at the contrast between her own narrow life and that of her spouse. Only in this book, for example, was she able to bring herself to relate an incident that had occurred the Sunday before his death:

> On the way home from church, we had the radio on. Just as Peter had brought the car to a halt before our front door, a radio announcer had mentioned the approaching St. Valentine's Day.
> Peter had reached across for my hand. . . . "Will you be my valentine, Catherine?" he had asked gaily.
> And I had withdrawn my hand and ruthlessly crushed his small moment of gaiety by replying sarcastically, "Oh, sure! I'll be your valentine, having a gay time all by myself here in Washington while you're in Des Moines. I hear you decided to accept that invitation, too."[44]

And she revealed—unconsciously, perhaps—the ways in which her thwarted desire for a writing career had found outlets during her marriage. After a vacation in his native land, for example, she had had her *Journal of a Trip to Scotland* beautifully bound for presentation to her husband as a Christmas present: her first book, published in an edition of one copy! During her two-year bout with tuberculosis she had written incessantly, though with no clear aim, and with the passing years, as we have seen, she had involved herself increasingly in supplying her husband with sermon ideas and outlines, though always unbeknownst to his public.[45]

Generalizing from all these experiences in a discussion of the painful self-knowledge acquired by widows like herself, in *To Live Again* Marshall

---

[43] Ibid., 15–16.
[44] Ibid., 12–13, 95.
[45] Ibid., 66–67, 228.

went as far as she would ever go toward espousing a view of woman's role radically different from the one she had inherited.

> The widow sees as never before that only when she is a whole person does she have enough to contribute to any marriage relationship. She sees that in marriage or out of marriage, she will be lonely unless she is taking definite steps toward finding herself, toward becoming the whole person she is meant to be.[46]

But such insights never fully effaced older convictions that Catherine Marshall had long held about her own nature and role. *To Live Again* is, in fact, an ambivalent, not to say confused, book. While conveying the frustration inherent in conforming to a definition of femininity that excluded large areas of human experience and achievement, and the exhilaration that came with breaking free of that role, it also made plain the emotional toll the process of liberation had taken: the nagging self-doubt as her fame spread, the suspicion that men did not much like the "new" Catherine Marshall, the psychosomatic illnesses that wreaked havoc with scheduled public appearances.[47]

For twelve years the essential terms of her existence had been defined by others, and then, unexpectedly, she had found herself on her own. The result was a distressing sense of being pulled in two directions at once. She was experiencing at first hand the psychic and tangible rewards of a successful career, and yet the lure of a feminine ideal that her husband had preached, his congregation (not to mention society at large) had reinforced, and she herself had embraced remained strong. The contradictory models offered in the favorite books of her childhood—the aspiring writer of *Emily of the New Moon* and the delicate plantation mistresses of the *Little Colonel* stories—had anticipated the poles of the dilemma:

> My ideal inner image of woman's role in the world—formed partly by the femininity with which I was born, partly by a Southern heritage, and partly by the years of my marriage—was definitely not that of the career woman. . . . [N]ot far under the surface was the little girl who had never had enough perfume, bracelets, and undergarments lavish with lace to satisfy her: who had disdained playing cowboys and Indians but had adored her dolls.
>
> The aggressiveness and independent attitude necessary to make a sally out into the world of successful careers seemed to me a contradiction of everything feminine I had ever known; . . . it was emotional anathema to me. Yet now circumstances which I had not sought were thrusting this genuinely distasteful

---

[46] Ibid., 118.
[47] Ibid., 98–100, 297–98.

role upon me. . . . The conflict in me was therefore basically a clash between femininity and the career that pressed in upon me. The woman and the book were in headlong collision.[48]

As *To Live Again* draws to a close the doubts multiply, and the same Marshall who had earlier urged every woman to strive to be a "whole person" draws back from the implications of such an aspiration for her own life. The divine mandate to carry on her husband's work, earlier offered as a justification for pursuing a career, now looms as a heavy cross to be relinquished as soon as possible. The book's final chapters strike a note of renunciation: God's purpose for one stage of her life has been fulfilled, and she can now retire to a more appropriate sphere.

She defends this conclusion in a soliloquy on womanhood and the question of whether women can "replace love with accomplishment, marriage with a career, or even combine a career with marriage."[49] The widow, she suggests, is uniquely qualified to answer such questions, for she has been torn involuntarily from the marital state and thrust into a rough-and-tumble environment that forces her to become tough, independent, and self-sufficient.

Through marriage, she writes, she and millions of other widows not only learned that "men and women were meant to be different," but also were made aware of the specific ways in which women were different: "our dependence; our passivity; the way our emotions ruled our reason; our delight in people rather than in abstract ideas; our compassion; our preoccupation with the minutiae of living—a flower arrangement for a party, the next meeting of the PTA, the selection of new draperies for the living room, a missing button on a shirt." But then came the husband's death, and the imperative need to develop a new relationship to society:

We who had known completeness only in our relationship with a man who loved us, were now asked to be complete within ourselves. In order to survive, we have had to do a hundred things we had never done before—handle money, sell and buy property, keep a man's working hours, try to be both father and mother to our children. We managed all this by summoning up latent masculine qualities we did not know we possessed—the necessity of accepting responsi-

---

[48] Ibid., 102. In a letter commenting on a draft of this chapter, Marshall observed: "I think that you caught accurately . . . the dichotomy that developed in me as time went on following Peter Marshall's death between what had been my attitude about marriage and a woman's life generally versus a career. Of course I came to enjoy many aspects of the career because I found myself in the deepest possible way through the process of writing. Yet I doubt that I will ever completely get over a sort of inner cleavage between wanting to spend my time in housewifely and gardening pursuits versus career matters." Catherine Marshall LeSourd, Lincoln, Va., to the author, July 19, 1977.

[49] *To Live Again*, 296.

bility, aggressiveness, competitiveness, drive, a partial submerging of feeling in favor of reason. . . . [W]e found treasured values slipping away. In the business world, we saw differences between the sexes blurred in a way we had not known in marriage. With the blurring, life lost something precious.[50]

Are the women forced by circumstance to develop their "latent masculine qualities" thus deviations from the natural order—admirable in adversity, perhaps, but certainly no model for emulation? Marshall had vacillated on this question, but in this concluding section of *To Live Again* she was unambiguous:

A true woman finds her reassurance, her reason for living, by looking into the eyes of a man who loves her. . . . I stood looking back over the way I had traveled since Peter's death and knew that my personal answer to whether or not a woman can replace marriage with a career and find it satisfying was—no, definitely not. The career left the woman still wanting to be—only a woman.[51]

The chapter which follows this declaration of dependence opens on a note of domesticity, as Mrs. Marshall describes an idyllic moment at "Waverley," the Cape Cod summer cottage where she and her husband had spent many happy hours, and to which she has now returned as a widow with her son:

I was sitting at the kitchen table preparing the vegetables for dinner. Since we had our usual quota of guests at Waverley, there was quite a pile of potatoes to be peeled, peas to be shelled. From where I sat, I could look through the windows into the back garden. Phlox, zinnias, and petunias were in bloom. A bird, with much fluttering of feathers, was giving himself a vigorous scrubbing in the birdbath.[52]

This is soon followed by another evocation of domestic tranquility, as she describes a visit to "Evergreen," the old Virginia farmhouse where her parents live:

As I write, spring has come to Evergreen. Mike, the collie, roams the greening hillsides, sniffing the air. The baby goat is growing. The duck is sitting on fifteen eggs. The drake (typical male!) wanders around disconsolately, lonely, feeling sorry for himself.[53]

---

[50] Ibid., 297–98.
[51] Ibid., 298.
[52] Ibid., 299.
[53] Ibid., 324.

In the book's final episode, we find Marshall fulfilling the classic female role: denying herself in order to be of service to a man. This time, the beneficiary is her son, Peter Marshall, Jr. As he prepares to leave home for prep school (Mount Hermon Academy in Massachusetts) she feels the pangs of separation but takes comfort in universalizing her experience: "Each generation of womankind has the same set of feelings. Life asks women to give and to give and then to give up, and to do both with equanimity and courage."[54]

She drives Peter to Mount Hermon, helps him unpack, meets his new roommate and his parents ("I noticed how Bruce's mother, all unconsciously, leaned on her husband's arm. . . ."), and then, reluctant to leave, finds a reason to stay: "The things they needed—that would be a handy excuse. When a woman is at loose ends, what does she do? She goes shopping for someone she loves."[55] After buying her son a chair, a plastic cup, and more clothes hangers, she stops at a farmhouse to pick up some maple syrup for herself. Again, the casual domesticity of the scene impresses her as pregnant with meaning:

> This was the family dining room. The round table in the center of the room was covered with pieces of tissue-paper dress pattern and cotton material. The two cupboards were filled with Early American pressed glass. . . .
>
> "The glass has probably been in the family always," I thought; "Antique dealers dream of finding places like this."
>
> The farmer came back with the syrup. . . . About him and his family there was an air of sturdy Americana. This was New England at its best.[56]

At peace with herself, she drives off into the sunset. A sudden thunder shower drenches the land, but then a rainbow appears: a renewal of God's benediction and blessing.

Sentimentalized as they are, these episodes of *To Live Again* are integrally related to the larger themes developed in Marshall's writings. They underscore her wish to return to the domestic security that had been shattered for her in 1949, to resolve once and for all the unwanted questions of personal identity widowhood had thrust upon her.

But the apparent clarity of her conclusion does not quite ring true. The evocations of domestic happiness have a distinctly "literary" flavor. She is an outsider, observing slices of "Americana" with an outsider's eyes: eyes that can shrewdly appraise the commercial value of heirlooms even as they recognize them as symbols of generational continuity.

[54] Ibid., 327.
[55] Ibid., 329, 330.
[56] Ibid., 331.

No doubt she was sincere in turning her back on her career at the end of *To Live Again,* but this was not to be the final word. True, she married the editor of *Guideposts* magazine in 1959 and settled with a new family of three children in a "sprawling white house with red shutters . . . set in the rocky, tree-shaded countryside of Westchester County,"[57] but her writing output continued undiminished: as Woman's Editor of *Christian Herald* (1958–60); "Roving Editor" of *Guideposts* from 1960 on; and author of a stream of inspirational books including *Beyond Ourselves* (1961), *Christy* (1967), and *Something More* (1974).

Like it or not, Catherine Marshall had become a modern woman. The old existence, obliterated at one shattering blow in 1949, was not to be restored. Ironically, the issues she was forced unwillingly to confront in the 1950s, when the domestic ideal ostensibly reigned supreme, were precisely those that would be eagerly taken up by an entire generation of American young women, including many ministers' wives, in the decades that followed.

[57] *Beyond Ourselves,* xv.

Contributors

Paul Boyer, professor of history at the University of Massachusetts, Amherst, was assistant editor of *Notable American Women, 1607–1950* (1971). His books include *Salem Possessed: The Social Origins of Witchcraft* (with Stephen Nissenbaum, 1974), and *Urban Masses and Social Order in America, 1820–1920* (1978).

Virginia Lieson Brereton, a doctoral candidate in American history and education at Teachers College, Columbia University, is one of the authors of a forthcoming study of the history of Protestant theological education in America. Her dissertation deals with Protestant fundamentalist education from 1880 to 1940.

Mary Maples Dunn is a professor of history and dean of the Undergraduate College, Bryn Mawr College. The author of *William Penn: Politics and Conscience* (1967), she is currently, with her husband, Richard S. Dunn, preparing a selective edition of Penn's letters and papers. She is a past president of the Berkshire Conference of Women Historians.

Alan Graebner is an associate professor of history at the College of St. Catherine in St. Paul and author of *Uncertain Saints: The Laity in the Lutheran Church–Missouri Synod, 1900–1970* (1975). His present research interest is women in the health professions.

Janet Wilson James is an associate professor of history at Boston College. She was formerly at Radcliffe College as director of the Arthur and Elizabeth Schlesinger Library on the History of Women in America, and associate editor of *Notable American Women, 1607–1950* (1971). She is presently working on the history of nursing as an occupation for women; her essay "Isabel Hampton and the Professionalization of Nursing in the 1890s" appeared in *The Therapeutic Revolution*, edited by Morris J. Vogel and Charles E. Rosenberg (1979).

James J. Kenneally, professor of history at Stonehill College, is the author of *Women and American Trade Unions* (1978) and several articles in women's history. He is currently researching the career of Joseph W. Martin, Jr., Speaker of the House, 1947–49 and 1953–55.

Christa Ressmeyer Klein, assistant professor of history at Lutheran Theological Seminary, Gettysburg, is coordinator and one of the authors of a forthcoming study, funded by the Lilly Endowment, Inc., on the history of Protestant theological education in America.

Sister Elizabeth Kolmer, associate professor of history and director of American Studies at Saint Louis University, is a past president of the Mid-continent American Studies Association. She has published in the *Negro History Bulletin, American Studies* (Taiwan), and *Social Justice Review,* among other journals, on topics of church history and women's and children's studies. Her current research interests are values in children's schoolbooks and the role of Catholic religious women in American society.

Gerald F. Moran is an associate professor of history at the University of Michigan, Dearborn. He has published articles in the *Journal of Social History* and the *William and Mary Quarterly,* and is currently completing a study of church membership and religious experience in colonial Connecticut.

Mary J. Oates, associate professor of economics at Regis College (Massachusetts), has written several articles on American economic history. She is the author, with Susan Williamson, of "Women's Colleges and Women Achievers" (*Signs,* 1978), and is currently engaged in a study of the role of Catholic sisterhoods in New England popular education after 1850.

Norma Fain Pratt teaches American history and women's studies at Mt. San Antonio College, Walnut, California. She is the author of *Morris Hillquit: A Political History of an American Jewish Socialist* (1979), as well as of several articles on Jewish women. She is presently at work on a study of the social and literary history of Yiddish women writers.

Mary P. Ryan, associate professor of history at the University of California at Santa Cruz, is the author of *Womanhood in America: From Colonial Times to the Present* (2d revised edition, 1979). Her book on the family, gender, and the making of the middle class in antebellum Utica, New York, will be published in 1981.

Laurel Thatcher Ulrich is a doctoral candidate at the University of New Hampshire, where she is completing a study of female role definition in New England from 1650 to 1750. She is the author of "Fictional Sisters," in *Mormon Sisters: Women in Early Utah,* edited by Claudia L. Bushman (1976).

Barbara Welter, professor of history at Hunter College, CUNY, has written extensively on women in nineteenth-century America. Her work includes a much anthologized article, "The Feminization of American Religion, 1800–1860," and the editing, with introduction, of *The Woman's Bible.* She is currently completing a monograph on the social and cultural history of American Protestant missionaries in the nineteenth century.